AF394772

SPEAKING EAST

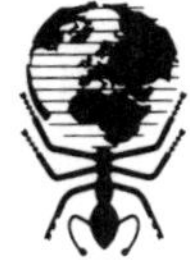

SPEAKING EAST

THE STRANGE AND ENCHANTED LIFE OF ISIDORE ISOU

ANDREW HUSSEY

REAKTION BOOKS

To Carmel with love, as ever

Published by
REAKTION BOOKS LTD
Unit 32, Waterside
44–48 Wharf Road
London N1 7UX, UK
www.reaktionbooks.co.uk

First published 2021
Copyright © Andrew Hussey 2021

Printed and bound in Great Britain
by TJ Books Limited, Padstow, Cornwall

A catalogue record for this book is available from the British Library

ISBN 978 1 78914 492 5

CONTENTS

Introduction:
'All Poets Are Yids!'

I met Isidore Isou only once.

This was in April 1999 when I was working on a biography of the 'Situationist' writer Guy Debord. I needed to speak to Isou because in the 1940s Debord and Isou had been close friends, with Debord in the role of disciple to Isou. For a short while Debord had been a member of the avant-garde movement founded by Isou, which he called *lettrisme* (or 'letterism' in English). They had quickly fallen out, however, and had despised each other since. 'Debord was like a Nazi,' Isou said to me, 'Worse than a Nazi.'[1]

Debord shot himself through the heart in November 1994. But this suicide only made things worse for Isou. In the 1990s Debord had become posthumously famous for his book *The Society of the Spectacle* – published in 1967 but by now considered a text that had prophesied the contemporary world of iPhones and social networks – the new 'civilization of the image' as he put it. Isou was jealous that Debord was now also being written about outside France, mainly in Britain and America. His work appeared on university syllabuses and his ideas were claimed as a major influence on all forms of counter-cultures, from the near-revolution of May '68 to punk rock and rave culture. For Isou, however, Debord was no great thinker; he was no more than a drunk, a plagiarist and a betrayer. Given the level of hate that had simmered away between them for nearly fifty years, I was amazed that Isou had agreed to speak to me at all.

Isou was then 74 years old. He had been in bad health for some time and had been unable to walk for months. He lived in Paris in two small rooms at the top of a building at 42 rue Saint-André-des-Arts. He had been here since 1965, never leaving the Left Bank except for a few trips to Israel. The legend was that he had paid off the mortgage by selling a sculpture given to him by Alberto Giacometti.

The apartment was simple and austere: a table, a chair, a bed, no paintings or other images on the walls. The bathroom was used to store paintings; the bath itself contained several medium-sized works (Isou preferred to use a public bathhouse). The three rooms of the apartment were laid out like a long corridor, with windows overlooking a courtyard. This was the common pattern of cheap Left Bank hotels, which was what the apartment had once been. Rather than being a home in which to live, this was a place to consume ideas and books, which passed through the apartment as fast as Isou could devour them.

The apartment was also dense with books and journals and I noted straightaway that Isou was reading two huge books simultaneously, the first a tome on Kurt Schwitters and the second a compendium of Dadaist texts. Isou had not left his apartment for two years and received no visitors apart from a nurse and his friend Roland Sabatier, a film-maker and artist who had tight control over the still-active group of *lettristes* in Paris.

The room was baking hot, becoming unbearable as the afternoon lengthened. Isou was taking medication for a degenerative condition, which made him sometimes drool and slobber and sometimes hard to understand. The black propaganda from Debord and his supporters was that Isou was totally mad, but it soon became clear, as Isou kept making sense, and even cracking jokes, that this was not the case. Happily, we quickly left Guy Debord and the tedious intricacies of avant-garde rivalry behind. Instead Isou began to tell me another, altogether more compelling story.[2]

Isidore Isou was not his real name. He was born on 29 January 1925 with the name Ion-Isidor Goldstein in the city of Botoşani in northeast Romania. His mother affectionately called him Izu, the Romanian-Jewish form of his name, which he precociously adopted as his avant-garde *nom de guerre* when he moved to Bucharest when still an adolescent. In his use of an alias he was following in the footsteps of another Jew from the same region of Romania. This was Samuel Rosenstock from the town of Moineşti, who had renamed himself Tristan Tzara and had come from this eastern outpost of Europe and conquered Dada and the Parisian avant-gardes in the 1920s. For a long time, Tzara was possibly the greatest man alive to the young Isou.

For most of his life Isidore Isou refused to even mention Romania by name. He gives, however, a vivid and intense account of his early life there in his first book *L'Agrégation d'un nom et d'un messie* (The Making of a Name, a Messiah). This astonishing work was published by Éditions Gallimard in the prestigious collection of the *Nouvelle Revue Française* on Isou's arrival in Paris in 1947, when he was only 22 years old.

In this book, the country of Isou's birth is never specified; it is only ever an inward-looking backwater – 'a small, insignificant country without culture'.[3] The same applied to the Romanian language, which Isou spoke fluently and which he scorned as a provincial dialect, 'a language with its feet cut off by customs officers.'[4]

As we spoke, I realized that nothing about Isou could be taken at face value or on trust. He was endlessly elusive, as you might expect from someone whose earliest hero had been Luigi Pirandello, the Italian writer whose characters are always changing, undoing or identifying with the text at will, and apparently at random. One of the first difficulties of reading Isou, therefore, is to work out how much is true and how much is invented. Isou was always full of contradictions, truths and untruths.

The same applies to his life as well as his art. To give just one example, having later claimed a conversion to Catholicism, he never spoke about his Jewish background to the staunchly middle-class Catholic family of his wife and indeed observed all the rites of the Catholic Church with reverence. At the same time, during this period he was talking to his psychiatrist incessantly about Israel, Jews and Jewishness. His work is almost always deeply imprinted with Jewish themes. We will never know whether the tales of Irina Galia or Bif, as recounted in *L'Agrégation*, are real or simply fantasies within fantasies. Similarly, Isou at first did not classify this early work as either an autobiography or a work of philosophy. Finally, he decided it was philosophy.

For all the reasons cited above, a critical biography of Isou is a daunting task. But it is not impossible. What I have sought to do is make a portrait of Isou, trying to capture something of his extraordinary voice, his ideas and his art, and thus his true place in the history of the twentieth century.

For all of his trickery, Isou's work is rooted in reality. One of the most powerful, and overlooked, aspects of *L'Agrégation* as well as other later works is how so much of Isou's writing, especially about Romania, is a true document of his life and era; a precise eyewitness account of the destruction of the Jewish world of Romania. His writings describe a coming of age in a place that was once paradise but has now become hell on earth.

9

Isou is physically attacked, made to work in a forced labour camp, keeps trying to escape, is caught up in massacres, and all the time hears rumours of the terrible slaughter of Jews in the north of Romania. Many of the names used in *L'Agrégation*, whether Romanian or Jewish, belong to real people – Jewish journalists, writers, landlords, shopkeepers. This is history, described in real time; a history that only now is being properly excavated by historians in Romania and elsewhere. This is why Isou's 'autobiography' plays such an important role in the first part of this book: my focus has been to uncover what really happened to Isou, and his role in the era.

During his time in Romania, for example, Isou crosses the path of another young chronicler of the age, Mihail Sebastian, since praised by the likes of Philip Roth for his account of what it felt like to be a Jew in a city where everyone wants you dead. According to Roth, Sebastian's book deserved to be on the same shelf as Anne Frank's diary.[5] Sebastian became properly famous in the 1990s when his novels and private diaries were published in post-Ceaușescu Romania. They became a sensation, revealing to a new post-communist generation the reality of the Romanian Holocaust, often dismissed by fascists and communists alike as a Jewish exaggeration.[6]

Isidore Isou knew the truth and wrote about it in *L'Agrégation*. Only the Zionists offered any real resistance in his view, and he asked them to help him get to Israel. The plan was 'fucked up', as he put it, when he got to the coast and there were no boats. Back in Bucharest, Isou hung out with his friends, visited brothels and got into fights, all the time hating the 'Christians' who wanted to kill him. In a darkened cinema, he is about to make love to a 'Christian' girl he has just picked up when he sees the first horrible images broadcast of the death camps in Eastern Europe. He recognizes himself in the piles of young corpses being swept into mass graves. 'Don't look at the Yids,' she says, pulling him back for another kiss. 'They deserve it. They brought it on themselves.'[7]

It was in this time and place that Isou had the series of revelations which would become *lettrisme*. The first illumination came to him on a Bucharest street on 19 March 1942, when he was seventeen years old.[8] It was clear to him that the 'old civilization' he had grown up in was now crumbling away before his eyes. The question was the same question being asked then in the newly born Israel: how to build the new world, how to found a new civilization?

The way out of this impasse was to invent a new language. A further revelation came to Isou while reading an essay by the German philosopher Hermann von Keyserling. He noticed that the word *vocable* had been incorrectly translated into Romanian as *voyelle* and that the original sentence had now been distorted beyond rational meaning. It now became 'le poète dilate les voyelles' (the poet dilates the vowels). This, like the best Dadaist poetry, was funny, strange and contained a new form of meaning; like the poetry of Rimbaud or even Tzara, it bent language out of shape into its real meaning: pure sound.

This, decided Isou, was the way forward; straightaway he composed the *Manifeste de la poésie lettriste*. In this, he defined the art and philosophy of *lettrisme* – a new way of making poetry that transcended all national boundaries, the source of all conflict in the world, by releasing humanity into the free space of pure noise. This was the new, truly democratic Republic of Letters. 'Il faut révéler le tout dans les lettres' – Everything must be revealed in letters.[9]

Lettrisme is not always easy to understand. I have been interested in *lettrisme* for over twenty years. But although I can discern a recognizable style and technique – the complex signs and symbols and sharp angular patterning of text and image – I have not always been certain what it is for or what it is about. Isou, with ludicrous grandiosity, compared *lettrisme* to the Renaissance. It was, he stated, no less than the complete reinvention of culture and what it meant to be a human being. He was serious when he said this.

He developed this notion in his book *La Créatique ou la Novatique*. The theory goes like this: societies develop not because of the human instinct for survival, but because of the desire to create. More than this, if creativity was the highest form of action, and art was its most visible form, then humanity was in charge of history. In this way, the artist took the place of God, the first Creator or artist.

You do not need to believe this theory to understand it. The comparison with the Renaissance is indeed less far-fetched than it sounds. Like the Surrealists, Isou was fascinated by the popularity of alchemy during the Renaissance. Alchemists practise 'experimental science and philosophy', seeking to turn base metals into gold, a universal cure for disease and the infinite prolongation of human life; most importantly alchemists believe that everything can be transformed.

This is *lettrisme* in action; it is how music becomes painting and painting becomes film and film become writing: all is endlessly mutable. This may all seem mad but it is not necessarily untrue. It has its origins in the French poetry of the nineteenth and early twentieth centuries – the abstraction of Mallarmé, the mysticism of Rimbaud, the myth-making of Apollinaire and the wild hallucinatory energy of the Comte de Lautréamont. Visually it is related to the early experiments of Cubism and the Futurists. It's based on the belief that art and life are the same thing – indeed, following the ideas of Marcel Duchamp, that life is the highest expression of art.

Isou particularly admired the Futurists because they aimed not only to revolutionize art but to totally undermine the world that they lived in. In the original *Futurist Manifesto*, launched by Filippo Tommaso Marinetti in 1909, they declared that they 'wanted no part in the past'. Everything, including painting, architecture, religion, poetry, music, clothing and even cooking, had to be remade to fit in with the spirit of the age – which was to be defined by speed, violence and technology.

Politically, *lettrisme* is also an heir to the Romantic Utopianism of the nineteenth-century philosopher Charles Fourier. Fourier was dismissed as a madman in his day but many of his ideas have passed into mainstream thinking: he valued women's rights, children's education and preached of tolerance towards homosexuals. Above all he hated the 'civilization' he lived in, which he thought of as violent, cruel and stupid. Fourier was later admired by the Surrealists and Walter Benjamin, among others, for his unshakeable belief in the redemptive power of human creativity.

This can seem naive from the perspective of the early twenty-first century, but it all makes sense in the context of the early twentieth century, as the belief in human history as an upward curve towards progress and improvement came to an end and was wrecked on the battlefields of Europe. The great projects of nineteenth-century capitalist 'civilization' had ultimately produced nothing better than machines for the mass killing of workers.

This rhetoric was common to all parties of the Left in Europe during the 1920s. It was also of central importance to the avant-garde groups of the period, which were emerging as the most powerful and dissident voices in Paris, Berlin and other European capitals in the aftermath of the First World War. The most strident of all these voices, both during and after the war, was that of the Dadaist movement, which had been founded in Zurich in 1916.

Dadaism was conceived as a negation of the entire system of moral values underpinning Western thought. It opposed reason, order, meaning and hierarchies in equal measure. It was not meant as an art movement but as a political weapon, carefully calibrated and loaded, aimed directly at the beating heart of the rotten capitalist order, the 'machine civilization' that had murdered so many millions. In his *Dada Manifesto* of 1918 Tristan Tzara spoke directly to a generation of young men and women who had grown up despising everything around them, to all those who lost faith in their homeland and its civilization: 'No pity,' he declared; 'After the carnage we are left with the hope of a purified humanity . . . there is great destructive . . . work to be done.'[10]

The parallels here between Dadaism and *lettrisme* are clear. It is also no accident that five of the original founders of Dada in Zurich were Jewish exiles from the same part of Romania as Isou (the invented name of one of these Jews, Tristan Tzara, actually means 'sad country', or 'ţară tristă', in Romanian). Dada has now entered history as a component part of Western modernity. But what this handful of Jews brought to Zurich was the influence of the Yiddish popular culture – mainly travelling cabarets. In these cabarets, the players often wore bizarre costumes and masks. The language of the comedy was often scrambled 'Jewish jargon' – of business or religion – which no one understood.[11] There was spontaneous stamping and roaring, the banging of drums and lids. The jokes were usually based on contradictions and double negatives. Performances were relentlessly sarcastic, antic, hilarious: everything was a target. This was obviously also how Dada worked. It was a series of calculated provocations that opposed and contradicted the logic of Western thought.

Dadaists and *lettristes* belong to the same family; they speak the same language in every sense. There is, however, one singular and crucial difference that separates them. The Dadaists had seen the massacres of the First World War. Isou had seen the Holocaust.

When he arrived in Paris in 1945, Isou began his career at the very height of avant-garde fashion. He was charismatic and good-looking, and he quickly gathered a pack of well-read young hooligans as followers. This new gang of *lettristes* was soon notorious for their punch-ups, their weird, threatening poetry, their girls and their arrogance. He dressed in the most stylish clothes of the era – usually *une canadienne*, a heavy felt coat designed for harsh Canadian winters, or an American-style sports jacket, an open-neck shirt and a scarf. The look was sexy and defiant: pure rock 'n' roll *avant la lettre*. Isou's reputation was boosted by the fact that he was soon published by Gallimard (the rumour was the *lettristes* had threatened to beat up Gaston Gallimard, the distinguished owner of the house, or at least firebomb his offices, if he didn't publish Isou).

Isou now socialized with and insulted the élite thinkers of the Left Bank, including André Breton, Jean Cocteau, Jean-Paul Sartre and others. The English artist Ralph Rumney was then only nineteen and new to Paris and hung around with the *lettristes*. He recalled that a favourite *lettriste* game was to knock the hat off the now elderly Tristan Tzara as he walked to a café for his morning coffee.[12] The new snotty young heroes of the avant-garde had no time for icons.

This is the self-created legend of Isou, which in the past few decades has been passing into literature and history. This is the Isou celebrated by the American writer Greil Marcus in his 1989 book *Lipstick Traces: A Secret History of the Twentieth Century*, about heretics in Western culture. Marcus celebrated Isou and *lettrisme* as avatars of a pure art of negation; their method, he said, was simple – to destroy to create, to say 'No' to say 'Yes'.

This was the version of news of *lettrisme* that in 1949 even got as far as the *New York Times* (actually the second time that Isou had been featured in the *Times*). A *Times* correspondent, Ralph Thompson, described Isou as 'chief Genius of the movement [*lettrisme*]' and reported that 'their poetry consists mainly of abstract sounds – peeps, grunts and squeals . . . when [Isou] finished there was a crash of applause. The air was foul. The drinks were bad. Everybody was happy.'[13]

It was no doubt one of these articles, along with other rumours of the new avant-garde, that in 1955 inspired a curious Orson Welles to interview Isou on film in the Librairie Fischbacher bookshop on the rue de Seine. In the film, Isou and another smartly dressed *lettriste* (Isou's then chief lieutenant, Maurice Lemaître) read out a sound poem about snow to a clearly baffled Welles.

This is a moment that would have appealed greatly to the Chilean novelist Roberto Bolaño (d. 2003), who has fast been establishing a posthumous reputation as one of the trickiest and sharpest writers to emerge in the early twenty-first century. Bolaño was fascinated by obscure avant-garde sects, and especially *lettrisme*. So Isou's ludic spirit keeps popping up in his writings, fictional and otherwise. In the novel *Woes of the True Policeman*, after a row between André Breton and Isou (which actually happened), Isou is denounced by the fictional magician and writer

J.M.G. Arcimboldi as 'a Romanian fuck-stick' on the grounds of his reputation as a seducer.

In real life Isou's reputation has never been higher and is getting better all the time. At the time of writing, a major retrospective of Isou's work was being planned for the Centre Pompidou.[14] Meanwhile his work was being shown in Tel Aviv, Bucharest and New York. His archive – dauntingly massive – was acquired by the Bibliothèque Kandinsky, the leading research library of modern art in Paris. Scholarly books and theses were being written about him in Stanford, Princeton, London, Cambridge and Berlin, as well as Paris, the consensus being that, whatever Debord and his disciples might have said, *lettrisme* was – or is – the missing link between Dada, Surrealism and Situationism. Unsurprisingly against this background, *lettriste* artworks and writings were being bought at a feverish rate by collectors, reaching dizzyingly high prices and increasing all the time.

In 2016, when I started writing this book, there was practically nothing left in Bucharest of the city that Isou had known. In the late 1990s I had spent some time in Bucharest and been disappointed in my quest to excavate the *Micul Paris* (the little Paris) that Isou had known. With my fellow writer Gavin Bowd, I had wandered across the city, down *bulevarde* and back alleys, criss-crossing the main avenues, drinking in the cafés and nightclubs, but there was literally nothing to see beyond the broken pavements, packs of stray dogs and crumbling concrete Soviet-style apartment blocks.

Like *Micul Paris*, the Jewish world where Isou grew up has long since disappeared. However, the story of how it disappeared – the story of the Romanian Holocaust – is still a controversial subject here. Although Romania officially acknowledged the Holocaust in 2004 by recognizing Holocaust Day, there were (and still are) plenty of people who say that it never really happened, or that if it did the Jews deserved it, or that Marshal Ion Antonescu, the Romanian dictator who led Romania through the Second World War, was secretly saving Jews from the Final Solution.

These arguments quickly grow violent. In 1991 a young professor called Ioan Petru Culianu, a scholar of Renaissance magic, was shot dead with a bullet in the back of his head in a corridor of the University of Chicago. Culianu had recently been writing about Romanian politics and excavating the Holocaust as well as the hidden fascist lives of eminent Romanian intellectuals, including Mircea Eliade, the great historian of religion. The theory was that Culianu was executed for his views by a group on the far-Right, or by Romanian intelligence, possibly former members of the Securitate. Entering the murky world of Romanian political hatreds, the FBI was soon lost. The crime has never been solved.[15]

In 2003 a former president of Romania, Ion Iliescu, started a diplomatic row with Israel after remarking that the 'Holocaust was not unique to Jews in Europe'.[16] He later grudgingly recanted, but cynics noted that Romania was at this point negotiating access to the EU and could not afford to be seen as Europe's last Holocaust denier. (I once shared a dinner table with Iliescu; he was clever enough to know what his Western audience expected but his real views, I suspected, were never far away.)

In 2013 another Iliescu, a respected elderly academic, was drawing huge audiences in Bucharest with a lecture that argued that the killing of 20,000 Jews in Romania (Iliescu's estimation) was 'not genocide' and that the 'Holocaust was a big lie'. Professor Vladimir Iliescu is right about one thing: the question of 'genocide' is complicated and hard to define.[17]

I had my own first-hand experience of how difficult this could be when in 1996 I interviewed a woman in Bucharest, with Gavin, called Paula Iacob. She was a lawyer who worked for the Ceaușescu family and we were there to interview her for the *Sunday Telegraph* about one of her clients, the recently deceased Nicu Ceaușescu, the drunken and murderous son of the communist dictator Nicolae.

Among other things, she had been defending Nicu Ceaușescu against charges of 'genocide' and took a careful, lawyerly view of what it did and did not mean. Since her death in 2015 it has emerged that Iacob, who was Jewish herself, had been working as an informer for the Securitate under the name of 'Gabriela' since 1952.[18] She had also lived through what had happened to Jews in the mid-twentieth century in Romania. Our conversation took place a long time ago but I do remember vividly an ambiguous remark when I asked about the history of antisemitism in Romania. 'If Romania is now a country without antisemitism,' she said, 'this is because it is now a country without Jews.'[19]

After the interview was over, trying to find our hotel, we got lost in a run-down area just off the main *bulevarde*. I was scared of the packs of stray dogs in the empty night-time streets. But I was spooked too by the swastikas and anti-Jewish graffiti. No Jews but Jew-hatred still visible.

Like Bucharest, Paris too has changed. It is certainly no longer the city of the late twentieth century where I met Isou. Isou's generation of Jews had come to France believing that, even if they were not universally loved, they were safe here. By the early twenty-first century this was no longer the case. As in Bucharest, Jew-hatred still lives on here and has even grown stronger and harsher in recent times. This is why throughout the 2000s Jews have been leaving France in numbers unprecedented since the Second World War.

Isidore Isou's last public appearance was in Paris, at the Amphithéâtre Liard in the Sorbonne in 2000, when he shared a platform with the Holocaust survivor and Nobel Laureate Elie Wiesel – a fellow Romanian Jew. Isou was quite ill by then, and the medication was making him slur his words more than ever before. Still, he finished his talk on creativity to rapturous applause before being taken away by ambulance back to his apartment.

Wiesel and Isou came from the same world. Like Wiesel, or the sociologist Serge Moscovici (who had been Isou's friend in wartime Bucharest) and many others, Isou was a member of a generation that had been obliged, through the experience of the Holocaust, to exchange Romanian identity for an imagined cultural and linguistic country, which had Paris as its capital but no real or literal landscape.

'I have never written in Romanian,' Isou explained to me when I mistakenly put it to him, in April 1999, that he was in the tradition of Mohai Eminescu, a poet whose real theme was his identity. 'And this is because I am a Jew from a country which hates Jews.' This turned out not to be entirely true – Isou did not master French properly until he came to Paris in his twenties, and so his first attempts at literature, and indeed his first published writings, were necessarily in Romanian.

Isou also said to me that he was not and never would be a French writer. He was in fact the direct opposite: a writer in French whose aim was to undermine the linguistic and cultural system within which he was operating. 'I had to write in the language of mankind, that is to say all Jews,' he said, 'so I chose French.'[20]

Someone else who made the same kind of choice was Paul Celan, who came from the same part of Romania as Isou, lived through the Holocaust and eventually came to France, where he chose to write poetry in German. He had made this decision in the work camp where he had been interned by the Romanian authorities. He wrote poetry, he said, to remain human. When Theodor Adorno made his famous statement that 'to write poetry after Auschwitz is barbaric' he did not mean that poetry should not be written but that it was wrong, 'barbaric', to persist in making art out of the European culture that had created the death camps. Celan was in torment about this fact; he wrote in German but was not German, he was a Jew. He prefaced one of his last poems with an epigraph in Cyrillic which read 'All Poets are Yids' – meaning all poetry, all culture, now had to be made from the Other, the outside.[21] In 1969 Celan could no longer find comfort in language or bear his guilt over his parents who had been killed in the Romanian Holocaust. He threw himself into the Seine. His body was found a week or so later; he was 49 years old.

For all his suffering, Isidore Isou went on to live a long life. He died in 2007 at the age of 82. Throughout his life he sacrificed everything – family, money, sometimes even his sanity – to the Great Work that was *lettrisme*. Right until the end, he lived and worked as an artist, an exile and a Jew.

PART I

A Romanian Youth (1925–45)

O, țară tristă, plină de umor
Oh, sad land, full of humour
GEORGE BACOVIA, *Cu Voi* (With You; 1956)

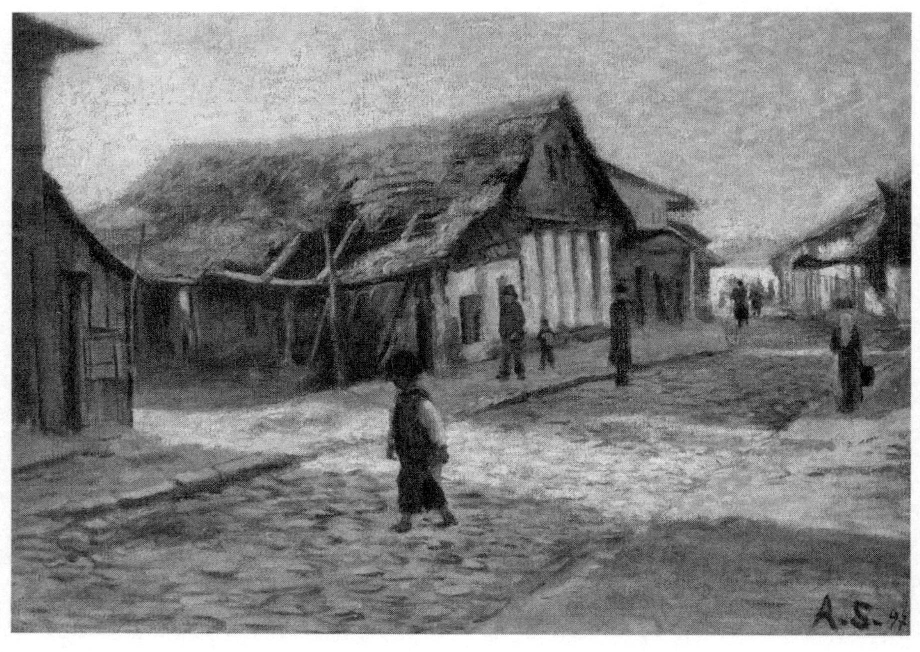

Arthur Segal, *Copil pe Stradă, Botoşani* (Child on the Street, Botoşani), 1897, oil on canvas.

one

Yiddishland

Botoşani was once a handsome town. The town that Isou knew was sometimes called 'little Leipzig' because the houses and shops on the main street, Calea Naţională, were built in the same style as those in Leipzig. This style is sometimes called *Leipziger* or *Sächsische Barock* (Leipzig or Saxon Baroque): it is characterized by rich, creamy ornamentation grafted onto the solid and squat buildings. Some of these buildings are still standing in Centrul Vechi (the old centre) of Botoşani; but most of the streets there are now half-wrecked and crowded out by communist-era grey or twenty-first-century steel and glass.

The rest of Botoşani is a dismal, half-built suburban sprawl. Botoşani is indeed now fairly typical of the 'Wild East' of Europe, closer to the Ukraine or Moldava than any of the great capitals of Western or Central Europe. Unemployment is high here and one of the few thriving commercial activities is smuggling, mainly petrol and cigarettes and also sometimes people, making for the migrant routes westwards.

At the southern edge of the town is the old Jewish cemetery halfway down Şoseaua Iaşului, a nondescript road leading out of Botoşani to the town of Târgu Frumos and then the regional capital Iaşi. The Jewish cemetery in Botoşani is vast and the new part is still used by the tiny band of Jews who continue to live here. The rest of the cemetery is impenetrable, overgrown and abandoned. Still the graves here are regularly desecrated.

The New York-based academic Mitchell Cohen came here in 1990, writing a book in pursuit of the town's lost Jewish past. He described it to me as 'a truly awful place'. He also told me that while speaking in bad Yiddish to one of the local Jewish leaders, he switched to Hebrew, which Cohen knew that they both spoke fluently. The man refused then to speak at all, avoiding any public usage of what was his own first language. 'This was not out of shame but fear,' said Cohen.[1]

When Isidore Isou spent his earliest years here, there were around 30,000 Jews living in Botoşani and its surrounding districts. Yiddish and Hebrew were as widely and openly spoken as Romanian, Russian or Ruthenian (a local variety of German). Botoşani was part of what was called 'Jiddischland', or 'Yiddishland', a term used by historians to describe the floating zone between Poland, Lithuania, Belarus, Ukraine, Hungary and Romania that, before the Holocaust, was home to 11 million Jews. In this part of Eastern Europe, several varieties of Yiddish were the first language of everyday life.

The typical Jewish market town in this region was called a *shtetl*, a Yiddish term derived from the south German word *Städtel/Städtle*, meaning 'little town'. The street life of a *shtetl* was mainly dominated by Jews and had a distinctly Oriental atmosphere – there were Jewish coachmen in high boots, with long, curly locks and rustic clothing, open markets with butchers and livestock, Russian or Romanian peasants, and a few Christian townspeople. The shop signs were in Latin, Cyrillic and Hebrew letters. An early photograph of Botoşani shows such scenes and a town built of two-storey houses with a shop on the ground floor and family apartment above. Nearly all of the houses were made of wood, apart from a handful of stone mansions belonging to the wealthy classes. The streets were, depending on the season, mainly mud.

The artist Arthur Segal – whose real name was Aron Sigalu – grew up in Botoşani and hated it. Segal came from a banking family and he led a relatively privileged life. But he despised the dull and brutish natives of Botoşani, as well as the Orthodox Jews, the Yiddish and Hebrew languages and the prayers at the synagogue. Eventually the way out for Segal was through Dada, as one of the founders of the Cabaret Voltaire in Zurich in 1916 – the cabaret where Dada was invented and first presented to the public. But when he started painting as a young man in Botoşani Segal was not yet a radical avant-gardist; his early paintings of the town and region are figurative and romantic. The tones are also dark, the mood is melancholy and you can sense that he was dissatisfied and angry that he had to live here.[2]

For a large part of his life, Isou would claim that he felt the same way about the place. But Botoşani was not quite as provincial as Segal, or indeed Isou, made out. For one thing it was famous as the birthplace of Mohai Eminescu, the national poet of Romania. Eminescu's ambition

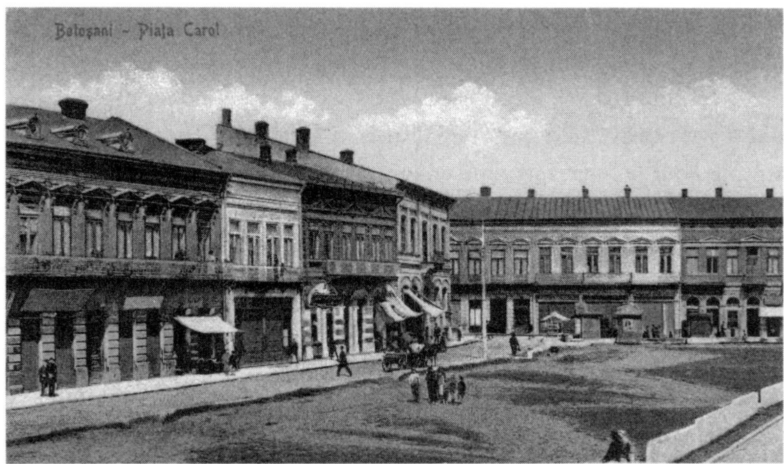

Postcard of Carol Square, Botoşani, early 20th century.

was to make the Romanian language a great language rather than a provincial dialect of Eastern Europe. Like all Romanian nationalists of the nineteenth century, Eminescu was also a passionate antisemite.

In reality, contrary to the grumblings of Segal, and later Isou, Botoşani was quite civilized by the standards of the era and region. The Marxist philosopher Lucien Goldmann, who made his name in post-Second World War Paris, was brought up in the Jewish life of Botoşani in the early twentieth century. In his unpublished autobiography, Goldmann describes '[a] town [which] probably differs little from many other Moldavian towns. Within it there were two communities which were numerically almost equal: Jews and Christians. Some [Jews] were quite rich but the majority was extremely poor.'[3] The Jews mainly worked in craft or commerce, while all the public positions in the civil and military bureaucracy were held by Christians, who were also manual workers and labourers.

As Mitchell Cohen describes it, Botoşani was a crossroads for trade passing back forth between Russia and Austria. As such it was prosperous enough to support a lively civic and cultural life; it had a good theatre and several high-quality publishing houses. It also had numerous Jewish houses of worship. The town's chief rabbi, Ezra Zuckerman, had an excellent library of Jewish ceremonial art.[4]

Botoşani was not, however, quite the model *shtetl*. As Lucien Goldmann also pointed out, its population was too mixed between Christians and Jews to properly qualify for this status. The Jew-hatred of the Christians – the 'true Romanians' – occasionally came to the surface. There were anti-Jewish riots in Botoşani in 1870; Jews were attacked in the street and businesses looted. More serious still was the so-called 'Peasants' Revolt' of 1907, which quickly spread across the region but began in Botoşani.

According to one account, peasants 'went on a rampage through the old town centre'. Old Believers (Russian Orthodox fundamentalists) emptied out Jewish stores and encouraged 'true' Christians to drive the Jews away from their territory. The populist newspaper *Moldava de Sus* (Northern Moldavia) called upon 'all true Romanians to save our ancestral land and our race from the infernal plans of the Yids'.[5]

Jews had no rights in this part of Romania until after the First World War. But they were allowed to be *arendaşi* – effectively managers on the estates of large landowners. Unlike the non-Jewish *arendaşi*, the Jews were not allowed to eventually buy the land they managed. This status made Jews doubly hated by the peasants: they were the instruments of the landlord's will but with no connection to the countryside. This was a dangerous position to be in; as Leon Trotsky explained it after a visit to Romania, this was how, 'while serving as a tool of feudal exploitation, the right-less Jew has at the same time to serve as the lightning conductor for the wrath of the exploited.'[6] When land reforms were introduced after the First World War, the *arendaşi* disappeared. But the resentment towards the *Jidan* (Dirty Jew) still lingered. Orthodox peasants cheered the Romanian troops, retreating from Russia, who took out their anger and humiliation on the Jews of the region.[7]

———

By the time of Isou's birth his family, the Goldsteins, had been established in Botoşani for three generations. They were Ashkenazi Jews and spoke Yiddish and Romanian with equal fluency. Yiddish (and some Hebrew) was associated with home and religion, and German, French and Russian with the outside world. When they spoke Romanian, like all the Jews from the region, they spoke with what Mihail Sebastian called 'a questioning lilt that comes from Yiddish'.[8]

Isou's paternal grandfather was a barrel-maker and the family was not rich. However, by the time that Isou was born the Goldstein family was wealthy enough to have two homes, one in the poorer and older quarter of Botoşani, where the family had its roots, and which was nicknamed *Calicime* (the Romanian for 'paupers' or 'beggars'), and the other in the new, commercial part of town. The family spent the dog-days of summer in the shade of the old town. The 'paupers' who lived here were mainly country people, still new to town life and who brought with them the habits and superstitions of the countryside. When business began once more with the bustle of the autumn harvest, the Goldsteins moved back again to the centre of the new town, to a parade of handsome two-storey buildings in the *Leipziger* style.

This is where Isou's father, Jindrich Goldstein, controlled his mini empire of shops across the Botoşani region. Isou described his father as the 'Romanian Félix Potin' – Félix Potin being a famous chain of Paris grocery shops. Isou despised his father for his money-grubbing. He was not above corruption – a house was burnt down by Jindrich to collect the insurance. Even though this was the kind of scam that ensured that the Goldsteins lived the good life, Isou thought it was mean and stupid.

He also saw his father as a show-off and a bore. Jindrich was a well-respected businessman with a taste for high culture. He was not Romanian but Hungarian (a nationality that made him doubly unpopular, as a Jew *and* a Hungarian, with the local 'true Romanians'). He was also extremely good-looking; when he made a first visit to the local kindergarten to check on the little Isou's progress, women clustered around him.

Jindrich was also well travelled, a fact that he often boasted loudly about in front of his friends and family. Among his businesses he ran a popular 'estaminet', or café, and he loved to hold forth to its clientele. He had been to France, Italy, Germany, Greece and Turkey, as well as to all the other Balkan countries. Isou was embarrassed about Jindrich's tendency to show off but most of all it made him wonder, from the earliest age, why did they still live in dreary Botoşani?[9]

Isou's first and greatest ally in the long war against his father was his younger sister Fanny. When arguments between the teenage Isou and his father turned violent – which was often the case – Fanny always defended her brother, calmly and without hesitation. Isou called her his Antigone – the grieving sister in the tragedy by Sophocles who, risking her life, goes against the king by ensuring that the body of her rebellious brother has a proper funeral. There was another younger sister called Ora (meaning 'my light' in Hebrew), born in 1936, who was also sometimes called Clarisse. But it was Fanny whom Isou loved best. She in turn stayed faithful to him to the end of both their lives, writing to him affectionately, now with her married name of Steiner, from her home to the north of Tel Aviv.

To reward her courage, Isou declared that he would give the entire proceeds of his first Nobel Prize to Fanny – this could not be far off, he assured her. He also promised to make sure that she married well, wedding a 'Young Lord' as 'young and beautiful as myself'. Fanny was an icon of feminine purity. Isou recalled an incident on a train in Sambothely (now Szombathely in Hungary) when he met a young girl who looked just like Fanny. He gave her sweets and bought her sandwiches. The following day, on seeing Isou kiss another girl, the younger girl burst into tears. Isou was deeply moved by this, and especially so because the younger girl 'had the same look as my sister when I used to slap her'.[10]

These statements are typical of the young Isou – provocative, amoral and grandiose. The model was not Romanian but the French poet Arthur Rimbaud, precociously gifted and defiant. Isou thought himself a revolutionary rebel in the same mould. Slapping his younger sister was no more important than making love to a girl whom he had just met and did not care about. But there was also obviously an emotional affinity. He adored Fanny for her gentleness. In this she incarnated a kind of feminine ideal, and most importantly this ideal was directly opposed to the boorish, masculine world of his father.

Isou attended a kindergarten and was mentored there by a certain Loewenstein, who was the director of the school and who encouraged Isou to read beyond his years in Romanian. Isou claimed that at the age of four he had a reading age of seven and that by the age of five he was easily accomplishing everything that children were just learning at the age of nine. This was only the beginning, said Isou, of his ascent.[11]

Most of his early schooling was, claimed Isou, a bore. He listened to stories of gods, angels and Romanian history with indifference. Isou's early years, like all Jewish children of his class and era, were entirely shaped by the regular, unchanging pattern of school, Sabbath, family obligations and religious festivals – all more or less common to the Central European Jewish bourgeoisie. He began his studies in the Botoşani Yeshiva – a Jewish educational institution devoted mainly to religious study. It was around this time (1932) that Jews were forbidden to speak Yiddish in the streets of Botoşani.

Around this time, Jews in Botoşani could expect to be insulted and sometimes physically attacked on a daily basis. The town was also home, however, to the Botoşani chapter of HaShomer Ha Tsair (the Young Guard), a Zionist and socialist youth movement that offered political, and sometimes physical, resistance to the antisemites. Inspired by the unlikely combination of Freud, Marx and Baden-Powell, this group was founded in Galicia, Austria-Hungary, and tried to imbue young Jews with a sense of moral perfection – a religious spirit without being religious.

The reading was eclectic: the Prophets, the Essenes, the Hasidism and the New Testament as well as the 'Romantic anti-capitalism' of Gustav Wyneken or indeed Constantin Dobrogeanu-Gherea – befriended by Trotsky when he visited Romania and described by the Marxist philosopher as 'Romania's Marx'.[12]

Other cultural influences in Botoşani included Zayde [Grandpa] Schwarz's bookshop, which stocked books in French, German and Yiddish and a few books in English.[13] This was a regular meeting place for young communists, who organized the 'Botoşani Reading Circle'. The shop was shut down in 1938 on the orders of no less than King Carol II, who was then starting to imitate the anti-communist and anti-Jewish positions of Adolf Hitler. Like most of the Romanian elite until this point, Carol had been staunchly Francophile. Now, he had decided to turn his back on his traditional allies and throw his hand in with Hitler. He was suspicious of 'communism' in both France and Russia and convinced too that the Germans would win any coming war.

King Carol II also loudly declared his belief that Jews in northeast Romania were really infiltrators from Russia and either communists or communist sympathizers. More to the point, he thought that they were all too ready to hand over Romanian territory to their Soviet masters at the first opportunity. Throughout the end of the 1930s, the propaganda from Bucharest intensified into a crescendo until it was believed everywhere across Romania that the Jews of Moldova were a Soviet fifth column, only waiting for the inevitable war to begin.[14]

It was easy to believe this because Romania was a place fraught with such massive tensions. In the words of Constantin Dobrogeanu-Gherea, it was 'a monstrous mingling of old and new'.[15] By this, Dobrogeanu-Gherea meant that the fundamental contradiction of Romanian life was that it was overwhelmingly a peasant, pre-capitalist society overlaid with legal and political structures that did not quite fit. The new and the old never met in Romania, in fact they were in perpetual antagonism: this was the fault line running through its history in the early twentieth century. Dobrogeanu-Gherea called the condition of the Romanian peasantry 'neo-serfdom' and pointed out that tensions in Romania all had their origins in the 'gap' between a tiny urban middle class and 'feudal realities'. The Jews were endlessly caught in the middle of these two opposites, as Trotsky had predicted, always the scapegoat on both sides.

In 1938 the situation suddenly got worse. Believing that the non-democratic countries, chiefly Germany and Italy, had the upper hand in the power play that was galvanizing Europe, Carol abolished democracy in Romania. The king had been profoundly disturbed by the French position at Munich – the French policy of appeasement not only deepened his pro-Hitler views, but made Romania vulnerable to ever-increasing demands from Germany to deliver more and more oil to feed its war machine. Carol was also now banking on German support if the Soviets threatened Romania's borders.

Carol's nearest rival was the charismatic fascist leader Corneliu Codreanu. Once an ally to, if not always a faithful supporter of, the king, he was 38 years old when he was killed by the king in 1938 on Royal Command as a potential rival and threat.

This was another decisive turning point; most of all it demonstrated not only the king's ruthlessness but his willingness to copy the thuggish style of the non-democratic countries he had thrown his hand in with. Hoping to impress the Germans, Carol began to draw up specifically antisemitic legislation. The first aim was to wage economic war against the Jews by excluding them from business and public life. Eventually the laws passed by Carol would discriminate against Jews not only as 'foreigners' in Romania but specifically on religious and racial grounds.

The snare grew ever tighter in August 1938, when Germany and Russia signed a non-aggression pact. This meant that Hitler had a free hand in Europe. The race to war with the Western powers now seemed unstoppable.

Almost immediately, Romania received a demand from the Soviet Union ordering the immediate concession of Bessarabia and northern Bukovina – the parts of northeast Romania with the largest Jewish presence. These stable communities, established here for centuries, were now suddenly under a severe threat. Many Jews believed that they were suddenly under sentence of death. This was when Jewish emigration from Romania became a flood. Palestine was a popular destination and underground Zionist groups started to operate throughout the country as antisemitic crimes became a fact of daily life.

In his later years, Isidore Isou very rarely spoke about his youth in Romania. His early life in Botoşani is, however, unusually and openly evoked by Isou in a novel called *Adorable Roumaine* (Lovely Romanian Woman/Girl, published in 1978). Isou wrote this book in 1975, at a time when he was undergoing psychiatric treatment. It was commissioned by a soft-porn publishing house and Isou only wrote the book to make some money, which at this point in his life he badly needed.

The heroine of the book – the 'Adorable Romanian' of the title – is Catinca, a child of the *mahalla*, the poorest area, of Botoşani. In Romania, it is always used with contempt. Traditionally, the inhabitants of the *mahalla* are also to be feared, partly because of their supposed command of sorcery and not least because of their mastery of the *mahalajoica* voice – a coarse and earthy form of invective in Romanian that comes from the *margine de oraş* (the edges of town).[16]

Catinca goes to Bucharest and then to Paris, where she is an all-conquering sexual adventurer. Isou appears in the novel as the author of the tale, an old friend of Catinca's from Botoşani, who also ends up in Paris, where he is a failed writer of avant-garde books (like this one!). Most importantly, however, the setting of the novel is obviously Romania in the early twentieth century. Among other things, Isou mentions the Peasants' Revolt of 1907, the rise of Romanian cinema, the cultural life of Bucharest, the Second World War, and the ever-present reality of violence from the fascist 'Legionaries' of the Iron Guard.

The Jews, and the violence against them which so marked Romanian history during this period, are, however, never mentioned. This did not mean that the Holocaust did not matter. Indeed Isou's head-on encounters with antisemitic violence during his early years shaped all of his thinking on politics, art and philosophy, as well as his identity, and ultimately his destiny. The Holocaust is never mentioned in *Adorable Roumaine* because it is a trivial novel, and the Holocaust could never be a trivial subject.

Shortly before he wrote this book, Isou's parents died in Israel. This came as a shock to Isou and he wrote the book partly to remember the life they had all known together. This was also the prelude to some of his most ferocious psychotic crises in the 1970s – when he felt that he was truly disintegrating as a human being. To keep himself 'safe', or 'whole', Isou returned to his memories of the 'Yiddishland' where he had grown up. When he talked about this to his doctors, Isou insisted that he was above all an *Ostjude*, a Jew from the Orient, and a Zionist. To do or say otherwise led to assimilation (he was angry with his father for this crime), which led to self-hatred (the great example here was Mihail Sebastian). Isou feared that self-hatred would lead to suicide, the greatest crime that he could imagine.

Isou did not deny or forget the Holocaust. But he refused to let its memory define him. Much of his psychotic illness in later life, as well as *lettrisme* itself, was a struggle against this fact.

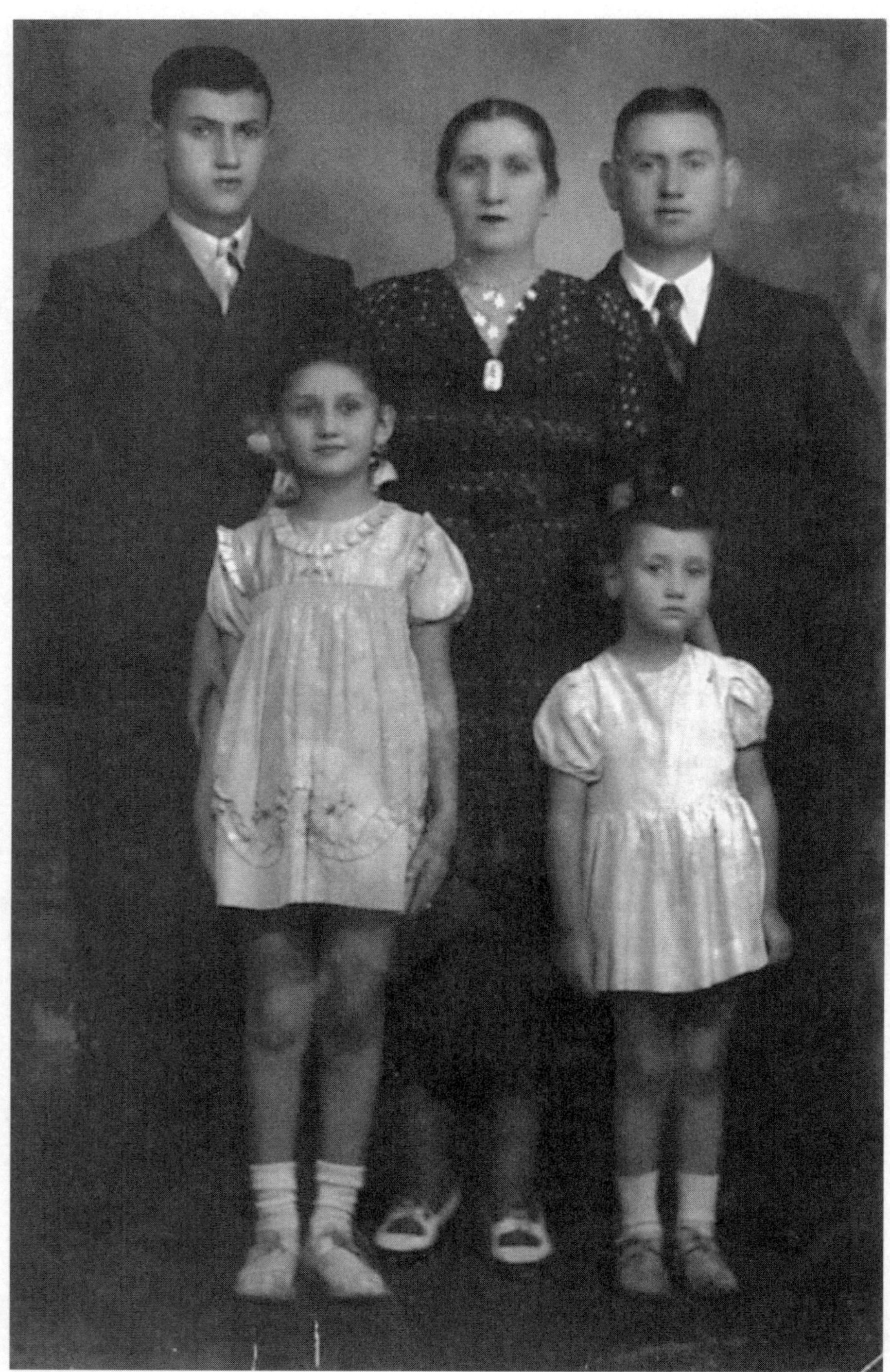

Isou and his family, early 1940s.

two

Young Savage

By 1933 the Goldstein family, like many fellow Jews from the same region, had moved to Bucharest. Jindrich Goldstein had long been planning the move, sensing already that anti-Jewish feeling in Romanian provinces was growing faster than ever before. Soon, by the end of decade, Jews would not be safe anywhere in Romanian territory.

The immediate feeling of Isou's family on arriving at the Gara de Nord was relief. If nothing else, the Goldsteins believed that among the large Jewish population of the city there would be safety in numbers. The idea was to get lost in the forest of Jews who lived in the mainly Jewish districts of Văcăreşti and Dudeşti in the centre of Bucharest. In the mid-twentieth century these central parts of the city were home to tens of thousands of Jews, many of them poor and, in Văcăreşti particularly, great numbers from the northeast of Romania, fleeing the massacres and the terror.

Although there was much poverty here in the cramped conditions, there were also large houses with English-style gardens commissioned by rich Jews in the early twentieth century. The Goldsteins took an apartment in a building in the heart of one of the less obviously Jewish quarters of Bucharest, at number 2 strada Pia Brătianu (now renamed strada Alexandru Philippide – after the well-known nationalist linguist who argued for Romania's Latin rather than Semitic roots).[1] It was large enough to reflect Jindrich's position in Jewish society. It backed onto an interior courtyard and with its balconies and elaborate facades that overlooked the cobbled streets beyond it would not have looked out of place in the 16th arrondissement of Paris. In the capital, the Goldsteins no longer had the social pre-eminence that they had held in provincial

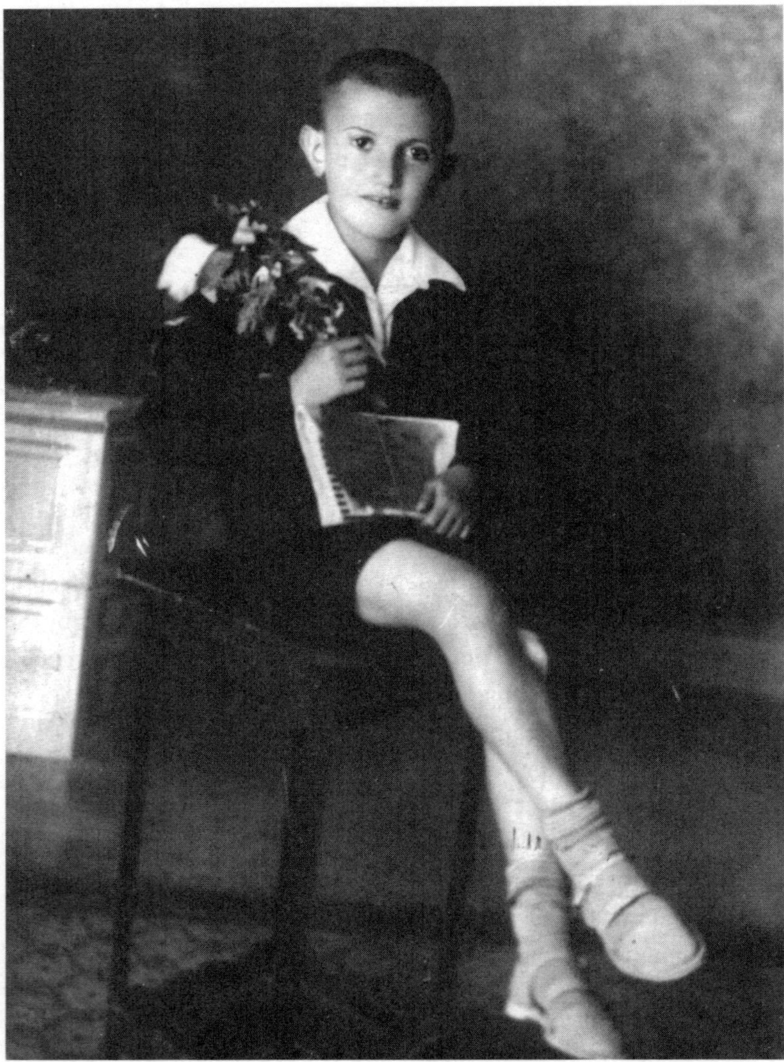

Isidore Isou as a child, 1933–4.

Botoşani but for now they felt that they were sheltered from the coming storms of anti-Jewish hatred in eastern Romania.

Isou claimed that was he was reading light novels at eight years of age, when he first arrived in Bucharest, then Dostoevsky at thirteen, followed by Marx, Proust, Husserl and Bergson. All of this, he says, without a dictionary in French or German – he had by now learned enough words not to need one. Furthermore, he said, he never read for pleasure – this was for foolish dilettantes – but for 'value', by which he meant the higher moral purpose of instructing himself in the great thoughts of mankind.

Now that the first part of the task was more or less finished, he argued with his teachers and his parents that there was no point in lingering with a pointless education that he had already exhausted.

At the age of twelve he brought into school a poem he had written himself and was unsurprised when the teacher, named Ion Dumitrescu, said that he should become a writer.[2] But this was useless advice for Isou: he knew already that he was a genius, but his destiny lay beyond that; he saw himself as a religious figure, predestined to bring illumination to humanity. So why wait? Why stay in school? His father did not agree and, until Isou learned how to fight back, would try and beat discipline into the boy.[3]

Isou was briefly sent away to study at the prestigious Liceu Aron Pumnul – named after a nineteenth-century writer from Transylvania – in Czernowitz, a town often called 'little Vienna' on account of its large Jewish population (Paul Celan was a native of the town and studied at the same school. It is now part of Ukraine). The young Isou felt that he was surrounded by stupidity everywhere. He recalled a school lesson during which the teacher concluded that God had decided to make Romania a country of contradictions and contrasts, linguistically and culturally, and this was why it was the envy of the world and therefore invaded so regularly and so often. For Isou this was ridiculous. He did not believe it for a moment; he could see, in his everyday life in the town and the school, that Romania was a land of division and hatred. He was regularly told that he could never belong here because he was a Jew. Sometimes he met such insults with his fists. His anger and contempt for stupid Christians hardened and deepened. Isou passed his final exams – the baccalauréat – with an overall average of six out of ten. He moved with relief back to Bucharest.

When the Germans – Isou always used the French term *Boches*, even in Romanian – began to move into Romania properly in 1940 Isou tried to join an underground resistance unit and asked to be involved in sabotage or assassination. Unsurprisingly, given his youth, his requests were turned down. Instead Isou and a friend called Harry Pantzer were given the task of sticking up posters and tracts on police and military installations. Sometimes they would try to stick the posters on a policeman's back – a dangerous, potentially fatal, activity. Isou soon grew bored with resistance activity:

> I think it's more difficult to cross a main street on a day of heavy traffic, taking a piss with your cock out, with no shame, as I did

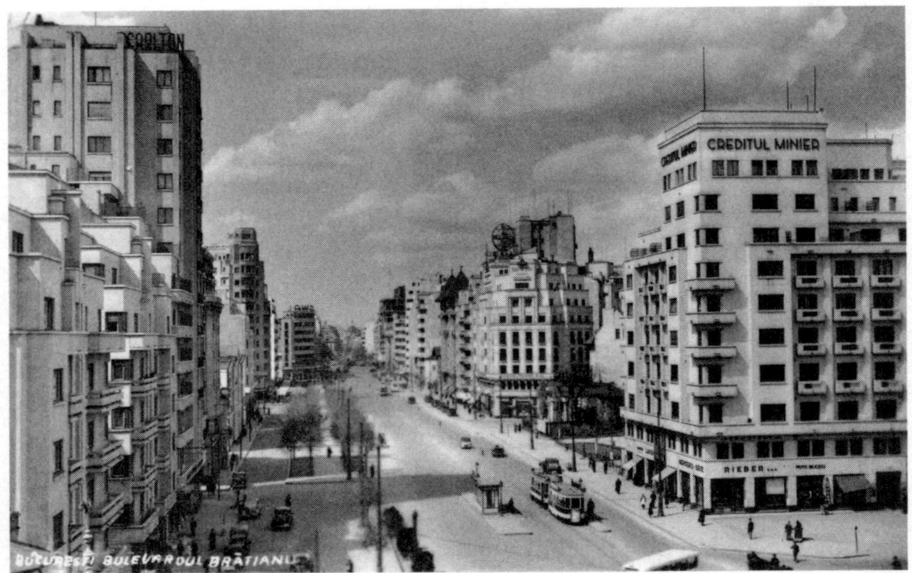

Brătianu Boulevard, Bucharest, *c.* 1939.

one time, than to stick up tracts. The first act demands an amazing self-possession, a total rejection of all conventional baggage, and the second requires only following orders which any cowardly person can do.[4]

He knew about the cruelty of the Germans and hated them for it. But he did not see what he could do to stop them that an army couldn't do. Instead, Isou swaggered and promenaded on the Calea Victoriei, attended the theatre and opera, took coffee at the Café Capsa and Café de la Paix, and seduced or tried to seduce *bourgeoises*. He frequented cabarets, which had a secondary role as upmarket brothels. Isou began to study French in Bucharest but he did not at first have any great feeling for the culture or the language. He had decided, however, that he was indifferent to the limits placed on him by knowing only a few languages, including French; instead he set himself the task of reading as much as he could in as many languages as he could. His method was: first, spend three months learning several thousand words from a dictionary, then read as much as you can, and then try to speak it. The accent did not matter – that was only sound; it was what you said that counted. With his newly acquired mastery of French, no matter how approximate, in his mind Isou was now the kind of cosmopolitan rebel that he had read about in Baudelaire and Rimbaud.

It helped that by the early 1940s, despite the war, Bucharest still had the remnants of a busy cultural life. Only a decade earlier the city had exhibited the likes of Picasso, Man Ray and Giorgio de Chirico. Stravinsky and Ravel had conducted its Philharmonic Orchestra. Marcel Proust was also well known and admired by the Romanian intelligentsia, not least because of his own fascination with Romania and Romanians – he collected them in Paris as friends and admirers and fantasized in his letters about distant and exotic Romania.

The young English traveller Patrick Leigh Fermor first visited Bucharest in 1934 and was fascinated by how casually well-read Romanians dropped the name 'Marcel', as if he were a personal friend. They did the same with 'Paul' (Valéry), 'Jean' (Cocteau) and 'Léon-Paul' (Fargue), among others. He also remarked that all of this pseudo-Parisian culture could feel like 'a ghastly nightmare'. He wrote that 'everyone seemed to be competing in a sneering marathon', describing his first experience of Bucharest café life, 'leaning back with a shoulder and an eyebrow raised, lip curled, waving an upturned palm over what sounded like *He!He!He!*, an unmelodious and jarring note'.[5] These arrogant young dandies were sometimes called *Bonjouristes* for their habit of greeting each other in French instead of with the Romanian *Buna ziua*. Leigh Fermor added: 'I hated them.' He felt as if he had been dropped into a bad French novel set in the Balkans.

In fact, the Romanian cult of France had its origins not in literature but in politics. In particular the Romanians had admired the way in which French diplomats had helped Romania gain independence and disentangle itself from the Ottoman Empire during the late nineteenth century. Encouraged by their new French friends, Romanian nationalists of the period began to believe a myth that Romania was a 'Latin' country adrift in a sea of Slavs; in their imagination France was the 'big sister' who would always nurture and help the 'little sister', Romania. During 1870 and the First World War, as Romania was establishing itself as an independent state, this love affair translated itself directly into architecture.[6]

With the Paris of the Second Empire as their model planners laid out great boulevards in Bucharest, which matched the loudly trumpeted ambition to be 'the Paris of the Balkans'. Bucharest had oil-fired street-lamps before Vienna and street lighting by 1882, well ahead of many Western European cities. In the same period more than 30,000 new buildings and about 120 churches were built. New areas were planned and developed – Delanvrancea Park and Domenilor Park were meant to equal anything in London or Paris. Large private villas were built around

Filipescu Park east of Şoseaua Kiseleff, the long boulevard running along the Herăstrău. French engineers and architects were commissioned to create a Western metropolis with open streets, open squares and modern houses and apartments – all were ornate, ornamental and self-consciously rejecting the Ottoman period.

New public buildings included a museum of popular art, the academy of architecture and the Palace of the Senate. The University of Bucharest in 1920 had 8,000 students, making it one of the biggest in Europe. The city had seventy primary schools and a whole host of grammar schools and colleges. Photographs from the early twentieth century depict a busy place, thronging with crowds wearing the latest European fashions, drinking in cafés, shopping in department stores, and attending shows and cabarets at music halls with Frenchified names. With its still visible Oriental past – shop signs in Hebrew, Cyrillic and occasionally Armenian script – and its overlay of French modernism, Bucharest looked like Constantinople rebuilt by Baron Haussmann.

This was always bound to be a flimsy edifice. Soon Bucharest was to be convulsed by an earthquake, a mini-civil war, anti-Jewish riots and finally deportations and massacres of the Jews. All of these events would have a great impact on Isou. But for his first months in the capital after finishing his school exams he was haunted by an image: the ghost of a girl he had tried to kill.

———

The girl was called Irina Galia. She was the same age as Isou and was a gifted student of mathematics. Irina walked with a pronounced limp, most probably as a result of childhood polio. He was first told about Irina by a mutual female friend, who told him that Irina had to spend long periods without moving. Isou was immediately intrigued by this; he was 'seduced' by the idea that Irina would remain motionless if he tried to make love to her; she would be detached and impassive, 'like a prostitute'.[7]

During this early period in Bucharest, Isou's greatest friend and intellectual companion was Serge Moscovici, a fellow Eastern Jew from the town of Brăila. After the Second World War, Moscovici would go on to become famous as one of the most distinguished social psychologists in France and a pioneer in Green politics (he later ran for the Mayor of Paris for the Green Party, *Les Verts*).

But for now, almost exactly the same age as Isou and renamed 'Solly' in Isou's memoirs, Serge was a disaffected rebel who admired Isou without reserve and through him fell in love with the avant-garde. Solly was also drawn to Isou because they had the same sort of origins; for all his worldly airs Isou was still a provincial: he walked in a heavy-footed manner – 'waddling like a duck' – had tender and cosy feelings for his family, despite frequent conflicts with his father, and laughed easily, for all his fanatical desire to be a metropolitan sophisticate. Isou was also already determined that he was a genius and acted as if he already was one; sometimes, says Solly, he acted as if he was mad, but he clearly wasn't and was also ready to laugh at himself.[8]

Having been thrown out of the Liceu in Bucharest due to antisemitic laws, Solly at first made a living by working as a welder in a factory. Both Isou and Solly immersed themselves in what avant-garde literature they could find. It was Solly's idea, inspired by his reading, that Isou should drive Irina to suicide. This would be Isou's first artistic work, his first great crime. Isou imagined the corpse of Irina as a living sculpture, comparing it to one of Marcel Duchamp's readymades.

Isou fantasized about himself chatting to admiring friends about the great trick he had played on Irina. So the relationship began with a phone call from Isou to Irina, with Isou begging her for a meeting above the shrieking voices of the clientele of the café where he used the telephone.

She finally agreed to see him but never turned up. Turning humiliation on its head, Isou said that he was glad about this – it taught him the truth, he said: that you only exist for other people if they choose to recognize your existence; that, like a character in a novel, you are both object and subject. In the same literary vein, on the day that Irina finally agreed to meet him, Isou also discovered the writings of Luigi Pirandello, devouring three of the Italian writer's plays and a novel in one sitting. Irina didn't at first know Isou's real name and nicknamed him 'Pirandello' because he talked so much about the Italian writer and his blurring of the real and imaginary.

When he finally met her, Isou saw that Irina was not a crippled monster who deserved to die: she was beautiful. Isou at first said that he was indifferent to her beauty, claiming that he was more impressed by her infirmity. But she was also an attractive and elegant figure: 'smoking cigarettes, the smoke wrapped around her like fur, like a lady in a fashionable English magazine'. He was attracted to her sexually. This was not why she deserved to live, however. Isou said that he recognized her as a fellow genius.

When they first met Isou persisted with Solly's plan. He talked incessantly about suicide, of killing yourself for no reason. He told Irina the story of a friend who had set fire to his hair. He wanted to 'burn his brain, turn his ideas into ashes'. Irina showed no reaction. Isou then told her about another friend, female this time, whose favourite game was to walk blindly into the heaviest traffic, ignoring cars, trams and buses. When she was finally run over and killed by a lorry she died without making the slightest cry. Another friend, a young man, stabbed himself in the chest on realizing that the meaning of life was that it had no meaning. Again Irina was unmoved, possibly thinking to herself that all of this had been invented, which of course it had.

Since he could not persuade her to kill herself, he decided that he had no choice but to kill her himself – in full view of other young men, to the sound of laughter, in bright sunlight. They took an outing to a nearby beach, probably at one of the Black Sea resorts then popular with fashionable *Bucarestois*.

Before meeting Irina, he had spent the previous night in a cheap hotel with a girl he had picked up by chance. Without returning home, he was first on the beach – tired, with a disgusting taste in his mouth. In the unreal haze of the sunshine, as Irina made sandcastles next to him, Isou began to terrify himself with the reality of his fantasy. He began to confess, saying that he had wanted 'to make something of her, to serve my own pride'.

Irina then picked up a copy of Martin Luther's *Table Talk*, which Isou happened to have brought along with him to the beach. She read aloud a parable that exhorted believers to pray against 'children of the Devil'. She then quoted Hrotsvitha, the tenth-century abbess of Gandersheim. Hrotsvitha's most famous work is the legend of Theophilus, an ambitious clergyman who is taken by a Jewish sorcerer to meet Satan, with whom he makes a pact. He later turns against the Devil and repents and is forgiven. Irina's meaning was clear: she understood exactly what Isou had been planning – her murder! – and it was now to be forgotten as a ridiculous adolescent prank. They both then lay on the beach coiled around each other. There was distant music, 'like an infinite tear'.

Unsurprisingly, after this misadventure, Irina never wanted to see Isou again. When she refused to take his calls he turned up at her house. On her father demanding to know the name of this young intruder, Isou responded: 'Is it obligatory to give my name . . . since I did not come to see you?' When M. Galia introduced himself as her father, Isou shot back: 'That is not my fault, and I'm sure it's not hers either.' Isou was immediately banned from the house. This felt 'like a kick up the arse' and Isou wanted go back and slap her father, or at least spit in his face.

When he was writing up Irina's tale for *L'Agrégation*, a young editor at Gallimard suggested to Isou that it would be more dramatic from a literary point of view if Irina actually did kill herself. Isou responded that the text already contained enough lies. One clue towards the unreliability of Isou's anecdotes lay in the name of an invented friend called Spoulber, introduced in the opening pages as a muse for the book, whose name was a play on the Romanian verb *a spulbera* – to blow everything up, which was what the novel, or autobiography, or whatever else *L'Agrégation* might be, was supposed to do. The tale was, in any case, not about Irina. To attract the reader's sympathy for Irina was a distraction from the real hero of the fable: an 'egocentric megalomaniac' – himself.[9]

There was, however, another, deeper truth behind the literary artifice. Irina had taught him that literature and life were not quite the same thing; even a genius like Isou had to face up to the human realities of friendship, empathy, even love. Isou thought he saw a girl who looked like her limping up the steps in the *métro* and, remembering the stupidity of his murderous plan, the sight of her sent shivers through him.[10]

———

Aside from killing Irina Galia, Isidore Isou's other great ambition on returning to Bucharest was to learn how to become a *huligan*, or hooligan. No one is quite sure when the English word 'hooligan' arrived in Romania. It had origins in nineteenth-century London to describe working-class ruffians, usually of Irish origin. It probably arrived in Romania from Russia, where it had been in use since the early twentieth century to describe the proletarian wreckers who would eventually create the Revolution.

Along the way on its journey to Bucharest, the word had changed class. By the 1930s, it was commonly used in Romania to describe a generation of young intellectuals who deliberately taunted and terrorized the older literary generation, and who declared that they hated anybody not born in the twentieth century. The venerable literary critic George Călinescu (who was born in 1899) detested them, describing them as 'snotty-nosed brats' and 'young savages'; they laughed right back in his face.[11]

These 'hooligans' were the main characters in the 1935 novel *Huliganii* (The Hooligans) by Mircea Eliade. They all dream of committing suicide, drink heavily, rape each other or are simply bored and sadistic. Life is pointless, art an illusion, philosophy is a dead-end and the civilization that made them is about to fall. Their philosophy was given voice by a student called David Dragu, who says: 'Only the barbarity of youth makes any sense; there is only one fervent debut in life and that is the hooligan's experience – to disrespect everything, to believe only in yourself, in your own youth, in your biology.'[12]

These were the role models that inspired Isou and Solly in their plan to kill Irina Galia. They also admired the writer Mateiu Caragiale, one of the most well-known 'young savages' of the era. Caragiale was the illegitimate son of Ion Luca Caragiale, one of the most important and respected playwrights in Romania at the beginning of the twentieth century. Caragiale *fils* hated his father and did everything he could to undermine his reputation. The elegant Café Capsa was overrun by his entourage of gypsies and bandits; he dabbled in occultism and drugs and was famous for his pan-sexual libertinism. Sometimes he deliberately sought out ugly women, and flirted with homosexuality and Sadism. He notoriously allowed one of his lovers to be raped by a stranger in the Cişmigiu Gardens in the centre of Bucharest. He was allegedly most sexually attracted to pregnant women, especially peasants, and trawled the country hospitals for vulnerable young women. Caragiale appears as a character in *Adorable Roumaine* under the name Mattei Cara, also nicknamed by Isou *Cara Nebunul* – 'Cara the Mad'.[13]

Isou admired Caragiale but his real teacher in this new anti-philosophy was a character nearer his own age and status called 'Bif'. One early evening Bif, Isou and some other friends were walking down an elegant *bulevard* in Bucharest, wondering whether to go to the cinema and then deciding it wasn't worth the effort; they were bored into fury by the banality of the people and the settings around them. Then, all of a sudden, Isou wrote, 'Something magnificent happened!'[14]

The 'something magnificent' was that somebody had spat right into the face of a woman promenading on the *bulevard*. Her face, Isou wrote, was covered in saliva 'like cellophane, disgusting and long like an earthworm, running down onto her fur coat'. Then a small mob of Isou's friends clustered round her, throwing her in the air, passing her from hand to hand so that it seemed that she was 'literally flying', each catching her just before she landed on the hard pavement. She was crying hysterically but no one knew what to do. The group of toughs, 'laughing, dodgy characters', looked as if they would 'rip open the belly' of anyone who interfered. Men stood back and watched, helpless. Women gasped with fear, 'their throats cut with emotion'. And then, as suddenly as it had started, with a word from the gang's leader, the game stopped. The leader of the gang was 'Bif'.[15]

After terrorizing the hapless *bourgeoise*, the gang went into a bar where they kissed and felt up any woman they wanted, whether they were obvious prostitutes or not, and in full view of their boyfriends, some of them army officers. They drank without paying, groping the breasts of the waitresses as a parting shot. No one dared move to stop them. Isou joined in with the 'hooligans', although he couldn't drink and never smoked (he never acquired these habits throughout his life). When a young man protested – as Isou pushed his girlfriend into the arms of one of the gang for a kiss – Isou smacked him hard, stunning the lad into silence. With this one daring act, Isou was now part of the gang.

They now swept down the *bulevard*, intimidating everyone they came across and stealing sweets and croissants from the street vendors. 'What we are doing is beautiful,' Bif said to Isou, 'Don't forget that!' Nobody dared challenge them. But they were now beginning to attract the attention of the police.

The quickest way to get out of the way of the gendarmes was to duck into the nearest cinema. Of course, they never paid. They didn't bother to watch the film either, launching into a chaotic free-for-all with the already seated paying customers. By the time the lights went up and the security staff tried to bring order, most of the gang had scrambled out of the auditorium. Isou stayed sitting, acting as respectably as he could and feigning disbelief at the *melée*. Shortly afterwards, back on the *bulevard*, Bif invited Isou to get involved in a test that was truly dangerous.

The plan was to go into a brothel and sleep with the most expensive girls without paying. The very real danger here was that they were no longer taunting the genteel *bourgeoisie* of polite society but tricking gangsters and pimps who knew how to use knives and guns. The 'adventure' was to occur in a place called Crucea de Piatra (The Stone Cross), where the most notorious and expensive brothels in Bucharest were to be found. Only three of the gang – Bif, Isou and a comrade called Antonio (a professional thief) – dared to do this, although the rest of the gang stationed themselves outside the brothel, promising to pile in if things got really rough.

If the plan was simple, the execution took courage. Wearing trench-coats and smiles, swaggering as if they owned the place or at least were regular customers, the three lads walked haughtily into the establishment, greeting Madame as an old friend. They browsed the photo albums – naked girls of every type, in all positions, some incredibly beautiful, others 'fascinating in their ugliness'.

With his chosen girl, a brunette, Isou tried to pass himself off as a man of the world but was all too aware that he was a mere boy. This was not the first prostitute he had known, but it was the first time trying to pull off a prank that could get him killed. He was panicky and after the sex was over he fumbled in his pocket to make sure he had enough money, 'just in case'. He needn't have worried. As their girls were getting dressed, Bif and Antonio appeared, grinning. In a single movement, they picked out coats from the cloakroom at random and were out on the street and gone, cackling as they tore down the darkened alleyways. Isou was breathless with fear and exhilaration. Beyond ideas, beyond books, this was how to live life as an 'adventure' – how to live properly and fully as a free human being.

Bif taught Isou how to steal and how to beg (this was simply another form of stealing, only 'with pity' rather than the cool-headed stealth needed to rob a house). Most importantly, stealing was a science. Isou compared it to the study of 'medicine' – divided into so many patients and maladies and species and sub-species of diseases; an infinite number of variables. Navigating your way through all of this took skill. As he advanced deeper into the art of thievery, Isou would abandon certain operations – stealing from a bookshop for example – because they were too easy. Stealing had to be a challenge in order to be true 'adventure'.

Eventually Isou fell out with Bif's gang. This was not just because of their cruelty – they would beat up strangers for no reason or organize a gang rape. The pretext was to defend his friend Solly, who had insisted on meeting for himself the gang of anti-social 'bandits' whom Isou apparently so admired. Isou didn't want Solly to come along; he knew that the gang had been drinking and were likely to beat up and rob such an obvious *bourgeois* student as Solly. They were also antisemites and Solly was very visibly a Jew.

They didn't beat Solly up but they did insist that Solly pay for all of their drinks at the end of the night. When Solly refused to do this, and Isou agreed with him, there was a fight. Isou was punched several times in the mouth before Bif stepped in. Isou couldn't be bothered with revenge, but from then on determined to work alone as a 'thief', hunting his prey 'like a tiger'.

Isou also admired Bif because he was a kind of poet. Isou noted that when Bif was drunk he tended to use a strange invented language that reminded him of Surrealist poetry. 'If the night is there,' he said to Isou one time, 'do not let her wait. Every night is like a new, empty bedroom waiting to be filled. That's your obligation.' On another occasion, Bif said,

> One night, trapped by the police, I broke a window, ready to jump out. I stuck my head out, to breathe in through the broken window, and I saw the sky, the stars, I all of a sudden became a poet. It was so beautiful that I forgot everything: the cops and the crime. I could see for the first time . . . I had the eyes of an owl, of a cat . . . eyes made to see the night.[16]

The reference to the Surrealists was no coincidence. Bif kept a journal full of paradoxical aphorisms that seemed to come straight out of a Surrealist manifesto. 'Getting old? It just means putting your cock in less and less filth!' read one of them; 'My face in the mirror? It makes me think of my head cut off, guillotined!' read another.

Bif also told stories. He invented a character called 'Hill' who set fire to himself and burned down his *liceu*. In his imaginary journal, composed by Bif, 'Hill' wrote that he admired the famous suicides of the Surrealist movement – Jacques Vaché, Jacques Rigaut and René Crével.[17] Bif (and Isou) also admired these 'joyful terrorists' – nihilistic dandies who had nothing but contempt for the shibboleths of work, family, politics and art. The leader of the Surrealists, André Breton, described their anti-philosophy as *umor* – a play on a supposed English pronunciation of the French word 'humour'. Above all, Breton's *umor* meant a 'superb indifference to life' and a 'hilarious trick'.[18] Bif and Isou could not think of a more perfect definition of the art of being a 'hooligan'.

Bif ended up in jail. Other members of the gang who had been arrested were condemned to death. But Bif had enough money to buy his way out and get an acquittal. Isou saw him on the street, fresh from prison. He was as cruel as ever. His final act, or boast according to Isou, was to impregnate a sixteen-year-old virgin with syphilis. The girl was called Médy and had been arrested for underground activities against the Germans. Bif paid for her to be sent to him. He literally fucked her to death.

Finally – at last – Isou was shocked. This was not an avant-garde prank – a 'hilarious trick' – but simple murder. He wanted to hit Bif or punish him in some way. But Bif was also by now a successful gangster in Bucharest, hardened by prison and notorious for a new level of ruthlessness and savagery, protected by a gang of real thugs. Isou was now disgusted by Bif but frightened too. Bif committed suicide after a robbery went wrong. Isou felt no pity or remorse.

———

Having exhausted school and schooling, Isou decided in the spring of 1940 that he wanted to learn about how the world worked. By this he meant the world of the present tense: 'the screech of motor cars, trams, men shouting in the street about the USSR!' Bucharest was a tense place at this time, ready to fall apart, or be torn apart by foreign powers. This was, according to Isou, what real history was supposed to feel like as opposed to lectures and sermons from teachers and history books. And so he went to work in a factory.

He was not interested in work in itself (this soon showed) but saw his sudden enthusiasm to 'do something' as an intellectual extension of his activities as a 'hooligan'; becoming a worker was a game and an experiment (and also extremely short-lived). He was first taken on in a weaving mill where there was a shortage of workers due to the mobilization widespread across Romania. On his first (and last) day, he was given the job of watching the power looms, looking out for warps ('like little farts', he said) and resetting the machine when he saw them. A boss gave him another job, carrying bundles up to the dyeing room, and a woman stopped to look at him with pity. He was unable to carry, or even lift, the bundle. When he did finally get it onto his back, he realized who he was: a well-dressed child.

He was shocked by the banter of the women workers in the mill. He could accept dirty jokes from his mates and other men, but was sickened by the appearance of these ugly, filthy women who made jokes about the size of his cock. He wrote that he felt like cutting off his dick at the root and throwing it to them, like throwing a bone to dogs.

Finally, he finished the day and returned home exhausted. Although he was still a self-avowed admirer of Marx and Lenin, he now also realized that he was no proletarian. He was put to bed by his mother and immediately went to sleep, lying with his back turned 'like a little baby pig'. He did not return to the weaving mill.[19]

This was not the end, however, of his adventures in the world of work. Using his contacts, an uncle got him a job in a hardware store. At first the manager didn't want to take Isou on – this was because the boy was the son of a prestigious and well-known businessman in the area – but the uncle convinced the store owner that Isou wanted to work and anyway would work for free. So Isou began his career in commerce by sweeping-up and trying to light the fire; he was incompetent at both and the girls who worked there laughed at him.

One of them took pity on him and showed him how to light the fire, but he never mastered the art of getting the gas to light up at once, so that flames 'appeared all at once everywhere, just as bandits do in a cowboy film'. He was then sent shopping for the lunchtime meal and cakes. He did this a few times, making a list and calculating how much it would all cost. He always got it wrong and even the lowest of the workforce, a snotty-nosed simpleton who mooched around all day, began to laugh at Isou.

His dire reputation among his colleagues was confirmed when they found him writing an avant-garde poem on the premises. If this was not enough, his lordly demeanour – never greeting customers or even his boss, refusing tips from kindly clients – made him seem like an arrogant lunatic to the other young people with whom he worked. Every evening the boss checked his staff as they left to see if they had been stealing. He didn't bother with Isou on the grounds that he was too useless even to do this; his workmates thought he was just the boss's pet. His humiliation was complete when a girl he knew – who liked him and had previously been impressed by his social standing – refused to dance with him or even acknowledge his presence because he had such low status as a worker. He lasted two more weeks in the hardware store.

It was finally Jindrich who could take no more of Isou's failing career as sweeper-up and dogsbody. Sensing that his son was the source of gossip and damaging his prestige, he installed Isou in an accountant's office, where he was set to learn the trade of numbers. He learned instead the art of 'subtle theft', becoming adept at making up figures and sums.

Isou's downfall was sex. He was sure that he had really only been taken on because his new boss's wife liked the look of him; she was less pleased when he started to sleep with the other girls in the office. He prided himself not only on his skills as a seducer and lover but as a dedicated masturbator. This was indeed his main activity, aside from reading Hegel, Bergson, Durkheim and Schopenhauer, and writing endless poems. A self-portrait drawn during this period depicts a thin, angular, intense face; it is not unlike the self-portraits made by Antonin Artaud during the heights of his madness. Isou was not mad, however – he was sure of this – he simply believed in his present and future greatness. Everything that had happened to him up until then – school, Irina, Bif and now this – were all part of his apprenticeship as a rebel, an outsider and eventually a prophet.[20]

In his memoir *Întoarcerea huliganului* (The Hooligan's Return, 2003) Norman Manea revisits his own youth in wartime Romania, and defines the *huligan* he finds there as 'an exile, a rootless, non-aligned vagabond', at war with the world around him and actively wishing for its destruction. These *huliganii* also often became fascists. Most of Bif's gang, for example, were antisemites who subsequently became fascists. They accepted Isou (and some other Jews called Goldberg and Moscovitz) because they were 'Israelites' who were destroyers; but they never believed that they were really the same people or ultimately on the same side.

In Eliade's novel *Huliganii*, the fictional character David Dragu is under the influence of André Gide, Nietzsche and especially a philosopher called Nae Ionescu. Ionescu was not fictional but very much real and alive; arrogant and aloof, incredibly charismatic and a forceful antisemite. Ionescu had a visceral hatred of Jews – he thought that they were ugly, physically weak and morally degenerate. The *huligan*, in contrast, was strong, and only violent because an excess of vitality made him so. This way of thinking was given the name *Trăirismul*, effectively a translation of the German term *lebensphilosophie* (philosophy of life), which emphasized the primacy of action and experience over reflection or theory: this was a philosophy that was influential in the early life of the Nazi Party in Germany.[21]

This philosophy also heralded no less than 'a spiritual revolution' in Romania. The soldiers who were to lead this revolution were the so-called 'Legionaries' of the Legion of St Michael, known also as the *Garda de Fier*, or 'Iron Guard'.[22] Unlike other fascist movements in Europe, the Iron Guard were not only anti-communist and anti-capitalist, but mystics. They believed that Romanian nationalism and the Orthodox Christian faith were inseparable; rather than the 'superhuman' dreamt of by the Nazis, they wanted a spiritual purification which would bring the nation closer to God. They wore green shirts to show their identification with nature. The organization spread its propaganda through a so-called *Echipa morții*, or Death Squad, which travelled through all of Romania, singing patriotic hymns in the face of violence, even the threat of death, from their enemies – the police, communists and Jews.

The most fertile recruiting grounds for the Iron Guard were the schools and universities. This was where young people found a way out of the rebelliousness and nihilism of the *huligan* in this new faith, which proclaimed itself as the living incarnation of the 'Romanian genius'. This only worked, of course, if you were not Jewish.

Nonetheless, there were Jews who had complicated emotions about the Legionaries. One of these was Mihail Sebastian, who claimed Nae Ionescu as a mentor and a friend and even asked Ionescu to provide a foreword to his book *De două mii de ani* (For Two Thousand Years, 1934), an account of the rise of antisemitism. Ionescu obliged with a venomous article in which he stated baldly that no Jew could belong to a national community. When he printed the article, still in awe of his teacher, Sebastian ran into a firestorm of hatred from his fellow Jews, who claimed that he was a traitor and a collaborator. He tried to explain himself in an essay, 'Cum am devenit huligan' (How I became a hooligan), but he couldn't get out of the trap he had made for himself.

Soon, however, both Sebastian and Isou would find themselves caught up in events beyond their control, and which forced both young men into a direct confrontation with the nature of antisemitism in Romania.

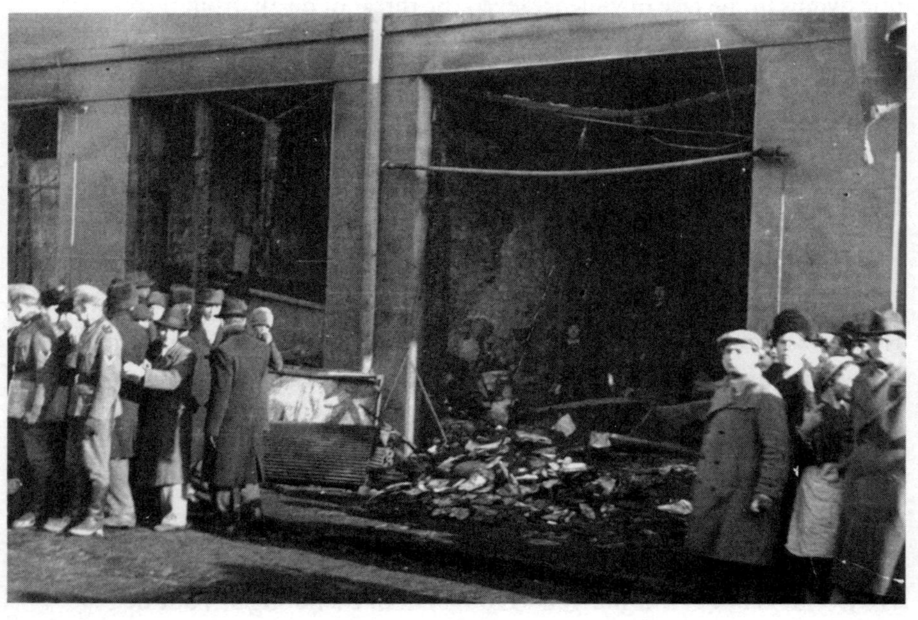

Jewish stores destroyed after a pogrom, Bucharest, 23 January 1941.

three

'God loves everything anti-Yid!'

Isou had not yet reached his sixteenth birthday when he was almost killed by the Legionaries of the Iron Guard during the night of 23 January 1941.

Tension had been building in Bucharest for weeks. At the beginning of January Isou had noticed that there were more and more pro-Hitler posters and pieces of anti-Jewish graffiti in the Jewish areas of the city – all the work of the Iron Guard, the members of which were now publicly expressing their anger with the government of Marshal Ion Antonescu. Antonescu, in their view, was not acting with sufficient speed and cruelty towards the Jews. The trigger for the revolt was the killing of a German soldier by a Greek citizen. A rumour went around the Legionaries that this was the work of British Intelligence, 'the British government of Freemasons', and that the slack government of Antonescu had allowed it to happen. Within hours armed Legionaries had launched a full-blown revolt, seizing government buildings and opening fire on the police. It also quickly became clear that their main target was the Jews and that the revolt was also a pogrom.[1]

On 20 January, the Goldsteins, like all the other Jews in the district, heard gunfire in the streets. They stayed indoors. Jindrich Goldstein hid the family valuables. Crouched behind curtains, they watched stray bullets ricochet across their street. The following day Isou hesitated before leaving home. He had just started working in the offices of I. Ludo, the writer Isac Ludo, one of the best-known Jewish literary figures in Romania. He had been invited to help Ludo edit a semi-underground journal called *Palestina*. Ludo's office was in a leafy residential district, at number 3 strada Doctor-Burghelea, in the same villa as the headquarters of the Federal Union of Jews in Romania (this building now houses the Danish Embassy).[2]

The morning was quiet – 'calm as an egg', as Isou described it (a description more Romanian than French). He watched other young Jews scurrying about and calculated that he would be safe. As Isou went to enter the building he was stopped by a young thug, whom he took at first for a street beggar. Isou fumbled in his pockets for change to give him. 'Are you Jewish?' the thug asked. 'Yes of course,' replied Isou. 'Come here!' the thug said.

Isou was shocked. What astonished him most was the sudden coarseness of the fascist's voice. It was as if, he wrote, 'an elegant woman was suddenly to spit in a smart salon'. 'Listen, you filthy Yid, I told you to get in here,' the fascist barked. 'Don't you understand our language, you dirty little Jew?' Isou gave the 'Christian' a look of contempt. Then he was pushed into the courtyard of the building with other Jews, men and women, most of them workers for the various Jewish organizations housed in the building. In the courtyard, they were encircled by guards, armed with pistols, clubs and machine guns.

At first Isou refused to be scared. When the young guards started spinning their revolvers around, evidently copying the cowboys they had seen in the cinema, Isou sneered at their childishness. Seeing this, one of the fascists, wearing heavy leather boots, kicked Isou hard in the stomach, knocking him to the ground. Isou began to moan, more 'out of shame', he said, rather than real pain. This was when Isou understood who and what he was in their eyes: less than an animal, a demon Jew.

As the group of Jews was divided into columns – 'partitioned like the notes in a piece by Satie', Isou said – he saw on the other side of the road a man who had been sent by his mother to find him. As soon as the man saw what was happening, he 'crumbled with fear' and backed into a wall, unable to move – 'suddenly like the burned-out husk of an almond', trembling and short of breath. He then ran off, gone as quickly as a 'fly crushed in the palm of your hand'. For the time being, Isou refused to feel frightened by these stupid 'Christians', posing as hard men and terrifying the women.

One of the 'Christians', evidently a kind of chief, stood forward and shouted for the keys to the office safe. Isou's friend, known only as C., who held the keys, began to wail uncontrollably with fear. 'Hey, I know you – you bastard Yid!' said the chief. 'You're the one who denounced me to the Prefecture for "financial irregularities".'

C. turned a 'pale, waxy yellow' and then bright red. His name was Sigmund Collin and he was the accountant for the Federal Union of Jews. He did not survive the pogrom – his mutilated body would be found in a heaped pile of naked Jewish corpses a few days later. Right now, Collin's jaw trembled, his whole body shook. One of the fascists picked up a small hammer and started tapping him with increasing force on both cheeks. By chance, Isou caught sight of the old concierge of the 'Palestine Office', an elderly man who had seen pogroms before, now shuddering, overcome with terror. Isou too was starting to feel the fear; it was unstoppable, overwhelming, spreading through his body 'with a roar', blanking out his mind.[3]

Then Isou was punched in the face. The blow came from one of the smallest of the thugs, who stood only at shoulder height to Isou (who was not tall). The thug spat on the floor and barked: 'Jews! Stand up!' He then went to each one of the Jews and smacked them hard in the face.

Isou wanted to hit him back but couldn't – standing behind the thug were armed men waiting for an excuse to shoot him – and so he burst into tears. This enraged the thug, who then started to properly batter Isou. The violence was steady; the thug took his time, flexing his muscles, picking out the places of maximum pain. The blows rained down on Isou like 'birds in a cage, flapping madly to get out'. He knew suddenly that he was about to be killed. And then, as Isou began to feel that he was 'drowning in a sea of blows', getting lost in 'a forest of pain', the beating stopped. Isou clung onto consciousness. He heard voices from the corridor and the words 'the Yids are in there to be beaten.'

With another Jew, Isou was picked out by 'an Orangutang' to sweep out the offices, now occupied by civilian 'Christians', men and women, laughing and kissing, celebrating their 'victory' over the Jews. One of the 'Christians', showing off to the girls, flew at Isou as soon as he caught sight of him, and began to hit him. A young girl started complaining, pleading with the young man to stop for the sake of pity. Isou was then dragged into a side office, obviously being used as an improvised interrogation room. By this stage, Isou was surrounded by a 'halo of nothingness', and was barely clinging onto life.

In the 'interrogation room' Isou was surrounded by a new group of thugs, who punched and smacked him with rubber truncheons. The first question was: 'So why do you want to go to Palestine, Yid? You don't like our country any more?' The second question was: 'Why do you want to stay here, Yid? Haven't you exhausted our country enough, you flea, you parasite, you vampire?' Then another voice: 'Teach this little Yid how to sweep up! He still thinks that he's in his mother's shit!' Isou now felt as if his body were on fire. The rubber truncheon was like a torch that lit fires in his lower back and buttocks. He was reduced to a throbbing piece of meat, barely a human being.

Still dazed, he was dragged into another room, packed with more Jews, where the 'Christians' began to justify their actions. One of them, in a strangely calm voice, almost like a teacher, said that all of this was because the Jews had killed Jesus Christ, that the Romanians were a Latin race, that Jesus Christ was their true King, and now his death was to be avenged on the Jews of Romania. God would not be happy until they were all dead. The Jews were then forced to chant, 'Long Live the Christians! Death to the Jews!'

The chant was interrupted by a Jew, who put a question to the guard. 'Why, sir, if God wants to kill us, does he use other people other than himself? And why does he wait and not kill all the Jews at once?' The teacher-guard seemed flattered and started to answer the question, slowly and carefully, saying that Jesus Christ was not killed at once, but left to suffer, and this too should be the punishment of the Jews – and the Christians were the instruments of God who would execute His plan.

Another Jew, encouraged by the lull in the violence, stalling for time, began to quietly argue back, explaining that the Bible was in fact a Jewish book. The guard was stunned. He took a Bible out of his pocket. 'Is the Bible written in Yid language?' he said. 'It's in Christian language. This is how God gave it to Jesus Christ to give to the Christians because he loved the Christians. God loves the Christians and Germans because they are antisemites. God loves everything anti-Yid!'

The discussion was stopped by wild screeching cries from a neighbouring room. They all knew at once that people were being killed. Then it was Isou's turn to go into the new room. His mouth was stuffed with a dirty cloth and he was made to lie down on the floor. He could barely stand anyway. He was kicked and battered with a riding crop and sticks. He couldn't cry out. He spat out the cloth and howled with agony before passing out. The beating stopped. The guards thought that they had finished him off.

When they picked up his limp body, they were surprised to see that he could still just about walk. Isou was taken downstairs to a cellar. His head was shaved by a huge blonde man who said he wanted revenge on the Yids for the death of his brother in the First World War. There were

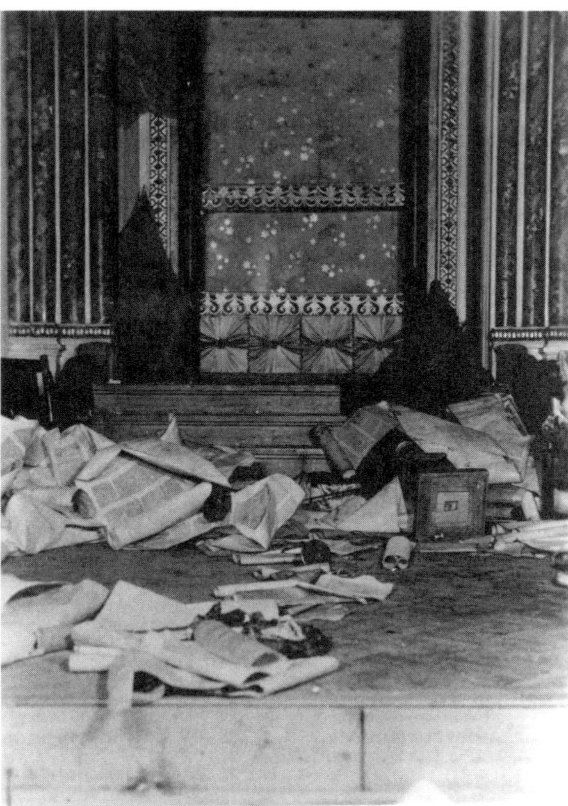

Torn Torah scrolls in a desecrated synagogue after a pogrom, Bucharest, 23 January 1941.

more questions from the blonde giant: 'Why do you think we have machine guns outside? Why do you think that we are antisemites?'

Isou could not breathe, let alone speak. He was beaten again, this time on the palms of his hand with a wooden club. He was then shoved into a pile of Jews, all lying on top of each other. The weak and the old were unconscious. Some were either surely dying or already dead. Isou thought of his mother, longing for her to be next to him. He tried to use logic to comfort himself. As long as he could feel pain – he reasoned – he was still alive.

A 'new cretin' came in and kicked Isou and all the other Jews strewn on the floor in darkness. Fatigue now began to overwhelm him and, unable to sleep, he drifted into a waking nightmare. An older Jew began to cry, begging the younger ones to finish him off. But none of them could do it.

Isou called out 'Mother, Darling Mother'. At least these words were real, even if they no longer brought comfort. Other Jews tried to comfort Isou; in their tenderness, he saw his mother in each of them. Isou became delirious. He cursed the guards: 'They will be punished, their time will come . . . Mother, do not pray for them!' The guards, ignorant and superstitious, crossed themselves against what sounded like a devilish Jewish incantation. Isou's muttered words became names; now he was chanting philosophers: Schopenhauer, Nietzsche, Plato, Spinoza. Half-recognizing these famous names – maybe Jewish saints or demons? – the guards were suddenly fearful.

There was a brief silence, broken by the entrance of an *Echipa morţii* (Death Squad), who marched in and started to sing patriotic songs. It was well known among the Jews that this was the ritual prelude to a massacre. One of the guards, an official 'Orator', began a speech claiming that all of the Jewish parts of the city were now in flames, 'red like Communist Flags'. All of the Christians were about to wipe out all of the Jews, like 'cigarette stubs'. Everything that belonged to Jews would now belong to Christians, even Jewish lives, because they had been born in Christian countries. Isou thought of his sister and then his father. For now, the guard went on, they would be safe. He said he didn't know yet if they were to be killed or transported and that all the transport at this point was full, taking Jews to be killed.

Not long after this, there were rumours that the 'revolution' was not going according to plan for the Iron Guard. There was still violence – kicks, punches, slaps. Isou was now put into a tiny room filled with old people who had been there for several days, endlessly tortured by lit cigarettes stubbed out on the soles of their feet, testicles beaten with batons to make them sterile, hands hammered out of shape. When they weren't being tortured, these elderly Jews told stories and anecdotes; the Christians were all imbeciles and the Jews always had the upper hand in these tales. There were smiles and tears. Isou said that this is where he learned the subversive power of laughter. It was like a 'certificate of good health'.

The next morning, Isou woke to find one of the guards trying to steal his shoes. When the guard saw that they were too small he moved on to another prisoner. There were whispers: the revolution had failed and the rebellion was over.

Another guard – the same one who had attacked C. – barked at Isou, telling him to get up and get out of the building. He was free. Isou didn't believe him. As he left the building he waited to be shot in the back. Walking down the street he thought he'd never see again, a guard called him 'Comrade' and wanted to walk with him. It was the one who had tried to steal his shoes. The guard was afraid to walk alone and assumed Isou was a fellow fascist. 'I am not your comrade. I am a Jew!' The man disappeared.

When Isou finally got home, most of the buildings in the quarter were still burning, about to crumble. The streets were packed with their former inhabitants. At first his mother, Saly, could not speak when she saw him. She had spent the night running from street to street like a madwoman. His sister Fanny embraced him and then – even though Isou later thought it was 'puerile and shameful' – they all collapsed into tears. They then waited for Jindrich Goldstein to return. He had been hunting for his son among piled-up bodies of Jews who had been slaughtered that night.

———

The days and nights of the pogrom in Bucharest in late January 1941 are some of the blackest moments in the story of the Jews in Romania. In 2016, however, there are still those who say that it never happened, and the rebellion was really an attempt to take power from Ion Antonescu, who was weak on 'communism'; that the 'excesses' of the Iron Guard Legionaries were an expression of frustration with the government, and they had the backing of Adolf Hitler; that any violence against Jews was simply 'Jewish Propaganda' and no more than a sideshow.

Isou was one of the many who saw what really happened. Another was a Jew who was also a journalist. This was F. Brunea-Fox, whose real name was Filip Brauner (he lifted the Fox part of his *nom de plume* from the Twentieth Century-Fox movies, which he loved) and who was one of the first to publish an account of what happened. This was an eyewitness journal called *Orașul măcelului* (The City of Slaughter), which he published in 1944 (and which was devoured and referenced by Isou straightaway). Brunea-Fox listened and watched from his house on strada Vasile Lascar as the Legionaries and their supporters (including trade unionists, school children, students and gypsies) launched attacks and riots in the districts of Văcărești and Dudești. Homes were set on fire and Jews were rounded up and taken to torture centres: the Iron Guard headquarters known as 'Green Houses'.[4]

One of the most sadistic leaders of the Iron Guard was Mircea Petrovicescu, who tied up male Jews and used them for target practice. He did the same to Jewish women, only with their backs turned to the firing squad. His men also sliced off women's breasts and used drills to kill them. As well as murder, there were countless rapes and other savage cruelties. These were the demon 'hooligans' of Mircea Eliade now come to life.

Brunea-Fox watched from his window as his neighbour, a lawyer called Millo Beiler, was arrested, 'struggling open-mouthed with a desperate and aphonic cry for help'. Everybody knew that nothing could be done to help those who were 'taken'.

One of the most shocking atrocities took place only a few hours before the end of the rebellion. This was the killing of fifteen Jews, including a five-year-old girl, who were selected at random by a group of Legionaries and driven in a truck from the Potsudeck sausage factory to the city slaughterhouse at Băneasa (now the site of a shopping mall and an IKEA store). There they were tortured, shot, skinned and their entrails hung around their necks, a breathtakingly vicious mockery of *shehita*, the *Kosher* practice for killing cattle.

Until now, Ion Antonescu had all too often described the antisemitic excesses of the Iron Guard as 'Romantic Incidents', lamenting them only as a combination of youthful zeal and well-intentioned if sometimes misdirected nationalism. But this was something else. Antonescu was never a friend of the Jews ('The Jew is Satan,' he once said), and ultimately responsible for the gravest crimes against humanity. Nonetheless, when the rebellion had long since been quelled, he appointed a military prosecutor, Reserve Lieutenant I. N. Vladescu, as part of a wider inquiry into the rebellion. Vladescu reported to Antonescu that he recognized three of his acquaintances among the 'professionally tortured' bodies (lawyer Millo Beiler and the Rauch brothers). He added:

Under the pretext of acting against a movement of a political nature, the Legionnaires committed mass murder at the city slaughterhouse, at Baneasa. More than a hundred people were butchered. Some were found with their bellies deeply cut open by the despicable assassins, who used butcher knives for this purpose. As masters in the art of torture, they had taken the intestines they had torn out of their victims' bodies and tied them like neckties around their necks. While this carnage took place inside the slaughterhouse, outside a large number of Legionnaires were singing and making a mockery of Jewish psalms and prayers. The German military attaché in Bucharest was collecting casualty reports ... In the Bucharest morgue one can see hundreds of corpses, but they are mostly Jews. They could no longer be identified as human bodies. In the municipal slaughterhouse, parts of bodies were hanging on hooks like carcasses of cattle. One witness saw a girl of about five hanging by her feet like a calf, her entire body was drenched in blood.[5]

The American Ambassador to Romania, Franklin Mott Gunther, also visited the slaughterhouse. He wrote to Washington: 'Sixty Jewish corpses were discovered on the hooks used for carcasses. They were all skinned . . . and the quantity of blood about was evidence that they had been skinned alive.'[6]

On Isou's terrible night of torture, Jindrich Goldstein had spent most of the evening at the morgue. Unable to find his son among the bodies scattered like so many 'spent cartridges', he was too shattered to leave the morgue until the morning. He was shocked that all the bodies were naked and even more shocked to think that he did not know what the naked body of his son looked like, and that he probably wouldn't be able to recognize him. As his father told him this, Isou, stretched out but sleepless on his bed, thought to himself that he would have been ashamed to have been naked and so would have hidden himself behind 'a pile of carrion'.

'Your death would have been the end of the world for your mother,' his father said. Isou reflected on this. This was the way that families – love – worked. One was never alone in a family, but when you died you left loneliness behind you, for the others who didn't die. That was what his mother was afraid of: solitude, loneliness.

Jindrich went on with the story:

A truck loaded with oil came down the street – people were shouting 'Death to the Jews!' I took your mother and everyone else in the apartment and went up to the second floor, to the neighbours' apartment. From the window we could see properly what was going on. They were looting, taking everything, clearing up as if they were stage hands in a theatre.

Isou reflected again that stage hands knew nothing about the spectacle that they were creating – but that it was the spectacle, the image of what they had created, that lingered in the mind of the spectator.

'You don't know what they did, Isou. They cut the throats of Jews in the slaughterhouse, and then strung them up, like icons. But nobody came to buy our soiled icons – they were too lifelike. And then the children were massacred.' Isou tried to smile. Mothers always clung to their children, like 'the froth on a glass of champagne'. Surely the children would be safe.

Jindrich continued, 'they killed the two sons of a Rabbi. They shot the Rabbi three times but couldn't kill him. The people cried out that it was a miracle.' This had taken place on 23 January in the forest of Jilava, to the south of Bucharest. The local Iron Guard commander had orders to exterminate all the Jews in the region. Altogether 92 Jews were shot in the forest. Rabbi Guttman survived the mass execution but no one knew how. The story quickly became a legend and was recounted by Brunea-Fox in his book documenting the massacres.

As his father spoke, Isou pictured the scene and said to himself that by now they all needed miracles. 'Jews were strangled in the toilets, drowned in shit.'[7] At this, Isou froze; this was a transgression that defied all humanity: to defile the dead, death itself. 'Old men had their beards ripped off. Women were raped and killed.' Isou had a brutal, almost unbearable thought: that maybe some of these women had died in unwanted orgasm, in bitter communion with their violators. 'Naked men were left in the snow until they froze.' With this, Isou's father was silent, unable to go on beyond the image of 'men became marble.'

After a long, heavy silence, his father said:

> Could it be one day that you will write, Isou? And that you will write down the name of every Jew killed, like a litany, like an obituary, so that each of them might live on. Even just in a small way. And this memory would be more beautiful than their real moment of death.

'No. Never,' Isou said. 'There are so many cadavers that they are already lost in one another. And I'm sure too that people will think of the death of Jews as a grotesque joke. Or they would think that it is at least normal and banal.'

Jindrich said nothing. Isou suddenly felt an immense sadness.[8]

———

The storm passed. Mihail Sebastian had spent the days of the rebellion stranded in his apartment on Calea Vitoriei, surrounded by Iron Guards and gunfire, agonizingly cut off from his family. In his journal, he noted on 24 January that the streets were quiet.[9] When he went back to his office for the first time since the start of the pogrom, he noticed that some of his colleagues in his office carried on as if nothing had happened, did not talk about the events of the past few days, were even bantering and laughing as if everything was normal. But for Jews in Romania there was now no longer any such thing as 'normal'. Like Sebastian, Isou too noted the quietness of the streets where he lived. But he thought that this apparent tranquillity was not really calm. It was fear. 'We had our mouths close to heaven,' he wrote. 'Some of us were already ready to commune with the Beyond.'[10]

The fear was soon compounded by stories of massacres in other parts of Romania. The first great pogrom took place in late June in Iaşi not far from Botoşani and the border with Russia. The trigger was a bombing raid on Iaşi by the Soviet airforce – a pre-emptive strike against the German invasion of the Soviet Union, which was then just about to begin with Romanian military support. The strike did not do much damage but it was soon rumoured that local Jews, in league with the Russian communists, had lit torches to guide the bombers. Iaşi was bombed again on 26 June and this time six hundred people were killed (including 38 Jews). On 27 June, Antonescu gave the order to 'cleanse Iaşi of its Jews'.[11]

Straightaway, the army and the police, aided by ordinary men and women, began rounding up Jews, raiding shops and houses. Many Jews went into cellars or other hiding places. To flush them out, the police distributed papers summoning Jews to local commissariats, promising that they would be free if they did so. They were met by machine guns and marched off for execution or herded onto so-called 'death trains', overloaded wagons that rumbled slowly and pointlessly through the surrounding countryside for eight days. Five thousand Jews died on these trains, either of starvation, thirst or sheer fatigue. Gypsy children sold the anti-Bolshevik tract *Romanul măcelarului roşu* (The Story of the Red Butcher) in the streets with the refrain:

Pleacă trenul din Chitila/Cu Stalin în Palestina
Pleacă trenul din Galaţi/Cu jidanii spânzuraţi.

The train will come from Chitila, with Stalin in Palestine.
The train will come from Galaţi, with Jews for hanging.[12]

The number of Jews that were killed in the following days and weeks has not been properly established, but no less than 13,000 were killed by the Romanian army. The Romanian troops were aided by civilians, gypsies and children, some of them 'shouting for joy' – according to an Italian eyewitness – as they mutilated corpses and lifted up naked bodies (clothes were stolen as a matter of course). Unlike many of the deadly pogroms that took place in Eastern Europe, which were often covered up or lied about, all of this slaughter took place in open daylight and was celebrated as a victory for Romanian 'Christianity' in the supposed war against 'Jewish Communism'.

Isou heard the rumours and read the facts in whatever foreign newspapers were still available in Bucharest. He was particularly disgusted by the way that Jews had been tricked onto the 'death trains', which were 'randomly sent out with no meaning, like a foreign language, endless, all the same, and incomprehensible'. He decided from now on to exalt the term 'communist' because the word was a mask used by 'Christians' for hating Jews, whose throats would be cut anyway. More than this, he decided, he would love everything that this 'Christian' civilization hated. It was a simple reversal. If God 'loved everything anti-Yid' then Isou, the 'Yid', in order to be free, had to love everything that was anti-God. He called this *Judaisme à l'attaque* (Judaism on the attack), declaring that Zionism did not go far enough, that it was in fact a way of giving in to 'Christians', who were in reality the true sub-humans, rather than the Jews.[13]

In March 1942 Isou and Mihail Sebastian were both detailed by the authorities to a work gang for Jews (although they had mutual friends they still did not know each other). That winter had been one of the hardest and coldest that Bucharest had known in living memory and packed snow and ice now blocked most roads, railways and pavements. Jews were organized into groups and sent out with brooms to clear the snow. Some were sent to camps but most, including Isou and Sebastian, were allowed to return home each evening. Work began in freezing cold at dawn and they returned home, often from distant outskirts of the city, late in the evening.[14]

Along with 'a thousand other' young Jews Isou had to sweep the roads for 'the tanks of the Boches or dig anti-aircraft trenches'. In the evening he worked piling defence fortifications. He blessed his luck that he was too young to be sent to eastern Romania – everyone knew how bad it was there. Sometimes he would bribe the overseer to let him slip out of the camp to rest and read. This was an extremely dangerous activity, sometimes punished by death. He read William Blake, Swedenborg, Rimbaud, Mallarmé and Leonardo da Vinci. All of these writers showed how you could go beyond the limits of everyday and mediocre human existence into immortality through creativity. This wasn't just a philosophy, it was a method; a lesson in how to recreate the world. More than this, by saving himself Isou was also saving the world. Looking at his surroundings, Isou saw straightaway how this could be applied, by turning tanks into tractors and war into peace. For now, however, this was just an idea, an impossible theory. Isou's reality was hell on earth, and Paradise was a very long way away.

In his journal, Sebastian complained mainly of exhaustion and the cold. Isou hated most of all the abject humiliation, degrading beyond belief. On the journey home, filthy, stinking, hungry and tired, the 'Jew Isidore Isou', as he called himself, was laughed at, called a 'Yid' and 'Dirty Jew'. The Jews also fought among themselves: 'too many geniuses together', said Isou. By this time, Isou still styled himself as a 'hooligan' but his 'hooliganism' had taken on a very different, opposite form to Sebastian's. Isou's response to the fascists was not to apologise, or cringe in self-hatred, but to hate them much more than they hated him. He also said that now God himself was ashamed, hiding his identity as a Jew, as if God too was scared to be a Jew. That's why he pretended to be an 'antisemite', to 'love everything anti-Jew'.

This logic was parallel to the reasoning of Elie Wiesel, a religious young Jew who at the age of fifteen was deported from the small town of Sighet in northern Romania to the concentration camps of Auschwitz and Buchenwald. When Wiesal heard his father praising God as he was crumbling into a slow death on a forced march in freezing cold, for the first time the teenager felt anger against God rising within him: 'Why should I sanctify his name?' If God chose to be silent, 'what was there to thank him for?'[15]

For Wiesel, being angry with God did not mean denying Him – much of Wiesel's work is indeed the opposite: understanding humanity, even forgiving it. This was, for Wiesel, the route back to the Divine. In his own crisis, Isou did not deny God either. But his faith was to take on a very different form. Isou hated the antisemites, but hatred was not enough. Most of all, during the pogrom, Isou had been terrified of being lost in the chaos of history, disappearing, nameless and unknown like the bodies of those Jews piled up in mounds.

He wrote about all of this in the chapter of *L'Agrégation* called 'Le Livre de desagrégation' (The Book of Disintegration/Unmaking), which as much as anything else – like the account of F. Brunea-Fox – is a historic document, an eyewitness account of events from inside them. Above all, during the days and nights of pain and terror everything that he had ever understood or believed in fell apart. As he described it in these pages, as I have tried to show in the detailed and redacted extracts above, he was literally unmade by the pogrom. For once, there is no literary artifice here, no attempt to play at being Pirandello, but as documented by a journalist at the time (F. Brunea-Fox) and other later historians, direct experience of the rawest form of anti-Jewish terror. This would be the emotional core of the rest of Isou's life and art.

This was of course the experience of millions of Jews during the Holocaust – those who survived the horrors commonly describe this as becoming a 'walking corpse', numb to feeling, thoughts, morality. They are caught between past and present; unable to live with the memories of what happened, and unable to live directly in the present tense. Suicide is common among such survivors.

Right now, Isou was determined not to die (the thoughts of suicide were to come later). He still believed in God, a Jewish God, but saw too that it was not enough to call on Divine help, to place your faith in a 'God-in hiding' from humanity.

four

Youth without Youth

As the war went on and the massacres multiplied, Isou started to look at the world in a new way. His starting point was that if the world was insane – which was obviously the case – then he, Isou, must be sane. Above all he had to avoid being killed by the Germans. This was not simply because he feared death (which he did) but because if humanity was to survive it needed the sane and not the mad. Following this logic, by saving his own life Isou was also saving the world.

These thoughts intensified during his time doing forced labour. He was scared not just of dying but of being lost among the dead. The Jews in Bucharest had already seen murder on their own streets. They also knew about the killings in eastern Romania and about the countless anonymous Jews who had already been swallowed up by the mass graves, lost not only to the world but to history. Nobody knew or remembered the names of these Jews; it was if they had never existed. It was this thought that transfixed Isou with terror.

Isou had even more terrible thoughts. He asked himself, what was the meaning of all of this slaughter? From his religious studies he knew that the Jewish race was eternal, but then why were so many now dying, being murdered, and with such brutal methods? Could it be – as in the Old Testament – that these dead Jews were sacrificial victims?

This thought darkened. The lesson of Jewish history was that such sacrifices were made in the name of a Messiah. And what if Isou, who was saving himself and so saving the world, was also the Chosen One? What if Isou – the young genius that had discovered *lettrisme*, and so the key to a new civilization – was the Messiah, and this was why the slaughter was taking place?

This was of course a desperate and fantastical belief system, pushing solipsism almost to the point of madness. But it was really founded on a way of fending off despair – the fantasy of a brilliant and melodramatic teenager who was scared that his life was about to end before it had properly begun. However, more and more, as the war intensified and the sense of unreality grew around Isou, the fantasy started to feel real. And if it *was* true that Isou was a Messiah, then this was also a terrible responsibility.

Isou later wrote:

> The War struck us every day, every night, without respite. Millions of brother Jews were dying of hunger, of thirst, on the over-crowded roads, stuffed into death chambers with skulls which cracked beneath the pickaxes of monsters, all my brothers killed for me. God slit the throats of thousands of musicians at Ebensee or in the ghettoes of Cracow to plunge me deep into their souls and to make me the greatest ever Musician. God was strangling thousands of philosophizing souls to build me up, into the Philosopher. To have a Messiah, my people paid a horribly high price. I had to be worthy: to be worth every single one of these sacrifices.[1]

Slowly Isou started to share these strange and terrifying thoughts with his friends. He would begin by explaining that a first step towards saving humanity would be to abolish Germany. At first when he said this, he was laughed at and told that this was impossible, that you couldn't just abolish a whole people. But, Isou argued back, this was exactly what the Germans were doing and all Jews in Romania could see that this was happening every day and that so-called 'true Romanians' were helping them. Jews were being slaughtered across the country in the name of a 'Christian Europe'. So why help the Germans and Romanian Christians in all of this by fleeing to Palestine? Why not fight back instead, and why not abolish their civilization, beginning by haunting it with the ghost of all the dead Jews that they had made? He wrote all of these thoughts in a journal he kept at the time.

Isou went one step further: one day the whole of humanity would be Jewish. This would be Paradise, when all men would know each other to be equal in the sight of God. This was his first teaching; this would be true Righteousness; all that was needed to get to this state was to imagine the exact opposite of the present civilization of death and discord. If his friends thought him mad, none of them could argue as fiercely as Isou, and none of them could argue either that he was wrong about the terrible times in which all Jews lived right now.

Such fantastical thoughts did not stop Isou getting involved in real political struggles. He gave a speech to the Jewish youth movement, the He-Halutz, a pan-European Zionist movement whose 'young pioneers' had been at work in Romania since the 1930s, helping to organize illegal immigration to Palestine through the port of Constanţa. He-Halutz also sent young 'pioneers' into the maelstrom of northern Romania to raise morale among the Jews there, but of course many of them never made it back, murdered for being 'racist and criminal Yids'. Like most Jews in Bucharest, Isou could tell those few who had been to the north and made it back to the relative safety of the capital: they looked stunned and scarred.

Isou's talk of saving humanity by leading it to Jerusalem – his Messianic duty – was in some ways not really so far away from the philosophical and political aim of the young Zionist pioneers. After his speech – anti-German and managing to link Zionism with communism, with no mention of being a Messiah or 'sacrificial victims' – Isou was approached by a young poet called Maké.[2] Maké was an anglophile who read Aldous Huxley, George Bernard Shaw and the Anglo-Welsh playwright Charles Morgan. Such Anglophilia was not unusual among young Romanian intellectuals; it was a way of escaping the pincer movement of Russian or German influence in the country. This was also, for example, the recently adopted position of Mihail Sebastian, who dreamed of an England after the war, inventing himself as a journalist, working away all day in the archives of the British Museum, taking holidays in foggy seaside towns. As part of his fantasy, Sebastian translated Shakespeare sonnets and quoted Shaw to himself.

Maké was not quite so besotted – he was just as in love with the French poets Rimbaud, Baudelaire and Francis Jamms as he was with T. S. Eliot, Shaw or Aldous Huxley. Isou and Maké found that they had in common a fascination for the French avant-garde. Maké wanted Isou to teach him about Marx and Lenin – Isou was a self-proclaimed expert on communism too. Isou agreed.

Isou insisted, however, that they could never discuss Marx or Lenin with reference to Romania. Isou had simply given up on the country. In the same breath, Isou also told Maké that from now on French would be the language in which he would forge his destiny. You can see this ambition taking shape in Isou's notebooks of the period where the French language edges out the Romanian from the 1940s onwards. These pages are dense with scribbled essays, poems and drawings. The oldest of them has a portrait of the pro-German King Michael 1 on the cover (King Carol had abdicated in September 1940 and been replaced by his young son Michael, who had been born in 1921).

In his tiny handwriting, Isou also follows the story of the war, writing that Romania had always been a country of fascists, and that is why he had to leave mentally (writing in French) long before real physical flight became possible. Inevitably, his first writings in French are littered with mistakes. But there is also a commitment to developing a true voice: 'which is most important?' he asked in clumsy French, 'the voice or the instrument?'[3]

Isou's first published writings were, however, in Romanian. These were articles commissioned by the writer and editor Ludo for his propaganda sheet. Isou first met Ludo at the same time as he was developing his friendship with Maké, and was deeply impressed by him. Before he even met him, Isou was fascinated and impressed by the bustle of Ludo's headquarters: mysterious packages of books, magazines and pamphlets seemed to be endlessly coming in and out of the courtyard where Ludo had his offices. People came and went and there was ceaseless, deeply serious conversation about politics, literature and philosophy. Listening at the door Isou heard the names of Goethe, Anatole France, Tolstoy, Walt Whitman and Ilya Ehrenbourg; this was where he wanted and needed to be. If not, Isou thought, he might as well commit suicide.[4]

Isou waited a few days before contacting Ludo, heeding the warning from Maké – who claimed to know Ludo well – that he was mean and bad-tempered. But then, upon hearing from a friend that one of Ludo's helpers had just left their job, he knocked on the door to ask if the writer, editor and publisher needed another assistant. He did, and Isou was immediately set to work next door to the great man.

Isou worked alongside another young lad called Herbert Sponder, who spoke German and sported a moustache that made him look like Don Ameche or Errol Flynn. Girls loved Sponder, devouring him with their eyes when he walked down the street. Isou started to spend his Sundays with Sponder, mainly as a way of picking up girls.[5]

It was around this time that Isou had his first case of gonorrhoea. He caught it from a girl he had picked up on one of the *bulevarde* with Sponder and who had asked him back to her apartment. Isou made love to her but not too successfully. He admitted to himself that although he was a master of seduction he was not yet a master of sex, and he thought of the gonorrhoea as a punishment for his incompetence. His father laughed when Isou told him about his embarrassing condition and sent him to a doctor who prescribed drinking beer to relieve Isou's aching balls, which had 'swelled up like oranges'. The beer helped even though Isou disliked drinking alcohol. He returned to his books, damning himself as incompetent and now probably impotent.

Finally he told his friend Harry Pantzer about his predicament. Harry was seven years older than Isou and far more sexually experienced. Like Sponder he sported a splendid moustache – which seemed 'to have a life of its own'. They often strolled together, trying to pick up housemaids. They went together perfectly – Isou the intellect, Pantzer the brawn; as 'perfectly matched as a cock and balls'.

Harry congratulated Isou on his gonorrhoea, saying that this was how a woman could truly make you remember her. Isou was more worried, however, about his lack of skill in, as he put it, 'finding the woman's hole'. Harry Pantzer knew the answer: 'If you can't find it, it means that you've got a knotty cock,' he said. 'All you have to do is spit onto it, rub it in, and it will slide into her like a wolf in winter. Spread her legs wide, until the secret eye of Cyclops sees the light of day (like a moon reflected deep in a well). Then blind the eye, stick your cock into it.'[6]

Isou tried this and it worked. He tried it first with a girl he had met while doing forced labour for the Germans – this time he had the relatively light task of clearing rubbish in a public park. He sneaked away with the girl into the vegetable garden; and then he was 'on the train: destination? A fuck'. Afterwards, he was thrilled to find that he had apparently delighted her with his technique.

Harry wanted to take his lessons in sex with Isou one step further. So he picked up an older woman – 'quite ugly' – and took her back to his apartment where both Harry and Isou would fuck her, with Harry going first to show the way. This woman had 'a cunt like the mouth of a dead fish', thought Isou, but it was still exciting to watch Harry with her. After they had both finished Isou asked the woman who had been the best fucker; she said Isou's 'cock was the biggest and hardest'. Harry later told Isou that he had paid the woman to say this to encourage him, but Isou knew that this wasn't true.[7]

He told this story later to another girlfriend (this was a girl called Anna, whom he met in Budapest), partly in an attempt to arouse her.

Anna asked him if he liked fucking in a group. Isou said no. The problem was that you had to put on a show for your friends, and as a natural leader he felt too much the responsibility of always having to be the best.[8]

———

Ludo was a kindly soul who saw himself as a literary mentor to Isou. His full name was Isac Iacovitz Ludo and he was a native of Iaşi. In the 1920s he had been the editor of *Ştiri din lumea evreiască* (News from the Jewish World), which concentrated on political issues among the Romanian Jewry and had an openly pro-Zionist agenda. By the time that Ludo met Isou, Ludo had established himself as the editor of an influential journal called *Adam*, devoted to Jewish literature and politics.

Ludo also had by now a reputation as a hard-headed polemicist, destroying his enemies with sarcasm – he was one of the leaders of the campaign against Mihail Sebastian for supporting the antisemite Nae Ionescu. After the war, Ludo reinvented himself as an anti-Zionist, serving the communist authorities. His former Zionist comrades treated him with contempt, as did eventually the Communist Party of Nicolae Ceauşescu, which never really got used to having Jews in their midst. Ludo died in 1973, an almost forgotten relic of pre-war Jewish Romania. Ludo was the first real writer that Isou had met, and he soon fantasized about Ludo as the prophet who would eventually introduce Isou the genius and Messiah to the world. Isou started off by doing errands for Ludo; he was soon entrusted with commissioning book reviews, and spent most of the day reading (and writing his own poetry). Ludo then commissioned an article from Isou for the yearly review of his magazine. Isou produced a stream of violent images: severed heads, dead bodies, murdered children. He justified the extremism of the piece by saying that the war was everywhere and that he was sure that he was going to die in the next few years and this was how this fact made him feel.

Ludo did not in the end publish the article but he praised it and even paid Isou. Isou gave the money to his mother. This fee, at least according to Isou, also caused consternation and jealousy among much more established writers who feared the arrival of a new and brilliant talent on the scene. The reality was that – having seen his poems and heard him speak – a number of Ludo's colleagues felt that they had to ask him if the new boy was mad. 'No, not at all,' Ludo would reply. 'He has a lot of talent.'[9]

Isou agreed with this description but thought too that his work had only just begun. Isou's ambition was not to be 'merely a writer' – this might be enough for Ludo but not for him – but to enter history, definitively and forever. He was already describing himself to Ludo as a Messiah, the 'chosen one who would finally bring happiness for ever to Humanity by leading it to Jerusalem'. Ludo took a wry view of all of this (it helped that in 1933 Ludo had published a book called *Mesia poate să aştepte. Cu maşina pe urmele profeţilor* (Messiah Can Wait: Driving in the Prophets' Steps) – an amused and amusing account of a Romanian Jew's adventures in Palestine.

Isou's best friend at this stage was still 'Solly' (Serge Moscovici). In many ways they were opposites: Isou was passionate, utopian, reckless, while Solly was moderate, careful, methodical and had few friends (unlike Isou, who was by now collecting friends whom he already thought of as followers). Isou's father laughed at Solly, who cut a lugubrious figure, was unattractive to women and the very opposite of his own impertinent but handsome son. Solly wanted to be an engineer and thought that humanity could be best improved by technology rather than philosophy. He was, said Isou, as far removed from the spirit of creativity (defined by Isou) as it was possible to be; yet, for all his moderation, Solly admired and looked up to Isou.

Isou started to become annoyed, however, when Solly began to imitate him. At first this took the form of copying Isou's style, in clothes, speech and attitudes. Isou could see this as soon as it started happening and was irritated. Then, as Solly began spouting Isou's ideas, he began to get angry. Isou was drawn to Solly by his calmness and his own original thinking – so often the opposite of Isou's own thoughts. But Solly was now starting to look and sound ridiculous, even grotesque. His speech, said Isou, was now 'rebarbative . . . always pontificating, dreaming up neologisms and talking all the time as if he were pronouncing a manifesto'. Isou refused to recognize himself and his 'historic thoughts' in any of Solly's 'stupid and endless babble'.[10]

In the meantime, another significant event was about to interrupt Isou's young life: the great French novelist and diplomat Paul Morand had arrived in Bucharest, appointed as the Vichy government's new ambassador to Bucharest. This was in September 1943, as Romania became the target for Allied bombing raids (Morand left Bucharest in 1944, as the raids grew heavier upon Bucharest; he departed in a special train loaded with art treasures from the French Embassy).

When Isou heard the news that an internationally famous French writer was coming to Bucharest, alone in his room he began to howl with delirious joy, banging his head against the wall, finally unable, literally, to stand still or upright due to his excitement. Until now Isou had only ever met Romanians who had been to Paris (including his father). This, however, was a totally new level of experience – a real Parisian intellectual. Isou was determined to meet Morand as soon as he arrived in Bucharest. He dreamt of a 'total victory' over Morand, convinced that the French writer would immediately recognize Isou's genius and arrange for him to leave Romania at once for Paris, so Isou would finally be free of the fascist 'jackals who barked at my heels, who wanted my body as carrion, who wanted me dead'.

The meeting did not go well. Morand came from a world that was completely unknown and alien to Isou. He was a member of Parisian high society, an intimate of Coco Chanel, Jean Cocteau and Marcel Proust, via whom he had been introduced to Princess Hélène Soutzo, who had been married to a Greek-Romanian millionaire, and who married Morand in 1927. Morand travelled the world as a diplomat and writer, often writing brilliantly but always with a lofty contempt for inferior peoples and races. This was not simply colonial prejudice but a deep belief in the racial superiority of the educated European, whose civilization was under threat from lower species of humanity.

Most of all he despised Jews and wrote articles attacking them in unrepentantly antisemitic language. None of this stopped him being elected to the Académie Française in 1968, although Charles de Gaulle – an open enemy of Morand, whom he saw as a traitor – refused to receive him at the Elysée Palace.

Isou knew already that Morand had a reputation as a fellow traveller of fascism, although he did not know about his associations with the far-Right journal *Action Française*, which was pro-Franco and pro-German. Morand's support for other fascist causes was well known in Bucharest and it was indeed widely rumoured in Jewish circles that one of the reasons he had been sent to Romania was to quietly help the Germans and Romanians clear the country of Jews. In fact Morand was sent in part because of his Romanian connections through his wife and because he already knew the country quite well. In 1931 he had published a novel called *Flèche d'Orient*, which was partly set in Romania, and in 1935 a travel memoir called *Bucarest*. In both books, Morand depicted Romania as partly the 'little Latin sister of France' and partly as Oriental squalor and chaos. These images of the country were not always appreciated by Romanians themselves.

To meet Morand, Isou had to sneak away from the forced labour camp. Meeting Morand was, however, worth capture and punishment. As he left from the camp to change his clothes and get ready to see Morand, his fellow Jews knew what he was up to and mocked him: he was a Jew, a sub-human to the likes of Morand; what could he expect, other than to be humiliated? Better to tell Morand to his face that he didn't give a fuck about him, to get back to the camp and have done with it.

Isou knew that they were right. He was only a poor Jew and Morand was a fascist aristocrat and it was impossible to 'jump across such extremities without breaking your kidneys'. But Isou couldn't stop himself dreaming of an unexpected, impossible result: that Morand would send him straight to Paris. He would travel in luxury and send back postcards from each station he passed through. When he got to Paris, Morand would make sure that he was published in the red and cream livery of the fabled Gallimard publishing house.

At the French Legation, Isou introduced himself to the concierge as someone who had known Paul Morand in Paris in 1937. He was not taken seriously but was insistent enough to get a more senior official to come and see who he was. This was a snotty young man with a condescending manner, 'probably a queer', dressed in clothes 'so well cut that they put your teeth on edge'. He gave Isou a thorough interrogation, testing him out to see if he was a member of the Russian Secret Services or the Gestapo (at this Isou expressed astonishment; a communist possibly, but a Nazi – never!). Before long, Isou was reduced to tears of anger and frustration.

Finally he convinced the lackey to give Morand a letter in which Isou appealed to Morand's curiosity and literary identity rather than his diplomatic status. 'I wish to see Paul Morand,' Isou wrote. 'But I have found that the Ambassador has replaced him. Is it not possible, Mr Ambassador, that Paul Morand could see me for a few moments without anyone knowing?' A reply came back almost at once: Paul Morand would see Isou that afternoon. Isou fell to his knees in joy.

By the time of the appointment, it had started to rain. Isou saw this as a bad omen. He was right to do so. As Isou was finally introduced to Morand, he noted that he was short, with a dark complexion and the stance of a boxer. Morand extended his hand in greeting to Isou and told him he was in a hurry and would have to leave for Constanța on business almost immediately. Morand then asked if Isou could explain his business in a few words?

Isou was already nervous. Now he was stunned, too. He wanted to explain to Morand that he had already discovered the secrets of creativity and existence, *lettrisme*, and that it was his duty to go to Paris as a Messiah, like the Dadaists before him, to bring the good news and to help usher in a new age for humanity. Morand might be a fascist but surely, as a literary man, a friend of the Paris avant-garde, he would understand precisely how important Isou was. But the words just would not come – and when they did they were like 'moles limping clumsily into the light, blinking, with broken knees'. Then Isou's words simply 'fell to the earth'. 'I can't explain everything to you standing up here like this,' Isou said. 'I'm afraid my suitcases are packed and ready,' said Morand. A female voice called to him from the next room.

'I am nineteen years old,' Isou lied. 'I am a Jew. I will make literary history and I wish to go to France to do this. Can you help me with the formalities?' 'This is impossible,' said Morand. 'As soon as you arrive in France you will be arrested. Why don't you wait for the end of the war? Then everything will be possible.'

Isou knew that it was more than likely that if he stayed in Romania he would be dead by then. The government lied all the time but the Jews believed the stories of slaughter across the country; they believed them because the Jews who made it back to Bucharest had seen it all for themselves.

Morand gave Isou a limp promise that he would see him in Bucharest on return from his business trip. 'He could have saved me, the Fascist,' wrote Isou, bitter after the meeting. 'But then he could have also saved all the Jews in the world.' Isou left the French Legation in tears, walking out into the cold rain, which 'purified' him. He was overcome with anger and humiliation, 'which invaded my body like a badly defended city, killing children, raping women, slitting throats'. He never saw Paul Morand again.

He did, however, go back to the French Legation, where he spoke again to the snotty youth who had sneered at him when he first went there. He managed to pick up a blonde French girl (possibly the snotty youth's sister? Isou wondered, fired up for revenge). It was the girl who told him that Morand actually wrote for *Action Française*.

She crossed herself while passing a church. Noticing that Isou didn't perform the same action, she asked him: 'Are you an atheist or a Jew?' Isou stiffened. 'An atheist and a Jew,' he said proudly. She kissed him. Isou asked when he could see her again. She laughed and said 'Never!' He asked: 'Why not?' 'A simple adventure has more charm,' she said and skipped off, away from him forever. The Legation concierge was now watching and smiling at Isou's second humiliation. He felt sad, devastated again.

———

Years later, Isou took his literary revenge on Morand. This was in the novel *Adorable Roumaine*, in which Morand appears in the fictionalized form of a French diplomat, Jérôme Dardanne – a would-be sadist who is in fact impotent (an insult which Isou applied to his enemies throughout his life).

Dardanne has an affair with Catinca – the man-destroyer from Botoşani – and falls in love with her. During a long night of talk and attempts at sex, Dardanne also reveals that his greatest sexual obsession is to kill someone, to kill *her*. Catinca allows him to act out his fantasy. He spits in her face as she is shaking with disgust; he burns her nipples with cigarettes as she twists in pain; he slashes her with a knife until she faints.

Catinca submits to all of Dardanne's fantasies, partly because she feels inferior and subservient to him, and partly because she wonders whether she might find in all of this cruelty some deeper understanding of what might lie beyond sex and love. She compares herself to a nun or saint, suffering torture from an executioner and awaiting some mystic insight. But no revelation ever comes.

After every fresh night of theatrical debauchery she awakes physically wounded and sick at heart. All of this is set against the historical background of the war in Romania. Catinca mentions the assassination of Prime Minister Armand Călinescu, a long-standing anti-fascist and supporter of France and Britain, who was killed in 1939 by members of the Iron Guard who were probably acting under German orders. She mentions too the Bucharest earthquake of 1940 when 267 people were killed when the Hotel Carlton collapsed. Their wrecked bodies were laid out in the streets around the hotel, spread out between the debris and bricks: a sight described in Isou's novel as 'a rag-picker's stall'.

Dardanne's rationale for murder is thoroughly intellectual. He tells Catinca that as a young diplomat in Mexico he had become fascinated with the Aztecs and their art of human sacrifice. Most of all he admired the fact that the sacrificer had to love the sacrificial victim – this is what gave the sacrifice its true meaning. Dardanne pleads with Catinca to let him kill her, 'so the weapon of my solitude might touch your heart'.

The Dardanne figure does not commit any sacrifice, real or poetic, but pathetically kills his pet dog instead of Catinca. He is in the end no Sadean superhero, but a 'vampire in pyjamas', a balding fat man whose eczema made his skin shed like 'sad confetti'. He ends up snivelling, pleading with her not to leave, and is laughed at in the street by passers-by as Catinca gets into a taxi and leaves him forever. Catinca then goes on to sleep with Germans, who are handsome, more truly wicked and sexually potent than Dardanne/Morand.

Ludo couldn't stop laughing when Isou told him what had happened. 'You went to see Paul Morand?' Ludo couldn't believe it. 'Are you by any chance totally mad?' Isou was defiant: 'when peace comes Morand will be banned from writing, and I will become the greatest man of my era. So people will be jealous that he ever met me. Even Morand will be envious of those who have known me more than he did.' There is of course no evidence that Paul Morand ever remembered the young Jew who came to see him in Bucharest, or indeed had ever heard of Isidore Isou.

For Isou, however, Morand was not just a fascist and an antisemite but now an artistic reactionary. The fact that Morand had rubbed shoulders with Cocteau, Breton and all the other 'greats' of the Parisian *beau monde* was now suddenly meaningless if he was so deaf to the obvious brilliance of Isou. What Morand had really revealed to Isou, however, was how small and insignificant he really was – a lost Jewish adolescent who was living on borrowed time in those fraught years.

Isou finished telling Ludo his story, swearing to his future immortality – a name that would enter history – and Morand's future obscurity. Ludo shrugged. 'Maybe it's the Germans who'll finish the story and kill us all,' he said. 'All of us. Including you like everybody else.'[11]

The war ended suddenly. On the night of 23 August 1944, the 22-year-old King Michael I of Romania, speaking on national radio, declared a ceasefire. He also announced that Romania was no longer at war with the Allied Powers but was now instead at war with Germany.

A few hours before he made this speech, King Michael had ordered his own faithful guards to arrest Antonescu, along with other senior members of the pro-Axis government. His declaration took considerable courage. In five minutes – as Mihail Sebastian described it – the king had completely reversed the course of the Romanian war. For Sebastian, it was also an omen that Paris had been liberated at almost exactly the same time as Romania turned to the Allies. Perhaps now, Europe could avert further disaster, although as all Romanian Jews knew a great catastrophe had already happened. On the night that King Michael saved the country, Sebastian himself was too fatigued to understand properly what had happened.[12]

five

Israelism

Leaving the war did not mean the end of danger. Although German forces had been steadily disintegrating since mid-1943 and were now obviously about to lose the war in the East, there were still heavily armed German units in and around Bucharest. To deal with these, King Michael called for Allied support, which came straightaway and which was then followed up by revenge attacks by the Luftwaffe. On 24 August German troops tried to storm Bucharest but were beaten back by the revitalized spirit of the Romanian army. The armistice with Great Britain, France and the USSR was signed on September. The Red Army accelerated its advance into Romania, and by the first days of September divisions were marching through the streets of Bucharest.

Isidore Isou was both surprised and exultant when he heard the king's broadcast. He was not alone. Bucharest erupted in a joyous festival minutes after the news of Antonescu's fall was announced. Sebastian described the night to come as 'delirium' as people screamed their delight across the city and drank whatever champagne could be found. Isou told how, within minutes of Michael's broadcast, everybody started shouting in the streets and kissing each other. Isou's first and most delicious thought – as he described it in his journal – was that his dreams had been restored and he could now return to imagining his future as the 'greatest man of his era' rather than as an anonymous dead Jew in a death camp.[1]

In the first days after the king's announcement, the Jews of Bucharest felt they had finally been spared. Isou described 'their cheeks reddened with joy', their unstoppable grins and hugs of relief as every radio broadcast brought more good news that the Allies or the Russians were on their way and the Germans were soon to be killed or expelled.

Not everyone in Bucharest shared their joy. There were 'Christians' who were anxious; Isou described them as 'like birds returning home in spring'. As they did so, they now knew that they had to give back the apartments, houses, offices and businesses that they had stolen from the Jews as part of Antonescu's official 'Romanianization' programme. Worse still, they would now have to pay the full price for 'every insult', every slap, every punch in the face of a 'dirty Yid'. There was now a new kind violence in Bucharest – new resentments and fears simmering just beneath the euphoria.[2]

All of these everyday crimes against the Jews also had to be measured against the even greater crimes that everyone knew had happened in the rest of Romania: the 'death trains', the deportations and the massacres. It was already known by now, from Russian propaganda and internal Jewish sources, that many more Jews than had previously been imagined had in fact been killed in Romania, and the Romanians had matched the cruelty of the Germans.

As they waited to be exterminated in turn, as the radio brought fresh news of yet another anti-Jewish atrocity, Isou thought that the guilty 'Christians' resembled 'enraged rats' who wanted 'to gnaw their way out of their cages'. These 'Christians' knew exactly what they had done – 'every knife in the back of the Jews, imprinted upon them like roses . . . nourished by the moans of the dying . . . the great daggers like flags spread out over the steppes of Russia.' In their fear, the Christians 'became like Jews'. Isou gloated over this.

There were of course also others among what Isou termed the 'Christians' who had fought against the Germans, fighting in resistance units, and had been locked up by the Gestapo like 'precious and rare objects in a safe'. According to Isou, these were soon no longer 'Christians' at all but honorary Jews, on the grounds that they had dared to hate the fascists, both Romanian and German. These were the 'Christians' who, when released from prison, joined the Jews lining the streets of Bucharest to welcome the Red Army as it entered the city. They hailed the Russians and called for revenge on their enemies.

There was still Jew-hatred clearly visible in Bucharest. An Orthodox priest watched Isou and his friends listening to the good news of the Liberation on the radio. He very clearly made a large 'sign of the cross', 'hexing' them and then 'disappearing diabolically' into the night, which 'happily swallowed him up'.[3]

The Liberation and the entry of the Red Army was a disappointment for Isou and his friends. Like everyone else, as the Russians first entered the city, they made their way to the Calea Victoriei, the most important *bulevard* in Bucharest, hoping to spend the night in celebration of their victory in what they imagined would be a wild and jubilant atmosphere. But the atmosphere was not really as jubilant as the Russian troops had supposed. The crowd was made up of well-known communists, and their chant of 'Jews, Jews, Jews' was political rather than festive. The communists and Jews tried to sing propaganda songs but 'hunger had destroyed their voices', and all that came out was a raucous out-of-tune noise like that of a 'hungry donkey'.

Later that night, Isou and his band made their way to a part of the city where they knew American prisoners were being held, hoping for some decent cigarettes at least (Isou sold them if he didn't smoke them). As they approached the guard-house, warning shots were fired in the air. The streets suddenly felt dangerous again. And so, in the early hours, deflated and bored, Isou finally trudged home. The house was firmly sealed shut by his father, who feared antisemitic reprisals, and it was only after loud protestations from Isou that the wary Jindrich opened up the front door to let him in.

The next day, hopeful again, Isou and his friends went down to the main *bulevard* early to see what was happening. There were newspapers everywhere, all of them proclaiming the end of the war and great joy. The reality of the city was much drabber than the news. The streets were dirty and smoky. The Russians, now circulating in patrols, looked young, tired and unshaven. Many of them were peasants who had never seen a city before, let alone a cosmopolitan city like Bucharest. They were not particularly friendly to the Jews, who had hailed them as saviours. Indeed, for many Russian soldiers, a Jew was to be hated even more than a German. There were still bands of Germans in the city too, most of them deserters but armed, undisciplined and dangerous.

Isou's friends Solly and Eddy soon went home, fearing the Russians and wildcat attacks from the Germans, but Isou still wanted action. He made his way to the offices of the Romanian Communist Party (Partidul Comunist Român), where there was an underground radio station and printing press. The headquarters was in the attic of a house in the district of Cotroceni, near Buzesti street, just west of the city centre. Isou found it quickly, noticing the bustle around a building there. Once inside, he grabbed a load of propaganda sheets and started giving them out in the streets. These depicted heroic Red Army soldiers being welcomed into Romania with slogans such as 'Traiasca Armata Roşie' (Long Live the

Red Army!) or simply depictions of a heroic-looking Stalin, friend of the workers and all Romanians (apart from fascists and capitalists of course).

The Romanian Communist Party had only just been made legal and its leaders only just released from prison in the past few hours. The official Communist Party journal *Scânteia* (The Spark) had also now been made legal. Its director was a Jew called Silviu Brucan. Brucan was a tough character who as a younger man had physically fought Iron Guard thugs and, conscripted as a border guard, come to know the lawless gangs who roamed the southern borders of Romania. As a veteran of the underground years during the war, he was now in fast ascent in the Party (he would later become Romanian Ambassador to the United States and the United Nations). Brucan was impressed by Isou's volubility and demonic energy in the attic office and immediately offered him a job. He was first of all asked to write articles that would, Isou said, 'wipe out men with words and wash the world with ink'.

Isou stayed in the Communist Party offices all day, writing and correcting articles, answering the telephone, giving out copies of *Scânteia*. The Party was in ebullient mood, rewriting history as far as they could to demonstrate their own historic role in King Michael's decision to take Romania out of the Axis and into the arms of the Allies.

As the day went on Isou was surprised to see people turning up at the offices whom he thought he knew reasonably well but had never suspected of being members of the Party. He was then shocked to see that a well-known antisemitic journalist was welcomed by the communists like an old friend.

No real fascist or antisemite would ever have dared set foot in the Romanian Communist Party headquarters – it would have literally been suicide. The 'antisemite' that Isou had seen was in fact Mihail Sebastian. Although Sebastian was a Jew and on the Left, he was still regarded by the likes of Isou as a traitor and enemy of the Jews.[4] The rumour was still alive in Bucharest in September that during his time in Paris in the 1930s Sebastian had even been a contributor to *Action Française* (when he learned of this rumour Sebastian laughed out loud).[5] In reality Sebastian had been an editor for *România Liberă*, a communist-affiliated propaganda sheet which, like *Scânteia,* had only just been made legal and used the same underground printing press.

By the evening Isou had already argued with Brucan about the presence of the 'antisemite' in their midst. Another Party member, hearing the commotion, eyed Isou suspiciously and wondered aloud whether Isou was a professional troublemaker, an 'agitator', and therefore maybe even 'a collaborator'.

Isou couldn't believe what he was hearing; the 'imbecile Christian' Sebastian, this other Party member, still hated Jews enough to believe that they were now undermining their liberators, the communists. He told them – Brucan and his assembled crew – that they made him feel sick. Brucan told Isou to calm himself, instructing him to 'lose his complexes'. Isou exploded at this and marched out, accusing each and every one of them – all communists, in fact – of 'cretinous simplicity'.

Out on the street once more, Isou noticed that many young men, Jews and Romanian Christians, were wearing stolen German helmets and carrying revolvers. This was out of fear. The Germans were still out there and could easily come back. Despite his run-in with the communists, Isou still felt the need to act in some way, so he rushed over to the other end of Bucharest, where he had been told a volunteer militia was being set up. When he got there – along with a group of other young Jews – he was told that the 'valiant Russians' were beating back the German enemy from the east of the city and that his services were no longer needed. As he was told this, he was approached by a young homosexual called Michel Grossman who (so Isou claimed) held a series of grudges against Isou, mainly 'fuelled by jealousy'.[6]

Grossman sneered at Isou: 'So now no more avant-garde literature? The time of Mallarmé and Huxley, that's all over!' It was, as Isou put it, as if Grossman had put 'a dirty finger into my coffee'. Grossman tried to get Isou to line up with the others in military fashion, to give himself an air of authority. It was again time for Isou to leave.

Back with his real comrades – Harry Pantzer and then Eddy and Solly – Isou felt terribly alone and abandoned. They all felt sad and didn't know quite why: this was the hour of victory and freedom, but they felt neither victorious nor free. They had been awaiting the end of the war with impatient glee, imagining that they – the young generation untarnished by the rotten recent past – 'would now finally be in command'. Instead, the past seemed more present than ever.

The next few days proved them right to feel this way. Jews in 'the quarter' were now regretting their gloating over the 'Christians'. Instead, they were waiting for the 'Christians' to come once again and inflict violence and terror. The Jews were now as 'jumpy as fleas'. The local police was made up of well-known faces: the same officers who had been responsible and notorious for massacres in eastern Romania. Jewish students were once again being beaten up at the University of Bucharest. In the Communist Party, Jews were changing their names to lose their origins and identity.

The Russians were by now also part of the problem. Mihail Sebastian had watched gloomily from the windows of his apartment as the first Russian tanks rolled into Bucharest. He worried about what would come next. He noticed that many Romanians were already muttering angrily about 'the Jews who had applauded the Russians', exactly as the Iron Guard and Antonescu had promised. It was hard if not impossible to lose a belief system overnight and for many Romanians the entry of the Red Army into Bucharest was all the proof they needed that the Jews were Bolshevik anti-Romanian traitors who wanted to destroy the country. Liberation did not bring a loosening of tensions but rather a tighter set of new emotions. The Iron Guard and Antonescu supporters did not go away overnight either. In apartments and offices across Bucharest, small underground cells formed, stockpiling weapons for the day when the signal would come to take on their real enemy: the Soviets. 'Incomprehension, fear, perplexity', reported Sebastian in his diary on 1 September 1944.[7]

For their part, the Russians had by now already started terrorizing the citizens of Bucharest, Jewish and non-Jewish. There were reports – all too easy to believe – of mass rapes. Shops were looted. Cars were stopped in the streets and passengers robbed and then left abandoned by soldiers who simply stole the vehicle in front of the astonished passengers' eyes. For some reason the Russian soldiers coveted watches in particular – an unheard-of luxury in the more rural parts of the Soviet Union – and muggings in the street were common. These crimes were committed by conscripts and officers alike: there was no discipline or safety.

When, in mid-September, Mihail Sebastian saw a propaganda film on the fighting between the Red Army and the Nazis in the Ukraine, and the terrible horrors that had taken place there, he decided that the lawless Russians in Bucharest were in fact acting like 'angels', given the carnage they had lived through.[8]

Isou, on the other hand, was disappointed that the Russians did not act with more violence in Bucharest. Isou, like Sebastian, had heard the rumours that Russians were stealing from the *Bucarestois* – especially watches – but when he saw an actual mugging in action he thought it was a mild, almost humble, operation. The Russians were stupid peasants and not the ruthless Revolutionary killers of legend. Isou wanted the Russians to cut the throats of fascists in the same way that the fascists and 'Christians' had been slitting the throats of the Jews. He wanted 'pyramids of dead Christians' to match the 'mountains of dead Jews'. Isou insisted that he was not alone with this fantasy; that this was what the whole ghetto wanted.

A friend remonstrated with Isou, arguing that Isou should forget the past, that he was making things worse and creating a new and dangerous form of racism. Isou argued back that all non-Jews had the killing of Jews in their blood, a 'kind of hereditary syphilis'. Isou's friend, a fellow Jew, argued back: 'If the world is anti-Jewish then the Jew must disappear. This is because it's the whole world which is right, and not just a single part of it. And I live here in this country, which has to become a country for everyone, not just for Jews.'

'I do not love this country,' said Isou. 'I cannot love any country where Jews have been killed . . . I demand pride and Jewish Anger.' Isou's friend accused of him of acting like the biblical figure Jacob, whose name was changed by God to Israel, 'the Prince of God', and who was known for his terrible anger and vengeance. Isou ignored this and went on: 'Is it my fault that I have been born in this country? You cannot know how much I hate this country. I wish I had been born somewhere else. But don't worry. I'll be leaving soon.'[9]

Isou wrote later that this conversation had exhausted him, that he was perpetually fatigued by Jewish defeatism. It made him feel as if he was being strangled. There were so many self-hating Jews – Mihail Sebastian for one – who thought that they had brought the massacres on themselves, that they had been too proud, too visible. Isou, on the other hand, refused to surrender his identity to the people who wanted to kill him. More than this he refused to forgive them.

When Isou said that his destiny was to lead his people, the Jews, his friend laughed at him and said that Isou could not be a prophet because he had no beard, and he could not be a Messiah because he had never committed miracles; he was too diplomatic and crafty, he liked women too much, and anyway he didn't believe in God. Isou's response was that miracles didn't matter – Jesus was no more than a street magician with his tricks – plus Jacob had taken as many wives and lovers as he wanted; and then he quoted Jacob again, who said that he believed in God as the Eternal Being. Isou did not believe in the 'Being' but he did believe in the 'Eternal' – that was his religion.

This was heresy, he knew, but it was still, he insisted, Judaism. 'I am so Jewish that it is perhaps the only word in my life that I will write with a capital letter,' he wrote. 'In the future I would like to be called Isou the Jew as Jesus was the Son of God, Blake the Visionary and Rimbaud the Seer.'

———————

Eddy, Solly, Harry Pantzer and Isou were now solidly established as friends, a self-contained 'gang of four' (Isou's friend Maké was only an occasional member of the group). Solly called the gang the *vitelloni*, or 'young bulls', and said that they were the only people who gave his life its meaning (in his memoirs Solly/Moscovici made sure to stress that there was nothing homoerotic in their love for one another). But they were already setting out on divergent paths. Eddy was falling in love with the cinema. Harry was simply falling in love with girls all the time. Isou was charting a path towards the unknown. They were equally divergent in their views on where they wanted to be: Moscow, Palestine or Paris, certainly anywhere but Romania.

According to Solly, Isou was easily the most intellectually gifted and certainly the most charismatic – although all of them thought that they would be great men one day. Isou was often jealous about his superior position in the group. He forced Solly to accept what they both called 'the Alliance of Bucharest'. This was the agreement that in future years, when they were both famous, Solly could dominate science and ethics, leaving philosophy, art and poetry to Isou.[10]

Together with Eddy and Harry Pantzer, they decided that they would start a new journal called *Generation 944*. They argued over the name of the journal – for a while it was called *Da* (Yes), with a deliberate nod to its ancestor the Dadaist movement. But they were less interested in the past than the future – which now belonged to the generation of 1944, hence the 944 in their new journal's name. Solly recalled that the journal 'was aimed at those who, like us, had lost their adolescence, but did not want to surrender. That was a new idea, in an environment sclerotic and little inclined to a refined social reflection.'[11]

These were fine ideals, but to set it up they needed money. This was easier to find than they thought. They lied to a would-be patron – 'a well-known and influential writer' (Ludo) – that they already had enough cash and just needed his political backing, followed up by a little more cash.

And with that they were now in business. They could foresee nothing but a great success and were already planning the future salaries that they would pay their workers when the journal properly took off.

Only four pages were produced in the end. There were two articles. A piece by Moscovici, signed with his real name Srul Herş Moscovici, on art and his theory of *lumièro-peinture* (light-painting) – now long forgotten even by Solly himself when he wrote his memoirs in later life. Isou held on to everything he ever wrote, however, including this early article on his philosophy – it was of course all of historic significance and to be kept for posterity. No copies of *Generation 944* survived the war but Isou kept all of his drafts and notes in his journals. In his notes for the journal, he declares in capital letters that he will be 'MARE OM DIN LUME!' – 'A Great Man in the World'.[12]

In these same notes, he described the origins of *lettrisme*, originally called *verbisme*. Isou writes that he is developing the work of James Joyce which 'does not yet exist' in Moldav-Walach dialect (this is his disdainful description of the Romanian language). This is his first early definition:

Nu e Dada
E Bada![13]

The translation is 'This is not Dada, it is Bada!' The pun only works in 'Moldav-Walach', or Romanian, where 'Bada' is an everyday interpolation, equivalent to the French 'Mais oui!' and meaning not 'Yes! Yes!' (Da! Da!), but 'Yes of course!'

The journal was well received at first by other young people who were ready for this new avant-garde, which seemed to be above the everyday politics of Left and Right which had reduced Romania, and Europe, to ruins. This was enough to anger the Communist Party. In the pages of *Scânteia*, the young Turks of *Generation 944* were attacked by one critic as posers and aesthetes, and the writer – a well-known 'cretin' who was trying to 'shipwreck' them, according to Isou – called for the journal to be banned.[14] Another rival, the poet Nina Cassian (later famous as the translator of Brecht and Celan), later denounced 'verbism' or 'lettrism' as a con trick in the journal *Studentul Român* (The Romanian Student). She noted with a sneer that Isou had been unable to come up with a name for his new movement; it was first called *motismul* (word-ism), then *verbismul* (verbism), before finally becoming *letrismul* (*lettrisme*).[15]

Jurnal.

Proiect pentru revista „Da", care pesemne nu va mai apare!

POEZIE DA! VERBISM

TEATRU NU E DADA CRITICA
E BA DA!

REVISTA GLOCULUI AVANT-
GARDIST.

Je dois partir forcément pour la Palestine. Je souviens
toujours de Zissu. Il voit beaucoup en moi et il m'a beaucoup
aidé. Vu comme je mange ce que je veux : halva, fromage,
beurre, café. Aurais-je ça tout ou je pensais tristement
au passé?
Ma mère a reçu mon premier argent gagné par l'écriture
15.000 lei. Elle a regardé plein de joie l'argent. Enfin,
elle voit quelque chose.
N'écris plus rien jusqu'au départ.

The attacks followed Isou to Paris, where an obscure critic called Dinu Stegarescu, with an obvious grudge against Isou, described him in 1947 as a pale imitator of Dada who was not taken seriously by people like Tzara. Still the journal was a success. Isou was even asked for his autograph in a restaurant: the first but not to be the last time, he noted. As he wrote his signature for his new fan, he added: 'This first autograph will take on its real value when other men will come and ask in vain for it.'[16]

The money disappeared. Jindrich Goldstein – who loved any form of attention that reflected well on him – was flattered when friends and business colleagues praised the 'genius' of his son. He offered to fund a second issue of *Generation 944*. But by now Isou had lost interest, and although his father was offering to 'buy the pilot's outfit', Isou no longer wanted to 'fly the plane'. Instead Isou went to Ludo and asked where he should go next to find a sponsor who would pay him properly. Ludo, smiling, suggested that Isou go and see a man called Zissu, who will 'pay you well'.[17]

This man was also known as Abraham Leib Zissu, or A. L. Zissu. He had in fact been one of the most well-known and active Zionists in pre-war Romania. Zissu was a religious Zionist, which meant that he saw the foundation of Israel as a promise from God and a prelude to Jewish, and ultimately universal, redemption, with the coming of the Messiah. At an everyday level he was against Jewish assimilation into 'Christian' society. He was a rich man who had varied business interests. He made a fortune from the oil trade and at one stage he had a specially commissioned house built for him in Berlin. His great loves, however, were politics and literature. He had sponsored young poets such as Benjamin Fondane and had written for, or edited, the most important Jewish journals in interwar Romania.

Isou had in fact already met Zissu once before. This was on a clear sunny morning in 1941 in Ludo's apartment. Ludo, who then had ambitions as a sculptor, was modelling a bust of Zissu. Out of boredom, Zissu started chatting to Isou, who was watching Ludo at work and enjoying the brightness of the day. Since 1937, Zissu had been banned by the Romanian authorities from writing or giving public speeches. Now at the end of the war and in his mid-fifties, he was a lively and dynamic intellectual who could not stop talking.[18]

Zissu began his chat with Isou by saying that Ludo had often spoken of the young author, and that by all accounts he was an exceptional talent. For this reason Zissu said that it would be interesting to discuss Judaism with him, to find out what Isou knew about it and what opinions he might have about the future of his people. Isou's immediate feeling was that this was an intelligent and important man and that soon they would be important to each other, although at this stage he wasn't sure why or how.

Isou thought it would be clever to answer Zissu with a paradox. 'You know, Judaism interests me for what it is now, and not for what it has been or what it was.' Isou went on, revealing already something of his own cult of himself, 'Things interest me only in so far as I can inscribe my Name into them.'

'And isn't Palestine such a place?' said Zissu. Isou answered: 'I would like that to be the case. So that I could be part of it.' Zissu then started digging into the details, trying to find out what Isou really meant. It turned out that Isou was against religious Zionism – making the Jews a separate people – and instead wanted to make the whole world Jewish. This is what Israel should look like – not a Jewish enclave but a whole world whose laws set men free and were universal. Zissu's response was provocative – God, and the Germans, had killed so many Jews because there were too many to go to Palestine. More than this, so many dead created a moral obligation for living Jews to go and complete the task of building their own country. Isou felt the need to visit the bathroom. 'Even great men have to do this,' said Ludo. 'No,' said Zissu. 'That's not true because when they are performing this act they are not great.'

Isou was impressed and intrigued by Zissu. He was mischievous, clever, sly, with a smile that would mysteriously come out of nowhere, and all his questions were loaded, as if only he had anything that resembled a proper answer. Isou described him as like 'a new pen ... with the noble clean cut of a new pen'. He was the only older man Isou had ever met whom Isou wished to be when he reached the same age.

After their first meeting, Isou asked around to find out who this magical figure 'Zissu' was who had so captured his attention? He heard the same thing from nearly everyone: Zissu was a rich dilettante who dabbled in literature and Jewish philosophy but who was incredibly tight-fisted, both with money and his friendship. Mihail Sebastian in particular disliked Zissu and felt especially humiliated when he had to borrow money from him. There were rumours too around Zissu – that he was close to the Germans (he was indeed friendly with an anti-Nazi member of the *Wehrmacht*), and that he dined with fascists and capitalists who had been leading the pogroms at the moment when German-language newspapers were predicting that by the end of the war there would be no Jews left in Romania.

Appraising Zissu objectively was made all the more complex for Isou by an inescapable fact: his wife was beautiful. Unlike Sebastian, Isou admired them both for their lofty indifference to the mundane world. They dressed well, went to the opera or theatre, and read the Talmud, in Hebrew, or the latest American experimental poetry. They were cultivated, said Isou, because they knew how to *concentrate*.

In 1944, with the end of Romanian support for the Axis, Zissu was allowed to write and publish again. He was also named president of the World Jewish Congress in Romania and as such was responsible for implementing the programme of mass emigration of Jews to Palestine, which the new Romanian government now allowed, and even encouraged, as a partial solution to its own 'Jewish Question'.

He was now working closely with Mossad, whose intelligence agents privately thought of him as an unreliable character and possibly a danger to the Zionist project. Still, by the end of the war it was estimated that he had been personally responsible for saving around 14,000 Jews from the Holocaust. Among other things, Zissu also wrote the preface for F. Brunea-Fox's book *Orașul măcelului* (The City of Slaughter) – the account of the 1941 pogrom that Isou had only just survived.

When Isou went to see Zissu to ask for money, Isou was now even more deeply impressed by him, surrounded as he was by secretaries, subordinates and advisers, cutting a truly presidential figure. Zissu remembered the argumentative but clever Isou. Isou had brought Zissu an article he had written (in Romanian) on the paintings of Moïse Kisling, a Polish Jew who had taken French nationality and established himself on the edges of Surrealism, even painting the famous model, muse and socialite Kiki of Montparnasse. Zissu read the article and straightaway offered Isou the job of editing the literary pages of *Mântuirea* (Salvation), the weekly journal of Romania's Zionist federation that Zissu had just restarted (the journal had been banned since 1922).

Although Isou was still – now even more than ever – an admirer of Zissu, he also noted and understood why Zissu had so many enemies in his own camp. For many Jews he was an intransigent troublemaker who never compromised on his religious beliefs. He particularly angered secular Jews, for whom Palestine, soon to be refounded as Israel, was a concrete political event and not the prelude to any Messianic drama. The communists called him a 'fascist'. (Eventually he would be imprisoned by them in the 1950s. He died in Israel in 1956, worn out by his harsh treatment in a Romanian communist prison.)

Zissu was incapable of diplomacy. He reminded Isou of the French Jewish writer André Suarès, whose great theme was the stupidity and brutality of war and who was known for his dogmatism. Zissu had a similar all-or-nothing approach to life. Isou's parents encouraged the relationship with Zissu, proud of their son's social success and pleased by Zissu's high standing in the Jewish community.[19] They were pleased too when the beautiful Madame Zissu began to take a maternal interest in Isou. She was kind to him, taking him to a café to cheer him up one day when he seemed particularly depressed. Isou resolved to one day write a madrigal for her as a reward.

Isou couldn't stop himself from being jealous of Theodore, the Zissus' eldest son. Theodore had been educated in Romania and Germany by the best and most expensive tutors. Isou growled that the unfairly privileged Theodore had somehow then ended up at the University of Oxford (actually it was Trinity College, Cambridge). Now thirty years old, Theodore had travelled the world and was at this point serving in the British Army. (He was also part of the British plans for slicing up Palestine and had given evidence to the Woodhead Commission, a British organization charged with the technical aspects of partition.[20])

Isou compared himself to Theodore and comforted himself by counting how many Nobel Prizes he would have already been awarded when he himself reached the age of thirty. What neither Madame Zissu nor Isou knew was that by now Theodore Zissu was already long dead; he was killed fighting the Germans during the Second Battle of El-Alamein in 1942.[21]

Under Zissu's watchful eye, Isou continued to write for *Mântuirea* and had started to develop a reputation, even a following, with his witty, occasionally incendiary articles on such diverse topics as Zionism, Stalin and why Jews dislike snow. Under Zissu's patronage, Isou progressed from the youth wing of the Jewish Congress to the Central Council. Once there, in classic *huligan* style, he began a policy of deliberately antagonizing the older generation, aiming to 'destroy the movement from the Left'. He annoyed his peers, too, by professing an admiration for Stalin, saying that one day, in the same way people spoke about Napoleon and Stendhal, they would describe Stalin and Isou in the same breath. Older heads in the movement described Isou as 'a hothead' and 'a little shit'. Isou was approached by the Communist Party, who suggested an alliance. It was Zissu who stepped in to calm tempers.

In the circles around the journal there was also much talk of going to Palestine, not simply as a form of escape but as a religious duty. Going to Palestine, in this sense, not as an exile but in fact going home. Isou remembered that his mother had told him as a child that his name, Isidore, also meant Israel in Hebrew. He and his people were one.

Except that this was not what Isou wanted. Palestine or Israel would never really be 'home' for Isou. Nonetheless Isou joined a branch of Hagsharah – one of the groups of young Jews who were preparing to 'make *aliyah*', or 'going up to Jerusalem', and so leaving for Palestine.[22] Isou did nothing but argue with the young Zionist pioneers, however, who called him *haver* ('comrade' in Hebrew) and who sang dumb heroic songs about picking oranges in the homeland.

Isou was not cheered either by a conversation with a 24-year-old English Jew, called Jacques (or most probably 'Jack'), who worked at the British Embassy and who had fought against the British with the Haganah, the Jewish resistance army in Palestine. Jacques was now delivering propaganda for the British; thus he told Isou and his friends how hard life was in Palestine, that although everybody fantasized that it was some kind of swish resort – like Nice, Cannes or Algiers – in reality it was a tough, dry place, with long, pointless dead seasons 'as useless as a pissing cock or cunt', as Isou summed it up. The only people who lived well there were the British.[23]

Isou also despised the fact that his Zionist friends, including Zissu, had been unwittingly misled. Zissu, for example, was a *Hasidim* – one of the 'illuminated Jews'; but he imagined Israel as a utopia based on a European model – a practical Western concept that was ultimately derived from the 'Christian and Hitlerian' model which had caused the deadly chaos in which they all lived.

This was not the way forward, thought Isou. If there was to be a utopia – the true Israel that the Jews had been promised – it was not going to be founded by boy scouts working in the desert. It had to be a totally new civilization. The problem was that this world, as imagined by Isou, lacked any geographical or historical reality. Isou would have to invent it all. To do this he had to get out of Romania and make his own *aliyah*, making for the new Jerusalem which was Paris.

Finally Isou exhausted the patience of the Jewish Congress, having deliberately provoked and insulted his comrades one time too many. He was also temporarily abandoned even by Zissu – who was anyway extremely busy with the job of negotiating with the new Romanian government the safe passage of Jews through and out of Romania. Exasperated but still loyal to Isou, Ludo found him a job working for an elderly Hungarian rabbi called Groos, who was in charge of an organization that petitioned for philanthropic aid for Jews.

Isou thought that the old man was dirty, 'like all bachelors', and 'very Hungarian' (in which way he no doubt reminded Isou of his father). Isou's job was to translate memoranda from the rabbi's German into French, which he would then send on to great men (Churchill, De Gaulle, Truman, Stalin), pleading for financial aid for Jews. Isou cringed; this was a pathetic, craven task. Worse still, watching the old man picking off a huge flea, 'like a tank', from his withered neck, Isou felt sick with disgust. It was while working for the rabbi that Isou decided once and for all that he had to be in Paris by 23 August 1945, the anniversary of King Michael's coup that had set Romania free. This was the very latest date he allowed himself.

In the meantime, he stomped bad-temperedly around the Goldstein house. He felt that each day more that he stayed in Bucharest, he was being starved of oxygen. It was now 10 May 1945, and he was wearing the same clothes that he had been wearing during the Occupation. The war was over but nothing had changed in daily life: same people, same hypocritical smiles 'fixed like muzzles'. He thought that even his own house smelled bad, like 'the armpits of an unwashed woman, a smell of goat'. Irritated, his mother told him off: 'You look at everything with disgust. But you'll soon see once you've left that you'll be covered in fleas, running all over you like a stream.' 'Yes,' he replied, 'but at least I'll be alone.'

Working for old Rabbi Groos had its advantages, however. One morning the rabbi decided that it would be a good idea to go and see personally the president of the Soviet Institute for International Relations. This was Alexandru Nicholsci, a Russian Jew friendly to Romanian Jewish interests and who would later lay the foundations for what would become the Securitate in Communist Romania. The president was new to Bucharest and somehow the rabbi had got hold of his address.

The pair presented themselves at the hotel at the earliest possible hour, with Isou introducing them both (in French) as important Jews who had a plan for the deported Jews that was to be sent straight to Stalin. Nicholsci greeted them with a sleepy smile, still in his pyjamas, and said that he would pass it on to his chief officer, who was still asleep. He ushered them into the hotel lobby.

There Isou was introduced to a beautiful dark-haired Hungarian woman, wearing the uniform of an American pilot. She was with an ugly older woman who 'looked like an armoured battleship', obviously some sort of bodyguard. This didn't matter; Isou straightaway began flattering and seducing the beautiful Hungarian who – Isou couldn't believe his luck! – worked for the United Nations, helping refugees. This was a miracle. If he fucked her well enough, Isou calculated, she could easily get him out of Romania, to Budapest if not Vienna. Then Paris. As easy as 'licking jam off a spoon'.[24]

When he got home after his meeting with the important Russian, Isou's mother calmly announced that Jindrich Goldstein had gone away to Budapest on a business trip. For the second time that morning, Isou howled with joy. This was another miracle. After years of living in Romania, which was like an open prison, a Jew, his own father no less, had managed to do the impossible and openly cross the border. It was another sign.

That same morning, Isou met up with Solly, who gave him the most astonishing news yet: Eddy had already left Bucharest, and was on his way to Hungary. Isou at first felt sick with jealousy and then elated. Eddy had not yet managed to get out of Romania, but he had been able to get on a train and get to a town in the mountains. This was the town of Oradea.

Eddy was trying to get papers and get to a village on the border with Hungary; this was already a splendid achievement. Solly had Eddy's number, so they rang him up to share his magnificent exit. It turned out to be a less glorious moment than they all thought. Eddy was quickly running out of money but didn't want to come back. Isou had his wages from Rabbi Groos, but it wasn't nearly enough for either Isou or Solly to follow Eddy. Then Solly had an idea: why not convince Eddy's parents that their son was in trouble? And if they gave them – his trusted friends – enough money they would save him from further disaster.

As she listened to the two lads babbling, with Isou taking the lead, Eddy's mother, skinny and tough 'like a tramp's cigarette', stared at them suspiciously. His father cursed Eddy as an ingrate and runaway. Isou could be persuasive, however: finally they coughed up the money.

Isou and Solly were suddenly rich. They celebrated by buying ice creams and first-class tickets to the town where Eddy was holed up. They spent the night carousing and showing off, and then at first light got the first train to the mountains. It was the first time that Isou had been on a train in five years and most notably without his parents. They ate in the dining car, feeling as if they were in a film or a dream. Solly smoked expensive American cigarettes. Isou had never smoked, but he tried a cigarette here – the glamorous surroundings almost seemed to demand it of him. He choked and quickly stubbed it out.

The glamour soon wore off and they started to get bored, complaining that there was no radio or entertainment other than staring at women, who looked back at them with contempt or did not return their gaze at all. Finally they arrived to find Eddy in the restaurant of the station, munching his way through a steak '[as] big as Joe Louis's boxing glove'.[25] They spent the next three days making plans. Then Eddy left to make his way to the border town where his parents were waiting for him, trying to persuade him to give up his plans and come home. Isou returned to Bucharest.

Solly and Isou never saw Eddy again. However, by getting out of their home city, which had felt like a prison, they had lived through a great adventure. Now they were ready for a longer and more dramatic journey.[26]

six

A Messianic Exercise

Back in Bucharest, Solly and Isou fell in with two Frenchmen at a dance. The Frenchmen were on their way back to France from forced labour in Nazi Germany. Isou was annoyed that they laughed at his accent when speaking French and made fun of his forced and elaborate vocabulary. He was disappointed that the Frenchmen were not men of letters, readers of Paul Valéry or the Surrealists, but simple apprentice butchers from Asnières. He did glean a piece of vital information from them, however. They were heading to Galaţi, a port town on the river Danube, where a boat was waiting to take them and other French refugee workers to Marseilles. Isou asked them to take him with them, which they refused to do.[1]

Two days later Isou telephoned a friend in Galaţi, who told him that there were still two boats at the dock waiting to set sail to Marseilles. If Isou could get there quickly enough there was a chance that he could get on board. There were also boats leaving for Palestine, if that was where he wanted to go to and even if he didn't he could try to arrange passage for comrades from the Hagsharah. Isou described these plans as 'Messianic Exercises' – it was his first chance to literally lead his people out of exile. He also changed plan – now it was Palestine rather than Paris where he would make his *aliyah*.

In 1945, taking a boat to Palestine from Romania was a dangerous enterprise. During the war the Romanian authorities had quietly turned a blind eye to illegal Jewish emigration to Palestine, mainly because it was in part a potential solution to the 'Jewish problem'. The British controlled the waters around Palestine, however, and the Royal Navy regularly sent ships back or to internment camps in Cyprus or other British territories.

Worse still, in early August 1944, only days before Romania changed sides in the war, an old wooden merchant ship carrying about three hundred Jews (no one knew the exact number) was torpedoed and shelled by a Soviet submarine. Survivors were strafed with machine-gun fire in the sea.

Isou knew this story and had heard others of drowning, sickness, starvation and dangerously decrepit ships. He had also seen at first hand the fierce arguments between Zissu and Mossad agents sent from Palestine. Zissu was angry that Mossad often cut corners – sometimes agents pocketed the money themselves or squandered hard-earned Jewish cash on bribes and sweeteners. Too often they provided cheap, half-wrecked shipping, which was then sent out into heavily mined seas with no thought of the lives of their Jewish cargo.

Isou knew all of this but was desperate to leave Bucharest and so took the first train for Galați. By now, he had run out of money and had to travel in third-class. The summer heat was overwhelming. To pass the time he stared out at the countryside and started chatting to a young man of roughly the same age, passing himself off as a medical student to his fellow traveller. Isou didn't know why he did this; it was just the first thought that came into his head. Isou appraised his travelling companion and gave him his learned medical opinion that he was in good health and would live a long life. Delighted with this diagnosis his companion fell asleep and began to snore loudly.

Isou hated the passing khaki-coloured fields – the same colour as army uniforms, he reflected. He hated the countryside because he was a Jew. Jews were urban creatures who delighted in towns and cities – the creative work of man. The countryside was the work of peasants, most of them Christians; stupid as the cattle they kept. Having settled on this fact, Isou set to work looking lasciviously at a woman in the same carriage who was reading a book. She could sense his stare and sneaked a few knowing glances back at him, occasionally treating him to a glimpse of her knee and her underskirt. So the journey passed.

Isou had orders from the Zionist youth movement in Bucharest to meet up with the local Zionist leader in Galați who was forty years of age, twice as old as Isou. They argued, shook hands and began a long battle about obeying the rules of the Hagsharah. He was then welcomed into the Hagsharah by a younger comrade called Iancou.

This particular version of the Hagsharah was really just a communal living hall with rickety campbeds and primitive cooking equipment. Isou was disgusted by the dirty linen, which lay around the place, and then by the food, which was so revolting that even though he was hungry it 'refused to colonize his throat'. They all ate with spoons rather than knives and forks, which Isou found barbaric. His new 'friends' visibly stiffened as they noted his awkward behaviour. Isou gave a false smile; he couldn't afford to make enemies here, at least not yet.

There were, however, Jews everywhere in Galați, following rumours of departure times and trying to get onto the boats. By the time that Isou got to Galați the ships for Marseilles had already sailed. The British were blockading the boats to Palestine. This was a wasted journey, 'a fuck up as usual' from the idealist but incompetent goons who called themselves Jewish patriots. Couldn't these Jews do anything for themselves?[2]

The Zionist pioneers supported themselves by working in the port, unloading cargo and other physical tasks. Isou was shocked that they seemed to have no cultural life: these were the first Jews he had met who were proud of not reading, they were almost as uncivilized as Christians. One of the pioneers called Mayer explained to Isou, 'we have come here to work, to eat and sleep.' Sometimes the pioneers had not even earned enough money to eat. Isou could not believe that Jews lived in such a way; he thought of 'hunger' as a useful poetic metaphor – to be 'hungry' for money, for sex – but not as a physical reality. 'We work so hard that we are too tired to read,' said Iancou. What the pioneers did do, like good Jews, was squabble endlessly among themselves.

They also had plenty of sex. The camp was made up of young men and women whose communal values included 'free love', and so Benny slept with Schelly and sometimes with Rachel, which so annoyed Schelly that she slept with Avram to get her own back on Benny. The problem was that the women only wanted to sleep with the best-looking boys. So the ugliest lads were forced to masturbate. This was soon declared an unfair humiliation, and the masturbators decided that they should be given a special fund to go into the town to find whores; this was, after all, only fair in the new socialist world of the Zionist pioneers! The masturbators had pre-empted a decision by already negotiating a group rate with a local brothel.

One of the chief masturbators was Mayer, who was 24 years old and engaged to a blonde Polish girl. The problem was that the girl was a virgin and refused to have sex until they reached Palestine. As Mayer was explaining this dilemma, the Polish blonde exploded with fury. 'Collective life? Ptiou! It's dirty! The whole town is talking about it . . . that the girls here are sluts, not proper Jews.'

Rachel was angry at this insult and began to cry. Isou thought this made her look ugly. His proposed solution for the group was to give a talk on 'Economics and Sexual Liberty'. They stopped arguing, listened for a while, and then all went to their beds, which were soon groaning under the weight of Isou's theories.

———

Meanwhile, Isou had his own sexual adventures to pursue.

On arriving at Galați he had managed to make a date with the girl who had been flirting with him on the train. They met up on a sunny 'honeyed afternoon' in front of a cinema. They both knew that the day would end with lovemaking in a hotel, but the cinema was the necessary prelude. The girl smelt good, and was as soft to touch as crepe de Chine. In the cinema, they dived right into each other: sucking, licking, chewing.

They were watching a newsreel of Allied propaganda, which was telling the story of the war. It began with the sound and sight of artillery, which forced them to stop kissing for a moment, and then, still clinging to each other, they watched footage of the Germans invading Poland. The girl started singing along with the patriotic songs being sung by the German soldiers. Isou looked at her in the darkness. She seemed lost in a trance.

It suddenly came to Isou that she had slept with Germans – that she had licked them and sucked on them in the same way as she licked and sucked on Isou; she spoke their language, she knew the words of their songs, and she had placed her tongue in German mouths before Isou's Jewish mouth. He shivered a little. The film continued; it showed the Germans in France, in Greece, in Africa, in Russia. The girl sighed softly to herself. She had no idea of what Isou was thinking or feeling.

All of a sudden the screen was filled with a huge tangled pile of dead bodies. 'These are the carcasses of Jews found in Buchenwald,' said the voice-over. Isou, like all Jews, knew what had been happening in the camps in Germany and across Eastern Europe, but this was the first time he had seen real images of what had really taken place. The images, made by an official military film-maker, were truly dreadful. Heaps of naked, skinny corpses, hollowed-out eyes, twisted and mangled figures, abandoned where they had died on the dusty roads alongside the camp. The whole cinema, including Isou's new girlfriend, fell silent, stunned and shocked.

The film seemed to go on forever. You could make out the hands and feet of Jews, but their heads and bodies were all scrambled up in the mass graves. Isou tried hard to make out individual details – a shattered skull, a blackened eye, a loop of hair. He wanted to find something that would help him recognize at least one person as a human being, as someone who had really existed before being slaughtered in this way, before being lost to memory, to history. But it was all too much; overwhelmed by horror, he could not focus.

He made a half-hearted attempt to get back to kissing the girl, as she squeezed him trying to get his attention. But he couldn't touch her lips; he was paralysed. He had to look again at the screen, where he thought he saw himself, with a broken spine, shaved head and twisted neck. He had the same sick feeling that he had experienced when his father told him about the night he had spent looking for him through the piles of corpses in the morgues of Bucharest; he feared then and now that this was how he might die, slipping into the darkness of eternity as a nameless, amorphous dead body.

He turned back to the girl, who was still excited, even sexually aroused, by the German songs she had been singing. Isou could smell the Germans on her breath. Her soft hands now seemed the hands of someone who could cut your throat, the hands of someone who cut the throat of the Jews at Buchenwald. The corpses on the screen seemed to be watching the couple – with contempt, sitting in judgement. The girl tugged at Isou and kissed him, trying to distract him, telling him not to look at the screen. 'Don't look at the Yids,' she said. 'They brought it on themselves. *We are Christians*!' It was this last word that forced Isou out of her arms, out of his chair. He had to leave the darkened cinema, scene of a nightmare; he stumbled as quickly as he could through the audience, breathless, and then staggered out into the street.

For the rest of his life, he never forgot this moment. Years later he could still see in his mind's eye what he saw then in the street, dazed by the afternoon sunlight; he saw a couple laughing, a drunken beggar, a cartload of apples. Everything was unreal, including himself.[3]

Days passed in Galați without any prospect of getting on a boat to Palestine, or anywhere. Isou had his hopes temporarily raised when he met a group of French people, three men and a woman, on the dockside.

They all looked gloomy but were at least friendly enough, and Isou chatted to them. He told them that he was French, like them, and that he was waiting for a boat to pick him up and take him home. He explained that his strange French accent was due to the fact that he had been abandoned in Romania as a child. The lies seemed to work and the French people seemed to accept him as one of their own. They too were waiting for the boat to take them home. Isou asked when it was due. They didn't know. They had been waiting for months. It could be weeks, probably months, none of them could say for certain. Isou left them, despondent once again.

Back in the camp, for all of the pioneers, boredom was turning into despair. Isou argued that going to Palestine was a waste of time anyway – that they would have to live there like peasants and no longer be Jews. This was a heresy too far for all of them: 'We will no longer be Jews but Palestinians,' Benny argued back to Isou. 'But that's how we will escape our broken lives here.'

Like any good Messiah, Isou decided that, whether he wanted to or not, it was his duty to help his people find the 'promised land', even if he was now beginning to think once again that it was the wrong one. He suggested to them that instead of waiting for a boat that would never come, they should sneak into Turkey. This was dangerous because it meant illegally crossing two borders, but once into Turkey they were safe and Jewish organizations would help them get to Palestine. Only Mayer, 'the gloomy onanist' opposed this plan, not because it wouldn't work but because it seemed to be breaking the rules, although he didn't know what they were. It was against the 'discipline' of the Hagsharah, whatever that was. They argued all night. By the morning it was decided that they would take the land route to Turkey.

Then Avram had another idea. Why not get taken on as deck-hands on a boat? They all knew that the boats were always short of crew, and wherever they ended up it was better than Romania. Even the women could work: Schelly, for example, who was 'comrade cook', could turn her hand to ship's rations.

The group marched off in expectation to the port of Galați. The harbour was half-destroyed by Soviet bombing raids. The boats were in no better condition. They spoke to the captain of a Romanian gunboat, who eyed them up and down sceptically and told them that they would be better off if they went to Constanța, which was a bigger port where ships were leaving every day. He wished them good luck and *au revoir*, as if he would surely see them one day in Sydney or Vladivostok.

They now had no choice but to go to Turkey. The route would take them down the eastern flank of Bulgaria, following the well-established route for migrants, to the Bărăgan steppe and then the Dobrudja steppe, which traversed the Romanian and Bulgarian sides of the border. It sounded easy but this was far from the reality. The Dobrudja was an empty and barren part of Romania and Bulgaria and disputed by both countries. Moreover none of the Hagsharah – all of them bourgeois Jews – had any experience of trekking or camping. The region was also wild and controlled by frightening bandits. This was a dangerous choice too for political reasons: since 1943 the Bulgarian authorities had been stopping Jews getting through. Now that post-war Bulgaria was in chaos, no one knew what the journey would be like. What was certain was that the group needed money for bribes, tickets and food. Isou asked the Jewish Congress for the money. They did not get much – 60,000 lei – but if they ran short they planned to sing in the streets or simply beg.

They took a broken-down launch from Galaţi down the lower Danube. As they boarded Isou wondered whether they would all drown, and why all Jewish journeys to Zion, even overland ones such as this, began with a passage across water. The Christians on board gave the group of Jews funny looks, assuming that they were on some kind of excursion. In the port Isou noticed a wagon loaded with German prisoners, 'swastikas in their mouths'. The sun was beating down hard and the Germans were sweating. It was going to be a hot day on board the rackety boat whose cheery, possibly drunken skipper had a 'head like an orange from Palestine'. As the boat left harbour, the young Jews all cried out 'L'Shana Haba'ah B'Yerushalayim' (Next year in Jerusalem) or 'Hazak Ve'Amatz' (Courage and pride). This was about all of the Hebrew that any of them could remember.

At about five in the afternoon, the group was unloaded at a small port further down the Danube. The only option was to get to Constanţa and from there try to catch a train to Varna on the Black Sea coast of Bulgaria. None of them had the right papers for this expedition but it was worth a try.

As soon as they had all got off the boat, they dashed to the nearby freight station, aiming to get on any of the freight trains for the coast. The trains were piled high with food supplies for the Red Army. They pooled their money to bribe the train guards and hopped on the first train they could find, sitting on sacks of fish and fruit, setting out for the far horizon, the train like 'the ring finger of a negress pointing the way'.

The train had no roof and they were soon being burned in the late afternoon sun. Now the train, slow, clumsy and uncomfortable, was like 'a circus elephant stumbling through a garland of flames'.

A ticket inspector clambered into the wagon and asked for papers. Isou tried to show off and argue his way out of it, shouting that this was a Soviet train anyway and trying to impress the inspector with his journalist's card. The inspector pocketed this, presumably to use it himself at some later point. The others showed him their tatty, blurred scraps of paper. This satisfied him enough to leave them alone. Isou regretted having given away his more flashy credentials, which the inspector finally returned, but decided that this was a lesson learned in not showing off on future escapades.

Avram began to hum an old Jewish melody but nobody knew the words in Hebrew and so he switched to a fashionable tango tune of the period. Such modern music was forbidden as sacrilege in the Hagsharah, but they all agreed that the tango had a slight Palestinian lilt. They soon forgot religion altogether and passed the time singing pop hits of the day. Finally, they all somehow fell asleep. They were continually awoken, however, by the persistent noise and smell of farts. The culprit was identified as Iancou, who, shamefaced, took himself off to take a not-very-private shit.

At the first station stop, a few hours down the line, they were joined by a suspicious looking character, obviously an illegal migrant but not a Jew. They all stayed awake, stayed silent and kept watchful eyes on their baggage. To their relief the man left an hour later and they all checked their kit to make sure it was all there. And now Isou needed to take a shit. Given that the train was on the move and the boys and girls were all clinging together, for the fastidious Isou this was a technical and moral challenge.

It was Iancou who showed Isou what to do. The trick was to position yourself between the wagons so you could aim your arse at the train tracks below. This was, Isou noted, a potentially lethal manoeuvre and an ignoble way for his career as a Messiah to end if he got it wrong. He got it right and prided himself on his accuracy and fearlessness. Now, around midnight, in a soft, warm rain, the entire Hagsharah began to drift into a real, deep sleep.

They were shaken awake by the train guards and the ticket inspector, who said that they could get them the right papers for 2,000 lei. They had expected this and paid up after some desultory haggling, which didn't work. A few hours later they all awoke, shivering in the glacial air of the dawn, 'having become hermaphrodites with our cocks frozen by the cold'. They arrived at Constanța at eight o'clock in the morning, genitals now unfrozen in the warming sun, and so all singing once again.

———————

Once in Constanța Iancou gave some cigarettes to a clerk in the train station to show them around the town. Benny bought some bread, which was unrationed here, and which they all devoured. They found a cart, which took them into the town and discovered that there was really no town at all, just a small cluster of buildings open to the sea. There was a smell of rotten fish everywhere.

Isou approached a passer-by who had 'a Semitic nose' to ask if there was a nearby Hagsharah. It turned out the passer-by was a 'Christian' who had no idea what they were talking about. Finally, a sailor showed them where to go, asking them what they were doing in Constanța anyway. 'We're here to go to Palestine,' said Isou. The man laughed in disbelief. 'Go hang yourself!' he said. 'There ain't enough of you for a new Crusade!'

They were welcomed into the safe house of the Hagsharah, where they washed and ate some more. A comrade loaned Isou a sailor's uniform, which he wore around the town. Although they were pleased to meet Zionist comrades, Isou and his friends were unsurprised to hear that in Constanța it was the same story as in Galați: there were no boats leaving for Palestine, the waters were entirely controlled by the British and if you were captured you were more likely to end up in foggy England than Zion. There was no alternative but to stick to the original plan, heading down to Mangalia and taking their chances with the Bulgarian border, which was only 10 kilometres (6 mi.) away. Once at the border, they planned to split up and to each follow a different route. As they set off again by train, Isou promised their new Constanța comrades, whom they were leaving, that once he had become known in Palestine as the greatest man of his era, he would return and show them the way there.

The carriages on the train were humid and sticky and so the gang decided to sleep on the roof of the train, lying as still as they could so as not to touch the electrified cables above them. The ticket inspector thought that they were mad and ordered them down. They were now running out of money and gave him what they could, which he accepted without a word.

The train was busy with Turks and Tartars returning home from the confusion of war. Isou struck up a conversation with a demobilized soldier who had lost a leg. 'Fuck it,' said the soldier. 'Losing a leg doesn't matter that much. In wartime you have no time to be vain, thinking just of yourself.' Isou gave him a superior look. 'You're still young,' said the soldier. 'There's a lot to learn.'

At one of the station stops, Isou got off the train to fetch water for an old Muslim lady, a Turk, whose mouth was on fire with thirst. He watched with curiosity as she slurped it down, her mouth full of sores and bad teeth. He then drank from the same cup, which did not bother him. These old Muslim peasants were like prehistoric creatures to him: almost another species. Isou thought that he could learn from passing among them. He was also still speaking to the soldier, who offered to show him safely over the border, claiming that he knew all the smugglers.

They arrived at Mangalia at six o'clock in the morning. The town was really just a village. The local peasants stared at the city people – the Jews – as they got off the train and walked down the muddy street, lined with carts and cattle.

The plan was simple: to go to the first bistro, start drinking wine, crack jokes, make friends with the landlord, and start dropping hints that these Jews weren't on holiday but trying to get somewhere else. The plan worked and before long the landlord introduced them to a sailor (there were sailors now everywhere in Romania as the Romanian Navy was at a standstill) who had come down into the village precisely at this early hour to look for customers to take over the border.

The sailor's first plan was to somehow hijack a Soviet vehicle (the Russians could go anywhere they liked both sides of the border), but this was thought to be dangerous. The sailor reached an agreement with them as he took a piss in the stable courtyard where he had parked a cart. He promised to meet the Hagsharah later to show them the way and take payment from them. In the meantime, the village was gearing up for one of its annual festivals and the Hagsharah began to cheer up at the thought of going to a dance, even if this was normally forbidden.

However, as night fell they all started to get more afraid than they ever had before on the journey, which suddenly seemed to be turning from a lark into a nightmare. This was because, as darkness fell over the village, they realized that the village was overlooked by a huge barracks, which actually seemed bigger than the village itself. The soldiers here were not going to be friendly to outsiders, especially such obvious city

Jews who were getting up to no good with sailors – never to be trusted by the army – or smugglers, and who might also be carrying large amounts of cash. As they wondered what to do, they were startled by a frontier guard who seemed to come out of nowhere, out of the shadows 'like some demon'. He spat on the floor and barked at them like a Nazi, warning them to watch out. And then he disappeared.

Finally, after waiting 'till our hairs turned grey', the sailor came back, much later than promised and with some pals. He told the band of comrades that the soldiers were suspicious and watching them; they knew that they were Jews and had noticed that they were all carrying haversacks. He told them that for now it would be a good idea to get out of the village and spend the night in a field a few kilometres away from the village. Now they were properly terrified.

The sailor encouraged them: 'There you go, lads, keep going and you'll get to Bulgaria soon. It's just over there.' No one wanted to move; Isou could see that Avram was frightened, Benny was frightened, Marcel was frightened, only Iancou was too stupid to see that they were in real danger. They could be shot in the dark and no one would know anything about it. Soldiers, sailors, smugglers – none of them could be trusted. The group fell silent and no one moved.

The sailor and his pals now started to get angry, watching their cash evaporate before their eyes. Isou tried to reason with them. This made the atmosphere even tenser; the sailor started shouting and threatening them – he would have made a good antisemite, thought Isou – and it seemed that the whole scene might end in murder.

Then they all froze. A voice came out of the darkness: 'Hands up!' In the shadows, they could just about make out the rifles that were pointing at them, and the soldiers who had surrounded them.

Isou thought of Bif: in a tough situation like this, Bif had taught him, it was most important to impose yourself, to take control of the situation. 'What's happening?', said Isou, in a calm voice. 'You'll see what's happening with a fucking bullet in your back,' said one of the soldiers. How would Bif behave? 'Could you speak more politely,' said Isou. And in an even calmer, impeccably bourgeois voice, 'We haven't yet been properly introduced to allow ourselves such improprieties.' His mates hissed at him to shut up; Isou would get them all killed. They all put their hands up – all except Isou. A soldier started to shout at him to put his hands up. 'Shut the fuck up. We're going to teach you not to cross the border.' Only then did Isou slowly raise his hands. He looked at the soldier with contempt.

More soldiers arrived on the scene. Isou knew that it was important not to stay silent, which would make them look as if they were guilty of something, so he went on arguing, shouting at the injustice that was happening. A shot was fired into the air to shut him up. But Isou was not afraid.

A corporal took charge of the scene and started at the assembled band of trembling young Jews. 'You bastard smugglers,' he bellowed, and hurled other insults so disgusting that Isou thought that the corporal's ancestors 'must have pissed and shat in his throat – now a sewer', so that everything that came out of his mouth was an obscenity. 'Speak politely,' Isou insisted. 'You are not speaking to rustics here.' Isou took out his journalist's card. 'The time of Germans and Collaborators is over; you have no right to speak to us in that way. You are acting as if they were still here. We will teach you to speak correctly.' The Corporal reached for a rifle and pointed it directly at Isou's head. 'Murderer', said Isou. 'You will die in prison.'

Isou gracefully held out his card. All of a sudden the corporal looked afraid, as if he had suddenly realized that he didn't know who he was dealing with, although he did not want to lose face either.

Avram, shaking with fear, said a few words to Marcel in Yiddish. When he realized that they were Jews, the corporal calmed down. 'You are Jews? You know times have changed. We used to shoot you under the Germans but now we have to behave correctly with you.' Then the corporal began a crude form of interrogation:

'What are you doing here?'
'We were going for a walk.'
'You go for a walk at this hour?'
'Free citizens can walk wherever they like, whenever they like. The restrictions have left with the Boches.'
'Near the border?'
'We didn't know it was the border. And anyway it's a new border that we couldn't have known about. When I came here before the war, the border was somewhere else. We were on our way back to the village when these soldiers stopped us and tried to arrest us. It's your fault that we are here and not in the village.'

At this the corporal scratched his head, not knowing what to do. He telephoned his superior officer, a captain. The captain was asleep and couldn't be bothered to get up. He ordered the corporal to lock them up and he would interrogate them in the morning. Back at the guard house, they were all thrown into the same cell.

As he drifted off to sleep, head wedged against his suitcase, Isou could hear the sound of music and dancing in the village. Last night he had slept on a pile of corn on a train, under the soft rain. Tonight he was in jail. He heard a dog barking in the distance. He was not afraid. He was happy.

So far, Isou's 'techniques of intimidation', borrowed from Bif, were working. Despite themselves the soldiers were wary of him, unsure of how important he really was – was he the son of an important politician or businessman who might have them sent to an even more obscure part of Romania, or worse. Above all they did not want to appear as antisemites. The Jews were not exactly in charge in Romania, but the Russians were ready to use any excuse to purge the Romanian forces of alleged Nazis.

The next day the Hagsharah were taken to see the captain. Isou was complaining all the way that soldiers were walking behind the group as they marched through the village, as if they were common thieves. In front of the captain, the other members began to lose their composure, stuttering and contradicting each other. Isou stepped in: 'You are terrifying my comrades with your manner which is like the Inquisition.' The captain told Isou to wait his turn. At this Isou grew furious, and, in deliberate imitation of the words of Émile Zola, slowly enunciated 'I accuse ... the corporal ... of having ... !'

Isou did not finish his sentence, confused by his own anger. It was now the captain's turn to be stunned by Isou's haughtiness and hostility. It crossed his mind that to be this fierce and fearless – not to say insolent – Isou really must be someone important. It was decided to pass this further up the line, to a colonel in Constanța, who had the authority to set them free and could take the flak if it all went wrong. They were given soup – quite delicious – and then taken in style in a horse-drawn cart to Constanța.

The colonel was not there when they arrived and they were met instead by a sergeant major. Isou complained at this, that the man's rank was not high enough to receive them. The sergeant major – an obvious antisemite – looked as if he wanted to smack Isou. But he didn't dare; like everyone else in authority he had been taken by surprise and intimidated by Isou, who threatened to walk away, or escape and risk being shot by these clumsy fools, who would then learn who he was (or in this case, who he wasn't).

Although he did not show it, Isou's nerves were also being worn down by this game; still he went on. To raise the stakes even higher, Isou insisted that the colonel should make a call to his general – a certain General Dima, who was also regional governor. Amazingly, Isou himself was allowed to make the telephone call to the general. He was told by his secretary that the general was asleep and so – now pushing his *chutzpah* almost to breaking-point – Isou insisted on waking the general.

The secretary refused to do this and so now Isou began to scream with frustration. The Hagsharah would again have to spend the night in a cell. Now Isou finally broke down, exhausted and shattered by the front he had maintained with such devastating energy; he railed against himself for being 'broken' and finally 'impotent'.

The cell was horrible. It was dark and full of shit and rats – 'the kind of runny shit that gets everywhere'. Isou tried to imagine that he was elsewhere, in a book or a story. Avram reminded him of where he was by moaning for a meal and a warm bed and blaming Isou for his woes. 'It's you who pushed me to go to Palestine. I should have stayed at home. You know what? I shit on Palestine! And I piss on Jerusalem!' Iancou slapped him. The others stayed silent. They were scared of saying anything against Palestine.

Isou still thought of himself as pure in his belief that he had been right – he was still 'a hard, unbreakable diamond'. He lay still, watching the night sky through the barred windows of the cell, 'drunk on the stench of the latrines, only a metre away'. He said to himself that this was a test for the new type of man, the 'Isouien' man he had prophesied. He recalled the poem by Paul Valéry, 'Patience dans l'azur', in which the poet, stretched out in the desert, stares out at the stars, the universe, which seem to be preparing his fate. He recalled the lines: 'each atom of silence is the possibility of a ripe fruit.'

He was angry with himself, but this was only to be expected from the occasional failures of a genius such as he was; it was no more than was a sort of 'calculated impatience', a form of spiritual discipline. He stayed awake all night and felt, as dawn approached, like a true mystic, that he was being mentally and physically transformed in his communion with the Cosmos.

At first light, two newcomers were thrown into the cell – a thief and a deserter. This was like a story from the Bible. The thief was dressed in tattered rags. The deserter was muttering to himself. Isou whispered to himself: 'If we're not out of here at six o'clock, it's time to break down the door.' He told his comrades that this is what they should do. So at six o'clock sharp they all began to batter on the door of the cell. The deserter and the thief were scared that they would all be beaten by the guards.

An officer arrived to see what was going on. Again Isou flashed his journalist's card, and in the haughty tones that were now well practised demanded that the general come and personally release them. The officer was now less intimidated by Isou; instead, filthy and with a manic look, Isou looked more like a mystic or a madman than a son of the *haute bourgeoisie*.

It was, however, General Dima who released him, genially asking Isou if it was he who had telephoned, and why couldn't he leave a man in peace. The doors of the cell and the barracks were opened to them. Speaking to the general – Isou had never spoken to a general before and didn't know whether he should call him 'Excellency' – Isou felt like Moses on the mountain speaking to God. Less grandly, the general said he would check their papers. Moments later, he laughed and set them free.

The adventure was not quite over; they still had to report back to the comrades who had stayed in Constanţa and then make their way back to Bucharest. Isou's shoes and clothes were wrecked and so, with his feet stinging with every step, he walked barefoot from the barracks to the town, still wearing the sailor's uniform that he had been given. He refused to feel ridiculous.

Isou lingered on for a few days in Constanţa after his friends had caught the train back to Bucharest. He went to a country fair, where he visited the circus and a freak show. He decided that this kind of thing – with its hairy women and cannibal dwarves – was a Christian aberration. There were no such creatures mentioned in the Old Testament. He recalled a visit to a circus in Botoşani when he was seven years old. His pregnant mother had been forbidden to look at the deformed freaks because it was a Jewish belief that if she did she would give birth to a freak herself.

He went to see a Jewish fortune-teller who told him he was loved fiercely by a woman but that he didn't know it and would never know it. He was relieved to be finally going home and decided to buy a bracelet as a gift for his sister Fanny. He remembered how much he loved her, and how much she loved him. He did not now regret his journey, but he remembered too that he came from a happy home, that – for all the fighting with his father – they were a happy family.

On the train back to Bucharest, Isou was in a compartment with a bearded university professor who looked like the notorious antisemite Nae Ionescu:

> one of those anti-Semitic Professors that we have here [in Romania], full of theological ideas and mystical racism; one of those who during the time of the Boches would certainly have demanded that I be thrown off the train with all the other filthy Yids, or at least held his nose if he even saw a Yid.

Isou couldn't stop himself from arguing with him. Although obviously nervous, the professor argued back. Isou went on the attack.

'I would cut my hands off if you could tell me the name of any Christian true creator,' said Isou. 'All Christians are imbeciles. They are all always stealing Jewish ideas . . . All Jews want to give Christianity a great big kick up the arse.' The professor was now quite frightened by Isou's open hostility. Isou continued: 'In France right now, there is a young man, a Jew, called Isou who is changing the world' (this was Isou's own prophesy). 'He is making France Jewish.'

The professor scolded Isou: 'But this is horrible, young man. God made us all from the same clay. Why do you hate Christians so much?' 'Don't you know?' replied Isou,

> By tradition, during the nights of the Easter festival, we eat the flesh of a 'goy' child, freshly cut into pieces – a nice pink Christian child, stolen the night before from its cradle or taken from the breast of the mother who had been feeding it . . . We cut them up and taste a little, but not much because it tastes of pig and we have to spit it out. That's how we learn to hate the 'goys'.

The professor laughed out loud. 'You really are splendid!' he said. Then it was Isou's turn to laugh. They were almost equals. 'You have courage because the Russians are here,' said the professor. 'If the Germans were here you'd speak differently.'

'Yes,' said Isou, 'I'd get baptized and become a Christian, to save my life. Like the Jews who became Muslims or Catholics to save their necks. We'll save ourselves so we can get our revenge on you in the end. You'll see.'

The professor now said nothing and looked a little discomfited. Later during the journey he offered Isou a cigarette which Isou didn't take because he didn't smoke but which the professor interpreted as a deliberate snub. At a station stop, Isou bought the man an orangeade. The man returned the gesture with sandwiches and sweets. They were on the point of becoming friends. Before the professor left the train he gave Isou his address and asked him to write to him. Isou took the scrap of paper and then threw it away.[4]

Finally in Bucharest, Isou felt as if the entire city was overjoyed to welcome him back. He felt the same intimate joy as he did when he put his hand up a girl's skirt. The tramway took him home to his mother. She was delighted to see him back, even with his dirty face, 'like melted chocolate', and the body-stench of a boy who had spent nights sleeping in shit-smeared prison cells in the dark.

seven

Facing West

Isou had only been home a few days when he heard the news that Eddy had managed to get over the border and into Hungary. Eddy had stayed at the Romanian-Hungarian border while his parents went back to Bucharest. As soon as they were home, he sent two telegrams to his parents, the first to let them know that he was finally ready to go and then to let them know that he had left. Obviously, their arguments and pleas for Eddy to return had not worked. His parents were distraught.

They blamed Isou for convincing Eddy that there was no future for either of them in Romania. Eddy's parents came to Isou's house. His mother screamed that Isou's mad and perverted ideas had sent her 'little Eddy' to his death. Isou pointed out that Eddy was older than he was, but this only enraged the woman. 'And what about our money?' she yelled, 'Whose going to inherit all our money now? This is money that we've worked for all our lives!'[1]

Isou noted that even in this moment of crisis Eddy's mother could not help herself telling the world how much money they had. Isou was annoyed that the woman was shouting at him and making such accusations. Secretly, however, he enjoyed playing the role of a 'corruptor', having always fancied himself as 'a bandit' since childhood. Eddy's parents only calmed down when Isou told them he was already making his own preparations to leave Romania, and that this would be soon, in the next few days at the latest. They seemed reassured that they were not the only people to have lost their son in the aftermath of war and that far from being unique in their loss and grief they were just like everyone else. Isou observed to himself that most unhappiness comes from feeling alone, an outsider.

It was Zissu who found the way out for Isou. By now Zissu was effectively in charge of the Romanian Red Cross, which among other things meant organizing emigration and not just Jewish emigration. Zissu tipped off Isou that papers were being organized for French deportees and that he could have a word with the man in charge of the papers – a personal friend – so that Isou could pass himself off as French.

The only snag was that – publicly at least – Zissu had fallen out with Isou for shifting to yet another faction in the Zionist movement. Privately, however, Zissu wanted to help this headstrong but talented young man. When Isou heard that Zissu was prepared to help him, he telephoned his old mentor and they were soon on better terms. When they met up, Madame Zissu was present and spoke to Isou sharply: 'Have you betrayed us?' she asked. 'No,' said Isou, 'I have been faithful. But because I am a genius I am also an opportunist. That's why Zissu isn't a genius; he doesn't know how to take his chances.' She laughed out loud, affectionately, at Isou's usual absurd arrogance.

The plan was to use the papers that Jindrich Goldstein had acquired during his pre-war visit to France to make out that he had been in France for the whole war. Isou also faked documents which stated that he had been with his father in France before the war and only taken refuge in Romania when the Germans had invaded France. Isou was now contacting the Red Cross so that he could get the documents which would allow him to rejoin his father.

Zissu hesitated for a while, but then signed the letter that would help Isou. After all it was not the first time he had lied – 'he was a free man,' according to Isou, and therefore 'free to lie'. The travel documents were duly prepared and signed by the Red Cross authorities.

Isou was now grateful to Zissu for having put up with his bad behaviour. In the days left before his departure, Isou stayed up late with Zissu, debating morality, philosophy, Judaism and Israel. As a parting gift, Zissu asked Isou to take any book he wished from his extensive library. Isou did not know what to choose and so settled on a collection of magazines he could read on his journey.[2]

Around this time, Isou also received a visit from 'Jacques', the British Embassy official who was also working for Mossad, and who had arranged for Isou and the others in the Hagsharah to get to Palestine. Jacques was furious that the first trip had been such a mess – a waste of time and money as well as putting agents like himself in danger. He blamed Isou directly for the fiasco, accusing him of 'deliberately fucking it up' with his own arrogance and stupidity. He was even angrier when he heard that Isou was now planning to go to Paris instead of Palestine. Jacques launched into him: 'So you're a traitor too,' he said, 'you've used our resources and now you're disappearing to France!'

Isou decided that the best response was to stay calm:

Listen, Jacques, what do you want me to do? I've heard voices and I don't think I'm mad. I'm declaring myself to be the Ambassador of the Jewish people on earth. Why shouldn't I be the Joan of Arc for the Yids? I have been sent from heaven in the same way that you have been sent from Israel. We are like each other. The only difference is that I don't want to make Israel into one scrap of land; I want the whole world to be Israel, Eretz Israel [the true promised land]. And if I fail I'll come back and see you in Palestine.

Jacques laughed. 'That's it! Isou the Talmudist, always arguing, always got the words.' Isou reminded Jacques that that was what it meant to be a Jew. He also reminded him that God had many names like the Jews – the Israelites or the Yids themselves. That's what made the Jews the Chosen People – they were like God because they lived in eternity. Although individual Jews lived and died, and their names died with them, they were immortal as a race. This was the meaning of the Holocaust.[3]

Jacques gave in. This was nothing like the politics or religion of conventional Zionism, but Isou was passionate, if misguided. He was also clueless about travel, as the Bulgarian adventure had demonstrated. He would need help from fellow Jews. Jacques eventually arranged for Isou to travel clandestinely with other young Zionists, through Budapest and Vienna, until arriving in Italy where they were to meet up with the Mossad-controlled Jewish Brigade. The others would then set off for Palestine; Isou would have to make his own way to France.

Isou went to see Solly and other young Zionist friends – Wladimir, Cerbou, Zolty, Boico. For Isou, this was another sign from the heavens – one way or another the time had come for them all to leave Romania. They talked for hours about what they would become, what the future held, the future of the Jews, dreaming of the 'infinite alchemy of time'.

Isou's mother collapsed into tears when she finally caught sight of the huge suitcase and the rucksack that Isou was packing to take with him. She put into his rucksack verses from the Torah and the *tefillin*, small leather boxes that carry said verses, which refer to God's intercession during the Exodus from Egypt, that he had not worn since he was thirteen years old. On the day that Isou was to leave, his father was 'red with emotion'. A few days earlier, he had said to Isou, 'I have no need of wealth if I have you. You have a value beyond yourself. Your value is in my eyes.'

Isou's father had already travelled across Europe. Now, Isou vowed to himself, because they were part of each other, it was Isou's duty to take his sperm further afield – to India, Mexico, Japan, the Congo; in spreading his seed he was also spreading the seed of his father. Before Isou finally left, his father said to him: 'I have great confidence in you.' Isou said that he was not yet worthy of his mother and felt full of shame, as if leaving her was a kind of betrayal.

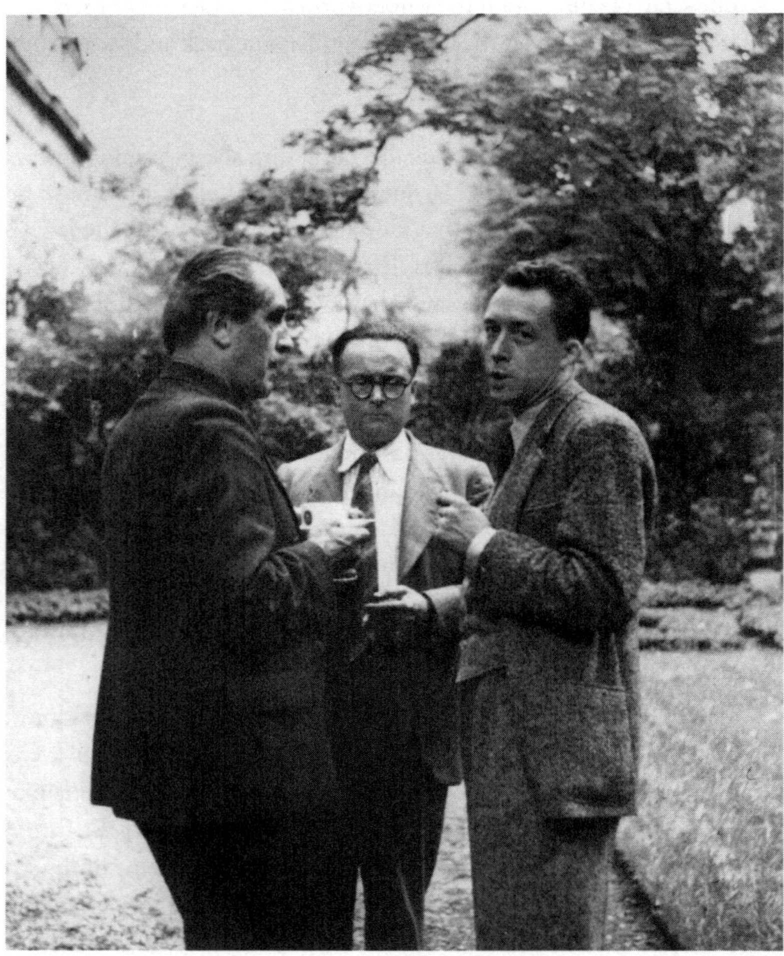

Jean Paulhan (left) with Marcel Arland and Albert Camus, June 1945.

That same morning Isou also spoke with Lucien Boz, a friend who was a journalist and who knew what was happening in the world beyond Romania. Boz was well connected in Paris and had fought for the French Resistance before being captured by the Germans. He had been interned at Drancy, the French gateway to the death camps of Eastern Europe. He was one of the few Jews to escape from Drancy and get back to Romania.

Boz told Isou that he had been told by a senior official in the Romanian government that the Soviets had now closed the demarcation line in Vienna. Nobody could now get through even with a proper passport and papers. The Iron Curtain was just about to divide Europe into two. Austria, and especially Vienna, was dangerous – a broken city of traffickers, spies and collaborators-in-hiding. 'You're young,' Boz said to Isou. 'It's still worth a try.'

Finally Isou went to see Zissu, who gave him a letter of introduction to 'a famous poet' in Paris. This was to Jean Paulhan, a former Director of the *Nouvelle Revue Française*, the most influential literary journal of the era, which was published by Gallimard. Paulhan was known to be a friend of the Jews and was a personal friend of Zissu. Urged on by Madame Zissu, Zissu reluctantly hugged the young man. Isou turned pale. 'Are you sad?' asked Zissu. 'A little bit,' said Isou.

Isou's uncle helped him take his bags to the headquarters of the young Zionists in Bucharest. His travelling companion, Zolty, was waiting for them. They took a taxi to the Gara de Nord. Solly was there to see his best friend off and wish him luck. Solly had decided to take his chances in Moscow; he had become a communist and feared the Soviets less than the 'Capitalists'. He asked: 'Will you write to me Isou?'

Isou spoke to his friend in French. He decided that he had already forgotten him. Solly's face was the emblem of the city that he now had to leave forever. He knew that he was being hard and that it hurt his friend and he was sorry for it. But he had no choice. This was real: he was leaving for Paris.

At four o'clock the train heaved out of the station.[4]

The train from Bucharest finally came to a halt in the early hours of the morning at Arad, a border town just inside Romania. Zolty and Isou had orders from the Zionists in Bucharest to make contact with the local Hagsharah, who would negotiate a way into Hungary for them. In the meantime they would camp out with the Hagsharah and wait for the signal to leave.

On the way to Arad Isou had already decided that he was now mostly French, although his identity was a lie. In his new role, he started to despise his fellow travellers – including Zolty – as Balkan peasants. At the first station stop – a long way short of Arad – a Polish deportee was kicked off the train by an inspector for having the wrong papers. When the same inspector approached him, Isou swore at him in French, which the inspector didn't understand. The inspector soon gave in.[5]

On arrival at Arad they met up with the local Hagsharah, who took them to a safe house. The plan was that they would make their way to Italy sheltered by the underground network of Zionists, who had safe houses, papers and contacts all along the way. They would have to stay for two days in Arad, waiting for the forged documents which would allow them to travel into Hungary. They were warned not to draw attention to themselves as foreigners to the town or as Jews – there were plenty of bitter ex-fascists here happy to settle scores with the 'Jewish-Bolshevik' menace.

Within a few hours, Isou was bored in the safe house. He asked one of the older women if there was a dance hall in Arad. It turned out that the woman was the wife of the local Zionist leader. This Hagsharah was an especially puritanical branch, and it was strictly forbidden to listen to modern music or go dancing, but the leader's wife told him that there was a dance hall and even where it was. On his way out of the safe house, in jubilation, Isou kissed a girl, 'a pretty little prawn of a thing'. She kissed him back and then giggled.

In the dance hall Isou quickly ran into trouble. He had picked up a local girl and started to dance a 'slow' with her when he felt a tap on his shoulder. He let the girl go and straightaway picked up another from a group of girls on a bench who were sitting in a row 'like a group of whores in a brothel'. He had only danced a few steps when he felt another tap on the shoulder. Now Isou was getting angry. He turned and squared up to the local young man and told him to get out of his way. The girl sighed with admiration for Isou.

Within seconds he was surrounded by a gang of toughs. One of the them, presumably the gang leader, stepped forward and tapped Isou even harder and asked why he wouldn't let the girl go. Isou again went into full *huligan* mode, the tactic of 'maximum assault' he had learned from Bif: who did these guys think they were, and what kind of place was this anyway where you couldn't dance a proper *slaou* with a girl? The gang was stunned and taken aback by Isou's attack. 'Where are you from then, stranger?' asked the gang leader.

'France,' said Isou. As he said the word – *Franța* in Romanian – he tried to make his mysteriously fluent Romanian now sound a little more fractured and Gallic. The ploy worked. 'France? You're a Frenchman. Ah well, that's different. Why didn't you say so?' The gang leader waved expansively to his mates. 'This guy's from France,' he said. 'Any of you lot who touch him will have me to deal with!' The rest of the gang then started shouting 'Vive la France!' Even though he wasn't technically French, Isou felt elated, as if he had actually taken part in the Battle for Romania, driven a tank and saved these undeserving yokels from the Nazis.

The dancing finished early by Bucharest standards and Isou was still bored and hungry for sex. He followed a girl into a church where she kneeled, crossed herself and began to pray. Isou propositioned her. 'What?' she said, offended. 'Don't you know how much that would cost? It's 500 lei to take me to a hotel. I'm not cheap.' It was now Isou's turn to be insulted. 'Nor am I!' he countered angrily. 'It would cost you at least 1,000 lei for me to fuck you. Maybe more!' The girl disappeared into the night.

Walking back alone to the Hagsharah safe house, he came across the 'pretty little prawn' and the leader's wife walking arm-in-arm down the street. 'We've been looking for you everywhere,' said the 'little prawn'. 'We wanted to go dancing with you but now it's late.' Then she kissed him passionately, 'as if they were lovers'. Somebody called her and she went back to the safe house.

Isou was alone with the leader's wife. He noticed that she was a statuesque figure. 'You are a very handsome boy,' she said. 'But the little one doesn't know how to kiss you . . .' Isou felt a sensation of danger, which always seemed to elevate him. This kind of seduction, from an older woman who was married to a powerful man, aroused him like nothing else. However, nothing happened that night. But the next morning, while the leader was away negotiating safe passes for Isou and Zolty at the customs post, the leader's wife invited him into their marital bed. This was a special, delicious form of betrayal, Isou thought, the best way to subvert authority; he was with her all morning.

That evening the leader, who was blonde – and, so thought Isou, possibly not even a Jew – looked at Isou with hatred in his eyes. The leader was hated by the rest of the Hagsharah anyway, reasoned Isou: he had fucked his woman in the name of the common good.

At dawn Isou and Zolty took a train, crossed the border and were on their way to Budapest. This was the first real foreign city on their journey. Isou described his first sight of Budapest as like seeing 'fleas on a comb'. The city was filthy and unpleasant and you felt contaminated by just seeing it. Isou also knew this was a very bad place for Jews. Nonetheless, having endured endless, boring countryside and peasant villages, Isou was relieved to be in a city again – one where there was a tramway, cinemas and proper cafés. Jews belonged in cities, even if they were as dirty and dangerous as Budapest.

Zolty and Isou again had orders to make for the local Hagsharah safe house. This was near the office of the Jewish Congress in the old Jewish quarter of Budapest. When the Nazis occupied Budapest in November 1944, this had been made into a walled ghetto, whose inhabitants could not get out and where many of them died of disease and starvation. In a last spasm of vindictive Jew-hatred, the Nazis and the collaborationist Hungarian government had sent around 130,000 Jews in cattle cars to death camps – this was out of a population of 200,000 Jews in Hungary. As late as January 1945, Adolf Eichmann was personally planning the 'elimination' of the rest of Hungarian Jewry. Even now, in the wake of the Liberation, the streets ran with dirty water, were littered with dead rats and faeces, and human corpses were a commonplace sight.

Once in the Hagsharah, Isou presented himself to his new comrades with a letter of introduction to a girl called Anna who was to take care of the Bucharest Jews. Anna was strong and well built. You could hardly tell that she had been through the war. She smelt good and reminded Isou of the sweet smell of 'a milk bar in a provincial town before 1939'; she smelt of innocence and the freshness of youth.

Anna led Isou, Zolty and another Romanian Jew called Pollatcheck on a short walk around the Old City. Zolty and Pollatcheck mocked Isou, telling Anna that Isou thought that he could conquer any woman. In his mind, Isou cursed them as 'impotent onanists'. 'Is this true, Isou?' she asked him. Isou loved the intimacy implied when she spoke his name; 'Yes,' he said, unsmiling.

They stopped at a cart where a peasant was selling fruit. Isou bought some apricots and compared them to Anna's breasts. Zolty and Pollatcheck laughed – again Isou silently cursed them. They should have disappeared by now. There was no time to flirt with Anna. They were leaving the next day on the train at noon. Isou wanted Anna, but he had to get rid of these clowns.

He took her by the arm. She pulled it away. 'You think you're so handsome,' she said. 'Well, I am – aren't I?' said Isou. 'Yes,' she said, 'but you're annoying too.' They slipped away from the two other comrades and went into a *pâtisserie*. They bought ice creams and, as they sat there, Isou began to stroke Anna's hair. 'Are you good at making love?' she asked. Isou looked at her, astonished. 'Admirably so,' he said after a silent few minutes. 'For example, I know exactly what you are doing right now with your legs. You are moving them because they are ready to be spread open.' Isou told Anna that he was leaving the next day and in the same breath that they should spend the night together. Anna said that he could spend the night in her room.

Back on the street, they were approached by a shabby man who was shaking and looked to Isou as if he might be a 'morphine' addict. He asked Isou for 20 poengoes (the local currency). Isou knew what the man was up to. Asking for a specific sum like this was another trick that Isou had learned from Bif: it gave you an air of certainty and respectability, nearly always ensuring that you got something in the end. Isou produced a bank note (100 poengoes) and, in a lordly voice, asked the man if he had any change. The man began to shake even more, probably in dire need of his drug; he had no change. Isou gave the note to him. Anna was shocked – Isou was an illegal stateless Jew and had no money to spare. Isou explained: he admired the man for trying to trick them rather than beg, which was demeaning. It was simply a question of style.

This was a philosophy which Isou also applied to sexual intercourse. Isou's belief was that you should make a woman feel grateful that she had slept with you, 'in the same way that you would be grateful if you had seen Henri Bergson or Paul Valéry give a lecture at the Collège de France'. He made love to Anna that night, so he wrote later, with 'all of the technical detail that I give to a *lettriste* poem'. He 'turned and twisted' his member inside her, 'taking her towards the mountains where' – approaching orgasm – 'she cried out to a distant and invisible mountaineer'. When she finally climaxed, she seemed to melt, whispering 'Isou-ou-ou' or 'Isou-ou-ou-ou' with every breath. There was a trickle of saliva on her lips, 'like a needle'. Isou bit her breasts, pulled her hair, and then he 'poured (his) liquid into her'. Then they slept.[6]

The next day Isou was exhausted, not simply because of his love-making with Anna but because his shoes were wearing through; his feet were sore from walking everywhere, his whole body ached with hunger and fatigue. He longed to be back in Bucharest, safe in the family home, adored by Fanny and his mother, protected by his father. He was slow to get out of Anna's bed, half-dreaming that she was his mother and that everything was all fine, as it always had been.

At noon he took the train to Graz, avoiding the potentially lethal snare of Vienna. The aim was then to get to Italy, where Jewish organizations, official and underground, were well established and reasonably well organized. This was the hardest part yet of the journey.

With a pack of other Jews, Isou was smuggled across the Austrian border at night through the Brenner Pass led by guides from Bricha (meaning 'flight'), a Zionist organization that was dedicated to moving Jews out of Europe and into Palestine. They travelled in wagons, escorted by friendly British troops, and then on foot.

Once in Italy, the Jews had to register at one of the United Nations camps in Milan, Rome or Bologna. Isou made first of all for Milan. There he had a crisis – his suitcases containing all of his treasured manuscripts and drawings was stolen at the train station, along with all of his money. He managed to get the manuscripts back – the thief had dumped them in a cellar – but he lost all of his money.

In Milan Isou also called on a poet called Giuseppe Ungaretti, another one of Zissu's literary friends. Ungaretti was a known fascist but he was not necessarily an antisemite, and anyway antisemitism had always been less fiercely ideological in Italy than it was in Germany or Romania. Ungaretti had also frequented Dadaist and Surrealist circles in the 1920s and was friendly with Tristan Tzara. Ungaretti's own poetic movement, called *Ermetismo*, owed much to Tzara's earlier experiments in dislocating sound and meaning. This was enough for Isou to declare later that Ungaretti was a fellow traveller of *lettrisme*, even if he was a fascist.

Isou smuggled himself on a train to Rome, where he registered at the UN camp in Cinecittà, the film studios just outside Rome, founded by Mussolini as a propaganda centre. Still using his false documents from the Red Cross, Isou claimed to be a displaced French Jew on his way home. He stayed for a few days with the other Jews at the UN camp in Cinecittà before catching a train along the coast to the French border. He was now travelling alone for the first time as his comrades either made for the boats to Palestine, or were temporarily billetted in the many camps for 'displaced persons' dotted across Italy.

Within a few hours of leaving Rome, in the nondescript port town of Livorno, he broke down. Arriving at the train station he could barely walk, overcome by fatigue and fear. For the first time ever in his life, he thought of taking his own life: he could not go on any more.[7]

He was saved, so he said later, by a miracle. This was the image of his mother's face, which, from nowhere, came into his mind and stayed there. He remembered that she prayed for him every day. Even if he were to be lost and forgotten in Paris, which was what he feared – he knew that his mother would love him forever. It was in this instant, he said, that he understood properly that his mother lived in him, like the 'mark made by a compass at the centre of a circle'.

He continued his journey and managed to get into France by wearing a battered American army uniform given to him by sympathetic soldiers, which helped him get across the border to Villefranche-sur-Mer. He was stopped in Marseilles, where he was arrested as an illegal immigrant and again thrown into jail. His father's face appeared before him in the freezing darkness of the cell. This was another image sent from God. His father said: 'What have you done with my creation – for you are my creation? You are wasting your time, which is my time, on this stupid adventure.'[8]

Isou was released after a few days, with the support of Jewish members of the Resistance, and given a new status as a Jewish 'displaced person'. Marseilles was now full of such Jews, waiting for boats to Palestine or even South America. Isou was still determined, however, to get to the French capital. He now had no money, but in the general confusion of post-war France it was an easy matter to slip onto one of the night-time trains travelling north from Gare St Charles.

By daybreak, he would be in Paris.

PART II

Paris Seen by a Stranger
(1945–68)

Parysis, tu sais, crucycrooks,
Belongs to him who parises himself.
JAMES JOYCE, *Finnegans Wake* (1939)

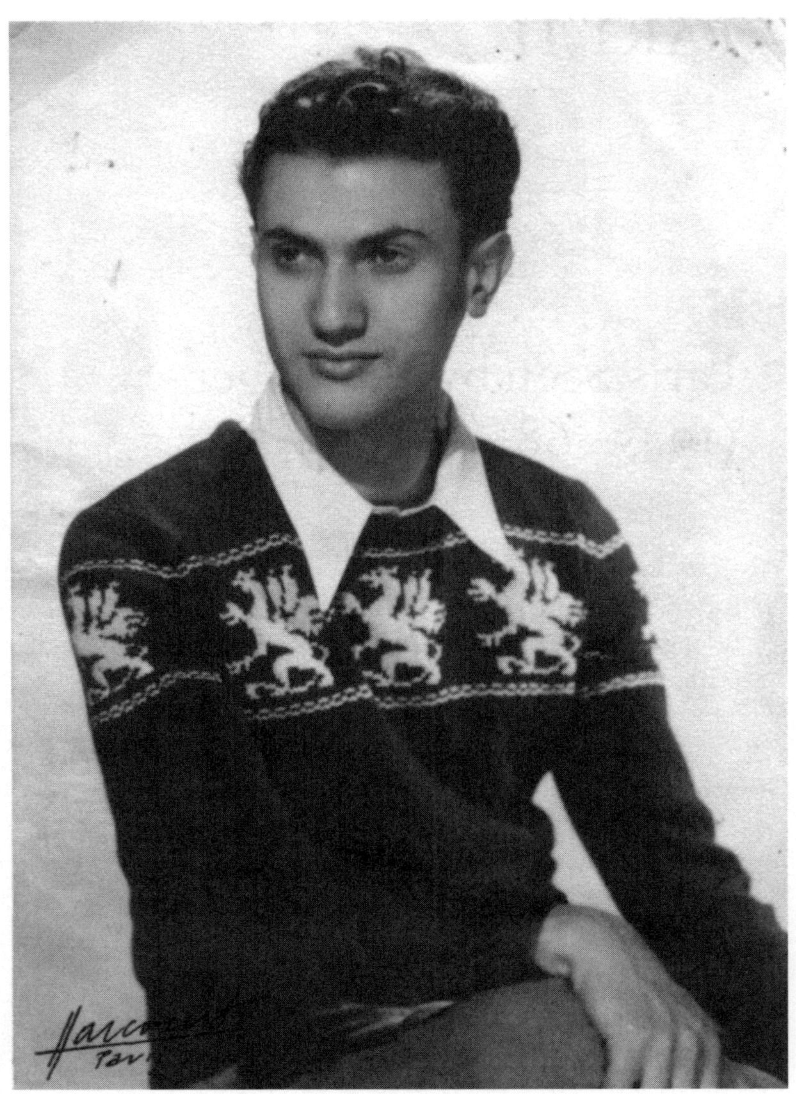

Isidore Isou, 1945, Studio Harcourt, Paris.

eight

Making a Name

Isou first set foot in Paris at first light on 23 August 1945, stepping down onto a platform at the Gare de Lyon. He was dirty, exhausted and scared. According to legend, he also had no time to waste. After only two days in Paris, lodging with Zionist comrades in Asnières, armed with letters of introduction given to him by Zissu and more recently Ungaretti, Isou made for the offices of Jean Paulhan, housed in the headquarters of the publishing house of Gallimard at 5 rue Sébastien-Bottin – one of the most elegant streets on the Left Bank.

Paulhan wasn't there – it was still quite early in the morning – but this did not deter Isou. He gleaned that Gaston Gallimard, the distinguished founder of the *Nouvelle Revue Française* and the house of Gallimard, was in the building. So Isou explained to the *concierge* that he was the most famous literary journalist in Romania and that he had come all the way from Bucharest to interview Gaston Gallimard. Somehow Isou was allowed into the building and ushered into the presence of the great publisher.

Isou introduced himself to the baffled Gallimard by declaring, in thickly accented French, that he was the most important poet since Charles Baudelaire. He also told Gallimard that he had come to Paris with a revolutionary new theory of poetry and music that would save mankind. This theory was in the form of a manuscript, in a battered haversack that Isou had brought with him from Bucharest. Isou took out the tattered pages and thrust them at Gallimard, describing them as 'a work of genius'. Gallimard promised to read the text and to pass it on to Jean Paulhan; it was sure to be of interest to him, Gallimard suavely assured the young man. Isou was euphoric. He spent the next few months expecting any day to hear back from Gallimard and take up his historic mission.[1]

In the meantime, Isou had to survive. To this end, his first destination
after the offices of Gallimard was the headquarters of the main Jewish
organization in Paris – the Alliance Israélite Universelle (AIU) – where
he registered as 'a displaced person'. The AIU, alongside American Jewish
organizations, ran kosher soup kitchens for 'displaced persons' and
returning deportees at the top end of the Marais, between the rue de
Saintonge, rue Rocher, rue Béranger, rue D'Elzévir and the rue Vieille
du Temple. This was the traditionally Jewish part of Paris known as the
pletzel ('little place' in Yiddish). After the war it was poor and dilapidated, but the soup kitchens served thousands of Jewish refugees every
day, and not only kept you alive but were a good place to meet other
Jews, to gossip and to plot, all without ever having to go to synagogue.
Isou lived in a hostel in Asnières but gravitated naturally to the centre
of Paris.

Isou did not, however, have to stay long in the *pletzel*. His Zionist
friends in Romania had given him yet another letter of introduction to
an address where he would be fed, at least for the next few uncertain
months. This was at number 9 rue Guy-Patin in the 10th arrondissement,
in a nineteenth-century mansion once owned by the banker Edmond
de Rothschild and which had been converted into a hostel for Jewish
students of various nationalities. It was run by the Comité de Bienfaisance
Israélite de Paris, a Jewish charity dating back to 1809.

The hostel's mission was to welcome Jews from all over the world –
although most of them came from French North Africa. There were
usually around a hundred beds, a library and seminar rooms. The hostel
was known as Le Toit familial, 'the family roof', and aimed to offer young
Jews two routes: to integrate into French society or prepare for the journey to Palestine. The place was, however, haunted by its grim recent past.
During the infamous raid of 10 February 1943, when the Paris police
rounded up Jewish children from all over the city, eleven of the hostel's
inmates had been handed over by the French police to be murdered by
the German authorities.

By the time that Isou arrived at the hostel, the standard of accom-
modation was high and roughly parallel to that offered by the Cité
Universitaire, the leafy international campus in the south of Paris. Le Toit
familial not only provided food and a bed but functioned as a kind of
Jewish Cultural Centre with talks, lectures and religious study groups.

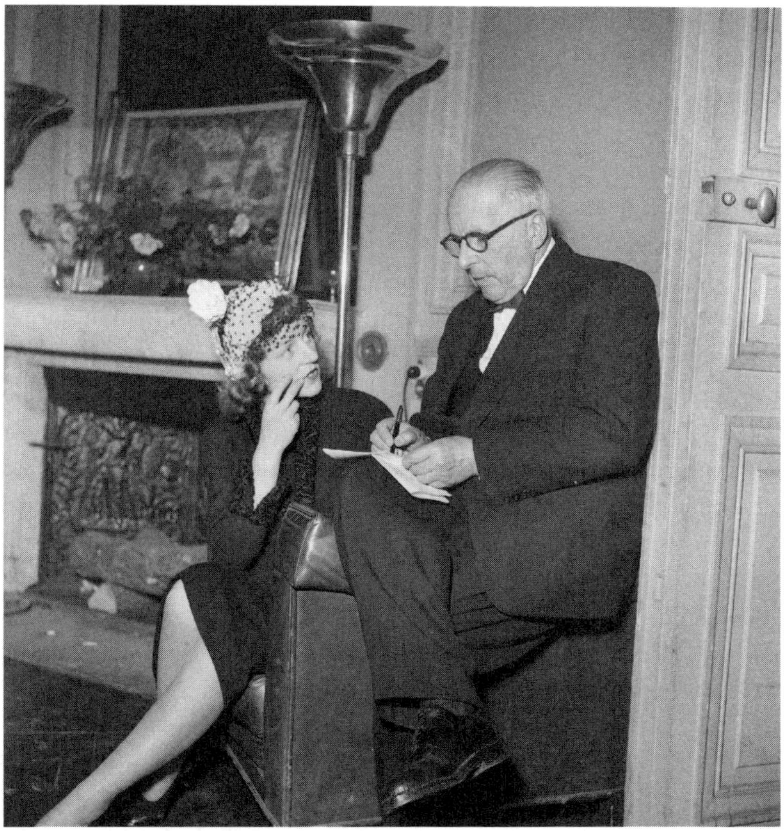

Gaston Gallimard in Éditions Gallimard on the occasion of the Prix Renaudot, 1951.

Religious practices were observed but were not compulsory, apart from the ban on smoking on the Sabbath.

Isou had no interest in travelling to Palestine, although he still described himself as a Zionist. He fancied himself rather as a student at the Sorbonne. He managed to get as far as registering his name there with the aid of a fellow Romanian Jew who had been resident in Paris during the last year and claimed that Isou was the first Jew he had met who had crossed from the East to Western Europe. By now Isou was living at a hotel called Le Gramont, which he paid for with a monthly stipend of 3,000 francs awarded to him as a foreign student at the university. This was about the average wage of a manual worker and he sought to supplement it working as a waiter and briefly in a shop. He was as disastrous at these jobs as any he had tried out in Bucharest.

Isou soon began to miss his parents and his sisters. He described himself as 'like a fallen angel', exiled from the earthly Paradise of his loving family.[2] He treasured a coloured birthday card, which was also a family portrait. In the photograph Isou is pouring tea standing over the centre of a table laden with flowers, and wearing one of his first ever grown-up suits. He looks nervous and shy. In Paris this became one of his few treasured mementoes of his previous life and he decorated it with silver glitter, giving each family member a silvery halo.[3]

Isou particularly missed Fanny, whose name is constantly written in capital letters in his letters and poems of this early period. 'Zennenne FANNY! Oi! Chema Israelle!' he wrote in a sound poem written during his first weeks in Paris, evoking the Jewish prayer from the first words of the Torah and placing Fanny at the centre of his yearning for home, for 'Israel'. 'Zou Isou! Issou Cathedral Craal', he wrote in another poem from the same period, ending the poem with the dying sigh of 'Christ, Staline . . . Isou . . . Isou'.[4]

Isou was not only homesick but often frightened in Paris. This made sense, mainly because political life in the French capital in late 1945 was so chaotic. This was the beginning of a period of revenge called *l'épuration sauvage* (wild purification), an orgy of self-hate and vengeance. The first targets were known spies or informers or black marketeers, who may or may not have been in the pay of the Germans. Most were summarily executed without trial. The violence soon spread to anybody suspected of collusion with the Germans, including women who were accused of 'sleeping with the enemy'. The scenes from this period include the terrible sight of hundreds of women having their heads shaved for so-called 'horizontal collaboration'. In Paris it was a common sport to join in with the crowd who attacked such women, tarred and feathered them, and daubed them in swastikas. The gaiety that accompanied such human suffering quickly became a taboo among 'Liberationist' groups.

In this atmosphere Isou found it hard to believe that the war was over. For Isou post-war Paris was a savage place where the dominant emotions were hatred and recrimination. The war had not changed anything; divisions between Right and Left were indeed now more acute than ever before. 'No illusions about the future', Isou wrote in his journal during those first weeks. 'The curtain falls on the bloody game of war, and a new tragedy begins – the intensified tension between a socialist world and a capitalist world.'[5] In a rare prose poem in French, written during those first few weeks, Isou recalled wartime Romania, deliberately blurring his memories with the reality of present-day Paris:

Dog-face ravaged humiliated sword anger battle enemy monsters horrible massacre coward warrior all in flames disaster honour dishonour inferior in number fear suffering tears insults conqueror conquered killed howling ambush forest blood wounds.[6]

During those first days in Paris, Isou was aware of the fact that, with his accent and dark complexion, he was very much an outsider here in a double sense: a foreigner and a Jew from the East. Unlike Bucharest, with its tens of thousands of fellow Jews, Isou was horrified to find that, beyond the reassuring safety of the *pletzel*, Paris was 'a wholly Christian city of bells, stones and prayers'. In war-battered Bucharest, Jews had been killed and beaten up and forced into work details, but they were still ever-present. In Paris, outside of their traditional quarters, Jews were barely visible. This was hardly surprising: out of 76,000 Jews who had been deported by the French and German authorities during the war, only 3,500 came 'home' to France, the majority having either been 'exterminated' in the death camps or chosen exile elsewhere.

Isou's greatest fear, like many Eastern Jews newly arrived in the West, was the coming of a new Holocaust. In his view, there were still too many French people who either denied any responsibility for Nazi crimes or thought that the Jews had it coming to them anyway. Isou saw 'daggers out for the Jews everywhere'.

Isou was alarmed by the drunken street songs of 'Christians', which he seemed to hear everywhere he went. The 'Christians' joked and shouted out 'Yids to the crematorium!' These cries could be heard all over Paris – in the Théâtre de l'Ambigu (actually a cinema on the Boulevard Saint-Martin), at the Opéra and on the Boulevard Saint-Michel.[7] There was always fresh antisemitic graffiti in the lavatories of even the best cafés. These places, Isou wrote, 'ought to be a place of repose, thought and sanctuary'; instead there was usually a Swastika scrawled on the wall, along with the slogan 'Death to the Yids!' At the sight of these graffiti, Isou felt a physical pain 'like an unsought for and unwanted erection'.[8]

Isou's frightened agonies were not without foundation. Most notably, official recognition of the Holocaust in France had been hesitant and nervous, although all Eastern Jews in Paris, like Isou, knew what had really been happening in the East.

The earliest French acknowledgement of the Holocaust came in June 1945, only a month or so before Isou arrived in Paris. This was when the newspaper *Libération*, which had been a Resistance propaganda sheet, published a pamphlet which contained eyewitness accounts of the death camps, alongside photographs of gas chambers and a man being burned to death. In the same month, the French government organized an exhibition called 'Hitler's Crimes', which was set up in the huge Grand Palais. In one of the rooms there was a timeline and catalogue of the Jews interned in the French camps of Pithiviers, Beaune-la-Rolande and Drancy in the Occupied Zone and Gurs in Vichy France. There were other images, on loan from the British Embassy: Bergen-Belsen, Buchenwald, Nordhausen, Mittelgladbach and Maidenek. The French public could now see the end-points of French collaboration with the Nazis. Significantly, however, this part of the exhibition occupied only a handful of the 29 enormous rooms of the Grand Palais.

Parisians had a more direct and visceral contact with returning deportees at the Hôtel Lutetia on the Boulevard Raspail. During the Occupation this had been a Gestapo headquarters and torture chamber. Now occupied by Allied forces, in the summer of 1945 it was a centre for repatriation where crowds flocked to look at the pasted-up photographs of those still missing. The deportees themselves were easily recognizable by their twisted gait, their blackened teeth and their limbs shrivelled to sticks. Many Parisians collapsed uncontrollably into tears at the sight.

This was, however, precisely the kind of emotion that made Isou nervous. Even the 'Christians' could not bear this much guilt, he reasoned. That was why they would kill the Jews again, to expiate the original crime. The same cycle had repeated itself for 2,000 years. This was why, in spite of, or perhaps because of, the Holocaust, you still heard the same old antisemitic slogans in the streets of Paris. Isou compared the experience of Jews arriving in Paris, or anywhere in the West, to that of Jews arriving in Palestine. They should never allow themselves to be victims again. It was time for Jews to fight back or die.

Isou was also horrified by the recent rise to power in France of the MRP (Mouvement Républicain Populaire), a Social-Democratic Christian party that was emerging as a newly influential force on the political landscape. The party supported Charles de Gaulle (although he never joined it) and aimed to bring together former *résistants*, socialists and Catholics in opposition to the Communist Party – which was also gaining support, mainly based on its members' prestigious activities during the war (the communists were always among the most effective and organized of Resistance cells).[9]

Isou thought that members of the MRP were hard-line Catholics and so fascists by any other name. There was no such thing as a 'new France' in the wake of the Second World War, only the 'old France' in disguise. This meant the 'old bastards' were still in charge. They were bound to be preparing the way to a 'cleansing of the Jews' – finishing the job that Hitler had started.

The Jews who didn't know this, or refused to see it, said Isou, were 'soft, cowardly, *ceruminous*, shitty Yids!' The use of the word 'ceruminous' is a scientific medical term describing sweaty or greasy skin, a perfect way, according to Isou, to describe a race traitor. These 'Yids', he wrote, were a 'shame to the race and religion!'

One afternoon Isou was making this argument to a fellow Easterner at a soup kitchen in the *pletzel* when a well-meaning French Jew told him to be quiet, saying that at least a soup kitchen was better than the camps. Isou exploded with fury. What could this 'French Jew, this *Western* Jew' know of what the Eastern Jews had seen and lived through? Was this happiness for Jews – Isou spat out his words – not to 'have your belly ripped open and be machine-gunned and then piled up in a heap of corpses? Should Jews be *grateful* for this?'[10]

Isou went on: couldn't these miserable French Jews, these *collaborators*, see that they were still in the ghetto – that these soup kitchens packed with filthy Easterners, from Galați and Moldova, were prisons too? And that the 'Christians' who were soft on the Jews now were just ashamed? They would soon be back to killing them once again.[11]

Isou was not the only young Jew in Paris who felt this way. Among those who heard Isou's call to arms and was impressed by it was a young French Jew called Gabriel Pomerand (real name Pomerans). Pomerand was almost exactly the same age as Isou. He had been born in Alsace and had moved to the Free French zone of Marseilles for the duration of the war. He had come to Paris in the confusion after the war but didn't quite know what he was doing there. He had vague notions of becoming an actor, but he had no experience or contacts in the city, although he did claim to have been trained by Marcel Marceau. He was also an avid reader of avant-garde poetry and in particular admired the poet Arthur Rimbaud as the ultimate rebel and visionary. He hated any form of compromise with authority and thought that the post-war government in France was no better than the Nazis – it was surely made up anyway of collaborators, liars and Jew-haters. The one defining point in his life was the fact that his mother had been deported and then killed by the Nazis.[12]

When he met Isou, Pomerand was selling cheap books – erotica and crime thrillers mainly – on the street to make a living. Pomerand was at first seduced by Isou's rage as well as his theories. Isou was a powerful and convincing orator. Isou's French was sometimes hard to understand. This was partly due to his thick Romanian accent and the Yiddish rhythms of his speech, and also partly because of Isou's florid, often obscure but also poetic, choice of words. Sometimes Isou would use a word that his audience might not understand – a Romanian word or a badly pronounced French word. But the audience felt the full force of its impact anyway, mesmerized by the endless flow of words and ideas. Pomerand was entranced:

> I have to say it was Isou who set loose this new phenomenon that manifests as my understanding . . . we wandered the streets together, deep in debate, and he filled my head with a mess of ideas in which the surprise of youthful poetry, of theatre, of erotology, of philosophy, of *metagraphics*, and perhaps, one day, of medicine, was expressed succinctly, too fast and mixed up for me to grasp.[13]

One of the first long conversations between Isou and Pomerand took place in a kosher canteen for refugees. The conversation was triggered by Isou's sight of a tatty edition of the writings of the nineteenth-century poet Lautréamont, which Pomerand took with him everywhere. Lautréamont had declared that his ambition was to overturn the world by poisoning the minds of fourteen-year-old girls with his sickly and satanic poetry. Lautréamont's revolt was not just against society, however, but against language itself, and he argued for using poetry as a way of undermining such illusions as 'truth' or 'beauty'; Lautréamont was not writing to improve the world but to spit on it.

Unsurprisingly, Lautréamont had been a hero first to the Dadaists and then the Surrealists, who revelled in his often impenetrable contradictions. The Surrealists in particular loved his absurd paradoxical aphorisms: 'As beautiful as the chance encounter of a sewing machine and an umbrella on an operating table' was a favourite maxim. Isou found a special totemic significance in the fact that he and Lautréamont shared the same name – Isidore.

Pomerand boasted to Isou that he had worked for the Resistance movement in Marseilles. This did not have, however, much currency with

Isou, who had already risked his life several times during the German occupation of Romania and then by smuggling himself to France. Nonetheless Isou was impressed enough by Pomerand to invite him to his lodgings, where he promised that he would explain to him the theory of *lettrisme*.

Pomerand was then sleeping in the streets and occasionally, if he was lucky, in a cell in a Rabbinical school. A friend who knew them both at the time described Isou as 'always well groomed, very sure of himself and very handsome'. Pomerand was, in contrast, unshaven, dirty and wild-eyed: 'a bard who would give his life for *lettrisme*'.

Pomerand eventually became an opium addict and killed himself in 1972 with an overdose, broken-hearted that he had eventually – and bitterly – been excommunicated by Isou (this happened in 1956). But for now, Pomerand was to be cast in a role – as Isou's first and most important disciple in his conquest of Paris. For this reason, Isou called him the 'Archangel Gabriel, the Archangel of Lettrisme', who would herald the good news that Isou was bringing to the world.

For his part Pomerand was impressed not only by Isou's torrential speeches, but by the way in which Isou was now also busy making himself known to the great writers of the day. Isou's calling card was that he was just about to be published by Gallimard and this book would be the first of many that would change society and the world. Isou let it be known that he had met Gaston Gallimard, who had admired the young Romanian straightaway, and that Jean Paulhan was reading his work with close attention, no doubt because it was so profound and earth-shaking. Nobody had any reason to doubt him.

On these spurious grounds, Isou was granted audiences with Jean Cocteau and François Mauriac. Isou was given 5,000 francs by the writer and critic Max Pol Fouchet, who did not read a word of Isou before meeting him but was overwhelmed by Isou's personality. The money did not last long in Isou's pocket; there was no point in saving money when he would soon be rich and famous anyway.[14]

One of Isou's first encounters with a major figure was with André Gide in November 1945. Gide was then in his late seventies and only a year or so away from being awarded the Nobel Prize in Literature. Gide received the young Romanian with courtesy, listened to him and patiently worked his way through Isou's manuscripts. He returned them to Isou via his secretary Gaston Criel. Criel also sent Isou a friendly note from Gide in which the great author declared: 'I am now a *lettriste!*'[15]

Isou was angry and disappointed at this follow-up to the meeting. Why did Gide not immediately offer Isou a publishing contract? Isou suspected that he was being patronized and fobbed off. He was reminded of his meeting with Paul Morand in Bucharest, and how he had felt bitterly humiliated by the fascist Morand's polite indifference.

From now on Gide was a sworn enemy and would be a favourite target for the *lettristes*. 'Since 1900,' wrote Isou, 'he [Gide] had been the favourite spittoon into which every new generation felt they had to spit, covering his epithets with saliva . . . But it was also something personal that meant that we too [the *lettristes*] wanted to cover his cheeks with shit and phlegm, this ignominious arse-licker.'

The real problem was, Isou later reasoned to himself, that Gide had been over-awed by Isou. Isou wrote in his journal:

> I had the impression that, faced with me, he [Gide] felt like a whore confronted with a huge cock that was far too big for her, and like the whore who didn't want to be raped, Gide tried to talk me down with words that he thought would excite me. I was supposed to ejaculate too quickly, to lose my hard-on and make him pregnant with yet another idea in his head.[16]

Gide was not, however, the only target for Isou. Through the autumn of 1945, late at night, all across the Left Bank, Isou and Pomerand – along with a handful of new recruits they had found in the dive bars of the Left Bank – pasted up cheaply printed posters and tracts announcing *La Dictature lettriste*, 'The Lettrist Dictatorship'. In their rants, they attacked the 'liars' of the French Resistance and the poets of the Resistance. The big names included Jean Cassou, Pierre Seghers, Paul Éluard and René Char – who mythologized themselves as rebels but who, according to the *lettristes*, were no more than self-serving aesthetic reactionaries, and therefore not much better than fascists.

Attacking the poets who had bravely fought for and exalted the Resistance was a terrible heresy. But that was precisely the point. In various impromptu meetings, Isou explained to his newly recruited *lettristes* that there was no middle way: democracy was always a failure, and ended for the Jews in murderous catastrophe. The only self-defence was attack. The '*lettriste* dictatorship' was meant as a reality and would be as absolute and total as any of the revolutions of Hitler or Stalin. All of this would of course be the concrete proof of Isou's theories that maximum and minimum effect were the same thing; and that by applying this theory you could create a new world by setting fire to the old world.

———

By late November 1945, Isou's forged papers had fallen out of date and were useless. His money had also long since evaporated. He was effectively stateless and destitute, despite his student grant. He now had no choice but to live off his wits, putting into operation once again the criminal arts he had learned from Bif in Bucharest. This was to be life lived as 'an adventure' once more.

Isou had no qualms about taking other people's money. This made him an excellent conman. So he set about borrowing money from people without any intention of paying it back. He prided himself on his ability to con complete strangers and was especially proud of having cheated a Catholic priest out of a substantial sum – proof of Jewish guile over Christian pity.

Isou decided to become a prostitute. There was not much difference, he reasoned to himself, between being a 'pimp, a gigolo or a young genius'. When he looked in the mirror he was 'stunned by [his] own beauty'. He was 'beautiful' and 'magnificent'. So why not use these looks to make money one way or another?

Isou drew the line at 'pederasts', although he was aware that he was attractive to older, richer men. Isou was sure that Jean Cocteau had been powerfully attracted to him; it would only be logical. Isou's only desire, however, was for Cocteau to help make him 'immortal'.[17]

Isou had no strict moral code against 'pederasty'.[18] He confessed to himself that he had often been tempted by the vampiric beauty of certain homosexuals and he enjoyed their company. On certain occasions, he said, it would not have taken much for him to have joined their ranks, in the same way that he did not exclude animals from his sexual universe. He admired blonde Polish boys as members of what he felt was obviously a pederastic race. His objection to homosexuality was that he had only so much sexual energy and that this was reserved for women. 'Pederasty' might too easily have consumed him. He had a vocation and duty instead to serve the world of women.[19]

Isou fancied himself as an elegant pimp, a criminal dandy adored by a stable of whores, taking advantage of every woman's natural inclination to sacrifice herself for a man. Lying in bed with Anna in Budapest, he had said that the pimp was 'every woman's ideal man'. Anna had shivered with mock disgust but Isou was serious when he said this and boasted that he had even played the role of a pimp in Bucharest just for fun. He also described how, at the age of sixteen, when he first saw a woman his initial thought was to get near her and wonder if she would kiss him. Then, at eighteen years old, he would make the same moves, but now wondering if he would get to sleep with her. Before long, he didn't care whether he kissed her or slept with her; his only thought was that his 'sperm was a commodity' and he had to get the right price for it. Finally he wrote that 'I prefer women who give me money without making love to me to women who make love with me and don't give me a penny,' although he added to this statement that sometimes he was so lonely in Paris that 'just a smile from a cutie' would do.

In the early evenings of November and December 1945, Isou made his way to Pigalle and loitered in the entrances of hotels where well-heeled *bourgeoises* were known to pick up young men. One of the most famous of these was the Hôtel d'Élysée des Beaux Arts on the rue Saint-Antoine, mainly a haunt of female prostitutes but also tolerant of a gay and female clientele looking to buy the bodies of handsome young men. This is where Isou had his first triumphs as a fully fledged prostitute. The going rate was 300 to 500 francs for a fuck. At first Isou said that he felt proud at his success but soon he felt degraded and debased when the woman, usually ugly, pushed the dirty, 'ragged and scruffed' hundred-franc notes at him over a café table.[20]

His success also attracted trouble. One evening he almost had his face smashed in by other male prostitutes who had been in Pigalle a lot longer than Isou and knew how to wield a knife. Isou wrote that, for all of these reasons, he soon tired of being a prostitute. Worst of all was not just the fucking, but dancing with the female client all night, giving her compliments and listening to her stupid chatter. He would lie awake, with his 'cock ever loaded and ready to go', because that's what the client expected, while the woman lay there snoring.

He preferred to be free of 'such cows' who not only 'suck your cock down to the bone but also your thoughts and ideas'. Being a gigolo was exactly like being a businessman, pretending to make small talk to make a sale; while all the time hiding the truth of the transaction that had brought both sides together. Isou felt like a commodity and, the greatest humiliation of all, he was unable to reveal his divine nature to these dim-witted bitches. He was sick most of all of ugly Englishwomen who had no money because of the exchange rate.

The English language, which Isou did not speak well, was everywhere in post-war Paris. The main reason was that the city was flooded with demobilized American soldiers who were able to stay on in the city due to the GI Bill of Rights programme, which allowed them to study there and live on a monthly stipend. Paris was also a magnet for displaced hustlers from all corners of Europe for whom American English, not French, Russian or German, was the new *lingua franca*.

In a poem written during this period, Isou makes a phonetic multi-lingual collage of the various languages you could hear on the streets of post-war Paris. The poem is called 'Paris vu par un étranger' (Paris Seen by a Stranger) and captures the immediacy of the city:

> PIGALLE! les catin lescatin
> Escourialle Chansélisée lesputains
> Les valins
> Les balins
> Sangermain BOULMICH
> Trichcoric sandouischcouchich
>
> Hélobeby obraytrédy Ianky doudl coudl
> Youdl fouky noudl
> OLRAITLEDY![21]

This poem comes properly alive when it is read out loud and you can hear the voices of the city's whores ('les catins', 'les putains') and Parisian hustlers accosting GIs with bad American accents that sound like Yiddish ('Youdl fouky noudl'). For all that he delighted in Parisian low-life, as celebrated in this poem, Isou quickly found out that being a gigolo was also an uncertain way to make money. So he found a more lucrative *métier* in petty theft. This was another craft he had learned from Bif in Bucharest.

In Paris, Isou improved his technique as a pickpocket by watching other thieves at work, mainly in the *métro*. During a stop at the station Barbès-Rochechouart, he marvelled as a young man, reasonably well dressed, stepped up at the last minute as a train was about to depart and snatched the handbag of an elegant lady before skipping off the train and disappearing forever in a crowd of commuters.

The trick was especially well played because Barbès-Rochechouart was an overground station and the thief would be several levels below the train, vanishing into the iron labyrinth of the railway bridge before anyone could even react to the crime. Isou also admired the sly way in which he had distracted the woman, staring at her knees and then into her eyes as if to seduce her. This was another technique which Isou immediately resolved to add to his repertoire.[22]

It was not long before Isou came to know the *métro* like a native. He travelled ticketless on long aimless journeys across the city, evading guards and especially the police, who might have asked him for his papers. It turned out that Isou was good at being a thief. It took daring, grace and agility and above all the ability to feint an opponent in what was really a game, or a sort of dance. It was indeed, he explained to Gabriel Pomerand, who was himself no stranger to petty crime, an art like any other.

In late November 1945, Jean Paulhan finally wrote back to Isou. He praised Isou's work and in particular expressed an interest in publishing *Introduction à une nouvelle poésie et à une nouvelle musique* (Introduction to a New Poetry and a New Music), the text which Isou had thrust at Gaston Gallimard, urging him that it was 'a great work of genius'. Paulhan was not convinced that Isou was 'a genius', but he was intrigued enough to meet Isou properly.

In the meantime, Paulhan had also passed Isou's manuscript onto Raymond Queneau, who was respected at Gallimard not only as a writer but as a sharp-eyed critic with a special understanding of the avant-garde. Later Queneau would be a strong supporter of Isou, defending him against charges of obscenity and praising him as a singular theorist. In 1961, with a group of like-minded intellectuals, Queneau founded an experimental group called OuLiPo (Ouvroir de Littérature Potentielle – 'Workshop for Potential Literature'), which shared Isou's interest in the confluence between mathematics, eroticism and poetry (Isou inevitably denounced Queneau as a plagiarist in all of this).

For now, however, Queneau had reservations about *Introduction à une nouvelle poésie et à une nouvelle musique*. The real problem for Queneau with Isou's text was in Isou's writing. More to the point, Queneau could not see any indication of literary talent. Isou expressed his ideas in a ceaseless, exhausting flow, often using strange comparisons or convoluted phrases that seemed to come straight from the Romanian rather than the French language. But there was none of the command over language that made the likes of the Surrealist Antonin Artaud, for example, a great artist as well as a madman. Isou's poetry itself was simply impenetrable. So Queneau hesitated.

Despite Paulhan's warm words of late November 1945, Isou could wait no longer. Finally, he put into operation his tactic of 'calculated impatience'. Isou demanded the return of his manuscript from Gallimard before Queneau had time to make a decision. He then sent it round other leading Paris publishers, shamelessly arguing that this was now their chance to steal a march on Gallimard and make Parisian literary history by being the first to publish Isou.

By the end of 1945, however, Isou had still not found a publisher. He had now been round all the leading publishing houses in Paris, each of which had expressed varying degrees of interest in his work but never enough to publish it.

Isou wrote an open letter to all the publishers who were ignoring him:

> Each generation brings with it a mass of new values which old bastards like you try to stifle. I'm warning you now that my friends and I will come and smash your faces in if you don't publish my work which will create great upheavals. I do not salute you, Isidore Isou.[23]

More graffiti appeared all over the Left Bank. One graffito read: 'Will your body be found at the corner of rue Sébastien-Bottin?'[24] This was an obvious threat to Gaston Gallimard, who had his offices in that street.

Isou had now been in Paris over four months and was still not famous. Panic and fury were now beginning to overwhelm him.

nine

Poets for the Atomic Age

Isou's anger had hardened even more by the first weeks of 1946. Isou and Pomerand in the meantime had attracted two new recruits – a young would-be musician from Paris called Georges Perros and Guy Marester, a young writer who had fought with the Resistance in Lyon – who would briefly be essential to operations.

With these new sidekicks, Isou and Pomerand convened a conference on 8 January at the Salle des Sociétés Savantes at number 8 on rue Danton. Previous speakers at this prestigious venue had included Lenin, Trotsky and the first Parisian Dadaists. A poster for the event announced 'New Poetry, New Music, New Art'; *lettriste* texts would be read aloud; Gabriel Pomerand was to give a talk called 'From Homer to Lettrism'; Isou himself would explain it all in his talk called 'First Epistle to the *Lettristes*'. The conference was touted as the historic moment when *lettrisme* would replace Surrealism as the most important avant-garde movement on the Left Bank.

Hardly anyone turned up. Most of the audience consisted of the inmates of a local orphanage chaperoned by the institution's director, who was – according to Guy Marester's account of the fiasco – a self-important and bossy widow. The group had evidently come to the meeting on the mistaken grounds that they would be attending an improving, educational talk on poetry.

The first thing that the widow did on entering the Salle (an hour later than the advertised starting time) was to order the *lettristes* to take down the 'hideous daubings' (their artworks that they had hung on the wall). The *lettristes* meekly did so, unwilling to lose their captive audience. Worse still, the orphans did not understand that Isou was reading out *lettriste* poetry; they simply thought that he was speaking Romanian, which they did not understand. The only representative from the press was the correspondent of the Right-wing Royalist journal *Lys Rouge*, who had apparently come to the wrong meeting (he had thought that he was attending a conference on Tibet).[1]

Isou was disappointed and angry that the conference had been such an embarrassing failure. It was obviously time to go towards more radical confrontation. A chance to do this presented itself only a few weeks later, on 21 January. Isou and Pomerand noted that on that date a new play called *La Fuite*, written by no less than Tristan Tzara, was opening at the Théâtre du Vieux-Colombier. Recently this old theatre had become a headquarters of the nascent Existentialist movement (Sartre's play *Huis Clos* had premiered there in 1944) and was therefore identified by the *lettristes* as a camp of a hated enemy (Isou particularly despised Sartre).

There were also other reasons why *La Fuite* was such a good target. The play, called a 'dramatic poem' by Tzara, was to be read by the actor Marcel Lupovici – another Romanian in Paris – and set to music by Max Deutsch, a Viennese Jew now exiled in Paris and close to Tzara and Jean Cocteau among others. It was to be introduced by Michel Leiris, who had so admired the play that he had almost resigned from the editorial board of Jean-Paul Sartre's journal *Les Temps Modernes*, which had refused to publish it.

This minor scandal around Leiris, Tzara, Sartre and their arguments ensured that the Théâtre du Vieux-Colombier would be packed with the cream of Parisian literary society – a perfect if unsuspecting audience for Isou and Pomerand. The main theme of the play too had special resonance for the would-be *lettriste* iconoclasts. It was the old Dadaist idea that the end of Western civilization was both necessary and inevitable: 'Bankruptcy, collapse, confusion . . . total chaos so that a new society can be born.' Isou and Pomerand dismissed this theme as *Résistantialiste* – a term the *lettristes* had coined to describe a mixture of Existentialism and Resistance mythology which, in their eyes, were both equally fictitious and out of date.

Isou and Pomerand bought tickets for all their followers – at least a dozen of them – and told them the plan was to wreck the evening; they were instructed to cause maximum disruption. The plan worked. As he began his introductory lecture, Leiris was met with a barrage of jeers and catcalls from the *lettristes* in the audience: 'Dada is dead, *lettrisme* has overtaken it!' Leiris said that he had never heard of *lettrisme* and was jeered even more loudly. Other members of the audience joined in: 'Fuck the *lettristes*,' somebody shouted from the back of the room. 'We have all heard of Dada,' shouted Isou from the audience, 'why don't you tell us about *lettrisme*?' Leiris said that he had never heard of it, which was met by more laughter.

At this point, with other-worldly self-possession, Isidore Isou strolled on to the stage. He announced that he was here to proclaim 'the Dictatorship of *lettrisme*'. Isou explained that while Dada had detached words from phrases, *lettrisme* would go one step further and detach letters from words. Isou began to read out a poem: 'Vagn bagadou kri kuss balala chimorabissss . . .' The poem was punctuated by someone with a sneezing fit, but this seemed to be in time and actually accentuate the impact of the noise that Isou was making. The evening disintegrated into chaos as the *lettristes* then noisily charged the stage.

The next day, Isou and the *lettristes* were the talk of the Left Bank. Most crucially, the journal *Combat* – then under the editorial control of Albert Camus – published an article by Maurice Nadeau, an intimate friend of the Surrealists and a literary power-broker on the Left Bank in his own right. Nadeau had attended the event at the Théâtre du Vieux-Colombier and reported it in fervid tones. Nadeau was amused by and approved of the 'youth uprising', declaring that the *lettristes* 'had put Tzara on the run!'[2]

Within weeks there was a rumour that a book contract and even a sizeable advance were on their way to Isou from no less than Gaston Gallimard himself. Isou was euphoric once again; the *lettristes* had finally accomplished their mission. Isou, the self-proclaimed Jewish messiah and genius, was at last about to enter history. This at least was the legend put about by Isou and his disciples.

Certainly, in the wake of the Tzara 'scandal', Gallimard was still interested in Isou. The reality was, however, that Gallimard, as well as Jean Paulhan, was worried about sales. At a second meeting in the offices in rue Sébastien-Bottin, Paulhan and Gaston Gallimard expressed their admiration for the young Romanian and conceded that it was quite remarkable that he had founded a movement which attracted so many supporters in only a few months. But his texts were badly edited and hard to understand.

After the meeting Isou began to doubt Paulhan's good faith. He wrote in his journal that Paulhan had a face which made him look like a Nazi and 'as if he might swallow you whole'.[3] His 'interest' in Isou was just as empty as the phoney promises of the Jewish Aid organizations, who were no better than collaborators. Isou's suspicions were fuelled by other rumours that Paulhan had been a passive collaborator during the Occupation and only wanted to publish a Jew to make himself look good. The same applied to Gaston Gallimard, who also carried the taint of alleged collaboration, and furthermore of being out of touch with the young post-war generation.

There was another meeting between Isou and Paulhan and Gallimard. The conversation was more heated and convoluted than the previous ones, not helped by the fact that Pomerand, who turned up as Isou's self-styled bodyguard, was swaggering about playing the hard man. Gallimard, in exasperation, turned to Paulhan and asked him to finally decide.

Paulhan had by now – according to Isou – developed a homoerotic fascination with Pomerand, who was indeed a powerful sexual presence attractive to men and women. Paulhan said yes, that they should publish the *lettristes* and the first contracts were soon drawn up. The initial books scheduled for publication were *Introduction à une nouvelle poésie et à une nouvelle musique*, the founding text of *lettriste* theory, and Isou's autobiography *L'Agrégation d'un nom et d'un messie*. Gallimard editors were immediately set to work making sense of Isou's complicated and contradictory manuscripts.[4]

Isou and Pomerand wasted no time over putting the new Gallimard contracts to good use. They first of all used them to secure credit from a friendly printer and began planning a series of publications. They now had at least two dozen followers who actively called themselves *lettristes*. It was time to turn all of this energy into something solid and real.

Isou decided that the *lettristes* needed an editorial headquarters. They courted two of their earliest admirers, a pair of book-dealers called Jean Caillens and Pierre Charpin, and persuaded them to let them use their shop, called La Librairie de la Porte Latine, as a base.[5]

Isou and Pomerand soon began to give out the name of the bookshop as their address. This was at number 1 rue d'Alger, a smart street in the 1st arrondissement, halfway between rue du Faubourg Saint-Honoré and the rue de Rivoli – one of the wealthiest parts of Paris. Soon the bookshop was regularly hosting talks by the *lettristes* and it displayed their artwork. It had the atmosphere of a clandestine underground movement, plotting the overthrow of the authorities; this suited Isou as it reminded him of his first literary adventures in Ludo's office back in Bucharest.

Isou wanted to spread the word of *lettrisme* as soon and as widely as possible. He was frustrated that the Gallimard books would not be ready for publication until 1947 – he really couldn't wait that long – and so decided to issue a propaganda sheet called *La Dictature Lettriste*. The publication had the subtitle *Cahiers d'un nouveau régime artistique*, and when it was published in June 1946 became the first official *lettriste* publication.

Effectively it was a collective manifesto, with contributions from all self-described *lettristes*, most of whom were soon to fade back into literary obscurity (the two notable exceptions here were Georges Perros and Guy Marester, who both went on to have distinguished careers as writers). Most of the pamphlet was, however, written by Isou, or composed under his orders. Most importantly, *La Dictature* set out what the *lettristes* stood for, who they opposed, who they hated and why. The tone of the manifesto was snarling and funny. It was also meant to start fights.

This meant not just a war of words but real brawls in bars and in the streets, mainly with Communists ('vile Stalinists') or so-called 'Existentialists', the young followers of Jean-Paul Sartre. Gabriel Pomerand was exceptionally good at fighting, with the streetfighter's knack of inspiring shock and awe in his opponents by letting them know that there were no limits to what he could do. Pomerand could in fact be truly vicious, punching at random, kicking over tables and chairs and lunging at his enemies with broken bottles.

When trouble kicked off, Isou would stand aside and watch the fighting, smiling and aloof, a general in command of his troops. One journalist, much to Isou's delight, described the young Romanian Jew as the '*lettriste Führer*'. A rumour that the *lettristes* might be fascists – and certainly they seemed to be using fascist tactics – was helped along by one *lettriste* poem, which was often chanted out loud with a chorus that ran: 'HeilHitlerHeilHitlerHEILHITLER'.

The use of the term 'Dictatorship' as the title of the publication was an equally deliberate and extreme provocation. A war had just been fought against the scourge of dictatorship; for this cause millions had died across Europe, including here in the streets of Paris as well as Berlin or Bucharest. By using the word 'dictatorship' to announce their movement, as one observer put it, the *lettristes* might as well have been wearing swastika armbands.

La Dictature Lettriste was relentless in its attacks on the older generation. Isou exhorted his young followers to 'smash the faces of the likes of Gide – no better than a German! Do this, even if they call themselves

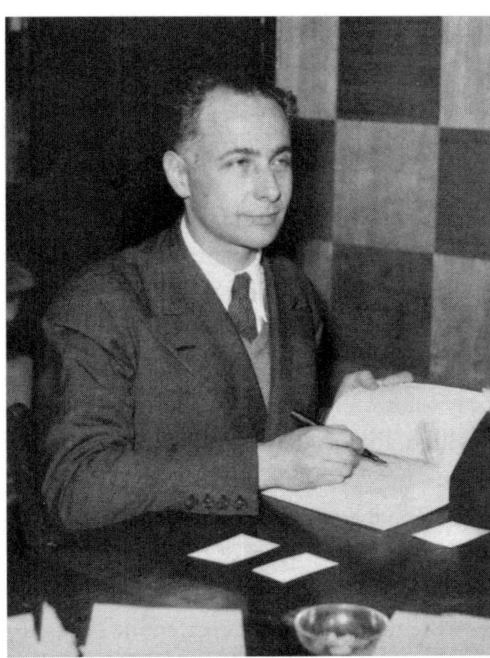

Louis Aragon, 1936, photographed by Henri Manuel.

Cocteau, Aragon, Pierre Seghers or Claudel.' This was not just iconoclasm for its own sake. Isou hated the way in which the older generation of these 'Resistance poets – '*Résistantialistes* to a man' – had adopted a high moral position, as if they and their readers were the only arbiters of ethical judgement during the chaos of war, as if they alone knew the 'truth'.[6]

Two key words in post-war Paris were 'responsibility' and 'commitment'; writers had to show moral responsibility by being committed to justice, truth, anti-Fascism and so on. Isou saw this as simple hypocrisy, a shibboleth which allowed the older generation to expiate their sin. 'Five million Jews weren't killed', he wrote, 'so that you could go on living as if nothing has happened.'[7]

Isou especially despised the poet Louis Aragon, 'the national pet Stalinist', who had become the most famous 'Resistance poet' of them all and whose ringing odes to France and patriotism impressed even the likes of Charles de Gaulle. Isou despised Aragon because he had originally started as an avant-gardist, a follower of Dada and one of the founders of Surrealism in Paris. He had, however, abandoned the avant-garde for the Communist Party and by the Second World War was one of the leading Communist intellectuals in France. Isou hated the fact that Aragon was now an establishment figure with a distinguished military record and political reputation.

For Isou, Aragon's greatest crime was, however, aesthetic: he had long since left behind him the experimental obscurities of the avant-garde for carefully modulated, classical poetry. What Aragon wrote, Isou argued, was simply 'anti-poetry'. Aragon was an 'arselicker' who made 'empty rhymes for the masses'.

Most damning of all, Aragon's new-found literary conservatism was a betrayal of the original aesthetic revolutions promised in the earlier part of the twentieth century – Dada, Futurism and Surrealism. This was not just about poetic technique but a moral and political issue; only by reinventing language could human life be properly transformed. Anything else, so Isou argued, was not revolution but betrayal and in fact a form of 'collaboration' – a word which, like 'dictatorship', carried a deadly, loaded charge in post-war Paris.

Isou did not say this lightly. The message he had to bring to Paris as the Jewish Messiah was that the 'old civilization' of Reason and Order had failed and had to be destroyed. This was the 'civilization' – Christianity and Enlightenment science – which had ultimately created the Nazis. To collaborate with the 'old values' was effectively to have 'collaborated' in making the Nazis. This was why *La Dictature Lettriste* was so important, wrote Isou, and had to be imposed as urgently as possible.[8]

In these same pages, Isou also turned on his present mentor Jean Paulhan. More specifically, in 1941 Paulhan had published a work of literary criticism called *Les Fleurs de Tarbes ou La Terreur dans les lettres* (The Flowers of Tarbes or Terror in Literature). The main argument in this book was that there were two opposing currents in modern literature: first, a tradition which referred back to older forms of writing and claimed to speak for history; second, a new tendency which sought to change history by changing language, especially the language of poetry. Paulhan called this second tendency 'Terrorist', taking his definition from the original use of the word to describe the 'revolutionary justice' of Robespierre and Saint-Just during the French Revolution, who advocated 'Terror' – killing the aristocracy – as a weapon for change.

Paulhan had sympathy with both camps, but this was not enough for Isou, who placed himself firmly on the side of the 'Terrorists'. Paulhan was attacked for his naive optimism and belief in old ideas and tradition – this made him the 'Candide' of French letters. Worse still, this made Paulhan 'a collaborator' like all of the others – Aragon, Gide and the 'whore Cocteau' (Isou called Cocteau this because it was rumoured that he had slept with German soldiers; this did not stop Isou cultivating him as a friend, ally and financial sponsor).[9]

Isou's attack against Paulhan was also based on rectifying a historical error made by the entire French literary establishment. Specifically, by the late 1930s and 1940s, Dada had been reduced to the status of a mere historical curio. The people responsible for this crime were those like Paulhan who characterized its 'terrorism' as naive and, worse still, the Surrealists, who had absorbed Dada into their history, where it had shrunk and become insignificant.

Isou thought that this was a trick played by the French literary establishment to castrate the 'true avant-gardes'. Paulhan was thus a collaborator twice over; with both the Nazis and the Surrealists. He looked 'like a toad, thought like a toad and wrote like a toad', concluded Isou.[10] His charity was not wanted or necessary; he was no better in fact than the Western Jewish Aid groups who claimed to care for the Jews from the East, but who in fact despised them.

———

Having so noisily declared war on the French literary establishment with *La Dictature Lettriste*, the *lettristes* inevitably began to attract the curiosity of the Paris press. One of the first pieces about them was in *Le Canard Enchaîné*, which had been satirizing all forms of pretention in art, literature and politics since its establishment in 1915. The author of the article was Henri Jeanson, then editor of *Le Canard,* and a lifelong pacifist with sympathy for avant-garde movements, no matter how deluded or daft.

Jeanson was in fact highly amused by the 'new school' – or perhaps 'an asylum' as he slyly put it – which called itself *lettrisme*. He described an encounter with a long-haired *lettriste* near the Tuileries, just across the street from the Librairie de la Porte Latine, who had a beautiful girl hanging off his arm and was chanting out *lettriste* sounds accompanied by maracas. Jeanson carefully quoted lines from a *lettriste* poem – 'Zelcar auoli lisar hédror / Tusis quilaf aresis capita / coli sti hisar, souliqué / Estali, Estali, cazouc'. Jeanson finished his piece with the sly comment: 'well, who could have put it better?'

Jeanson's real target was not the *lettristes*, however, who were young and rebellious but really not so different from the Dadaists or Futurists, but Gaston Gallimard, who was an old fool with a 'franchise in hermeticism', who was financing the whole thing in a desperate bid to keep up with new fashions. Jeanson concluded that the *lettristes* were quite possibly mad, but also to be admired because they talked real nonsense; this was not the case with any other poet sponsored by Gallimard, such as René Char, 'who has nothing to say but doesn't know it'.

The mass circulation daily newspaper *France-Soir* sent its resident cultural expert, Marcel Augagneur, to interview Isou in the offices of the respected literary critic Frédéric Lefèvre, who had become fascinated with Isou. Augagneur was taken aback to find that Isou was so unashamedly looking for fame and accused him of '*arrivisme*'. Isou did not care about this insult; all that mattered, he said to Augagneur, was that his name was now becoming known to the intellectuals who mattered and to the wider public.

Most journalists who went to speak to the *lettristes* found them highly entertaining but also hard to take seriously. Visually, the *lettristes* looked like 'Zazous' – dandified young Parisians who wore baggy American zoot suits, listened to American jazz (the name 'Zazou' came from a Frenchified attempt to imitate the scat singing of the jazz singer Cab Calloway) and were generally provocative and anti-authoritarian.

For Marie-Louise Barron, writing in *Les Lettres Françaises*, Isidore Isou had a 'name like birdsong and the swaggering shoulders of a boxer'. Otherwise she was relieved to find that in person he was quite well behaved, well dressed and that 'his mother could be proud' of his elegant clothes and courteous manner.

The same could not be said, however, of Gabriel Pomerand – a truly disturbing presence, 'a savage dionysiac', apparently suffering from some kind of 'derangement' which was possibly 'gastro-intestinal in origin'; he was 'a Rimbaud with bad digestion'. In other articles, Pomerand was variously described as 'hideous,' 'dirty' and 'writhing'. 'You have to have the nerve of the Devil to get published,' Pomerand said in one piece. 'We're so important that only Gallimard can publish us.'

The most detailed and sympathetic article on the *lettristes* was written by Paul Guth in *Le Littéraire*. It was a fairly long piece, spread over two pages and illustrated with cartoon portraits of Isou and the other *lettristes*. Guth was a sensitive critic with a sense of humour who had decided, for all their bluster, to take the *lettristes* seriously, or at least to let them have their say. He went to interview them at Librairie de la Porte Latine, where among the orderly shelves and rows of classic works he found a sect who were 'preparing a holy war against all forms of human knowledge'.

Like every other journalist, Guth was first of all shocked by Pomerand, who had a face that was 'ravaged with ardour [with] a stitched-up mouth that kept its secrets behind gaping yellow teeth'. Pomerand had 'the body of a demon in the clothes of a coalman, covered in dust . . . eyes, eyebrows, hair, all anthracite black'. He spoke in explosive, staccato bursts of laughter or poetry. This was quite unlike 'Geoffrey', a medical student at the psychiatric hospital of Sainte-Anne, who calmly explained that words 'led to lies' so that the reinvention of human life, promised by the *lettristes*, had to start from 'chiselling' down to nothing; starting again from zero.

The bookshop owners Jean Caillens and Pierre Charpin nodded along, as if hypnotized. Guth did not dismiss any of it. He understood in fact that all of this was not so far from recent discoveries in particle physics, in particular the splitting of the atom, which not only revealed the infinite depth of the universe but released a terrible potential for destruction. If, Guth suggested, such powers could be discovered in science then why not poetry? Guth called the *lettristes* 'poets for the atomic age'.

The main event in Guth's story was of course Isou, sharply dressed and again described as 'swaggering like a boxer' as he strolled into the shop. He was 'Romanian, olive-skinned, be-quiffed and eyes aglow with the certainty of someone about to be published by Gaston Gallimard'.

Isou began to explain to Guth that *lettrisme* had already been around for a long time – you could hear it in the nonsense rhymes of children or the wailing of Sioux Indians. All the other *lettristes* in the shop fell silent, as Isou began a recital. He made noises 'like a saw, the trotting of carriage horses, guttural howling'. He ended on the apparently erotically suggestive sounds – at least this was how Guth understood them to be – 'Cafoufou Pantaloun'.

Outside the shop, the world went about its business. But Guth had the feeling, so he wrote later, that he had just been at a séance and had heard the sound of the end of the world.[11]

————

Isou was of course delighted with all the press attention, but he was not really surprised. It was no more than what he deserved and he had in any case foreseen all of this back in Bucharest. He was not alone in believing this: Isou had by now also convinced his *lettriste* comrades that his, and their, historical mission was not to seek mere fame but immortality. The task now was to make it happen.

The next step towards this was the second *lettriste* conference, which was held on 14 November 1946 at the Salle de Géographie, towards the southern end of the rue St Jacques, a short walk from the Luxembourg Gardens. Unlike the fiasco of January, when hardly anyone had turned up to the first conference, the room was packed with the newly faithful and the curious, some of whom were famous. It was rumoured that André Breton and Jean Cocteau would be there along with the former Dadaists Raoul Hausmann and Kurt Schwitters, who had also heard of the *lettristes*. Hausmann, simultaneously entertained and appalled by the *lettristes*, went so far as to record a very funny imaginary interview with them, complete with guttural grunts and farting noises.

The conference began with Isou climbing onto the stage, without saying a word. He was surrounded by his closest *lettriste* comrades, who all fell into a respectful silence as he took his position centre-stage. Isou remained silent as the performance began.

Gabriel Pomerand began to read out a text called 'On the Historic Necessity of *Lettrisme*'. Much of this was an attack on *lettriste* enemies,

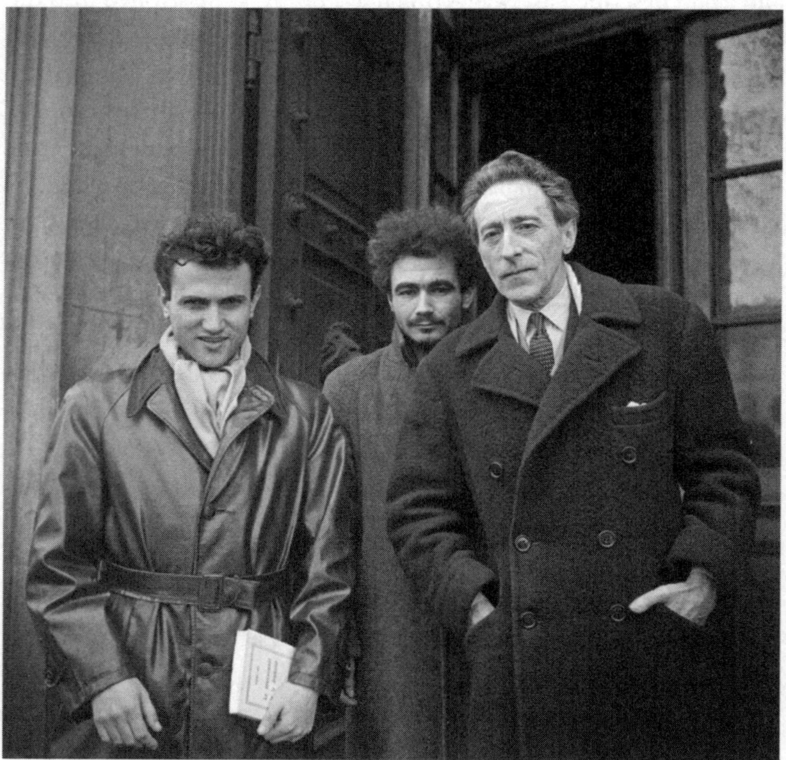

Isidore Isou, Gabriel Pomerand and Jean Cocteau, Paris, 1950.

which was now quite familiar to anyone who had read their posters or pamphlets, or the profiles and interviews in the press. Pomerand's first sally was against Jean-Paul Sartre and his followers and in particular the notion of the writer's 'responsibility' to write in an ethically correct manner. 'Poets will cause confusion in their tiny minds,' thundered Pomerand, 'and will plunge a dagger into the meaning of this word "responsibility".'

Next in the dock for Pomerand the Inquisitor was Louis Aragon and 'his teacher friends', who 'shit on the flag and talk about France, all so they can join the Académie Française'. Pomerand returned to the theme of ethics, justice and political commitment, all the values so prized by the generation of 'Resistance intellectuals':

> To kill in the name of Good is worse than killing in the name of blood and the eagle. I would always refuse to hang a man, even if he had killed my mother. You live amidst pigs who argue that they are acting in the interests of Humanity. Me? I shit in their faces.[12]

Pomerand's speech shocked his audience, who did not know that his own mother had been killed by the Nazis. To many in the audience Pomerand sounded like a pacifist and possibly a Nazi supporter, or at least an appeaser. In his own mind, however, he was arguing for abolition of the twin categories of Good (the Resistance) and Evil (the Nazis), both of which fed off each other and so sustained an endless, pointless dialectic. The 'historic necessity of *lettrisme*' was to destroy it all and start again, with *lettriste* poetry as the agent of destruction.

Pomerand was a hard act to follow. Jean Caillens read out a lecture called 'Manifesto for *Lettriste* Painting'. Geoffrey read out poems by Isou. Then the performance was over. Isou had still not uttered a word. This felt less like a literary event than some kind of religious meeting, with Isou in the role of priest or even a divine being to be venerated.

Not everybody who attended the conference took it so seriously, however. A rumour grew that Isou didn't speak not because he was an illuminated genius, but because his French was so bad that no one could understand it. Isou was indifferent to these rumours and insults. By now he had already accomplished enough miracles to know that he was an exceptional being, and anyway, he was now poised to publish his first Great Works with Gallimard.

ten

Hatred of Poetry

The year 1947 was easily the strangest and most extreme for France since the shaming defeat of 1940. This was first of all because it was the year when Europe properly and irrevocably split into two camps between East and West, between the communist-led sphere of influence with its headquarters in Moscow and those countries under the influence of the former Allied powers. France was caught in the middle of this division, as Centre-Left and Centre-Right parties sought to prevent a drift towards a communist revolution that would almost certainly have brought Paris under the control of Moscow.

It was partly to prevent this disaster that the United States announced the so-called Marshall Plan. The overall aim of the Marshall Plan was to lift the whole of Western Europe out of the economic wreckage left by the war by diverting hundreds of millions of dollars to shore up its battered industries. In France, the relief was immediate, particularly as the winter of 1946 had been a freezing one, and food shortages were as acute as at any period during the war.

But most people also knew that the Marshall Plan was essentially a thinly disguised attempt to prevent a communist takeover. Even those who weren't communist supporters resented this, and the brief moment of post-war pro-American sentiment was quickly lost, soon to be replaced by a wave of traditional French anti-Americanism, as well as suspicion of the British.

Against this background, boosted by the high prestige they had acquired during the war as organizers of the French Resistance, the French Communist Party launched a wave of strikes in the autumn of 1947. The riots which accompanied the strikes were as violent as any since the 1930s. Although the strikes had collapsed by early December of 1947, Paris was by now a bitterly divided city with a large population that felt angry, disgusted and betrayed by its own side.

The main focus for this anger was the attempt by the remnants of the Paris *bourgeoisie*, who had survived the war relatively unscathed, to establish a return to something like pre-war normality. Mostly this meant cocktail parties and new fashions (this was the year that Christian Dior launched the so-called 'New Look', much to the disgust of Parisian working-class women who attacked some of Dior's models in the streets). Most ordinary Parisians survived in the meantime on meagre rations in a dark, dirty city that was still physically and emotionally damaged.

In his notebooks from 1947, writing in Romanian and French, Isou described the blasted political landscape of post-war Paris as being like the Warsaw ghetto. The Liberation had not yet happened, and it wouldn't happen until politicians and ordinary people confronted the true horrors of the war, the greatest of which was the Holocaust.

In the opening weeks of 1947, however, all of this was secondary to a singular event of world-historical importance: on 26 January, Isou and the *lettristes* were featured in an article in the *New York Times*. This was in a piece called 'The Gallic Literary Scene: A Report from Paris' by a certain John Lackey Brown. As well as being an occasional literary correspondent for the *New York Times*, Brown was also a suave and well-connected diplomat whose contact book contained names such as Albert Camus, Josephine Baker, Marc Chagall and the like. He was obviously amused by the *lettristes*, if not entirely convinced. He wrote: 'A band, led by a 21-year-old Romanian whose pen name is Isidore Isou, has created "lettrism". The Lettrists, determined to do Dada and the Surrealists one better, aim at the renovation of poetry not only by the invention of new words but of new letters.'[1] Brown then noted drily that so far they had invented eighteen of them.

Brown's ironic wit was not lost on Isou, but he didn't care. This was the *lettristes*' most startling propaganda coup yet. The only thing that mattered was that already *lettrisme* was crossing the Atlantic and getting ready to soon take over the world. Back in Paris, Isou wrote to himself that his duty now was to prepare himself mentally and physically for his coming victories.

The first of these came on 25 April 1947, when Isou published his first book with Gallimard. The book was his *Introduction à une nouvelle poésie et à une nouvelle musique*. This was a book that Isou described as one of the founding texts of *lettrisme*, and was therefore a book that would change history forever.

The book begins with a warning to the reader, stating that although this Book of Books was written between 1942 and 1944, it was composed 'far from any participation of events considered or produced' during that time. To explain the book's apparent 'timelessness' Isou had attached a series of appendices to each of the three central books of the text, which made up the theoretical core of the book.

He had then attached a collection of *lettriste* poems under the collective title 'Grave and Joyous Recitations' and finally a score for 'the first *lettriste* symphony', written in a new musical language that Isou had invented. It was called simply *La Guerre* (The War) and had four movements called 'Menaces', 'Nazi Victory', 'Lord, Please Grant Us . . .' and 'Tomorrows Which Sing'.

The title of this last movement was borrowed from a final letter written by the French communist Deputy Gabriel Péri before he was shot by the Nazis in 1941. The letter appeared in Péri's autobiography, published in 1947, and contained a clarion call for the young people of the world to rise up and create 'tomorrows which sing'. Isou had obviously been inspired by this while the rest of the symphony, which expressed horror and revulsion at the war, gave the lie to Isou's earlier warning that the contents of *Introduction* were not specifically linked to contemporary events.

This contradiction also applied to a poem in the section called 'Grave and Joyous Recitations' entitled *Cris pour 5,000,000 de juifs égorgés* (Cries for Five Million Jews with Their Throats Cut). This was a musical sound poem composed in Yiddish, German, Romanian and French and meant to be read out or chanted by a '*lettriste* choir' made up of young Jews, using drums and tambourines. This performance was meant as a concrete demonstration of the theory of new music and poetry outlined in Isou's book – the soundtrack to an apocalypse.

The central chorus was the chant:

Adonoi ADONOI
Himler, guimère, meringue, jimlère, jéringue
Auschwitz – schwitz – schwitz
Auschwitz – schwitz – schwitz

BERGEN-BELSEN
BERGEN-BELSEN.[2]

Isou described this poem as being part of the spiritual core of *lettrisme*. Put simply, for Isou the singular importance of the Second World War was that it was a racial war against the Jews. Everything else – the conflict between nation states, capitalism and communism, patriotism and treason, all the geopolitical rivalries – were all secondary issues. Seen from this point of view, Stalinism was just as bad as Nazism. The French Resistance belonged to the 'old world' just as much as any other of the 'old ideologies'. For all of these reasons, the 'new poetry', mostly made but not exclusively so by Jews, had to come from the Jewish experience. Anything else – any 'non-*lettriste*' form of poetry – was a betrayal of the Jews.

Aside from the politics, there was also an aesthetic theory at work here. This was the application of the twin principles of the *amplic* (amplification) and *ciselant* (chiselling, or paring away), which he claimed to have discovered in Bucharest in 1942 during the time of his *lettriste* 'illuminations'.

Isou describes these principles in the opening chapter of *Introduction*, which was entitled 'Spiritual Evolution of Poetry'. This is where Isou explains that the *amplic* and 'chiselling' are diametrically opposed, but also interchangeable. Isou goes on to explain these concepts with reference to poetry, especially French poetry.

He begins with a discussion of how Homer had laid down the template for poetry – that it should be epic, dealing with the great themes of love, death and war. In French literature this *amplic* phase had reached an end-point in the poetry of Victor Hugo, which was epic but also overblown, pompous and empty, and therefore not poetry.

From then on, after Hugo, French poetry had turned in on itself. Baudelaire's poetry was about anecdotes, small intimate events, Rimbaud was about the inner life, Mallarmé's and Tzara's poetry was about symbols, poetry about poetry, and with Breton it was finally nothing, literally meaningless. It had chiselled itself into non-existence.[3]

Isou produced diagrams to demonstrate the historical process of this 'discovery' and proof of why and how *lettrisme* was the way out of this apparent philosophical dead-end. The solution was in *lettrisme*, the 'new poetry' in which words must be replaced by sound. 'Isou' – he referred to himself in the third person – was here to restart the *amplic* process, with noise replacing words.

Ultimately this philosophy would be applied by later *lettristes* to all forms of human knowledge that reached their *amplic* phase and needed to be reinvented. But for now it was about poetry, which was anyway, according to Isou, the highest form of art. Isou also claimed, among other things, that in this way he was turning philosophy into poetry and poetry into philosophy.

Similarly the 'new music' came from the sound of the human voice. Instruments were to be abandoned as creating too much nuance and as a distraction from the main event, which was the creation of noise from the human body. This was hard to understand at first, Isou conceded as much, but there was also no doubt, if you saw a performance by Pomerand for example, that these methods could produce powerful and disturbing art.

There was not a single review of Isou's book, either in any of the important Left Bank journals or in the mainstream press. The main reason for this was that for most readers, including assiduous followers of the latest avant-garde trends, the book was convoluted, fragmented, and largely unreadable when it was not incomprehensible or possibly even insane.

Isou sent *Introduction* to André Breton, hoping for a word from the celebrated founder and leader of Surrealism, but Breton made no comment on the book – which loudly declared that *lettrisme* was about to overtake Surrealism and Isou would take Breton's place as the leading theoretician of the future. At this stage, Isou was still in thrall to the old Surrealist leader and even wrote a long poem in homage to him. The opening lines began, 'Gnaaaaaaaa! Gnahuta gnahuta iahata ha!'[4]

A new *lettriste* conference to announce Isou's book was held on 3 April 1947 at the Salle de Géographie. The conference was a disappointment for Isou. This was mainly because he was unable to perform his new 'symphony', *La Guerre*, because it was unfinished. Other *lettriste* poets who spoke at the event, however – Poulot, Brasil, Lambaire, Hirsch, Dufrêne, by now all quite fashionable 'sound poets' – were received with loud applause.

Isou was furious that Pomerand and other poets had plagiarized him and overshadowed him. At one point they all quarrelled and Isou insisted that the word *lettrisme* should be replaced by the term 'Isouian'. But by now, with the *lettristes* on their way to becoming famous and the word now well established in the Left Bank lexicon, it was too late to turn back.

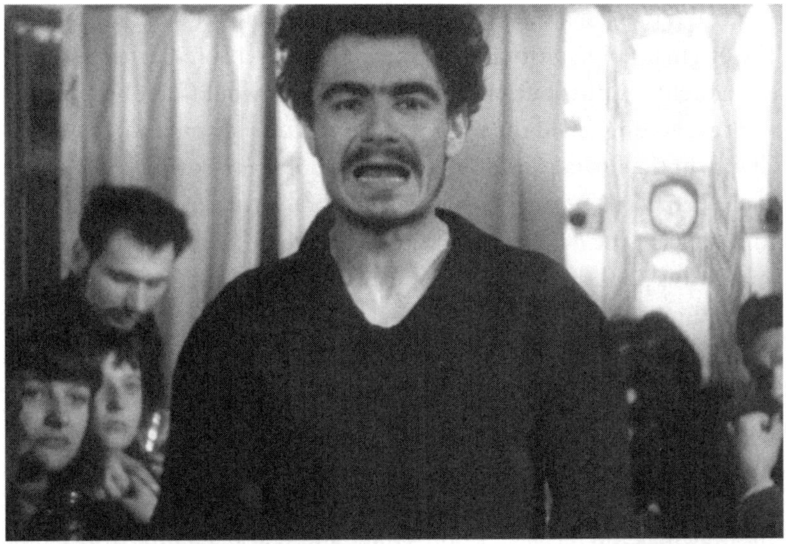

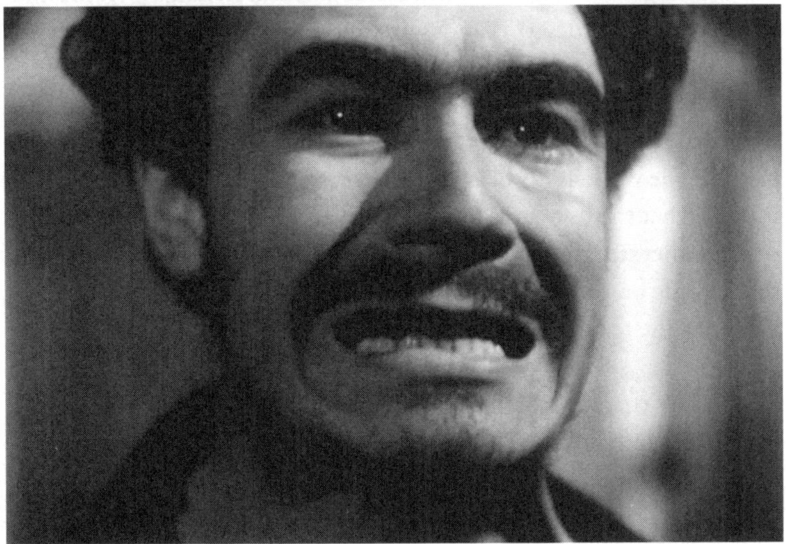

Gabriel Pomerand in Jacques Baratier's short film *Le Désordre* (1947).

Isou was jealous too of the way in which Pomerand was fast becoming known in Left Bank folklore as a 'character' – even something of a
'star' – as well as the public face of *lettrisme*. Instead of the street, he was
now occasionally sleeping all night in the Café de Flore or the Deux
Magots or under a bridge down by the Seine.[5] Pomerand also appeared
as the main character in a short film called *Le Désordre* by the film-maker
Jacques Baratier with a script by the writer Paul Guth, the journalist who
had been a *lettriste* sceptic – now turned into an admirer.

This film is a snapshot of the unruly tumult of Left Bank life in 1947. The original script, written by Pomerand, was 'censored' when the film was bought for distribution in 1949. This script would later become the text that accompanied the images of *Saint ghetto des prêts. Grimoire* (St Ghetto of the Loans: Grimoire), a 'metagraphic' work which is without doubt Pomerand's greatest achievement as well as one of the most important works in the *lettriste* canon. It has been hard to find and little seen since it was published in 1950, but it captures beautifully and brilliantly the paranoid chaos of post-war Left Bank life.

In essence, it is 120 pages of a prose poem on the left-hand page accompanied by pictographs – a visual puzzle sometimes referred to as a 'rebus' – which are the representation in images of the text. This is what is meant by a 'metagraphic work': one work that functions on many different levels at once, in this case a poem that is a painting, and vice versa. The drawings and images are both comic and skilful, ranging from child-like depictions of desert islands, girls and imaginary animals to cryptic mathematical formulae in several alphabets all at once.

Pomerand called the book a 'grimoire', a book of spells and invocations that are meant to have a transformative effect upon the reader. He justified the work as his ultimate statement. Greil Marcus, for his part, thought that the book was both magical and a historic document: each page another step through the illuminated labyrinth into the secret utopia that was life on the post-war Left Bank.[6] The utopia was also an illusion, however; the text of *Saint ghetto des prêts* ends:

> Besides there's no Saint-Germain-des-Prés.
> There's only scenery . . .
>
> Saint-Germain-des-Prés is like Donogoo-Tonga, a neighbour-
> hood specially built for the needs of foreign clients – like Venice
> for American tourists – . . .[7]

The film *Le Désordre*, with or without Pomerand's script, is similarly a fascinating historical document set in this false 'utopia'. Other 'characters' who put in an appearance include Jean Cocteau (who is pursued and publicly 'insulted' by Pomerand in the film), Simone de Beauvoir, Juliette Gréco and Orson Welles.

The film opens with a '*lettriste* choir' chanting an 'Oratorio' led by Gabriel Pomerand; in another opening scene a beautiful young girl performs a jerky *lettriste* ballet in the lift of an apartment; the occasional novelist Boris Vian plays the trumpet; a child and a dog wander through bombed-out streets looking at memorials to the anonymous dead of the war. It is, however, Pomerand who is undoubtedly the most charismatic figure in the film. He saunters through the streets of Paris's Saint-Germain-des-Prés quarter, which were still as dark and dusty as they had been during the German Occupation; he stares hungrily in the window of a kebab shop, saying in a voice-over that he lives 'like a skeleton'; he declaims poetry from the rooftops; with other *lettristes*, he imitates the sound of machine guns and burns a Picasso print.

Other *lettriste* comrades are filmed in the Boulevard Saint-Germain in ripped clothes, which had been torn and sprayed in graffiti reading *Ratés* – 'Losers' – and with excerpts from *lettriste* texts. These images and the style of clothing would resurface some thirty years later in London, in the clothes shop Seditionaries on the Kings Road. This is where Malcolm McLaren and Vivienne Westwood placed photographs of the *Ratés* and *lettriste* texts in the windows and set about defacing the clothes that they were making, inventing the style that would eventually become the

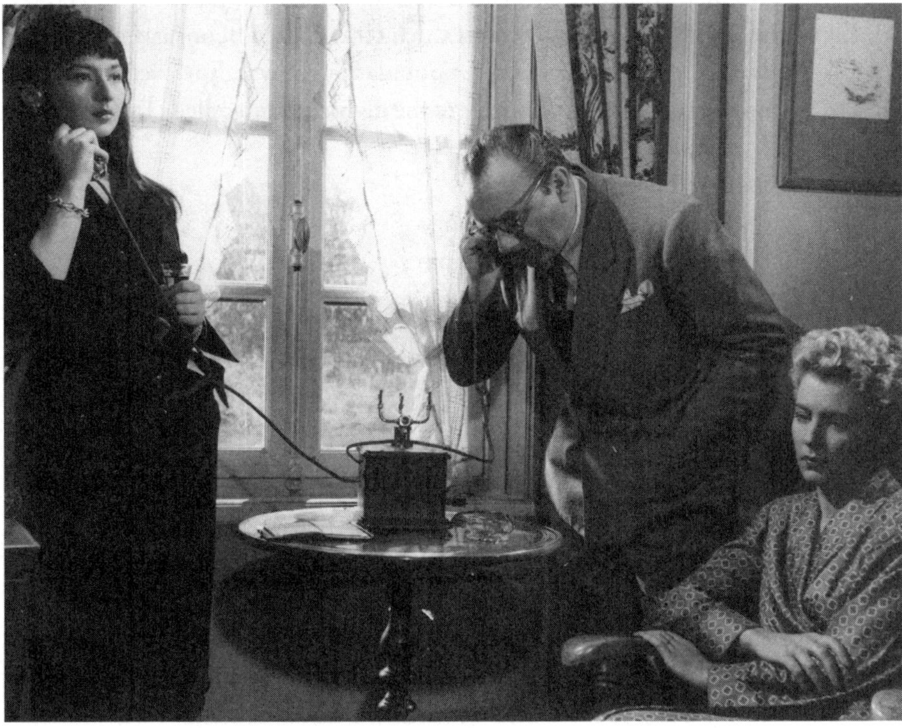

Juliette Gréco in Jean Cocteau's *Orphée* (1950).

cultural revolution that the world would soon know as punk rock – a perfected art of negation, saying 'no' to say 'yes'.

The most compelling and most menacing moment in *Le Désordre* is, however, when Pomerand glares through the barred window of the Bar Vert in the rue Dauphine – then one of the most fashionable haunts on the Left Bank. He seems genuinely dangerous and deranged. He declares to the startled, well-heeled customers in the bar: 'Saint-Germain is a ghetto, everyone there wears a yellow star in his heart!'

Pomerand leaves, the crowd in the bar laugh nervously; the film moves on to shots of wastelands and ruined buildings.

When it was first shown on the Left Bank, the film made Pomerand a minor celebrity. He even became a tourist attraction when he was invited by Bernard Lucas, the owner of the newly opened jazz club Le Tabou, to give a nightly recital of *lettriste* poems.

Pomerand would usually take the stage when the writer and trumpeter Boris Vian had finished his performance. Pomerand lived up to every tourist fantasy of the wild Left Bank bohemian. One of his favoured performances was Isou's poem 'Lances rompues pour un femme gothique' (Broken Lances for a Gothic Woman), which ended in a powerful coda with the lines: 'IAHAHAAA!IAHAHAAA! / Bounjagaa, Bounjagan, Bouguerga'. Pomerand's most popular poem was, however, written by himself specifically in homage to the nightclub and called 'Tabou'. It read:

Yam Bambo Yam Bambo
Roum Pika Il congo sa longo
Roum juke il nada bial nana
Baila yamba combi al kié
Maka Roumba Caussa Samba
Yambambo Yam Bambo
Yam Bambou[8]

Late at night, or in the early hours of the morning, with Pomerand in full shamanic flow, chanting to an audience that was half-drunk or stoned on hash (easily available from the nearby rue Xavier-Privas), the poem perfectly matched the fast and ferocious crashing rhythms of the jazz band that sometimes accompanied him.

Once the poetry was over, Pomerand would go into the crowd, asking for money. Sometimes he made as much as 10,000 francs a night. Usually the money was handed over straightaway to Isou to fund the *lettriste*

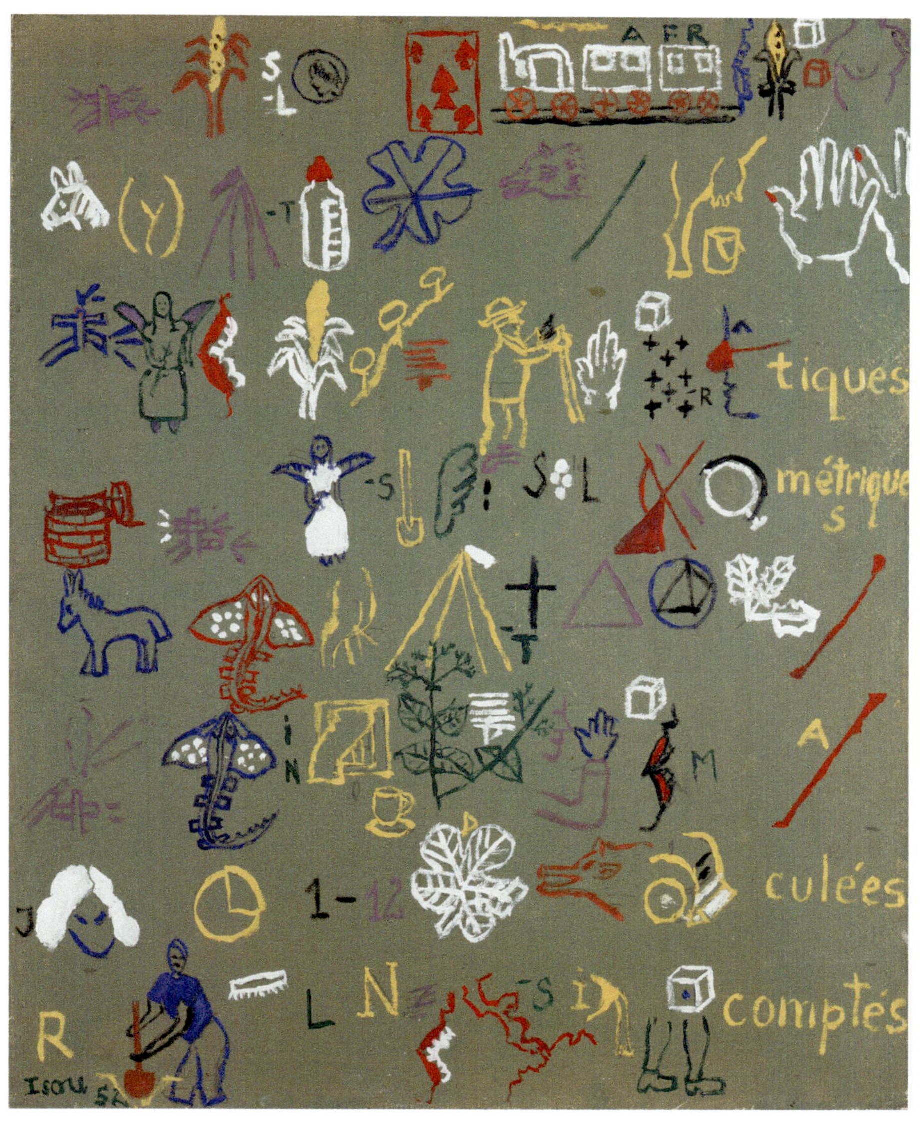

Isidore Isou, *Les Nombres, no XXVIII*, 1952, oil on canvas.

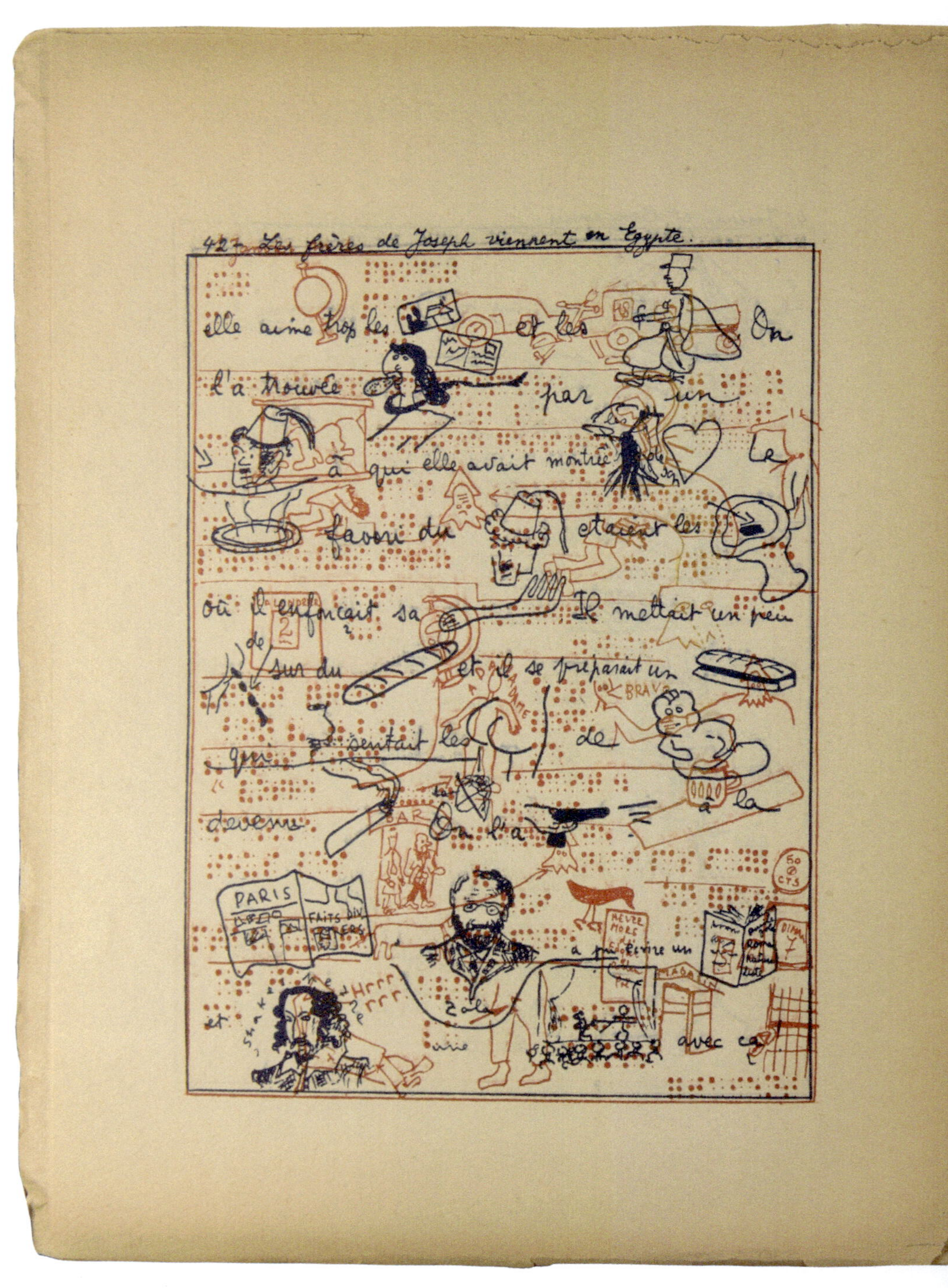

Plates 42–3 of *Les Journaux des dieux* (The Gods' Diaries, 1950).

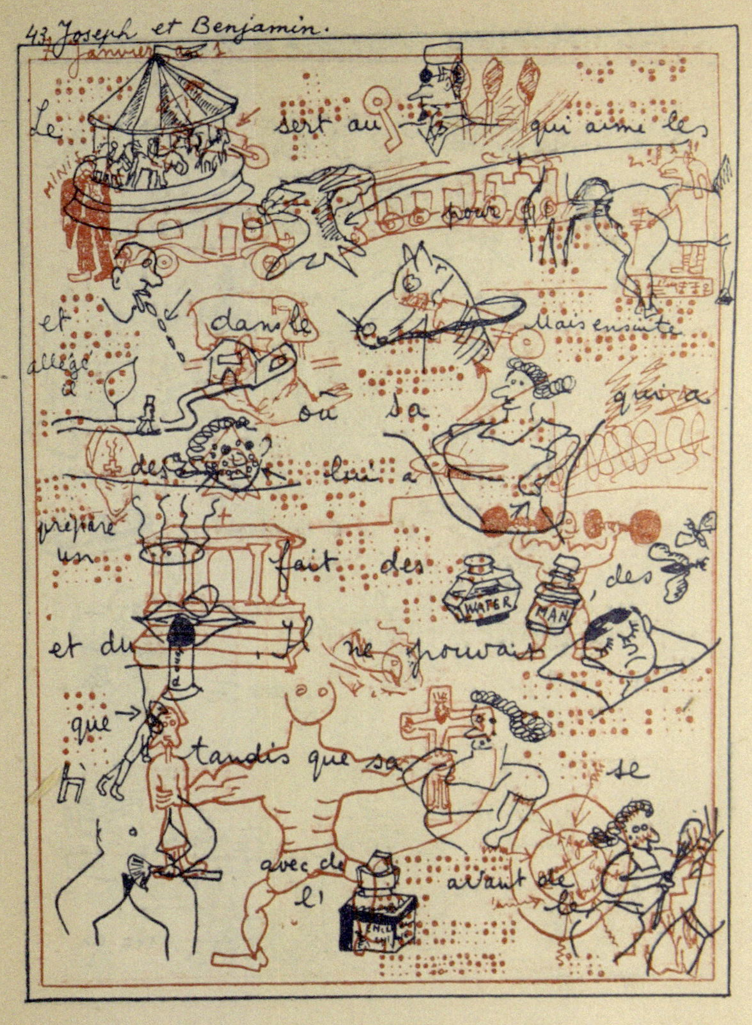

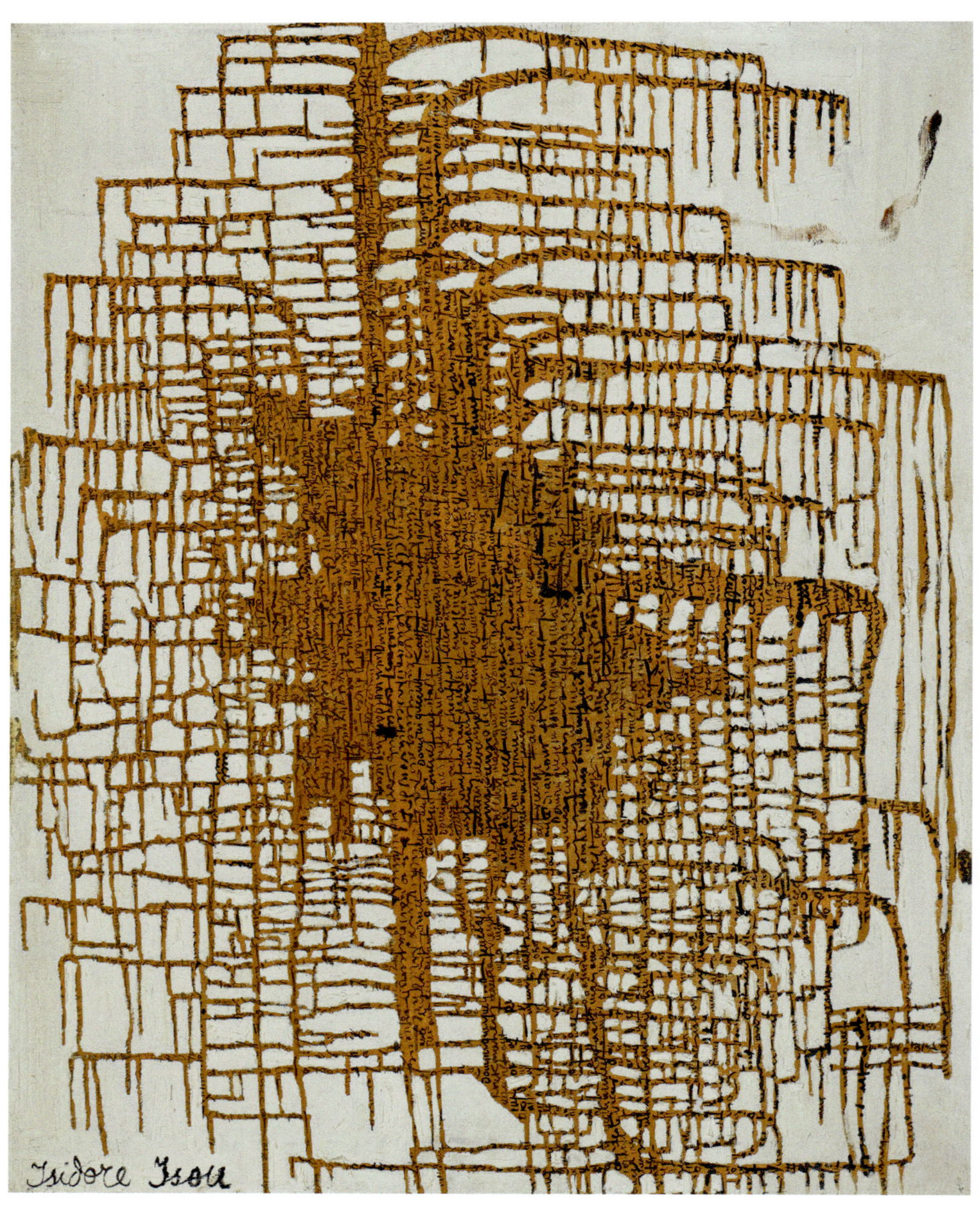

Isidore Isou, *Réseau centré M67*, 1961, oil on canvas.

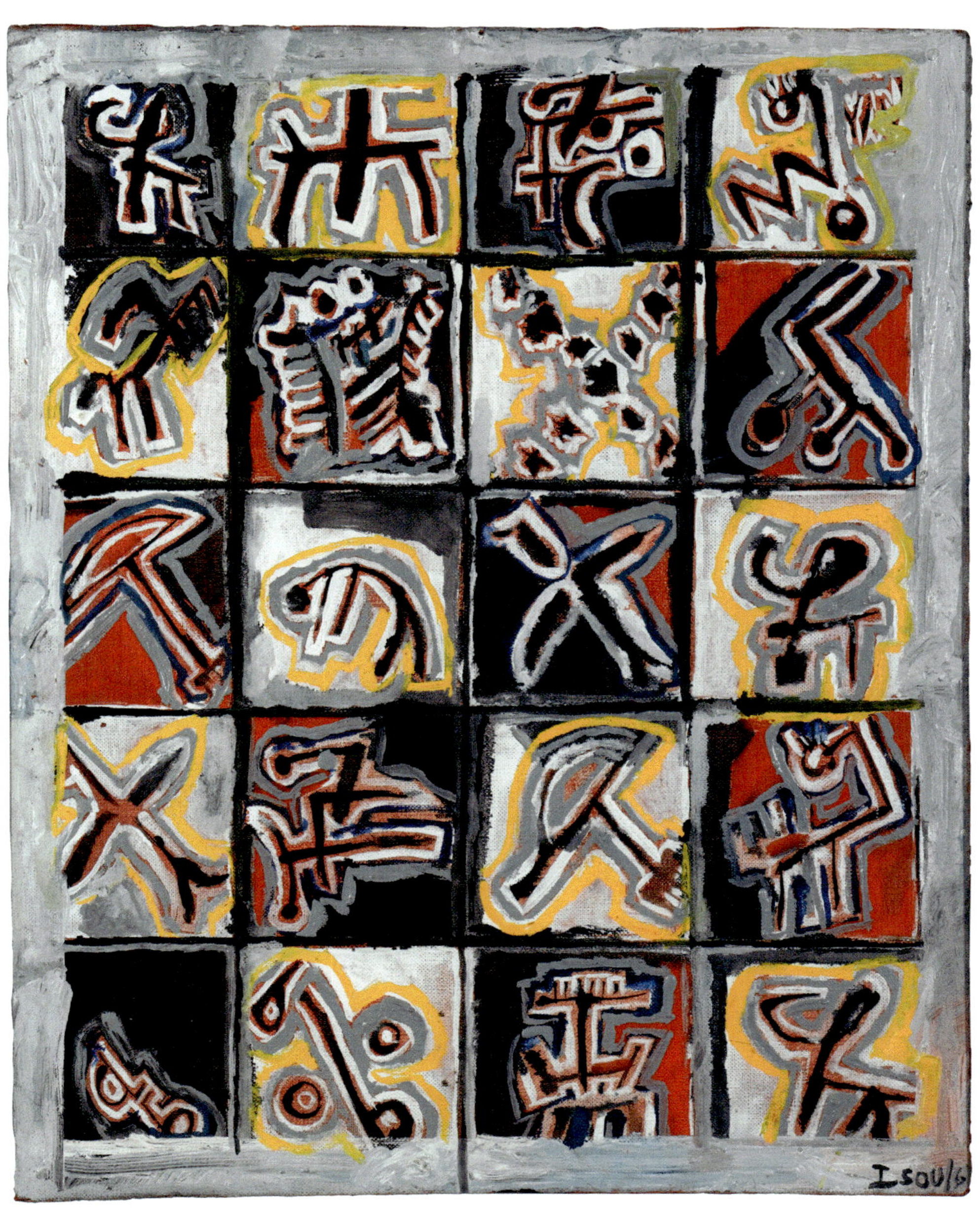

Isidore Isou, *Signes fauves*, 1961, oil on canvas.

Dans L'Agrégation d'un Nom et d'un Messie (N.R.F. 1947)
j'ai introduit le judaïsme dans la littérature novatrice et
immortelle, mondiale en général, française en particulier, qui étaient
polythéistes, chrétiennes ou athées. Depuis cette date,
... d'autres auteurs m'ont imité, mais comme ils ignorent
la méthode de création, leur judaïsme est arriéré et banal,
réduit au raisonnable moral et aux lieux - communs de
l'acquis.

L'Homme à la loupe, portrait sup-
posé de Baruch Spinoza, attribué à
Rembrandt van Rijn, par plusieurs a-
mateurs dont le Docteur Guy Maruani, qui
m'a demandé de réaliser pour lui cette
oeuvre, dans le cadre de ma série de
tableaux « Dialogue avec Rembrandt »

Je propose au docteur Guy Maruani de me suivre, en dépas-
sant ses passions insuffisantes : a) la vision logique du monde de
Baruch Spinoza, laissée en arrière par la vision de l'invention
et de la découverte permanente, dévoilée par mon système La Créatique
ou la Novatique (etc) ;B) le messianisme de Sabataï Zwi, celui de la piété
statique et sclérosée, laissé en arrière, par le messianisme isouïen
celui de la création multiplicatrice, avançant vers la société
édénique du cosmos. Isidore Isou 189

Isidore Isou, *Untitled* (Portrait of Baruch Spinoza), 1989, oil on canvas.

Commentaire sur Van Gogh (19)

Dans cette toile, j'ai essayé de reproduire l'oeuvre de Vincent, La route aux cyprès.
Il m'aurait été facile de faire de nouveaux signes, des incrustations, de leur donner d'autres couleurs, tels qu'ils ont été réalisés dans tant de mes tableaux : ce qui m'était difficile,

c'était d'avancer dans le figuratif, de m'approcher de la peinture de Van Gogh, de la "conquérir", dans un certain sens, de l'intégrer dans l'hypergraphie. Considérées sous cet aspect, ces oeuvres représentent un pas en avant par rapport à mon accomplissement plastique antérieur et incarnent un échelon de mon évolution. Isidore Isou/85

Isidore Isou, *Commentaire sur Van Gogh (19)*, 1985, oil on canvas.

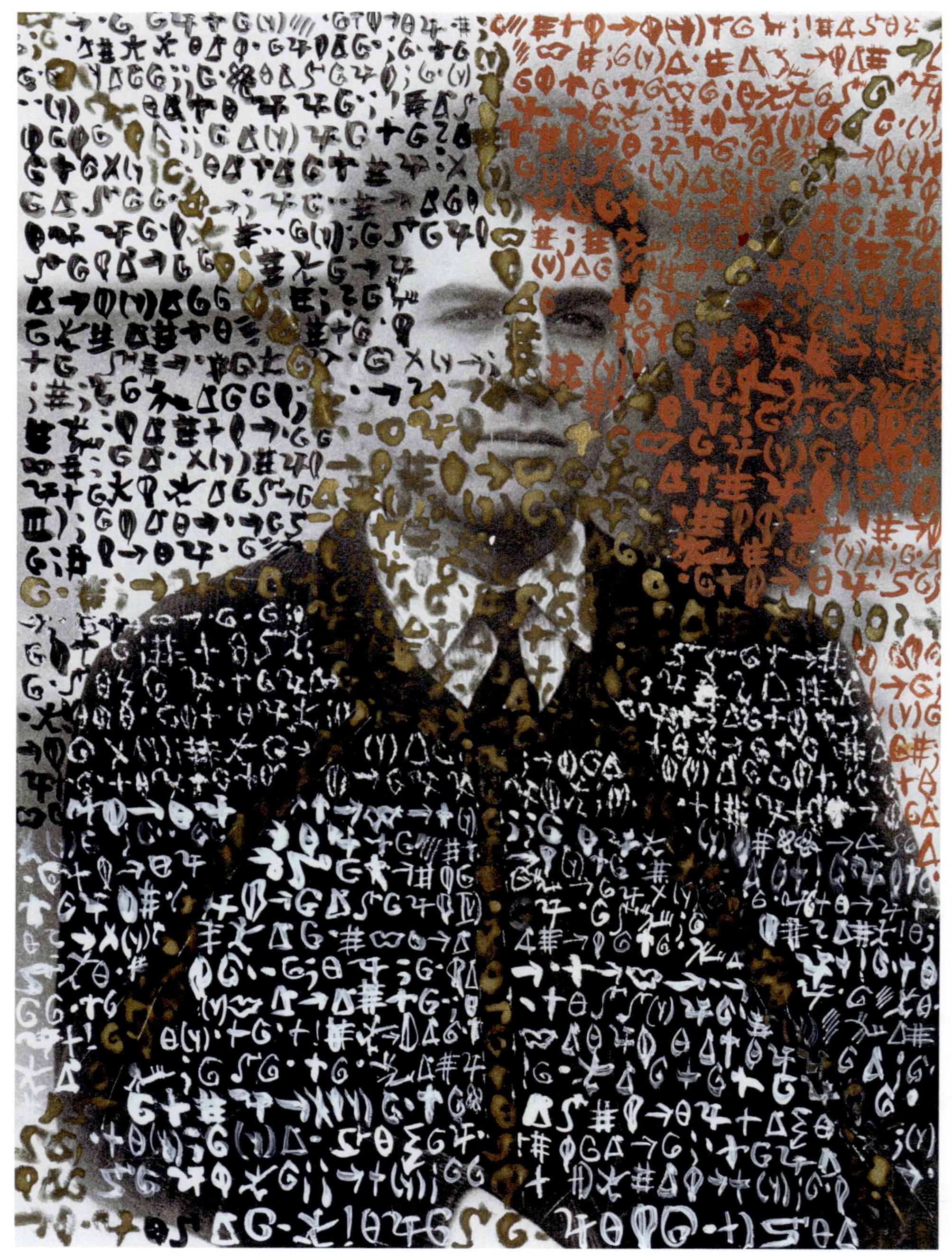

Isidore Isou, *Amos* (Portrait of Maurice Lemaître), 1952, lacquer pencil on photography.

project. Occasionally, however, Pomerand would spend the whole amount in one night on women and drink. He would be so destitute the next morning that he sometimes had to sell the sheets of the dive hotel where he had spent the night.

For Isou this was a serious breach of *lettriste* discipline. There was already a growing tension between the two comrades as Isou feared that his disciple might one day usurp him. The tensions grew ever sharper with every new act of disobedience from Pomerand.

A crisis point was reached when Pomerand fell in love and tried to sleep with a wealthy young woman whom Isou had first seduced and then persuaded to finance his adventures. Without any explanation or excuse, Pomerand found himself excommunicated from the *lettriste* inner circle by Isou. The excommunication did not last long – women would always be less important than men in Isou's inner circle – but it was enough to teach Pomerand who was properly in charge.

The real argument between Pomerand and Isou at this stage was that Pomerand – who revelled in all the attention he was attracting – thought that *lettrisme* could only be realized in practice: performance, conferences and so on. Isou thought instead that the written page was enough, and that in fact *lettrisme* was still a theory in its most protean form, which had to be nurtured and developed. What Isou wanted to achieve was not the discovery of a new form of poetry, but a new form of communication, and ultimately a new form of being human. He was also visibly annoyed that Pomerand was being filmed, written about and hailed as 'the new Rimbaud'.

——————

Despite these failures and new tensions among the *lettristes*, it had been nonetheless a kind of success for Isou that this latest conference of 3 April had been attended by the Surrealist leader André Breton, who after much prodding from Isou was finally intrigued enough to attend.

In the wake of this conference, Breton began slowly and cautiously to develop a friendship with Isou. A cordial private meeting between them took place at the Rhumerie Martiniquaise on the Boulevard Saint-Germain.[9] Breton was quite as pompous in private as Isou had feared he might be. He seemed 'enchanted' with the young man – at least according to Isou's own account of the meeting. Certainly, Breton was curious about this new pretender who, so it was claimed, was seeking to 'eliminate' him. Isou boasted that a peace treaty of sorts was now agreed between the *lettristes* and the Surrealists. If this was the case, then it was not to last long.

Isou, in the meantime, had also found new enemies. These included a Russian Dadaist called Iliazd who claimed that Isou was stealing all of his ideas and that *lettrisme* was a confidence trick. Iliazd was almost thirty years older than Isou, a native of Tbilisi who had lived through the great convulsions of the twentieth century before landing in Paris where he lived in permanent exile.

Outraged by what he saw as Isou's straightforward theft of his method for writing poetry, Iliazd launched a campaign against the young man which culminated in a fist-fight at an 'anti-*lettriste*' demonstration organized by Iliazd at the Salle de Géographie on 21 June 1947, where the artist Camille Bryen, who had the misfortune to admire both Iliazd and Isou, was beaten up by Isou's supporters for 'treachery'.[10]

One of the first major figures in Paris to take Isou seriously was Georges Bataille. This was by writing the first (and only) long review of *L'Agrégation*, which was published by Gallimard as Isou's second book in October 1947. The review was published in the prestigious journal *Critique*, founded by Bataille in 1946 and which took as its model the seventeenth-century *Journal des Savants*, a review whose remit was to discuss 'every important idea of the era'.

In post-war Paris Bataille was also perhaps the only figure in the Paris avant-garde whose influence could rival that of André Breton. Both of them were veterans of the avant-garde wars of the 1920s and '30s and, once rivals, they were now forming a friendship and loose alliance against the new usurper Sartre and his 'Existentialist' followers. Bataille's initial reputation had been established as a subversive thinker, the author of sulphurous pornography and a kind of dissident Surrealist (the art critic Patrick Waldberg famously described Bataille as 'the black surrealist of catastrophe').

In the 1930s Bataille had been accused of flirting with fascism, and there were even lurid rumours that he had planned a human sacrifice with the other members of the secret society *Acéphale*, which he founded and led and which venerated the Marquis de Sade, Nietzsche and Hegel. There was of course no murder, but Bataille, who had a dark and sardonic sense of humour, enjoyed the rumour and encouraged its persistence.

In the 1920s André Breton had been suspicious and critical of Bataille. The main reason was entirely political: Bataille had a powerful and strange charisma, which attracted many of Breton's followers to his own groupings – first the art magazine *Documents* and then *Acéphale*. Certainly Breton was threatened enough by Bataille to devote several pages to denouncing him as a 'liar' and 'a pervert' in the *Second Manifeste du Surréalisme* of 1927.

By the 1940s, however, Breton conceded that Bataille, his old enemy, was one of the few men alive whom he truly respected. Most importantly, both Bataille and Breton agreed that in the post-war world, the meeting between politics and philosophy, as espoused by Sartre, was not enough, that the task of the pre-war avant-gardes was not yet over and that a new religious spirit was called for.

This was why Bataille was interested enough in Isou to write about him at some length. Bataille's article was called 'La Divinité d'Isou' and unlike almost all of the other press on Isou and the *lettristes*, he took this unknown Romanian seriously and at face value.[11]

Most importantly, Bataille grasped that when Isou wrote about his destiny as a Messiah it was not meant as a joke or metaphor. In his own writing, for many years, Bataille had been pursuing a kind of mystical mission. Bataille's original vocation had been to become a priest until he lost his faith; but although Bataille no longer believed in God he never lost his belief in the structures of thought of Catholicism. More to the point, like Nietszche or William Blake – both of whom were heroes to both Isou and Bataille – he understood the paradox that even though God may be dead, the mystical impulse, the will to communicate and commune with the beyond, never quite leaves humanity.

Bataille described *L'Agrégation* as 'an often superb tale'. He especially admired Isou's fearlessness as an individual who aimed relentlessly at exceeding the limits of his own being. He concedes that Isou, for this reason, might properly be described as a 'genius', and even that, after Isou, the term might be exhausted – meaning that Isou had changed our concept of what 'a genius' is or might be.

Most importantly for Bataille, Isou was indifferent to 'literature' – the old-fashioned idea that books were in themselves a force for moral goodness. Isou's book was not supposed to instruct you, improve you or make you feel good but, like any true document of religious experience, to make you *feel*.

Isou's book contained many emotions: it was, wrote Bataille, a book which was 'frightful, stupid, a failure, puerile, genius-like, as laughable, as troubling and embarrassing as a bared arse'. Isou's 'stupidity' was 'sublime';

his need to cry out loudly to the world was both pathetic and tragic. Isou was a young man whose acute and painful intelligence had driven him to 'pure disorder'; the question Bataille then asked was whether this feeling was the edge of madness or a truly mystical experience? Bataille's conclusion was that Isou had not yet gone far enough over the edge to know the answer.

The stumbling block for Bataille was also Isou's Jewishness. More precisely, Isou was still locked into the Jewish tradition in which the Messiah who announced a new world was still a prophet, recognizably still a human entity. In the Christian tradition, which Bataille obviously knew far better than Judaism, the Messiah is also part of God. Isou's tragedy was, for Bataille, that his method so far did not, could not, make him into God. Put simply, *lettrisme* therefore did not work. Bataille quoted the example of Marxist thinking, which, like *lettrisme*, aimed to give men divine attributes with economic and technological liberation but was limited and finite in this ambition, lacking a metaphysical dimension. In this sense, for Bataille, Isou's book – for all its 'charm' and brilliant and moving 'absurdity' – was only the first halting step on a spiritual journey.

Isou himself did not disagree with this analysis. He immediately grasped that Bataille, alone among Left Bank critics, had properly understood him. Bataille was from now on a kindred spirit for Isou. He would often quote Bataille, tearing pages from Bataille's books for reference, and quoting Bataille's notion of a 'Hatred of Poetry' – by which Bataille meant that all poetry was sham, and a kind of lie, when it could not be reduced, like prayer, to the silence of contemplation. Bataille was one of the few critics of this period who was left unscathed by Isou's sarcasm and contempt.

The same could not be said of André Breton, however. The 'peace treaty' between them, as described by Isou, would soon be drawing to a close. Isou was impatient for the great man's attention and, more than this, fully expected Breton to announce him as the heir to Breton's position as revolutionary leader of avant-garde Paris. Breton was friendly but guarded and this was never going to be enough to satisfy Isou.

The breaking point came one evening at the Café de la Place Blanche, where Breton usually met with his acolytes and disciples every Wednesday evening. As soon as Isou arrived he immediately picked up on an unfriendly atmosphere. Surrounded by his followers Breton had reverted to playing to type as the imperious and high-handed leader whose opinions could not be challenged. Isou had anyway already offended the Great Man by arriving half an hour late. Breton said openly that this was unbelievably rude. Isou did not apologize. From this point on, the evening only got worse.

Isou's chief antagonist was the painter and sculptor Victor Brauner, a Romanian Jew who came from Piatra Neamț, a town not too far from Botoșani with the same Jewish culture that had nurtured Isou. Brauner was then in his mid-forties and had passed through Dada and communism before establishing himself as a follower of Breton's Surrealist movement.

Isou remarked to himself that Breton seemed to like to surround himself with cronies who, like a group of 'old women, wilted like dead flowers'. Brauner famously only had one eye (he had lost his right eye in a brawl in a Paris bar in 1938) and with this he squinted fiercely at Isou. Brauner, said Isou, was like Breton's personal 'nail file', never missing a chance to polish his boss's ego. He left 'slimy, humid trails', which made Isou uneasy.[12]

Every time Brauner spoke, he 'chewed on slanders like an old witch, gnashing his rotten rack of teeth and gums'. At each fresh observation from Isou, who was making a point of disagreeing with Breton to show that he was not subservient to him, Brauner would join in 'barking against the enemy': Isou. Isou despised Brauner, partly because he was such a sycophant but mainly because 'he was one of those foreigners who love to squirm and wriggle to please their patrons.' As a foreigner himself, and proud of this fact, Isou was disgusted by this blatant display of arse-licking aimed at seeking the patronage of Breton, a 'ridiculous fat vegetable'.

For all this, Isou was sure that Breton, despite his *hauteur*, was listening carefully to Isou and was impressed by his genius, especially his theories on youth revolution, the end of civilization and the need to reinvent everything. Isou then had an immediate revelation: he suddenly realized that Breton was actually a deeply mediocre man, who had made a career out of stealing the ideas of geniuses such as himself. Isou, now aware of this, abruptly stopped speaking.

Now it was Breton's turn to speak. 'Like a haughty old monk', he accused Isou of being a self-seeking glory-hunter, an *arriviste*, who used his friends in the service of his own reputation. Breton said that he refused to find new recruits for Isou, which would only enable him to build his own cult. The meeting was finished.

Isidore Isou, *Swing*, 1947, pencil drawing.

Breton was now added to Isou's growing list of important literary enemies. If Isou had simply wanted Breton to come to his events for publicity, Isou said, then he would have preferred someone who actually was famous, like Laurel and Hardy – or even better Rita Hayworth, who at least had long, luscious legs.

For Isou, Breton was a hypocrite, flabby and out of breath. Isou had noticed this straightaway when they had sat down together for the first time at the Rhumerie Martiniquaise. Breton was 'a fat Monsieur-Madame, but more Madame than Monsieur'. Isou described him as like those tuberculosis patients who, coughing and spitting at café tables, 'do not realize that they are spitting in their neighbour's coffee'. Never mind: history would soon forget Breton, concluded Isou, who from now on would look at the old man with contempt but no pity.

All in all, 1947 had been a momentous year for Isou and the *lettristes*. But for all their achievements, Isou was still restless. After the meeting with Breton he was more sure than ever that Surrealism had failed as a revolution by becoming known merely as a technique in art and literature, a cipher for the appearance of Freudian or Marxist undercurrents in any given work.

To avoid this, Isou had at all costs to move in the opposite direction. Thus far the *lettristes* were becoming known as poets and painters (and less convincingly as composers of music). The highest praise had indeed been accorded to *lettriste* painters who had exhibited at the Librairie de la Porte Latine. These included the likes of Guy Vallot (who was in fact a young Romanian woman called Rodica Valeanu), who displayed genuine virtuosity. But all of this was a trap. Talent was a trap. It was now necessary to go one step further than art or poetry – to do the job of politicians, revolutionaries and armies. *Lettrisme* from now on would be a fully fledged political movement at war with society.

This war was also the theme of the final *lettriste* conference of 1947, held in early December once again at the Salle des Sociétés Savantes, and entitled 'The *Lettriste* Movement Enters Political Battle: The Economic and Social Bases of a Youth Revolution'. The emphasis was on the violence and cruelty to be used against the enemy, which meant everything which represented the prevailing social order. All of this was perfectly in tune with the mood of insurrection that had, by the end of 1947, spread throughout France as conflict between communism and capitalism, East and West, seemed inevitable.

Gabriel Pomerand followed up the *lettriste* conference with a lecture of his own in the same hall on the 7 December during which, with his usual venom and fury, he barked:

I announce to you now that it is time for the circulation of blood, the time of mines under your shoes, assassinations at the dinner dance in the town hall. Being is the cry, the howl, and the spirit of pure contempt. Our revolution will crack heads as other heads were chopped off in other revolutions.[13]

eleven

Sex, Prison and Revolution

In the first half of 1948, Gabriel Pomerand was stricken by a series of respiratory diseases, brought on no doubt by his reckless lifestyle and taste for sleeping rough. By midsummer it really did look as if he might die of this mysterious condition, which was finally found to be tuberculosis.

He now spent much of his time in a hotel room, where he was sometimes nursed by Juliette Gréco. This was almost certainly when he began to develop an opiate habit, which would turn out to be a lifelong series of addictions. In order to alleviate the relentless coughing fits, Pomerand started to take elixirs and syrups made up with morphine and its derivatives. These were easily found in Paris at the time, sold over the counter in pharmacies.

In the early spring of 1948, Pomerand moved to Leysin, a small Swiss village at the eastern end of Lake Geneva, about an hour from Lausanne, in search of a purer climate and fresher air. His condition worsened, however, and in July he was hospitalized with a bleak prognosis.

Isou had no sympathy, however, for Pomerand and his illness, or even the fact that he was near to death. In fact Isou had already made the decision, whatever happened, to break with Pomerand and exclude him from the *lettriste* movement. This was mainly due to jealousy, both sexual and artistic. In the first instance, Isou was angry because Pomerand had seduced the wealthy young woman whom Isou had already targeted as a possible sexual conquest and future benefactor of the *lettristes*. This turned out to be the Swiss woman who had taken Pomerand to Leysin, financing his medical treatment.[1]

Second, Pomerand was now developing a reputation as the most daring and flamboyant of the *lettristes*, with many admirers assuming that he was the real genius of the group. They publicly declared themselves as Pomerand supporters and called themselves 'ultra-*lettristes*'. In February 1948, Isou and Pomerand appeared together in print in the journal *Hikma*, published in Tunis, with Pomerand appearing under the pseudonym de Pol Meyra. It was to be the last act of solidarity between Isou and Pomerand for some time.

The reason for this was that in the same month, Pomerand published a book called *Le Cri et l'archange*. This was a *lettriste* work in the sense that it strictly followed Isou's theory that the sound of a letter was more important than its meaning. Pomerand went one step further by announcing that shouting or howling was an almost mystical practice, a way of bringing mind and body together in a primal scream. (Isou himself would return to this theme in the 1970s, when he claimed he was being 'tortured by psychiatrists' and argue that the 'primal scream' was a way out of neurosis. By then the term 'primal scream' had of course been made famous by John Lennon, who had undergone 'primal scream therapy' in the early 1970s. Isou's psychiatrist, Guy Maruani, told me that he was familiar with all of this but did not pursue it with Isou.)

Pomerand's slim volume, with apparently unconnected texts printed on opposing pages, attracted approving critical attention. The well-known and well-respected writer Joë Bousquet wrote, for example, that he had devoured Pomerand's work with great pleasure. By now Pomerand was making no attempt to hide his ambition to become a millionaire and a member of the Académie Française, if the tuberculosis didn't finish him off first.

All of this was intolerable for Isou. He decided straightaway that all of Pomerand's work in fact belonged to him, Isou, the genius who had rescued Pomerand from oblivion, probably death, and given him the role of John the Baptist to his own Messiah. On 23 July, two days after Pomerand was hospitalized and said to be close to death, the journal *Arts* published an open letter from Isou in which he declared that he was the real author of *Le Cri et l'archange*.[2]

The journal *Combat* refused to publish the letter, on the grounds that it was tasteless and cruel to open a public debate with a weak and dying man. Isou could not care less. Pomerand said that he found the whole affair very funny and would have laughed, if he had any time left to him for laughing. Instead, in August, near death, or so he thought, Pomerand drew up both a legal and a literary will.

Following in the tradition of the fifteenth-century poet, criminal and chronicler of Left Bank life François Villon, he began composing his own literary *Testament*, an ironic homage to his own life and times (a typically absurdist entry read: 'I leave all my dances from now on to all those girls who are never invited to dance').

By the end of the summer, Pomerand was, however, on the road to recovery. He had moved further south to Cairo, where he met and married a woman called Roxane (to whom he dedicated *Saint ghetto des prêts*). Roxane was the daughter of a Greek financier who worked for King Farouk of Egypt. Under the influence of his new wife, Pomerand began converting from Judaism to Greek Catholicism. Despite Pomerand's exile and excommunication from Paris and the *lettristes*, this was not to be the last that Isou would hear of him.[3]

In the summer of 1948 Isou followed Pomerand's trail to Switzerland, to Lausanne, partly to renew contact with Pomerand's Swiss lover in the hope of funding for the *lettristes*. In Lausanne, Isou gave a series of talks to groups of students at the University of Lausanne who, having heard the good news of the *lettriste* revolution from Paris, were keen to see Isou in person and in action. Isou was not officially allowed into the university, as he had not officially been invited, so gave his talks on the steps of the building.

The group of admirers who attended the talks later became a self-funded publishing house who, under the name of Éditions aux Escaliers de Lausanne, were to publish Isou's next few books. In the meantime Isou had been dropped off Gallimard's list. He was never told the reason for this. Off the record, it was whispered by insiders at Gallimard that for all his fame and notoriety, and the relative success of his books, Isou was just too much trouble, and was quite possibly mad.

The simple fact was that, having only been in Paris for three years, Isou was almost famous but had also already irritated enough people to last him a lifetime. His admirers stood fast. But those he had had offended wanted to punish him and sought revenge. Happily for his enemies and detractors, the notion that Isou was an egomaniac and out of control was apparently confirmed by the publication of his next book, which was called *Isou ou La Mécanique des femmes* (Isou; or, The Mechanics of Women).

This book had originally been intended as part of *L'Agrégation* but was turned down by Gallimard on the grounds that it would very likely be banned for obscenity and cost the publisher a heavy fine. Isou managed to get backing, however, from his admirers in Lausanne and so, with the substantial financial investment of his chief cheerleader in Switzerland, a businessman named Charles Favrod, *Isou ou La Mécanique des femmes* was published by the invented house of Éditions aux Escaliers de Lausanne, in a cover jacket that deliberately mimicked the famous cream and red livery of Gallimard.

The contents of the book were devoted to teaching the young generation 'erotology', or the art of sex. It was Isou's duty to spread his expert knowledge of the subject as part of the new, wider remit of *lettrisme*, which was now transmuting from revolutionary poetry into the reinvention of all human knowledge. With his now familiar Messianic joy, Isou called his method of fucking *le baiser Isouien*, the 'Isouien method of fucking'. Like *lettriste* poetry, it was a new form of expression that would change the world. The book was prefaced with the warning that it should not be read by anybody over the age of forty, mainly because very few people at this advanced age knew what sexual desire was anyway – it was entirely the business of youth.

According to Isou, nothing could be more fundamental and important in the sexual act than knowledge of how women enjoyed sex. This was something that most young men found mysterious or baffling. Making women enjoy sex was, however, an art that everybody could master if they followed Isou's rules and principles. The key to understanding female desire was to understand that women were sexual creatures too. Many young male virgins failed to grasp this, believing the propaganda of books and movies that all women wanted was comfort and love and they despised sex or pretended not to know what it was.

In actual fact, as soon as you revealed the rawness of your own sexuality, women responded to you; most women loved maleness, the smell of sweat and cocks, and they loved to feel a man inside them. Sexual equality for both sexes would come when men started to understand this and stopped pretending that women were innocent or afraid of sexuality. You only had to read the Marquis de Sade to find out the truth about men and women – that they loved fucking in lots of different ways – and then to put it into practice.

The book picks up Isou's story from the end of *L'Agrégation*, as he starts to make his way towards Paris. Most of the book's content is devoted to the few days he spent in Budapest with Anna, the young Jewish woman he had been introduced to as part of the Zionist network helping Jews

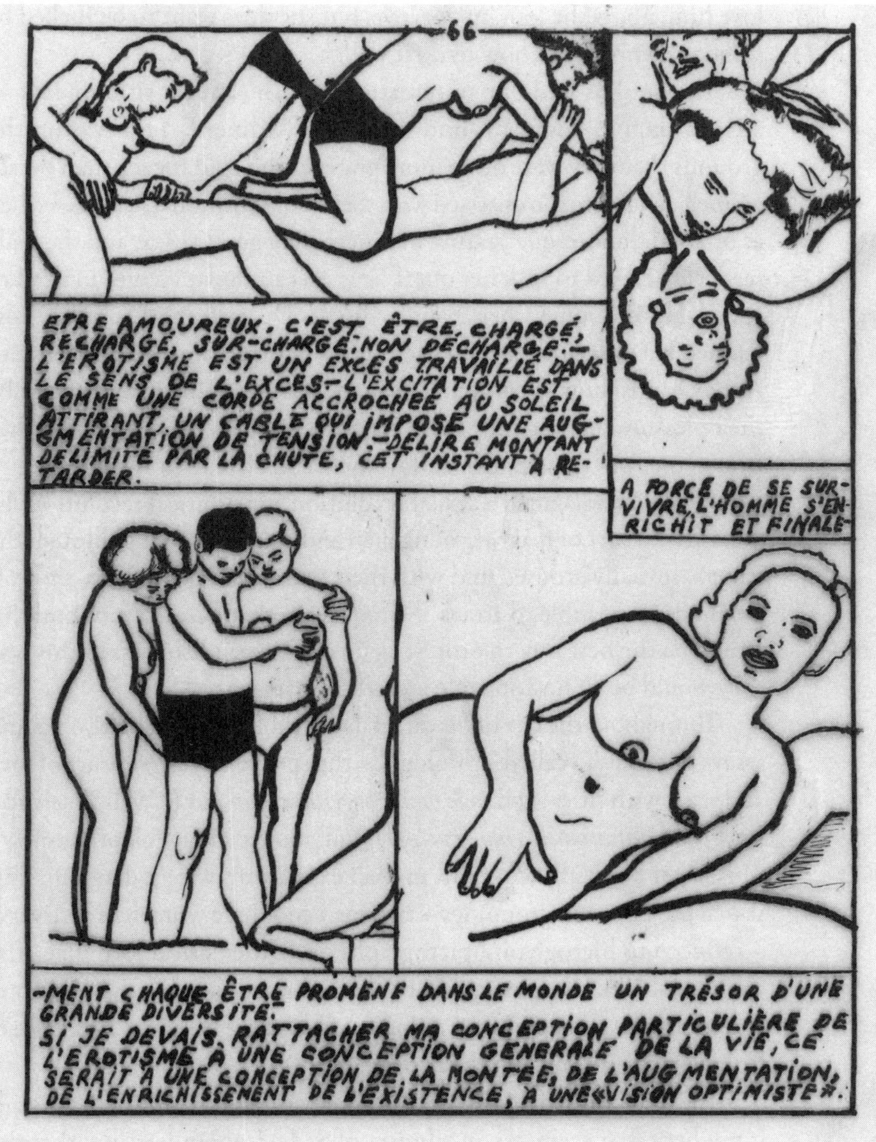

Original plate (tracing paper) used for Isou's novel-treatise on eroticism,
Initiation à la haute volupté (1960).

get out of Eastern Europe. She is both in thrall to him and his disciple,
and it is through making love to her in a variety of positions, using different techniques, that he teaches the reader how to please a woman. She
also teaches him about the ways of women; she is his interlocutor for the
scattered philosophical digressions that pepper the text. She does not

love him, nor is she looking for love, but she does want to be fucked by someone who knows how to do it well.

The book is laid out systematically with chapter titles meant as advice, such as 'Hang around with Ugly Women!' This was on the grounds that they were often more grateful and avid for sex than pretty women, who were too obsessed with their looks. Anna herself is described as of 'solid, Juno-esque' stature but incredibly good at sex, and the male reader is advised to seek her out if he is ever in Budapest and in need of sexual gratification. Other chapters discuss Descartes and Spinoza; how women become greater than themselves in orgasm; masturbating into Anna's hands; how what excited Isou most was hearing women describe their pleasure and watching them masturbate. The whole point of all this, Isou wrote, was to help men and women articulate their own desires.

Finally he imagined a sexual revolution as a political revolution; he visualized 'a sort of mass of young men and women walking through the streets', sexually aroused and with their stimulated genitals on show. It would be impossible to attack them or resist them, Isou wrote, and this would be the best way to protest against 'false prudishness'. In this way they would be an unstoppable insurrectionary force.[4]

Throughout the rest of his career, Isou regularly published books and essays on what he called 'erotology' – the specifically *lettriste* art of love and sex – with titles such as *Je vous apprendrai l'amour* (I Will Teach You Love) and *Initiation à la haute volupté* (Initiation to High Voluptuousness). This latter book also contains myriad explicit drawings, diagrams and sexual postures and groupings – two men and three women or vice versa – reduced to hieroglyphs, pictographs or mathematical formulae. The women look like the pin-up fare of the 1940s and '50s, but their faces are real, as are the faces of the men portrayed, and are based on Isou's lovers from within and without the *lettriste* group.

The reduction of group sex to mathematics is not quite so strange as it might at first seem. As an admirer of Sade, Isou understood that the eighteenth-century age in which the Marquis lived was both the age of pornography and the age of mathematics; this notion surfaces in the later works of Sade, who finally became more interested in mathematics than sex, and whose fictional gang-bangs are often punctuated by severe commands for clearly numbered and regulated acts of transgression.[5]

Later on in his career, Isou also wrote many 'erotic' novels, often under a pseudonym to make money as much as anything else. He saw himself, in these fictional works, as carrying on the Surrealist spirit of

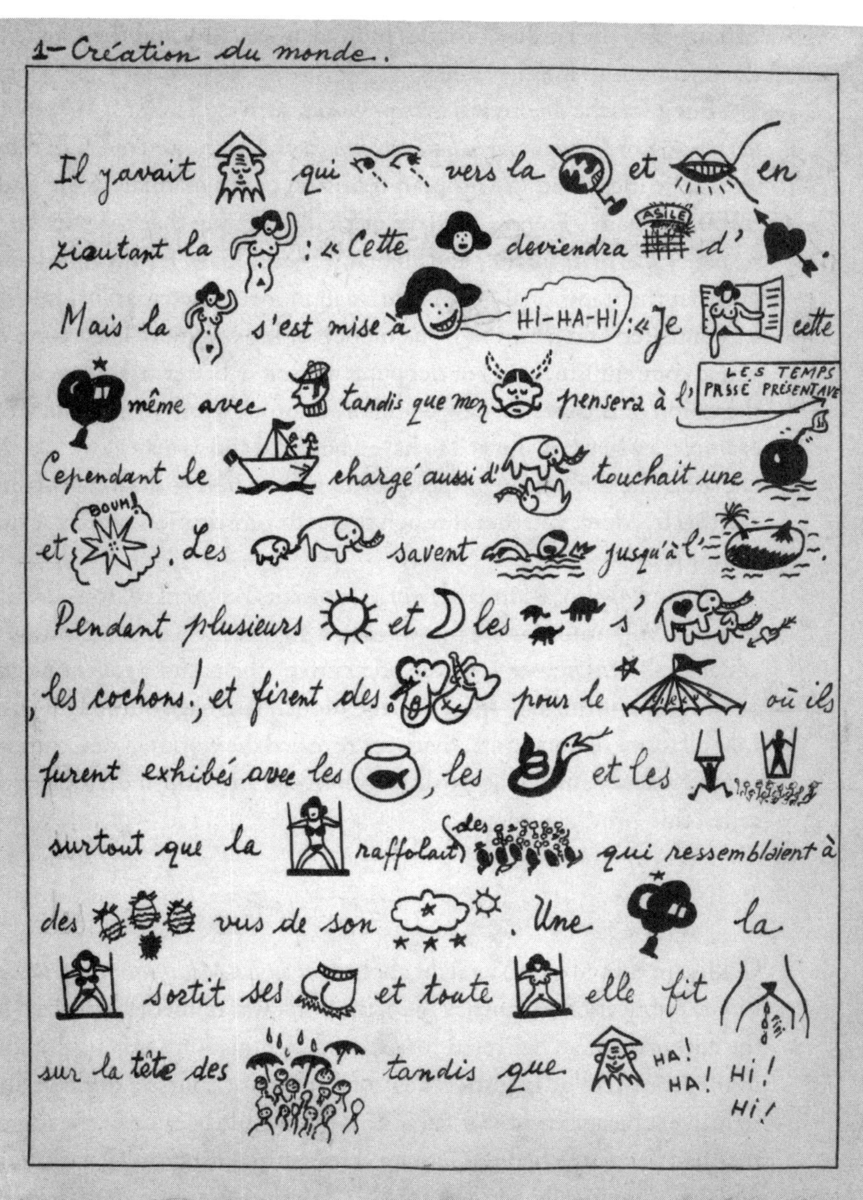

Isidore Isou, 'Création du monde', plate 1 of *Les Journaux des dieux* (1950).

enquiry into the endless varieties of human sexuality and their links to the unconscious mind.

But it was the theoretical *lettriste* works, such as *Isou ou La Mécanique des femmes* or *Initiation à la haute volupté*, which counted most. In these works, he identified the utopian tradition of sex manuals, from Sade through Charles Fourier to Havelock Ellis, arguing that the science of sexuality was in its infancy and all that we really knew for the time being was that the traditional Judeo-Christian model of heterosexual fidelity was outdated and harmful. Isou's model for sex was more like a form of sexual communism, or as Fourier put it in 1808, a 'better arrangement for the union of the sexes', a new world of 'amorous freedom' in which, for example, a woman is allowed to have a husband and as many lovers as she chooses. The duty of the male, according to Isou, is to actively encourage this freedom, whether through orgies or prostitution or new sexual techniques.

There was also, again as in Fourier, a mystical content to Isou's dreams of 'High Voluptuousness '; this was like a 'higher form of consciousness' and, like all *lettriste* activity, from poetry to mathematics, a route towards hearing, and ultimately speaking, the hidden language of the Universe. Like all forms of human creativity, sex revealed the workings of Creation: *lettriste* sexuality made the two categories, Man and God, indivisible. Isou called this 'prodigious love'.

———

Gallimard turned out to be right about *Isou ou La Mécanique des femmes*. On its publication in January 1949, the book was immediately seized by the authorities and delivered to 'a special commission for consultation' in the Ministère de la Justice. Censorship was of course a difficult and sensitive subject in post-war Paris. This was mainly because of the stigma that had been attached to German censorship during the Occupation, which automatically banned anti-Nazi or anti-German material that might provoke Resistance 'terrorism' or revolt.

As it was, the authorities in 'liberated' Paris were constantly and deliberately being provoked and tested by a new generation of writers who stood for literary freedoms in all its forms, including the freedom to write about sex and violence. These freedoms were, however, opposed in roughly equal measure by conservative, mainly Catholic forces, who wanted a return to 'moral order' in post-war France. It was this mood which in part explained the so-called Loi Marthe Richard of 1946, a new law that led to the shutting down of the 'Maisons de tolérance', the semi-offical brothels which had been operating in the capital since before anyone could remember.

Marthe Richard was a conservative politician who had been a prostitute and a spy in her own youth, but caught the public's imagination, or at least that part which didn't frequent brothels, by arguing that it was precisely this sort of decadent activity which had led to the Fall of France in the first place. It didn't help that brothels had reported thriving business during the Occupation and that they all too often welcomed Germans as more favoured clients than Frenchmen.

Isou ou La Mécanique des femmes was obviously at odds with this moral climate. But in fact Isou fell foul of another new law which was aimed specifically at banning books that deliberately corrupted or 'demoralized' young people by encouraging 'crime, lies, theft, laziness, cowardice or debauchery'. The main targets of the law were the French translations of American comics which used sex and violence as their selling point and were flooding the market. Literary works were, however, also being proscribed. Among the first books banned by the authorities during this period were Boris Vian's *J'irai cracher sur vos tombes* (I Will Spit on Your Graves), a pastiche of the 'hard-boiled' American thriller, and Henry Miller's rawly autobiographical *Sexus*. Partly as a reaction to this wave of moral conservatism, the publisher Jean-Jacques Pauvert was just beginning a career setting new boundaries for literary expression by being the first publisher to publish Sade under his own name. Pauvert would later go on to publish such literary monuments as Georges Bataille and Pauline Réage (*The Story of 'O'*).

Isou knew full well that he was courting trouble with his book. *Isou ou La Mécanique des femmes* transgressed almost all of the prohibitions enshrined in the new law and more, and given that Isou was the rising star on the Left Bank it could not be ignored as an obscure work by an unknown author. More to the point it aimed directly at leading young people to 'debauchery', even if this didn't exactly 'demoralize' them in the way that the law imagined.

The most offensive scenes, in the eyes of the censor, were not only the most explicit but those that described taboo acts such as anal sex. 'Yes, my phallus is large and heavy,' wrote Isou in a central section.

I like it like that, like a knife planted between my legs, with hatred, like a public challenge, like a hand thrust out of a train in a Fascist salute . . . I could not hold back and began to caress Anna once again. She turned her back towards me. It was stronger than me. I spread her out with my foot and buried my organ, covered in sweat, in her behind. Her hole squeezed my organ tightly. She gave a start. Isou, Isou, no! no! But I went deeper. She struggled and wriggled – It makes me sick! . . . The pleasure is so great it makes me sick.[6]

Isou was arrested on 6 April 1949 and then sent for a month to the prison of La Santé on the Boulevard d'Arago before his trial. He took his imprisonment in his stride, telling the newspaper *Samedi Soir* that he was very happy there, preparing a revolution and studying for a degree in philosophy. He had known worse in Romania and Bulgaria. He was indeed proud to be a public martyr, and immediately placed himself in the tradition of Apollinaire, who had also served a sentence in the same prison. Apollinaire had indeed written a heartbreaking poem about his time in La Santé in 1911, when he was briefly (and falsely) imprisoned for art trafficking. He described the 'hours passing like those at a burial'.[7]

La Santé also had a controversial recent history. During the war, the Germans had imprisoned members of the Resistance here. Eighteen of them were either guillotined or shot by firing squad during this period. The Occupation ended with a riot during which 28 prisoners were shot on the orders of the German regime. Even more recently, Jean Genet had been imprisoned repeatedly in La Santé through the 1940s. In 1946 Genet published the semi-autobiographical book *Le Miracle de la Rose*, which had been inspired by his incarceration in the penal colony of Mettray, near Tours, and completed in La Santé. Genet passed his time in his cell dreaming of the 'erotic charm' of prisons and their special 'aura', which encouraged homosexuality.

Isou was sanguine about his fate. Prison was no more than a 'detail'; he was indeed pleased that the book that had caused all this trouble was serving the cause of promoting Isou's name and the *lettriste* cause. *Isou ou La Mécanique des femmes* was indeed turning out be a mini-bestseller on the Left Bank, with all profits going to Isou. Better still, Isou was now officially a public martyr, a hero and an example to the bohemian youth of the Left Bank. He was medically examined by a psychiatrist called Dr Gouriou, who concluded that Isou was quite sane although obsessed by sex.[8]

A campaign to release Isou was mounted by his *lettriste* comrades and an open letter calling for the sentence to be quashed was signed by such luminaries as André Breton, Raymond Queneau, Jean Cocteau and Simone de Beauvoir. They didn't all agree that Isou was a genius and a Messiah, although this is what the *lettriste* faithful still believed, but they were against all forms of censorship, especially censorship of sexual material on the grounds of obscenity. In its own way this campaign signalled a minor step forward in the history of French censorship and marked a milestone in what could and couldn't be written about sex. On 25 April 1950 Isou was given a fine of 200,000 francs, which he couldn't pay, and a suspended sentence of eight months in prison.

Not all of those who supported Isou while he was on trial did so because they thought he was a great or even competent writer. They supported him because they had to: it was unthinkable for any right-thinking Left Bank intellectual to hold any position other than that of opposing government sanctions on writing about sex.

But support for Isou could be grudging, sarcastic and hostile. In the English-language journal the *French Review*, the literary critic Henri Peyre witheringly remarked that prison had been the making of many a good writer, so there was still hope left for Isou. In the journal *L'Esprit*, Chris Marker, whose real name was Christian Bouche-Villeneuve and who would go on to a distinguished career as one of the radical critics and film-makers in post-war France, opposed Isou's sentence, but he also observed that Isou's megalomania and lack of talent made him look ridiculous.

These were the first expressions of outright hostility towards Isou and the *lettristes* from the literary establishment but Isou didn't care. This sarcasm was in fact only to be expected from 'the old and the impotent', those who could never join in Isou's imagined insurrection. It was time to intensify the *lettriste* revolution by making it a truly political and violent insurrection. The pressing issue now was to raise the level of antagonism, applying the tactic of maximum tension, which had also served Isou so well, to create a truly hostile atmosphere, when the *lettristes* and their followers would only be one or two steps away from real, raw violence towards their enemies.

This new turn in the history of *lettrisme* was to be the revolutionary movement that he called 'A Youth Uprising!' He had already argued for this in 1947. Now, in 1949, it was to be made a reality. Posters appeared all over the Left Bank announcing that 12 million young people would soon be coming down into the street 'to make the *lettriste* revolution'.

Isou described his views in a pamphlet that was published, again by Éditions aux Escaliers de Lausanne, in 1949, under the title of *Traité de l'économie nucléaire. Soulèvement de la jeunesse* (Treatise of Nuclear Economics: Youth Uprising!). His big idea was that until the Second World War, youth as a social category had always been associated with sport, fitness, serving society and above all obedience. You could see this in youth movements from the Boy Scouts to the Hitler Youth to the junior Legionaries of the Iron Guard. Isou had, however, glimpsed a different way, a different future. Youth could be savage and cruel but above all free; all the young had to do was to refuse to believe in the so-called civilization they lived in.

This was Isou's conception of 'youth' as a new revolutionary class. As a young 'hooligan' in Bucharest, Isou had seen that 'youth' could also be a rebellious and dissident force. It was simply a question of channelling the energy and savagery of 'youth' into a coherent strike force. This was one of Isou's ideas that had so intrigued André Breton.

The *Traité de l'économie nucléaire* was also widely circulated in the dive bars of the Left Bank, where Isou easily found a constituency among the self-styled *ratés* ('losers' or 'dropouts') who had colonized the district. This was a parallel universe to the smart cafés of Saint-Germain-des-Prés, where the likes of Jean-Paul Sartre, Camus and all the rest of the 'professional thinkers' of the era pontificated on history and responsibility. The *ratés* were runaways, delinquents, army deserters, refugees and down-at-heel students whose lives were predicated on irresponsibility, chance and just surviving. They couldn't have afforded a drink in the posh bars of Saint-Germain-des-Prés anyway and delighted instead in the alternative Paris which they had set up only a short walk away from the most prestigious cafés.

It was here, in bars with names such as Le Bar Bac, Le Pichet, La Chope Gauloise and Le Bar Vert, that Isou announced in his frequent 'spontaneous' speeches that 'youth' was excluded from the economy because it had no exchange value; without employment, family or capital, youths were not people but 'luxury items' or 'utensils'. Revolution would be made, argued Isou, by all those who realized that youth was an economic construct and nothing to do with age. This made youth, or at least the economic definition of youth, the new proletariat, the new revolutionary class. A by now familiar theme was the attack on the *Résistantialistes*, the smug old bastards who had pretended to fight the Nazis, while it was the young generation whose lives had really been in danger. He elaborated: 'Every reform must start with the resolution of millions of pre-agents who make up the "sickness" of society.'[9]

By the 'sickness of society' Isou meant all those who, through age, boredom, drunkenness or alienation, found themselves excluded from the economic life of society. According to Isou they were in fact harbingers of freedom from family, work, money.

As soon as the new class realized this and unleashed their revolutionary potential, the constructs of state, government and finance would melt away. 'We will call young any individual, no matter his age, who does not yet coincide with his function,' wrote Isou, 'who struggles to attain the realm of activity he truly desires, who struggles to achieve a career and a form of work other than that which was planned for him. These are the young who have nothing to lose. They are the attack. They are the adventure!'[10]

Isou was not the first or only young man of his generation to call for a 'Youth Uprising'. In the late 1940s, throughout Europe and America, there were already the stirrings of what would become the rock 'n' roll culture of the 1950s and the counter-culture of the 1960s. But he was one of the first to understand the power of youth as a force for political as well as cultural change; this of course would be one of the defining characteristics of the events of May '68 in Paris, as well as their aftershocks.

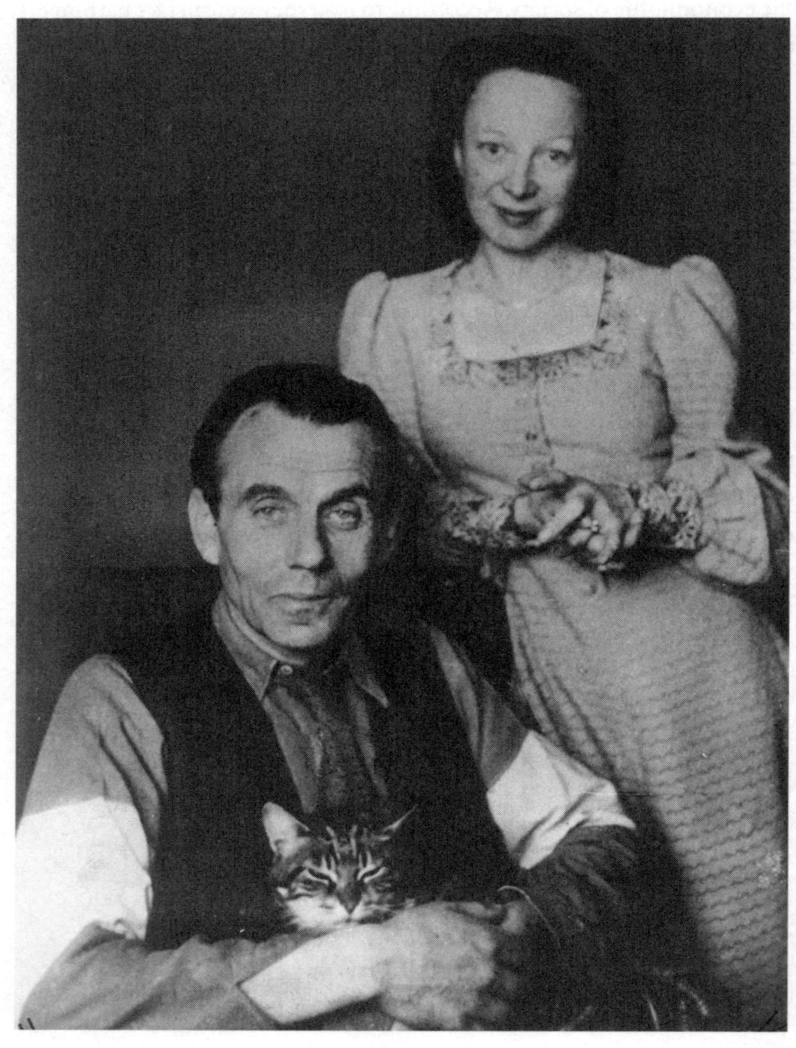

Louis-Ferdinand Céline with Lucette in Denmark, late 1940s.

twelve

The Heroic Period

In December 1949, Isou met another young Jew who was immediately convinced by Isou's call for a youth revolt. This was a young man called Maurice Lemaître, already a committed anarchist, who would very soon replace Gabriel Pomerand as Isou's most trusted lieutenant. He would occupy this position until Isou died in 2007.

Maurice Lemaître was born with the name Moïse Bismuth in 1926 in Paris to Felix Bismuth and Suzanne Lemaître. The Bismuths were a respectable *petit-bourgeois* family (Felix was a haberdasher) who lived at first at rue de Trévise in the 9th arrondissement, before moving to rue Marie-Stuart in the 2nd arrondissement, where Maurice's sister Christiane was born in 1943. Like Isou and Fanny, Lemaître loved his sister deeply and they were lifelong companions, outlasting all of Maurice's marriages and countless love affairs. In 1939 the family moved to 13 rue de Mulhouse, another nondescript street in the 2nd arrondissement. Lemaître never moved away from this apartment, which he named the Centre de Créativité.[1]

Lemaître learned his politics during the Occupation. He had a vivid memory of his father being forced to wear a yellow star. At this point he was the only one in the family who had to do this. When the family were stopped on the street and asked by a policeman what they were doing walking with a Jew, Maurice's sister Christiane, no more than a child, turned to the policeman and declared with great pride that this man was her father. It was not long, however, before Maurice too had to wear a yellow star and saw his identity card stamped with the word 'Jew'.

Lemaître was caught up in the infamous 'rafle du Vél d'Hiv', the rounding up of some 13,000 Jews on 16 and 17 July 1942, led by the Paris police following German orders, who were taken to the Vélodrome d'Hiver, the cycling arena on the rue Nélaton. This was one of the most disgraceful moments of the Occupation, not only because thousands of Jews lost their lives or were deported to death camps, but because so many Parisians, clearly complicit with the crime, looked away and denied any responsibility. Lemaître somehow avoided capture but he never forgot how close he had come to death or deportation, and that the traitors had been his fellow Parisians. He lost his friends and his childhood sweetheart in the raid. Some 55 years later he recalled the trauma in a film called *Merci Pezou, pour Nina Nadolna*.

During this period Lemaître was a student at the École Nationale Supérieure des Arts et Métiers. He tried to involve himself in Resistance activities but did not get far: he found it impossible to take orders or respect a hierarchy. In 1944, during the Liberation of Paris, attempting to join in the free-for-all as the Allied forces retook the city he was knocked over and injured by an American jeep.

Lemaître was clever as well as ambitious. He published his first article in 1946 in the prestigious journal *L'Homme et l'Architecture*, edited by no less than Le Corbusier. He did his military service in Germany that same year and on his return to Paris in 1947 registered for a degree in philosophy at the Sorbonne. By now he was already a convinced anarchist, fired up with hatred towards all forms of authority. He began to mix with such well-known anarchist figures as Georges Fontenis and Maurice Joyeux, joining the Fédération Anarchiste and contributing to their journal, *Le Libertaire*. At the same time he was developing an interest in occultism and mysticism and was briefly a member of the circle around the Italian poet Lanza del Vasto, then in exile in Paris and known as a follower of Gandhi, an advocate of non-violence and an adept in the thinking of the philosopher and spiritual guide G. I. Gurdjieff.

Isou and Lemaître met for the first time in December 1949 at the offices of Louis Pauwels, who edited a journal called *Aux Ecoutes* which had its headquarters on the Boulevard de Madeleine.[2] Pauwels was an admirer of Isou. He was also interested in Gurdjieff and varying forms of mysticism but was at the same time a hard-headed journalist. He would soon go on to edit the journal *Combat* and then have a long and distinguished career in the French media.

Outside France Pauwels is most famous for a book he wrote with Jacques Bergier in 1960. The book was called *Le Matin des magiciens* (The Morning of the Magicians) and among other things claimed to reveal the occulist interests of the Nazis and the link between atomic physics and alchemy (Bergier claimed that he had met the legendary and mysterious alchemist Fulcanelli, who was admired by no less than André Breton). This book became a bestseller in the 1960s, was a major influence on the Anglo-American counter-culture, and made Pauwels and Bergier, who may well have been hoaxers, very rich.

Whatever the truth of the matter, Bergier certainly had a colourful past. He was a Russian-born Jew trained as a chemical engineer who was also alternative in his thinking, a member of the French Resistance, a spy, and claimed to have worked on the secrets of atomic fission. Bergier was also a survivor of the Mauthausen–Gusen concentration camp in Upper Austria, which was nicknamed 'the bone-grinder' by the Nazi authorities and dedicated to the extermination of intellectuals.

In 1949 Louis Pauwels admired Isou because he thought he was an authentic genius, although as an inconsistent Catholic, Pauwels had yet to be fully convinced about Isou's status as a Jewish Messiah. More to the point, Pauwels was intrigued by Isou's uncompromising arguments for the supremacy of Judaism and joked, with seriousness in his voice, that he would use Isou's ideas as the starting point for his own book promoting antisemitism. The meeting between Isou and Lemaître was a great success. A photograph taken shortly after this first meeting shows the two young men, elegantly dressed against the cold, walking up the Champs-Élysées, as Louis Pauwels lurks in the background. It is clear already from their confident, business-like expression and their determined stance that these are two young men who are ready to take on the world.[3]

The meeting between Isou and Lemaître was brokered in part by Pauwels so that they could all discuss their views on the novelist Louis-Ferdinand Céline.[4] In 1949 Céline was languishing in exile in Denmark, having fled a warrant that had been issued for his arrest on charges of collaboration during the Occupation. Having been one of the most successful writers of the 1930s, Céline was now one of the most hated men in France. The plan was for Lemaître and Isou to launch a campaign to defend Céline.

This was meant partly as a severe provocation to the right-thinking intelligentsia on the Left Bank, who were so hypocritical and so quick to condemn Céline while many of their crimes went unpunished, and partly because Lemaître and Isou admired Céline as the most authentic and best writer of the age. Isou placed Céline on a par with James Joyce as a 'true creator', a linguistic magician who could transform the language of the gutter into poetry.[5]

Céline was also a ferocious and unrepentant antisemite. Between 1937 and 1941 he had published a series of pamphlets that are made up of the rawest antisemitism. In these pamphlets – which look like popular paperbacks, and amount to more than a thousand pages – Céline's ideas are those common to many pre-war French antisemites: he rails against Jewish-Bolshevik vermin, sees Jewish conspiracies everywhere and praises Hitler. These are savage texts. Céline declared that the arrival of the Germans in France was a 'necessary tonic'. Céline's only regret by then was that the war had not been devastating enough. Long before the Nazi machinery began to construct the Final Solution, Céline called for the extermination of the Jewish race: 'If you really want to get rid of the Jews,' he wrote, 'then there are not 36,000: racism! That's the only thing the Jews are afraid of: racism! And not a little bit with the fingertips but all the way. Totally. Inexorably. Like complete Pasteur sterilization.'[6]

Although Isou and Lemaître both had the same views on Céline, it was Lemaître who led the way for his defence. This took the form of a series of articles written by Lemaître and published in the anarchist journal *Le Libertaire*. The first of these was entitled 'What Do You Think of the Trial of Louis-Ferdinand Céline?' It featured a variety of responses from the leading intellectuals and writers to whom the question had been sent.

Céline received a sympathetic hearing from Jean Paulhan, Albert Paraz, Jean Dubuffet and Marcel Aymé, who generally agreed that Céline was the victim of a witch hunt. Others such as André Breton were less friendly; indeed, Breton wrote that he could not support any artist who did not have the character to match the excellence of his work.

Céline himself was, however, delighted with the efforts of the young Jew he called the 'admirable Lemaître'; he wrote to his friend Pierre Monnier about him: 'Fuck! He's firing directly at them, the lying cunts!' Céline asked his publisher to send a copy of his latest book, the novella *Casse-Pipe*, to his Jewish supporter, noting that, given the overwhelming superiority of the forces ranged against him, Lemaître was also bound to be 'shitting himself a little bit'.[7]

Lemaître, like Isou, did not, however, lack courage when taking on his elders. He wrote in *Le Libertaire* that certainly Céline had a case to answer, but 'Justice in France is derisory!' So who had the right to judge him? Lemaître went on to argue in the strongest terms that the real criminals were the politicians, the financiers, the factory-owners and the writers and intellectuals who had profited from the war and who were now pointing the finger at someone who was not only the best writer of them all but the most honest. Céline's Jew-hatred was at least real and authentic – unlike 'the madness of public opinion', which was irrational and capricious and 'the truest relation of antisemitism and racism'.

Even more provocatively, Lemaître now signed his articles under the aegis of the 'Committee of Israelite friends of Céline', which was meant to include Isou. He and Isou sent a letter defending Céline in the name of this committee to the Court of Justice in Paris where Céline was being tried *in absentia*. Delighted with this new line of attack, Céline wrote directly to Lemaître congratulating him on his audacity: 'This is true genius. The great Rabbi now mixed up in it all, whether willingly or by force! A Baptism of Fire! You will need this on the Supreme Council! You have the age and the talent!'[8]

Isou and Lemaître were pleased and flattered at this attention from the most demonized French writer of the age. But what really brought Céline and the young Jews together was that they both shared a special contempt for Jean-Paul Sartre. More precisely all three of them had been particularly incensed, for parallel reasons, by an article Sartre had published in 1945 in the journal *Les Temps Modernes* called 'Portrait of an Anti-Semite'.

In this article, Sartre, whose life and well-being had never been in serious danger during the war, claimed with his usual high moral authority that he knew how to diagnose who or what an antisemite was and, furthermore, to prescribe a possible cure or antidote. For Isou and Lemaître this was the perfect example of what they had already called 'Résistantialisme' – the high-handed pomposity of Sartre's 'Existentialist' argument that the 'Jewish problem' would be solved if the Jews assimilated into the true democracy that was Universal Humanism.

Isou, in particular, was angry that Sartre dared to make this argument from the safety of post-war Paris, while Isou's brothers and sisters from Eastern Europe were fighting and dying in Tel Aviv, Jerusalem and Gaza for the simple right to exist. Most importantly for Isou, Jewish assimilation was achieving the goals of the Holocaust with words instead of gas chambers. The whole notion of a 'Jewish Question' was a fiction anyway, invented by the *goyim*.

Céline had even more concrete reasons to be angry with this piece. More precisely, in this essay Sartre deliberately made the claim that if Céline had supported the Nazis it was because they had paid him to do so. In 1949, to be paid by the Nazis was a direct act of treachery that could earn you a death sentence. Céline turned on Sartre in print, snarling back that if he hated Jews, which was not a crime in itself, he did not need to be paid by the Nazis to speak against them. Céline said this in a short pierce of superbly poetic invective called *À l'agité du bocal* (The Crackpot).

Céline sent this text first to Jean Paulhan, who ignored it, and it was finally published in a private limited edition of two hundred which was distributed across the Left Bank. Céline called 'Jean-Baptiste Sartre' a plagiarist of his own literary language, who had borrowed the style of the early Céline for his first novels, but was worse still a new form of traitor. Sartre was like 'a tapeworm, blind and stupid' crawling up Céline's rectum into his shit and entrails, where he could poison and destroy him, and this, in the world of the late 1940s, when every so-called *résistant* was also now a *massacriste*, amounted to calling for Céline's death to the soundtrack of 'the choirs of the hangmen of Nuremberg'. Céline called Sartre a 'true monster' and 'an assassin'.[9]

Isou, Lemaître and Céline could never be on the same side but they were dissenting voices who knew what smugness and self-righteousness looked like. Isou was writing directly to Sartre when he wrote: 'But you won't have our skin, you fucking undertaker, so long as there is a young Jew left alive who is not afraid to live and to live life till it's exhausted. No, you won't have our skin!'[10]

If Gabriel Pomerand – now in distant Cairo pursuing his new love affairs with his new wife and opium respectively – had been 'picturesque', Isou found in Maurice Lemaître 'a man of action'. Lemaître was tough-minded and practical, and, as the first adventure with Céline had demonstrated, knew how to turn ideas into deeds.

Isou now gathered round himself, with the help of Lemaître, a new generation of *lettristes* who were either extremely talented artists – most notably Gil J. Wolman – or were characterized by their daring and willingness to pursue actions to their ultimate extremes – two notable figures here were Jean-Louis Brau and Serge Berna. Brau had already made friends in 1947 with the poet and actor Antonin Artaud, who was then writing poems and scripts that consisted of sounds rather than words.

Artaud had been close to the Surrealists, and was much cherished by them, but by now he was also physically and mentally ill, always teetering on the edge of psychotic meltdown. Brau and the other *lettristes* of course venerated him as a great visionary who was on their side in the historic struggle against rationality and meaning. Inspired by Artaud, one of the first actions of this new trio in the *lettriste* group was to form a 'commando' and to launch an attack on the Cercle Paul Valéry, which was meeting in the more fashionable Left Bank cafés to honour Valéry. They did this by reading sound poems through megaphones until they were manhandled and booted out by the waiters.

In February 1950 Lemaître published a text on the 'Youth Front' in the *Libertaire* and a few weeks later organized a conference on the subject with his anarchist friends. The alliance with the anarchists did not last long and Lemaître pledged his full allegiance to Isou. The proof of this allegiance came a few weeks later when Lemaître, along with Berna, Brau and Wolman, was one of the leaders of the so-called 'attack on Auteuil'. This was a raid by the '*lettriste* youth' on a Catholic orphanage in the chic Paris suburb of Auteuil.[11]

As well as the obvious ringleaders led by Lemaître, the '*lettriste* youth' were in fact a motley band of students, petty criminals and drunks rounded up from various bars with the promise of a fight and some drinking. The excuse for the riot, according to the *lettristes*, was 'a so-called provocation' by the authorities. This was the arrest and latest confinement of Éliane Papaï, a beautiful and insolent teenage runaway of Romanian origin who had been in and out of the Auteuil orphanage most of her adolescence, and who had fallen in with the *lettristes* during her latest break-out. Her return to Auteuil was, for the *lettristes*, akin to an enemy raid in which Éliane had been captured. Retaliation was the only option.

The *lettristes*, fuelled by drink, drugs and the possibility of a scrap, set off in the late afternoon for the suburbs. Once in Auteuil, the '*lettriste* youth' hurled abuse and bricks at the orphanage staff and started a small-scale riot in the courtyard of the building. The police arrived, skulls were broken and many of the '*lettriste* youth' were hauled off for a kicking in the cells. Serge Berna remembered that as he approached the orphanage with his comrades he was covered in sweat, fearing the worst, but not knowing what that might be. Priests and policemen – there seemed to be hundreds of them – battered the young *lettristes* with whatever came to hand. The orphans themselves were terrified by the scenes of violence. The raid began as a kind of joke but turned into something else: a direct confrontation between the 'Youth Front' and the forces ranged against them.

Isou was not directly involved in the attack on Auteuil but it was well known that the 'action' had been directly inspired by his rhetoric and ideas. Lemaître, the tactician, made sure that everyone knew this. At *lettriste* headquarters in a Left Bank bar, the action was judged to be an interesting prelude.

———

There would soon be more 'adventures' to come. In late March 1950 a meeting was called by Serge Berna and other *lettriste* fellow-travellers at the Salle des Sociétés under the rubric 'Meeting des Ratés' (Meeting of the Losers). The meeting was attended by other like-minded individuals, all very young, including Maurice-Paul Comte, who edited a respected art journal called *Osmose* (contributors included the likes of Jean Cocteau) and a failed Dominican monk called Michel Mourre.

The mood of the meeting was shaped by a tract which took its cue directly from Isou's 'Youth Front': 'We are losers!' it began. 'We're told that we're idiots, and we are. We are nothing, but we are still here. *NOTHING AT ALL*. And we are *NO GOOD. INCAPABLE, USELESS, IDLE, RAGGEDY-ARSED BOOZERS*. Come and meet us at the *MEETING OF THE LOSERS*.'[12]

Serge Berna opened the meeting by describing himself as 'a syphilitic of the Left' who had served in the Waffen-SS (extremely unlikely given that he was only 25 years old). He made little secret of his plan: to launch an anticlerical attack at the altar of Notre Dame during High Mass on 9 April, which was Easter Sunday.

So it was that at 11 a.m. Michel Mourre, the failed monk turned *lettriste*, stepped forward towards the altar at Notre Dame as Mass was about to begin. He was in disguise as a priest, wearing the correct robes and having convincingly tonsured his hairstyle. The plan was that he would walk up to the microphone and read a prepared text, written by Serge Berna. As well as the congregation in the cathedral, there was an estimated audience of some 10,000. In its entirety, the text read:

> Today, Easter day of the Holy Year,
> Here, under the emblem of Notre-Dame of Paris,
> I accuse the universal Catholic Church of the lethal diversion of
>   our living strength toward an empty heaven,
> I accuse the Catholic Church of swindling,
> I accuse the Catholic Church of infecting the world with its
>   funereal morality,
> Of being the running sore on the decomposed body of the West.

Verily I say unto you: God is dead,
We vomit the agonizing insipidity of your prayers,
For your prayers have been the greasy smoke over the battlefields
    of our Europe.
Go forth then into the tragic and exalting desert of a world where
    God is dead,
And till this earth anew with your bare hands,
With your PROUD hands,
With your unpraying hands.
Today Easter day of the Holy Year,
Here under the emblem of Notre-Dame of Paris,
We proclaim the death of the Christ-god, so that Man may live
    at last.[13]

Mourre had barely begun his oration when the great organ of Notre Dame roared into life. Serge Berna, Jean-Louis Brau, Ghislain Desnoyers de Marbaix and other *lettristes* had infiltrated the congregation and at this point rushed out towards Mourre, trying to smuggle him away and out of Notre Dame.

The Swiss Guards, guardians of the cathedral, now exploded into action, drawing their swords, which they meant to use in real anger against the blasphemers (one *lettriste* comrade was left with a head wound and a scar for life – the Swiss Guard were aiming to kill). The gang was captured by a crowd that pursued them towards the Seine, fully intent on lynching them. They were rescued by the police, who immediately arrested them, almost certainly saving their lives.

In the end Mourre was the only member of the gang to be properly charged and detained. He was put into a psychiatric hospital where he was diagnosed with several conflicting personality disorders. Much was made of the fact that he had also been a supporter of marginal Right-wing parties in the post-war period, his sexual guilt and shame (he was found to be 'orthosexual' – a heterosexual). Most damning of all, according to the press, was the fact that he professed to be an admirer of Sartre's novel *La Nausée*, then the most well-known 'Existentialist' guide to alienation and loss of faith and a book that was largely unread but still notorious to the world beyond the Left Bank.

The 'scandal of Notre Dame' made headlines across the French-speaking world; the consensus in the newspapers was that this kind of very deliberate blasphemy and hooliganism was the inevitable consequence of the amoral and rebellious world of free-living youth on the Left Bank. For his part, Isou was pleased that once again the *lettristes* had so directly taken the fight to the enemy and, through the power of scandal, transmitted the *lettriste* message to the widest possible audience. Isou was delighted with the incident. It was at once an attack on 'the impotence of celibate priests', but also more personal: it was Isou's revenge on the antisemitic 'Christians' who had tried to kill him in Bucharest.

Most importantly, major writers on the Left Bank were taking this new avant-garde, *lettrisme*, led by this unpredictable young Romanian Jew, as a force to be reckoned with. *Combat*, for example, despite a finger-wagging editorial, opened its pages to a debate with contributions from Jean Paulhan, Louis Pauwels, André Breton and Maurice Nadeau, Gabriel Marcel, Benjamin Péret and René Char. Breton conceded that the *lettristes* were now living out what the Surrealists had only dreamt about.

All the major figures agreed that, one way or another, *lettrisme* represented the authentic voice of post-war youth, and that it signalled the end of the lingering influence of the pre-war avant-gardes. Isou was not to be trusted: he was an egomaniac, dangerously reckless, and the cult of violence was disturbing. But no one could doubt that *lettrisme* had arrived.

———

At this point Isou once again became jealous of challenges to his control over the group. Tensions soon emerged between the 'artistic' wing of the *lettriste* movement and the 'actionist' factions, who were soon accused by the 'artists' of seeking notoriety for its own sake. Isou did not take sides, but enjoyed his control over both factions, whose mutual antagonisms ensured that Isou remained in complete control of the group.

Towards the end of 1950, the living propaganda of the 'actionists' was matched by a flurry of artistic activity from the 'artists'. These included the publication of a slim volume called *Précisions sur ma poésie et moi. Dix poèmes magnifiques* (Precisions on My Poetry and Me: Ten Magnificent Poems). This was mainly written in the third person and contained chapters entitled 'Why Isou Is the Greatest Contemporary Poet' and 'Why Isou Is Not Only as Great as Baudelaire but Greater Than Baudelaire'.

Isou wrote that he had already found the secret of his 'Immortality'. He did not need the approval of other men to know this as he was already above and beyond such mortals. He wrote

> There are days when I am really so happy that I want to burst,
> I want to cry tears of joy, I have the impression that life is worth
> living for this single hour, and I fall apart and almost feel sick.
> But if you think about it, it must be admitted that I am at least
> for now the most beautiful boy who is making 'great literature'
> today.[14]

He followed up this statement by publishing his most important work so far. This was *Les Journaux des dieux, précédé d'un essai sur la définition, l'évolution et le bouleversement total de la prose et du roman* ('Journals of the Gods', preceded by an essay on the definition, evolution and complete overthrow of prose and the novel), the world's first ever 'hypergraphic' novel – a new form of artistic expression which would take writing and thought beyond even Joyce's *Finnegans Wake*.

The ambition is staggering but the work is also beautiful and hypnotic. The 'hypergraphic novel' consists of fifty plates of text, diagrams and drawings in a variety of colours, over-laying each other as 'unreadable' but fascinatingly cryptic puzzles. Isou composed the book with the help of Maurice Lemaître, who used the skills he had acquired during his apprenticeship making prints in the École Nationale Supérieure des Arts et Métiers. The result was stunning. This is undoubtedly one of Isou's most original and moving works. If you can find it in a rare-books bookshop, it is worth paying whatever high price the dealer is asking for it these days. To hold it in your hand is to feel and see the awakening of a creative, visionary intelligence that does indeed seem to convey some sort of religious significance.

The *Journaux des dieux* was met by critical silence. This was, however, irrelevant to Isou, who in August 1950 started work on what was for him a totally new art form which would take *lettrisme* into an even deeper and wider dimension. He had started making a film.

The film was called *Traité de bave et d'éternité* (Treatise on Slime and Eternity) and soon would briefly take Isou and the *lettristes* to new heights of fame and notoriety. To do this, Isou and the *lettristes* travelled down to Cannes in May 1951 to the annual film festival there. They intended to cause enough trouble to get Isou's film shown, even though it had not been entered for the competition and in fact no one had actually seen it yet.

Isou started work on the film on 15 August 1950 and finished it on 21 May 1951. The sections of the film that were shot in Paris were filmed through the winter of 1950 and 1951, which was as hard, cold and poor as any winter since the war. The main figure in the Paris shots is Isou, whom we first meet dressed in an American-style fringed jacket. His hair is immaculately styled in a Tony Curtis quiff, his lower lips are full and sensual; he prowls the streets, indifferent to the shabby passers-by in their drab utility clothes. He looks like a young Elvis Presley ten years before the world had heard of Elvis.

The Cannes Film Festival was an ideal target for the iconoclastic fury of the *lettristes*. It had been founded in the 1930s as a response to the Venice Film Festival's tendency to give awards to films of marked fascist tendency. By the late 1940s, Cannes was a runaway success, which reflected the post-war French love affair with the cinema. Although the *Nouvelle Vague* (New Wave) had yet to be born, and the French public in the 1940s was mainly flocking to see Fernandel comedies or rehashes of films based on Colette's stories, in its four years of post-war existence the Cannes Film Festival had come to be regarded as a prestigious and powerful showcase for French culture in its most official form.

The Paris press were on full alert to the *lettriste* presence in Cannes, gleefully anticipating perhaps a scandal like the 'attack on Auteuil' – which of course had made the press – or even the now legendary 'Assault on Notre Dame'. No one was sure if Isidore Isou would actually attend the festival in person and some journalists cast doubt on whether 'Isidore Isou' really existed or was just another made-up name by avant-garde pranksters set on subversion.

Isou was not happy with this rumour and set in motion a counter-rumour that the original celluloid, all 2,500 metres (8,200 ft) of film, would be shown as a physical object to anyone who wished to inspect it. In the pages of the journal *Le Film Français* Isou said that he was taking his films further than those of Orson Welles or Rossellini and that '*Traité de bave et d'éternité* will change cinema drastically and push it towards unexpected paths. It requires only that juries lend it an *attentive ear.*'

Maurice Lemaître was the first *lettriste* to actually arrive in Cannes, having gained accreditation as a journalist for *Le Libertaire*, bringing the prints of the film with him. Isou followed on a few days later.

In a photograph taken in a street in Cannes during the first week of the festival, the *lettristes*, with Isou at their head, look like a pack of street young hooligans – young, casually dressed and looking for trouble. At the back of the gang you can see the young Guy Debord, the future leader

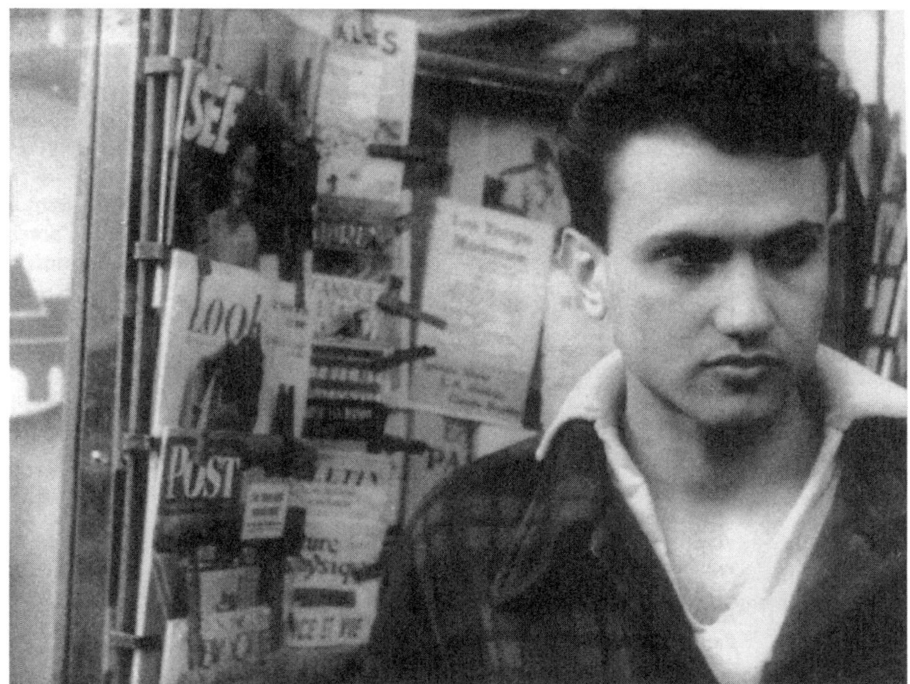

Isidore Isou in *Traité de bave et d'éternité* (1951).

of the Situationists and soon to be Isou's lifelong enemy. This was Debord's first encounter with the *lettristes* and the avant-garde in full attack mode. Debord was soon to learn a great deal about the art and science of provocation as well as how to make a film that was an assault on its audience: art as a deliberately constructed 'situation'.

In the course of a week of agitation and interruption, the *lettristes* finally disrupted enough meetings of high-powered executives to win a screening on 20 April at the Vox cinema. It turned out that the film was unfinished and the second part of the film was no more than a blank screen accompanied by dialogue. According to *Nice-Matin*, there were scuffles when the film finished and Isou was slapped in the face by the film critic Sonika Bo. Others seemed equally disconcerted. Nonetheless, on the whim of Jean Cocteau, who was on the jury at Cannes, along with the writer and film-maker Curzio Malaparte and the actor and footballer Raf Vallone, the film was awarded a specially invented prize called *Prix de l'Avant-Garde*. The film critic of *Combat* was astonished and appalled; to him the 1951 winner of the Special Jury Prize, Joseph L. Mankiewicz's *All About Eve*, and Isou's barbarism, had effectively proved that the cinema, if not dead, was entering a terminal phase.

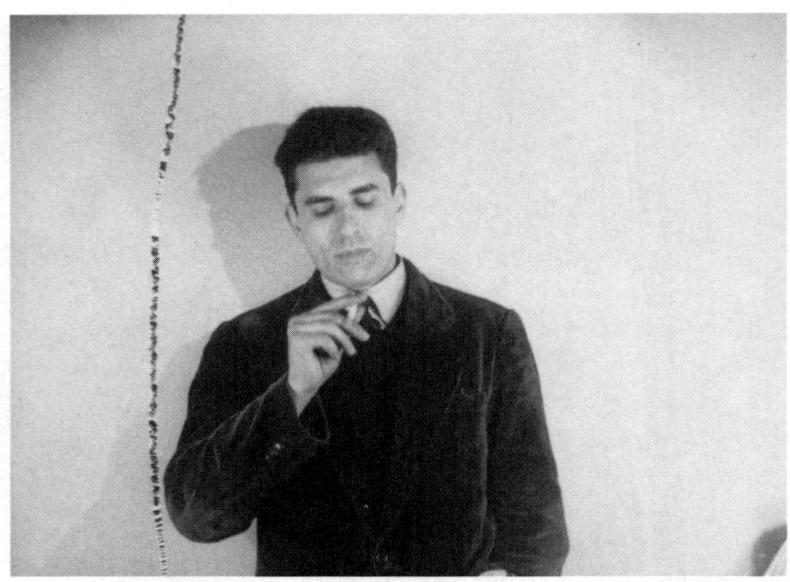

Maurice Lemaître in *Traité de bave et d'éternité*.

Isou was totally indifferent to such views and returned home to Paris in triumph. Once back in the capital, he announced a full screening of the 'finished' film (now four hours in length) on 23 May at the prestigious Musée de l'Homme, overseen by the well-known film writer Armand Cauliez, and then followed by a full week of screenings at the Studio d'Étoile near the Champs-Élysées. The film was advertised as featuring the distinguished actor Jean-Louis Barrault and Jean Cocteau, both of whom, needless to say, had nothing to do with it. Cocteau was, however, persuaded to design the poster for this Paris screening.

The Paris press was, like the audiences in Cannes, mostly baffled or enraged by the film. A headline in the pages of *Le Figaro* read: 'Applause, booing and insults greet the film of Isidore Isou.' Most of the reviews were unrelentingly negative, noting the film's relentless 'verbal delirium' and that 'at five minutes you laugh; at ten minutes you are bored; at twenty minutes you leave.' The far-Right journal *Rivarol* did not bother with film criticism, delivering a straightforward antisemitic insult, describing him as 'a little Jew called Isidore Jewel' (*Bijou*) and saying that the film was no more than desperate self-promotion.

There were others in that first audience who were, however, paying attention to Isou. Among those who came to see the film were Alain Resnais, Chris Marker and Jean-Luc Godard, all soon to become luminaries of the *Nouvelle Vague* – a film movement whose aesthetic values were

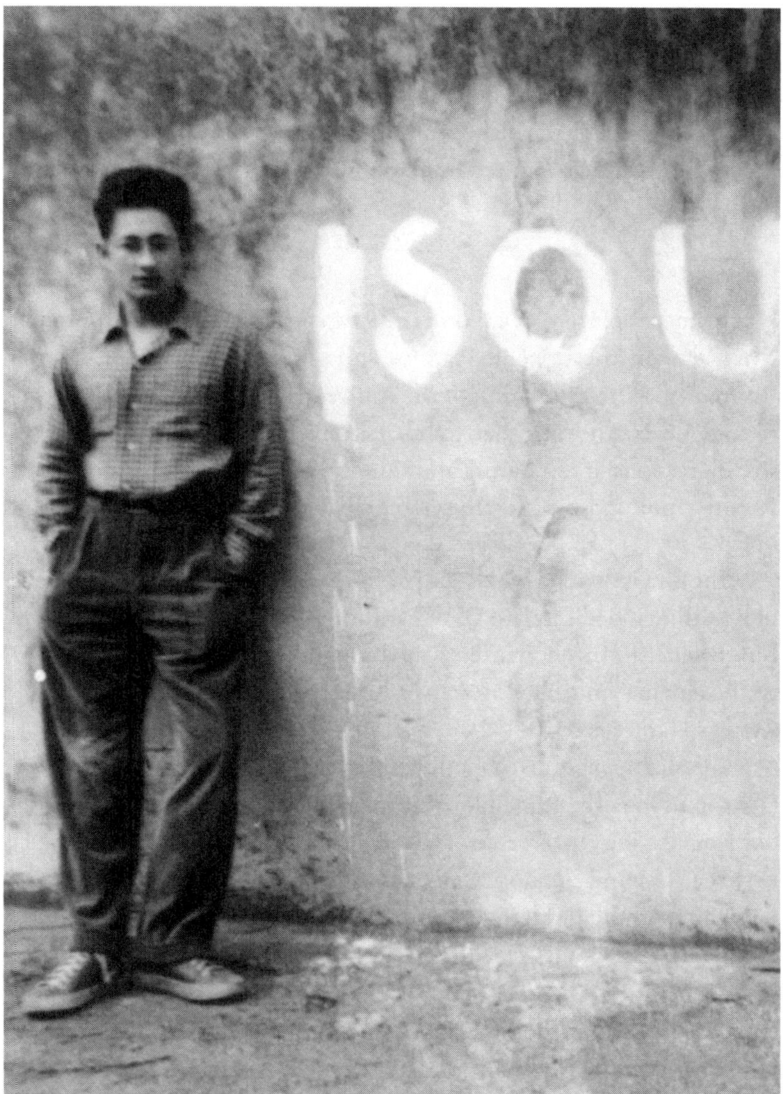

Guy Debord in Cannes, 1951.

often mirrored by *lettriste* theories on alienating the spectator. Jean-Luc Godard and the painter Yves Klein were also impressed enough by the film to attend and take part in various *lettriste* meetings.

A sympathetic review was even published in the *Cahiers du Cinéma* – the bible of the *Nouvelle Vague* – by a certain Maurice Schérer, which was the pseudonym of Éric Rohmer, soon to be another leading light in the *Nouvelle Vague*. Rohmer mocked Isou's ambitions and pretentions but he also recognized that this was a serious and innovative work. He admired the 'provocative variety of tone' in the film and the care taken with every shot. He concluded: 'It is my duty to say that the first chapter, in which we see Isou walking on the Boulevard Saint-Germain, "hooked" me a thousand times more than the best non-commercial films I have ever seen.' Most of all, Rohmer admired Isou's 'desire to see things as they really are'.[15]

———

Not many people have seen *Traité de bave et d'éternité* since the moment when it won the prize at Cannes and entered French film history. Rohmer and the generation of the *Nouvelle Vague* were right, however, to recognize at the time that, for all its convoluted arguments and obsessive digressions, it is a daring and innovative work – all the more so, as Rohmer pointed out, for the fierce dislocations between sound and image.

The film is divided into three parts. The opening sequence announces that the film is dedicated to D. W. Griffith, Abel Gance, Sergei Eisenstein, Luis Buñuel and other masters 'who brought something new or personal to the cinema' and then presents a brief panorama of Isou's published works so far.

The film then begins properly with the intertitle *Chapitre 1: Le Principe* (Chapter One: The Principle). The main protagonist is not Isou himself but Isou playing out the role of an alter ego called Daniel. Isou/Daniel is first seen leaving the doorway of a *ciné-club* on the Boulevard Saint-Germain and then walking, deep in thought, through the streets of the Left Bank. The soundtrack is the debate in the *ciné-club* which Isou/Daniel has left behind. As he walks out of the *ciné-club*, we hear Isou/Daniel compare himself to the Marquis de Sade, and especially Sade's demand for 'total freedom' to finally make the true Revolution. A man's voice answers: 'He's a Democrat! So, he must be a Jew!' A girl's voice calls on the crowd to 'smash his face in!'

There are several voices at work all at once. Behind everything there is the percussive sound poetry of a '*lettriste* choir' which falls and rises as the backdrop to the action, much in the tradition of a conventional orchestral movie soundtrack of the period. The voice of Isou/Daniel is played by Albert Legros, and a commentary delivered by Bernard Blin, both *lettristes*. The narrative moves back and forth in time. The conversations and monologues, accompanied by jazz music and *lettriste* chanting, rarely match the images on the screen (the soundtrack was also deliberately recorded on vinyl to give a rough, scratchy edge to the sound; as you watch the film, you can hear the needle crackling on the plastic).

After the opening section, the film is made up of 'found images' of Vietnam, Algiers, Paris, mainly from Pathé newsreels. These images have been scratched or deliberately damaged with scrawled 'hypergraphic' signs made by Isou or Maurice Lemaître. Isou called this the *cinéma discrépant*, a filmic practice where sound and image did not always meet. The vandalized figures were a form of 'chiselling' into the film, making the spectator aware of two things at once: that this is not real life, and that you can destroy the illusion of reality that cinema creates.

Running parallel to all of this is a third layer of narrative – a love story between Isou/Daniel and a girl called 'Eve'. Isou is imperious and magnificently handsome, particularly in still photographs wearing a long leather trench coat or fashionable and expensive suits. Eve is blonde, Nordic and beautiful: a pure Aryan. Eve and Isou/Daniel walk by the Seine and he says that if he has ever been rejected by a woman it is because she knew from his look, his dark complexion and thick lips that he was a Jew. He could not stop being a Jew, however, and did not want to be anything or anyone else. This was why he had to hate antisemites with such extreme passion; it was the only way of stopping them having any power over you; in this way Isou/Daniel says that he 'will never be a victim of history'.

He explains his philosophy of 'the perverse' to Eve. This is an art which he has again borrowed from the Marquis de Sade. He explains that, back in Bucharest, he could not understand why the French Ambassador's daughter, an elegant and refined blonde, preferred the oldest, smelliest cheeses – Roqueforts and old Camemberts – that revolted him. Then he understood that revulsion was just another form of desire, a higher form of desire in fact than mere love or lust. This was what it meant to have a higher palate – to want that which disgusted you.

This is why, he says, he understood why Sade ate the shit of his lover. Ultimately he loved her shit more than the woman herself. He loved what she had produced, what she had *created beyond herself*. This was how the artist too had to love his art; like shit or slime (*bave*) it was outside of himself; revolting but pure and his or her own creation. The concepts of ugliness and beauty were fictions to keep men and women in line and subservient to the lies of Christianity.

Like Nietzsche (here quoted by Isou) the *lettristes* were announcing a new set of values, a new morality. The key to understanding *lettriste* poetry was to remake the world in its own image rather than simply reflecting the world as beautiful or ugly, good or bad. When men (and women) had discovered this, that they too could themselves be creators, their own creations, they would discover also that they could walk with God as 'the companions of Creation'. This is the revelation, from Isou the Messiah, that ends the film.

This statement was also the culminating point of Isou's heroic period – the thousand-mile-an-hour acceleration which, in a few short years, had taken him from an obscure provincial town in Romania to the heights of French cultural life. He was still only 25 years old. What he did not know was that this exalted status would not last forever, or even for long.

thirteen

Traitors

In contrast to the intellectual confidence that had surged through the Left Bank in the immediate post-war period, the new mood in Paris through the early 1950s was one of uncertainty. This was mainly due to the various failures that were shaping French politics. The Fourth Republic, established in 1946, staggered from one crisis to another under a constitution that had hardly moved on from the 1930s. The French colonial empire was in the process of breaking up, and in Algeria there were the first stirrings of a war that would soon bring France to its knees. At the same time, as the Cold War hardened across Europe, the political divisions within France deepened.

This was nowhere more visible than in the famous public rows between Camus and Sartre, the great thinkers of the 1940s, who now separated over their political allegiances – Sartre to the Communist Party and Camus to a self-invented form of liberal humanism. Although intellectuals on the Left Bank still grappled with the great issues of the day, there was the sense that even the finest of them – including Camus and Sartre – were losing their way in the post-war order, which no one seemed to properly understand. It was already clear at the beginning of the 1950s that the freewheeling bohemian Left Bank life of the 1940s, where Isou's avant-garde antics had been nurtured and had made him famous, would soon be over for good.

In his journal of December 1951, Isou recorded that he was now becoming tired with the Left Bank, the place where he had made his name. His notoriety there was not 'real' fame, he wrote, but just noise and gossip about his adventures and activities. He was frustrated that no one seemed to understand he was just about to become a world figure, a world-historical hero.

The most recent proof of this, he noted, was a letter he had recently received from Japan enquiring about his 'activities'. He knew no one in Japan and obviously had never been there. But the good news of his message was travelling wide and fast. Saint-Germain-des-Prés would soon be merely an irrelevant stopping post on his global conquest. He complained too that it was now becoming overcrowded, packed with gawping, foreign tourists. The so-called intellectuals – Sartre, Gide, Mauriac and all the rest of them – reminded him of walking corpses, all getting ready to dig their own graves.[1]

———

Inspired by the success in Cannes and bolstered by the backing of Cocteau and others, Isou and Lemaître decided to concentrate *lettriste* activity away from literature and into the cinema. This was a way of reaching a wider audience beyond the late-night clubs and impromptu poetry sessions. Most importantly, however, Isou had decided that the cinema, like poetry, had reached the end of its *amplic* phase. By this he meant that 'the cinema of Hollywood had exceeded itself' and was now reaching the period of its inevitable decadence. This condemnation did not stop Isou himself from enjoying the movies: he went several times a week to the cinema to see films, Hollywood or not, and enjoyed not only the sexual pleasures of going there with girls but was a fan of the directors Orson Welles and John Ford among others.

Although Hollywood was the enemy, his real targets were more local and at hand. These were the *ciné-clubs* of Paris, centred mainly on the Left Bank. In the pre-television era the *ciné-clubs* were not only a popular and inexpensive form of entertainment but had a massive audience. The idea behind them was that their members paid a subscription to see all manner of films, including non-commercial cinema as well as Hollywood movies. They were generally owned and run by local town councils.

The *ciné-clubs* were also important in rural France, where the main cinema chains – Pathé or Gaumont – did not go, and they were often central to the cultural life of a town or village. At one stage their membership numbered 100,000 across 150 clubs throughout France. Most of them were, however, clustered in Paris and other big cities, where they were an integral part of youth culture.[2] Isou hated this official domestication of the energy and rebelliousness of youth – the qualities which he thought were essential for the coming Revolution to be made by the *lettriste* 'Youth Front'. He wrote: 'We must always finish with the word *tomorrow*.'[3]

The new offensive against the cinema was launched with the screening of Maurice Lemaître's film *Le Film est déjà commencé?* (Has the Film Already Started?). This was shown for the first time in Paris in November at Le Musée de l'Homme, followed by its 'official' premiere at the Ciné-Club du Quartier Latin at the Cluny Palace on the Boulevard Saint-Germain on 7 December 1951.

Both performances involved no less than Maurice Lemaître himself cutting through the screen with a knife at approximately 47 minutes in. This was accompanied by a *lettriste* chorus and a voice-over which states that this act is the beginning of 'a mass of cinematographic inventions' as the abstract scenes filmed on camera flap around wildly, tattered and torn but still there, tinted orange, pink, red or green; the photographs, moving images or designs seeming like a living painting.

Isou claimed that this was 'le premier film en relief vivant' (the first film with living sculpted relief).[4] Unsurprisingly, Lemaître had dedicated the film to Isou, who was prophet of all that would come next. Isou, for his part, had already agreed that this was the only true second *lettriste* film, the worthy successor to his own *Traité de bave et d'eternité*.

Lemaître also described this film as *cinéma ciselant*, applying the *lettriste* method of chiselling words and images 'down to the bone', to their component parts. In the voice-over he described himself as 'one of the most cynical men alive'; this was not, he said, a film, but the 'performance of the cinema', which was turned into a three-dimensional art happening with 'interventions' taking place through the cinema itself, from the lobby to the showing-room. This was not the flat representation of reality, which was normally what the cinema showed, but an experience, a lived situation, which had no natural meaning or conclusion. *Le Film est déjà commencé?* was not conceived of as a film but more like a 1960s 'happening', described by Lemaître as *syncinéma*.

As such it mirrored reality more closely than 'film' ever could. The 'performance' ended with the 'interventionists' and indeed the film-maker himself, Maurice Lemaître, being kicked out of the cinema by the police. They did not go easily, and the 'performance' soon became a near-riot. There was of course nothing new in this. Avant-gardists had been using the cinema as a deliberate form of provocation since its invention, culminating in 1930 with the 'scandal' around the showing of Luis Buñuel and Salvador Dalí's film *L'Age d'or*, which was interrupted by violent Right-wingers objecting to its depraved and corrupt morality; a view that entirely satisfied the film-makers' desire to cause trouble and gain publicity. Unfortunately for Isou and Lemaître, *Le Film est déjà commencé?* was met mainly by critical indifference.

Among those who had been totally impressed, however, was Guy Debord, who had finally made it to Paris in September 1951. Debord's first friendship there was with a fellow *lettriste* he had met in Cannes who was called Marc'O (and whose real name was Marc-Gilbert Guillaumin). Marc'O had been an ardent *lettriste* since his first encounters with the group in Le Tabou. He was one of the youngest members of the *lettriste* movement but he was physically tough and obdurate; he had been a *résistant* and *maquisard*, fighting undercover in the *maquis*, the harsh countryside in the Auvergne, and had been seriously injured there in a shoot-out with the Germans. It was Marc'O who helped Debord find his first lodgings in Paris and brokered his first meetings with Isou.[5]

Debord planned to rent a room for 9,000 francs per month in the same hotel as Isou. They read parts of *L'Agrégation* together and Debord was totally convinced that Isou was the Messiah. He wrote to his friend Falcou – then Debord's best friend outside Paris – that he thought that, after a discussion with Isou that lasted five hours, he had met in Isou a young god. Debord declared that he was ready to 'throw himself out of the window' for Isou. Debord was less keen, however, to follow Isou's orders to go and beat up a well-known thief on the Left Bank who had robbed Gabriel Pomerand. This was on the grounds, Debord admitted to himself, of 'pure cowardice'.[6]

Debord had been in Paris less than a month when Marc'O invited him to contribute to a new *lettriste* journal called *Ion*, whose first issue was to be dedicated to the cinema. The opening essay was to be by Isou and called 'The Aesthetics of Cinema'; it argued that the destruction, or 'chiselling down', of cinema would herald a new civilization of vision rather than image.

Debord's written contributions to *Ion* were an essay and an outline for a *lettriste* film which were entirely in keeping with what he had learned from Isou so far. 'The decomposition of the cinema', wrote Debord, would simply be a prelude to 'displacement of the values of creation towards the spectator'. The planned film would be a paring down of language which would 'destroy the cinema' by breaking it down to it constitutive elements. Isou helped Debord plan the film and worked on ways of improving it with him.

Debord's other contribution to *Ion* is a photograph taken in June 1951 to mark his completion of the baccalauréat, which he had celebrated with a fake funeral Mass card. In this photo, Debord, wearing a sports jacket and a polo shirt, the most stylish clothes of the period, leans back against a wall, slightly away from the camera. Most importantly, borrowing the technique of using purposely damaged film from Marc'O and Isou, Debord has reshot the original photograph to blur and destroy the image. The idea was to signal the beginning of an offensive led by Debord against the cinema.

In the meantime Isou had put Debord to work by enlisting him to promote *Traité de bave et d'eternité*. In an insult thoroughly approved of by Isou, Debord wrote to the film critic Simone Dubreuilh, who had the cheek to criticize the film in the pages of *Libération*, 'I read your review of Jean-Isidore Isou in *Libération*, but you are horrible to look at and so you shouldn't put your big feet into intellectual questions.'[7]

Isou was also reassured by the fact that Jean Cocteau had telephoned him several times to tell him that there was nothing else like *lettrisme* in Paris and that, most importantly, the showing of *lettriste* films like *Traité de bave et d'eternité* was always at least 'an event', loaded with 'atmosphere' and thus was the direct opposite of the dry and boring premieres of the latest neo-Realist Italian or Russian movies. Cocteau and Isou could often be seen together in the Café de Flore or Les Deux Magots.

Notwithstanding, through the early part of 1952, the *lettristes* continued to cause trouble in the world of French cinema. In April a *lettriste* commando team, without Isou but with his blessing (and with Guy Debord in their number), set out once again to the Cannes Film Festival with three films: *L'Anticoncept* (The Anti-concept) by Gil Wolman, *La Barque de la vie courante* (Navigating Modern Life) by Jean-Louis Brau and *Le Tambour du jugement dernier* (The Drum of the Last Judgement) by François Dufrêne. The festival organizers were by now well-informed in advance about the *lettriste* hooligans and managed to defuse potentially difficult situations by refusing entry to anybody in the *lettriste* number who had been recognized from the previous year, or who had not been able to pass themselves off as journalists or film producers.

Incensed by this, a group of twenty or so *lettristes* attacked the press office where tickets were being handed out. The struggle was violent, the police were called, but eventually the *lettristes* were kicked out. Eleven *lettristes* were arrested. To make matters worse (from the *lettriste* point of view), the French press decided that they had seen all of this the year before and chose to maintain a bored silence in the face of *lettriste* provocations. Back in Paris, Isou fumed at the media blackout, but was glad that he had not been personally humiliated in Cannes.

Lettriste anger was also fuelled by the fact that, earlier in April, the French government had effectively banned Wolman's film *L'Anticoncept*. The film had already been premiered at the Musée de l'Homme in February and was one of the most extreme *lettriste* statements yet, stretching Isou's concept of the negation of art to the limit. Wolman did this by projecting an alternate sequence of black and white circles onto a barrage balloon. Seventy minutes of this visual torture was accompanied by a text which Wolman read aloud as a featureless drone. The text began as meaningless babble, language 'chiselled down' in *Isouien* terms, and hypnotically took on a mysterious meaning for those in the audience who had come armed with hashish, booze or ether.

The French censorship board, the Commission de Contrôle des Films Cinématographique, did not like any of this at all and was fairly sure that anything which brought together such a drunk or drugged rabble on the Left Bank, and indeed anything associated with the known pornographer and megalomaniac Isidore Isou was not in the best interests of the Republic. No reason was given for banning *L'Anticoncept* other than the word *interdit*. The film is actually officially banned to this day. Most bizarrely, but also much to their amusement, the *lettristes* found themselves listed alongside American-made primitive porn classics such as *Behind the Green Door*, *The Dirty Girls* and *A Bedroom Fantasy*, as well as Italian-made fascist propaganda and other corrupting material. The failed *lettriste* assault on Cannes in 1952 had been an attempt to right this wrong.

The greatest threat to Isou in 1952 did not come from the French authorities, however, but from within his own ranks. This was from Guy Debord, who had by now evolved from Isou's devoted disciple and propagandist into his deadliest rival.

The beginning of the break between Isou and Debord was the screening on 30 June 1952 of Debord's first film *Hurlements en faveur de Sade* (Howling in Favour of Sade). The title of the film was most likely an appropriation from Georges Bataille, who had originally given his early essay on Salvador Dalí, 'Le Jeu Lugubre' (The Lugubrious Game), the title 'Hurlement en faveur de Dalí'. The visual content of *Hurlements en faveur de Sade* begins with a blank white screen that turns black; the film was only twenty minutes or so of flickering nothingness. When the screen went black at the end, there was silence. At the first screening of the film,

Debord and fellow conspirators had hidden themselves on the balcony with bags of flour, which they proceeded to drop on the audience. The end of the film was to be a piercing scream, let loose by Debord's girlfriend Michèle Bernstein, who claimed to have a voice that could break glass and who was literally howling in favour of Sade.

This first screening of Debord's film was, however, a damp squib. It began badly with the audience members hurling abuse at the blank screen. In the end, after all Debord's grand planning, nothing had happened. Worse still, Isou and Lemaître had not attended the screening and made no defence of the film, claiming loftily that it was of no interest to them. Marc'O, who was already cold-shouldering Debord, slipped quietly into the shadows. Debord was being taught to know his place and learn *lettriste* discipline. He returned to Cannes to lick his wounds and start again.

From Cannes Debord wrote to Isou, accusing him of treason. For a few days, Isou ignored the letter before responding with a critique of the film, which he said plagiarized his own work, and stating that he had originally wanted to introduce the film but Debord hadn't asked him to. Anyway, Isou said, the film was so badly done that it undermined all the victories that the *lettristes* had won so far. Plagiarism was not innovation or creation; Debord should have known this before he started making the film.[8]

Within days of hearing this, Debord had decided to cast Isou aside and found his own movement, which would obliterate the 'cult of Isou-worship' while taking *lettrisme* to a new, more advanced level. During a trip to Brussels in July 1952 (ostensibly to help with the showing of *Traité de bave et d'eternité* in the Belgian capital), with Gil Wolman as his chief lieutenant, Debord secretly founded a group which he called the Internationale Lettriste. This was to be the 'extreme Left Wing' of the *lettriste* movement. In a parallel movement, Marc'O had set up a rival group of *lettristes* called the *externalistes* – they aimed at 'actions', such as the planned assault on Notre-Dame, rather than art, and thought of themselves as the public face of the group.

At first there was a level of cooperation between the three groups: Isou thought that he was really still in control and that such sectarianism was only natural in new movements. But Debord was pulling further and further away, muttering that Isou was out of control and mad.

Isou was stunned. His moods started to grow even wilder, from vowing violent revenge on Debord to finally comparing Debord to a neo-Nazi and his followers to the kind of vermin who blindly followed leaders towards murder and destruction (Isou claimed that he was in fact the first person to use the term 'neo-Nazi', and that this was in reference to Debord). Debord was an antisemite, but not just an antisemite: he was the most evil kind of assassin, aiming to wipe Isou out of history.

Maurice Lemaître remained faithful and unperturbed, convinced that none of the breakaway factions could even begin to understand the genius that was Isou, and were therefore doomed to failure. Throughout the summer of 1952 he quietly steered Isou towards his vocation, which was to make art and change the world with his art. Isou was never placated – his anger at this betrayal burned for several decades in fact – but he refused to lower himself to even admitting these factions were any kind of real rivals.

Debord's faction was greedy for attention, however, and desperate to make their mark outside the Left Bank. The chance came on 29 October 1952. The occasion was a press conference called by Charlie Chaplin at the Ritz Hotel in Paris.

Chaplin was on the French leg of a world tour and had called the conference to thank the French government for awarding him the Légion d'Honneur. Having been denounced in the United States (then in its most McCarthyite phase), Chaplin had come to Europe to promote his latest film *Limelight* and found himself banned from re-entering the United States, branded as a 'Communist' and 'fellow traveller' for sympathizing with the political movement. On his arrival in Paris, Chaplin found himself the darling of the French press and a cultural hero to the anti-American Left. In the clamour outside the Ritz, as Chaplin was deafened by the cheers and applause of an adoring crowd, Serge Berna and Guy Debord charged forwards and blocked the entrance to the hotel, as Gil Wolman and Jean-Louis Brau darted through police lines, shrieking insults at Chaplin and throwing pamphlets over the heads of the crowd.

The pamphlet was entitled 'NO MORE FLAT FEET!' Its main charge against Chaplin was that his films were a form of 'emotional blackmail' and his sentimental worldview robbed the oppressed of the urge to rebel. For this, he was described as a 'fascist insect'. In Chaplin's famous rattan cane, Debord and his cohorts claimed to see 'the nightstick of a cop'. Poverty, however, was no joke. 'For us, the young and beautiful,' screamed the pamphlet, 'the only end to suffering is revolution.'[9]

An hour or so after the 'action', Isou, not quite understanding the nature of the Internationale Lettriste, commended them as exemplars of revolutionary intervention. He changed his mind, however, during a

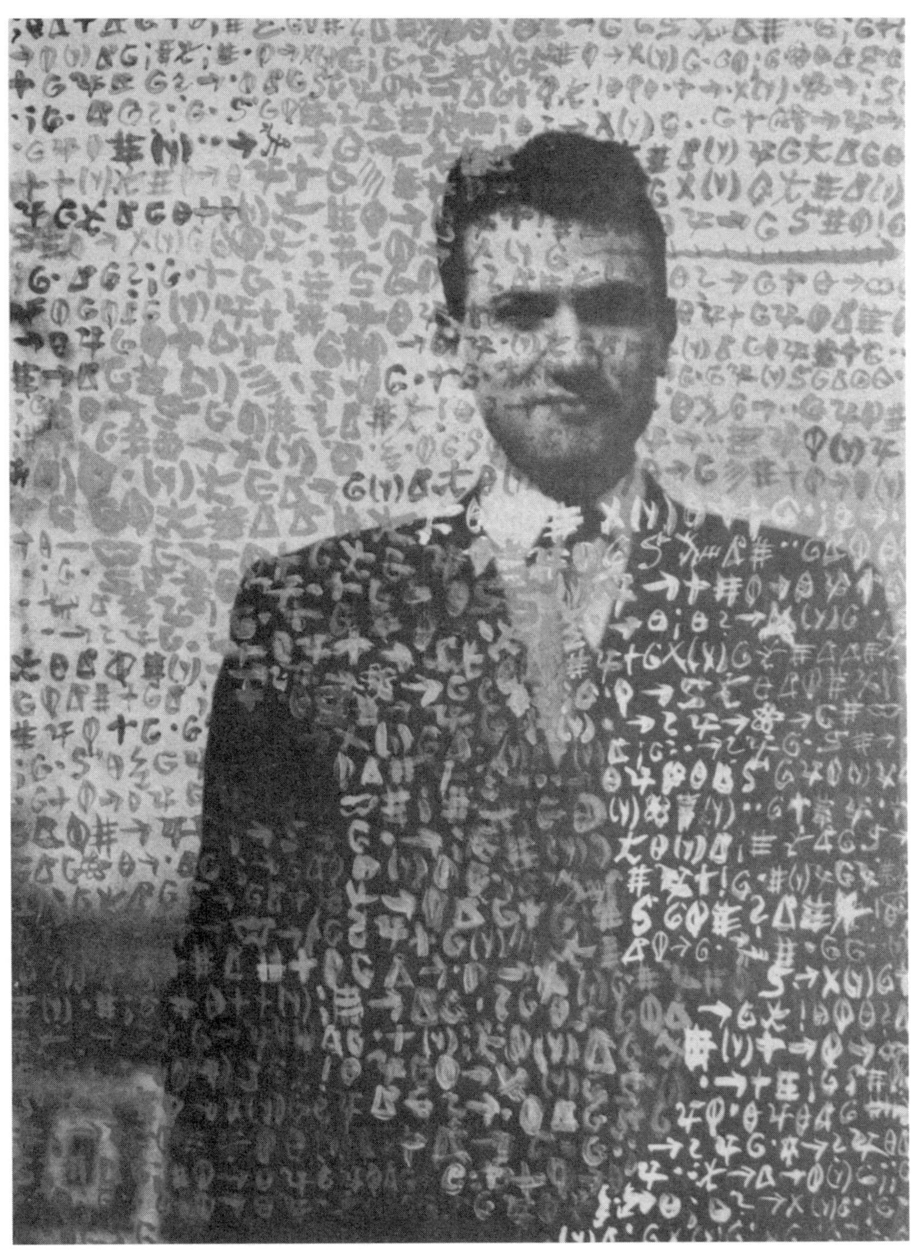

Isidore Isou, *Self-portrait*, 1952, lacquer pencil on photography.

meeting with other *lettristes* who convened the next day to prepare a public statement. Most importantly Isou now grasped that the attack on Chaplin was also an attempt to destabilize his authority. In a letter published in *Combat* on 31 October, Isou denounced the Internationale Lettriste as being 'extreme and confused in content'.

The Internationale Lettriste fired back, with open letters sent to *Combat* (but never published). Jean-Louis Brau wrote to Isou accusing him of 'meanness and childish cowardice', adding that the 'nullity of your personality is compensated for by the Great Work, but your route towards an initiatory mysticism and the deep imbecility of some of your disciples has a disgusting stench which sickens me.' For Guy Debord, Isidore Isou was now to be destroyed.

Isou did not lack physical courage. Debord, in contrast, was not physically brave although he did like to cultivate a reputation as a tough guy. At this stage, he had already started his lifelong habit of being accompanied by 'minders' – in this case two hard-nut Algerians who went along with him for free drinks and the promise of trouble. When Isou next crossed Debord's path in Paris, a few weeks after the initial arguments, Isou paid no heed to the Algerians, took off his glasses, and flew at Debord, battering him into the ground. Debord was left bleeding and bruised.

The bitterness between the two men would last for decades. Debord was vengeful, with all the spite of a disappointed lover. He declared to his fellow comrades in the Internationale Lettriste, 'It is as if Jean-Isidore was nothing to us.' In a registered letter to Isou, meant to cause maximum anger and hurt, he wrote: 'You know that you're a failure . . . Your looks are now gone, so you won't be able to even make a good marriage.' Debord wrote to a mutual friend that he had often seen Isou in the morning at the Café Bonaparte, reading *Le Monde*, alone and deserted by his friends.[10]

This was not quite true. Although Debord had taken with him some gifted and dedicated artists, Isou was still the better known of them all, and still attracting sponsorship (and glamorous women). Isou was, however, shocked by this great betrayal. He had always known that as the Messiah it was inevitable that he would be betrayed; but when it really happened it felt unreal, 'cold and brutal', as if he was no longer in control of his world.

Isou soon recovered from Debord's attack, however, and continued with an unstoppable pace of work. His activities included his first solo exhibition called 'Les Nombres' (The Numbers) at the Galerie Palmes, which took place in late 1953 and consisted of 36 'hypergraphics'. He followed this up with forays into the theatre, first of all with a text called *Fondements pour la transformation intégrale du théâtre* (Foundations for the Integral Transformation of the Theatre).

This text was of course ignored and left unread by most theatre critics and practitioners, even though many of Isou's ideas were close to those of Antonin Artaud, whose theory of the 'Theatre of Cruelty' had great prestige in post-war Paris and who was now considered one of the most influential thinkers on the theatre in France. Undeterred by critical indifference to his theories, Isou went ahead with plans for the then 22-year-old Jacques Polieri to direct his first play, *La Marche des jongleurs* (March of the Acrobats). Polieri would go on to become one of the most prominent actors, directors and theoreticians in French theatre, but at this stage he was an outsider, like Isou, and admired Isou for the ferocity of his arguments as much for his dramatic skill.

Mainly due to Polieri's persistence, *La Marche des jongleurs* premiered on 19 January 1954 at the tiny Théâtre de Poche in Montparnasse. The play ran for six weeks, finishing in disarray with the three actors in the play left unpaid and Isou claiming that they didn't know how to read their lines. The script called for actors – two men and a woman – to dance, take off their clothes, read a newspaper. The problem was that none of them could decipher Isou's phonetic poetry to Isou's satisfaction. This poetry was the whole point of the play and was to be read aloud as Isou's one and only film was projected onto the set behind them.

Isou was, however, pleased that on the posters for the play his name had appeared in bold, black capitals above – and much larger than – the play's title. Critical reception was muted or confused. None of this stopped the unflagging Polieri inviting Isou and his crew a year or so later to theatre festivals in Marseilles and Avignon.

Despite the painful betrayal by Debord, Isou's star was still on the rise in the first half of the decade. The Italians in particular were impressed by the 'new Da Vinci' who was described as 'il papa del lettrismo' (The Pope of *Lettrisme*) in the *Gazzetta del Popolo*, a progressive Leftist newspaper based in Turin, and approving reviews of his work appeared in magazines and journals, painting him as a leading poet and painter on the Left Bank of Paris.

This status was confirmed in April 1955 when Isou made his first (and only) appearance on British television. This was in a documentary called *Around the World with Orson Welles*, part of a six-part travelogue written,

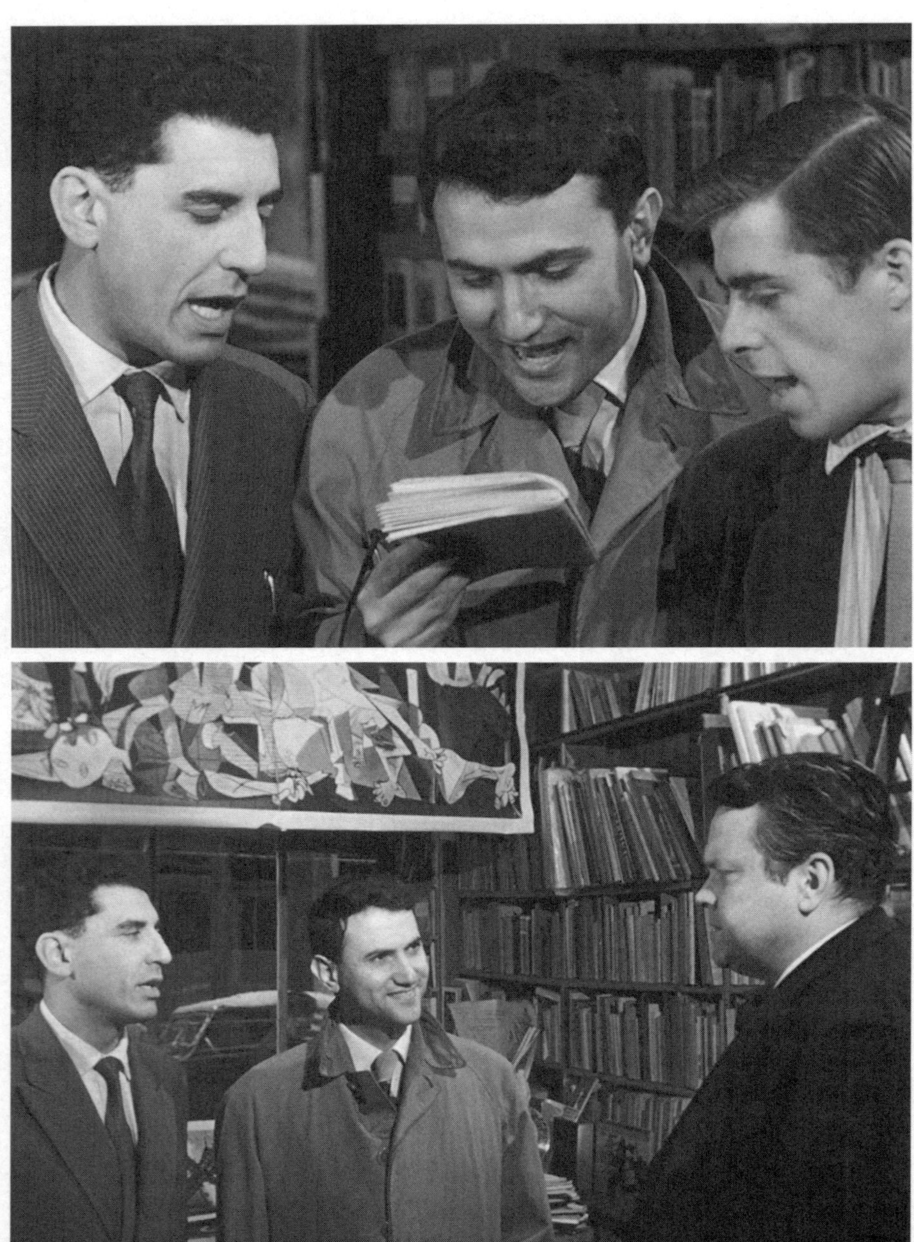

Maurice Lemaître, Isou and Jacques Spacagna with Orson Welles in 'St Germain des Prés', the fourth episode of the documentary series *Around the World with Orson Welles* (1955).

directed and presented by Welles and commissioned by the newly launched ITV network in Britain. Other programmes in the series featured Kenneth Tynan and Welles at a bullfight in Madrid or Welles retracing his travels in Vienna. Isou (and Maurice Lemaître) appeared in the fourth programme of the series, which was about the eccentric denizens of Saint-Germain des-Prés.

These included the American poet, sculptor and philosopher Raymond Duncan, brother of the dancer Isadora Duncan, who appeared in a home-made tunic and sandals, explaining his philosophy of artistic creation and self-sufficiency. Other Left Bank characters who appeared in the film were Juliette Gréco, Simone de Beauvoir and Jean Cocteau, then just about to be elected to the Académie Française, and – much to Isou's ire – Gabriel Pomerand (who appeared in segments filched by Welles from the documentary *Le Désordre* when Welles ran out of material for his own documentary; he did the same with the images of Cocteau, Gréco and Beauvoir).

The *lettristes* are filmed in the Librairie Fischbacher, a bookshop specializing in art which dates back to 1872. The film begins with shots of the veteran journalist Art Buchwald – then a young rookie writer based in Paris – typing out his column, called 'Paris after Dark', for the *International Herald Tribune*. This was basically a gossipy running commentary on salacious goings-on in bohemian late-night Paris. He introduces the 'Letterists', as he calls them, writing that this is the latest form of poetic expression which needs to be 'heard to be believed'. The film then cuts to a trio of smartly dressed *lettristes* led by Isou chanting a poem.

Lemaître then goes on to explain the main theories of *lettrisme* to Welles in perfectly fluent English – 'each sound has strength,' he says. At this point Welles, usually more than a match for his interviewees, seems confused and looks around in bafflement as Lemaître describes the *lettriste* alphabet. Lemaître then snorts and makes other noises with his mouth to make clear what he means. This is followed by Isou, smirking, reading out the poem 'Neiges' (Snows) from his collection *Dix poèmes magnifiques* (Ten Magnificent Poems), beginning: 'Khneï Khneï thncapata thnacapata, Eï, Eï, thagahaté thagahaté'.

Both Welles and the audience had no idea whether the *lettristes* were for real, or whether they were mocking Welles's credulity. In the end, none of this mattered. They had appeared on international television with a famous personality and brought *lettrisme* to the world. Isou was an admirer of Welles – he even thought of him as a kind of hero, a creator in the lineage of Joyce or Picasso – but he was pleased that in the encounter it was clearly he, the genius Isou, who had the upper hand over the hitherto greatest film-maker in the world. At this point in his career, Isou still thought that he was untouchable, destined for immortality, and driven in the best way by a mind on fire.

fourteen

A Letter from Gaza
and a Marriage in Paris

Prompted by the encouragement of his Jewish friends and colleagues in Paris (who at this time included the young journalist Elie Wiesel) Isou was keen to see what the Promised Land really looked like. Isou was ambiguous about Israel – he had long discussions with his family about living in Israel or the United States but thought of Paris as his true home and headquarters. He still thought of himself as a Zionist and was enthusiastic about the establishment of Israel. But he was also worried that the Jews were only there because they had given in to the Gentiles, and that as long as Israel existed as the Jewish homeland the Gentile Europeans would never have to face up to their true role in the Holocaust. It was a country built on the guilt of the Gentiles as much as the Jewish religion.

In the end he went principally to see his parents and Fanny, who had moved there as soon as they could after the war. From 1948 onwards, the Romanian government had allowed 4,000 Romanian Jews a month to leave Romania, partly because the World Jewish Agency had paid a huge bribe to the now communist Romanian government. In all some 115,000 Romanian Jews moved to Israel, many of them supported by the Israeli government with special funds to compensate businessmen who had been made 'economically redundant' by the war.

The Goldsteins settled in Be'er Sheva, one of the most southerly towns in Israel, only 40 kilometres (25 mi.) or so from Gaza. Although Be'er Sheva had been conceded as Arab territory under the 1948 agreement which established Israel, it lay safely within Israeli borders, having been seized from Egypt in October 1948.

By the time that the Goldsteins arrived there it was already being built into a new town, soon to become a city, made up of raw-looking housing projects designed on the European model. It was in one of these developments that the Goldsteins settled around 1950. When Isou finally visited in the early 1950s, Be'er Sheva still had a Bedouin population, along with a picturesque old town and a weekly camel market, but it now also had, however, a new Jewish population of some 25,000, and growing daily. Although it was surrounded by desert and still physically for now not much different from its biblical origins, Isou felt at home in this population; despite being mostly non-European – the population of Jews were mainly from Tunisia, Algeria, France and Morocco – French was widely spoken and French speakers treated with great respect.

Isou was surprised, and slightly annoyed because of jealousy, that Fanny had found herself a husband, a high-ranking officer in Israeli military intelligence. Isou still thought he was, or should be, the most important male in her life. He ignored or mocked his recently acquired brother-in-law, arguing to himself that because he was an artist, he had higher status than the highest military officers. Nonetheless, the intelligence officer and brother-in-law, largely to please Fanny, offered to take the quarrelsome and arrogant Isou to visit nearby Gaza from Be'er Sheva during one of his visits in the late autumn of 1956.[1]

Gaza had only just been captured and occupied by Israel and it was hard to imagine a more highly charged time to visit the territory. Until 1956 Gaza had effectively been occupied and administered by the Egyptians, although the Egyptians had maintained a hard border (making life much harder for the Palestinian refugees who had flooded into the territory after 1948). The Israelis attacked Gaza as part of the general offensive launched against Nasser's Egypt by Israel and an Anglo-French Expeditionary Force in response to Nasser's nationalization of the Suez Canal. Gaza was one of the front lines in this mini-war. Only a few weeks before Isou's visit there were rumours of a massacre perpetrated by the Israelis at the Egyptian garrison town of Khan Yanis, a short distance from the Gaza–Egypt border.

Isou wrote an account about his adventures in Be'er Sheva and Gaza at war in the Franco-Jewish journal *L'Arche*, published on 1 January 1957. *L'Arche* was founded and directed by Michel Salomon, who was roughly the same age as Isou. Salomon had little patience with Isou, remembering him even into his old age as 'an unfunny jester, such a pain in the arse'.[2]

Although there is no *lettriste* theory or extrapolation in Isou's essay, it also offers no analysis or journalistic commentary. It is simply a first-hand account in real time of what he saw and felt there. Isou begins by describing how his sister Fanny had long wanted to visit 'Aza', the Hebrew name for Gaza. This was, he said, because she was basically a snob and always wanted to be ahead of fashion; so she wanted to see Gaza as a day out by the sea in much the same way that Parisians enjoyed a day-trip to Deauville.

Fanny woke Isou up early one morning to announce that they were going to Gaza. He was then greeted by his brother-in-law, wearing a broad smile and carrying himself with all the adventurous gait 'of a Malraux character'. They got into a military jeep, drove to the local barracks and picked up two more soldiers, and then set off on the road to Gaza. 'The sun was shredding the countryside,' wrote Isou, 'and the road spurted off in a straight line and the only thing you could make out was the waves of dried mud, gathered up like ancient scrolls.' This was the border of ancient Israel, Isou was told by one of the military men.

Isou had by now also managed to irritate his military companions. He had been informed that one of the men had just been promoted to sub-lieutenant from the ranks, a rare honour. The promotion had been awarded because the man had carried a wounded comrade on his back for more than 7 kilometres (4 mi.). Isou remarked that this was not a remarkable feat and that you could see such 'meagre gestures of courage' every day in war films in the cinema. It was nothing. Isou said that he had earned the right to say this because he was an artist and a genius whose station was far more elevated than that of lowly soldiers. Isou's travelling companions described him to his face as *Schwitzer* – an Israeli Yiddish term meaning pain in the ass.

Isou's first impression of Gaza, when they arrived after several hours of fractious travel, was that it was a filthy place, hardly worth capturing. It was Oriental and squalid, like the dirtiest and poorest parts of Botoşani but worse: 'women were veiled in dirty habits and had scrofulous legs on show – proof of the lamentable and backward race they belonged to.' The Israeli soldiers, in contrast, erect and shining with cleanliness and purity, were like classical statues, markers of a higher civilization.

They drove past a Muslim cemetery and were assailed by children selling cigarettes or 'the sweetmeats called *rabat-loukoum*'. Isou noted that the *rabat-loukoum* came in tins adorned with the smiling face of Nasser. 'To a Parisian,' Isou remarked haughtily, referring of course to himself, 'the whole scene was rather sordid.' He was now looking at the East through the eyes of someone from the West.

They moved on to the Great Mosque of Gaza in the Old City. Isou noted only the crenellated minaret and that it had been built on the site of an ancient Jewish temple, rumoured to be the burial place of Samson. The surrounding Old City was not in the slightest picturesque or of any interest to Isou. He wrote: 'Horrible streets seem to have been locked into misery and poverty for all eternity. There were children in dirty clothes playing barefoot; old men with bleary eyes, with the body and head covered in a robe and complicated turbans, sat on the dusty floor.' Isou declared that he was shocked by all of this.

Later, Fanny introduced Isou to an aide of Sgan Aluf Haim Gaon, the present governor of Gaza (Sgan Aluf is roughly equivalent to the rank of lieutenant colonel), who addressed him in an Israeli Hebrew, which Isou did not understand. He nodded his way through the conversation, watching from the corner of his eye a man driving an ass which had floppy ears like a rabbit. 'This is such a great pleasure,' said Fanny to the group but no one in particular. 'We had been told that the *fedayim* (Palestinian or Egyptian soldiers) would kill us if we came here. But instead I feel as if we have won the whole town.'

The governor showed them around his residence, which until recently had been the palace of Mohamed Fuad el Djnali, the Egyptian governor who was now a prisoner of the Israeli army. They marvelled at the luxury but also the emptiness of the place. They also shivered at the massed bottles of potassium cyanide, which looked like salt and were meant for the Jews, poisoning their water.

They went down to the beach, via the '*quartier chic*' where they were introduced to a woman, high in politics, who looked to Isou like a cross between Gina Lollobrigida and Marilyn Monroe. She led the party to the beach, where they were stopped by Israeli soldiers and asked for their papers.

Isou walked away from the group down by the sea; he thought of the indifference of the sea and the sky to the activities of humankind. The sea, he thought, was like 'a fleeing belly button, explaining nothing of the smooth belly in which it lies'. His thoughts became ever more poetic: 'this was like a belly smooth with happy harvest, hidden abundances, suns of salt and drunken runaways, secret engines hardly making a murmur.'

A few moments later, as he turned to leave Gaza, Isou regretted the mad exultation of his thoughts, 'which had neither the finesse of reptiles or the eternity of the sky'. As the jeep left to go back to Be'er Sheva, passing through more military checkpoints, now within range of Egyptian artillery, he spied in the near distance a young Jewish woman, no more than a girl, preparing an evening meal for her *Kibbutz*. The girl looked totally unlike the Arabs; more like a sturdy, rosy-cheeked peasant in a Viennese comedy, thought Isou to himself. Isou regretted that he didn't speak enough of the local Hebrew to get down from the jeep and make love to her, right there and then, in the encroaching half-darkness of the surrounding desert.

This trip to Be'er Sheva was only one of many that Isou would make to Israel. This early visit was, however, one of his most powerful and lingering experiences there. Even when his parents had died Isou continued to return to Be'er-Sheva, staying in a hotel near the cemetery where they were buried and visiting their graves three times a day. Israel meant family and love to him. Romania was now more or less impossible for him to visit legally but there was no one or nothing left there which he could call home. He had brought the Romanian language with him.

For these reasons – sometimes at least – Israel seemed to be a place beyond politics and history. It was where he went, he wrote, to disconnect from his destiny as a Messiah. Here, as he put it, he understood the distinction between the demands of everyday life and his duty as a 'Creator'. By this he meant that, when with his family in Israel, he could relax back into the safety of his family unit, reverting to being the same precocious young man he had always been in provincial Romania or Bucharest. His family doted on him as usual; Israel was a place where, as long as he was with his family, he never had to grow old.

Back in Paris, however, Isou had indeed already started realizing that in fact he was growing older. This was no tragedy – he was only 32 and still handsome and an inveterate lothario – but he also thought it was time to move into a different phase in his life. For all his avant-garde theories, there had always been a side to Isou that was socially conservative. He did not drink or smoke, partly because he associated these activities with being 'adult' while he thought of himself as a 'youth', but also because he thought such activities to be 'vulgar'. Nurtured and encouraged by his pleasant excursions to the Middle East, Isou decided that it was now time for 'Isou' to put away childish things and to take his place in the adult world. And so, in July 1957, Isidore Isou got married.

His wife was Jacqueline Enger, who was tall, blonde and elegant. She had crossed Isou's path in one of the cafés near Place Saint-Michel which she frequented at lunchtimes with her friends from the nearby Faculté de Médecine (Jacqueline was studying there to be a medical auxiliary).[3] She was intrigued by Isou from afar, thinking that, with his fastidious manners, elegant clothes, haughty manner and foreign accent, he was 'something or someone special'. During one lunchtime, when Jacqueline was on her own, he offered to buy her a coffee. Isou was very attentive and charming. They chatted, met some more, and Jacqueline started to feel deeply for Isou. She was impressed too that he seemed to know everybody on the Left Bank and that even quite distinguished or famous figures treated him with respect. This was hardly surprising to Jacqueline since he had told her early on in their relationship that he was Professor of Philosophy at the Sorbonne and that in his own country he was one of the most famous poets and philosophers of his generation. All of this happened during the spring of 1956.

Jacqueline was from a middle-class family from the outskirts of Paris and a devout Catholic. There was therefore no question of sleeping with him. Isou delighted her by saying that this had not been his intention and instead proposed marriage. He met Jacqueline's parents who, like her, were impressed by his apparent social status, his learning and his exquisitely good manners. Jacqueline's mother, Raymonde, who thought she knew a thing or two about men, said to her daughter that she could easily imagine Isou as a son-in-law, if not a true son. There was only one problem: Jacqueline was a Catholic, and Isou was very much a Jew.

Isou, however, was not one to let his religion or his ethnicity get in the way of his libido. Jacqueline was now even more desirable and beautiful because she was so elusive and so far out of reach. So Isou decided to convert to Catholicism. Conversion from Judaism to Catholicism is not a quick or easy process. It takes months or years and many Jews struggle with their conscience, particularly because it was always traditionally Christians who were their persecutors in Europe. With Jacqueline it was different – she was apparently, in Isou's eyes, 'worth a Mass'.

He was vague about the details of his conversion but somehow, a month or so before the wedding was arranged, he managed to get hold of a baptismal certificate; Jacqueline thought she had successfully blackmailed him. So, the couple were then married on 27 July at the Église Notre Dame in Jacqueline's home parish of Pavillons-sous-Bois, then a

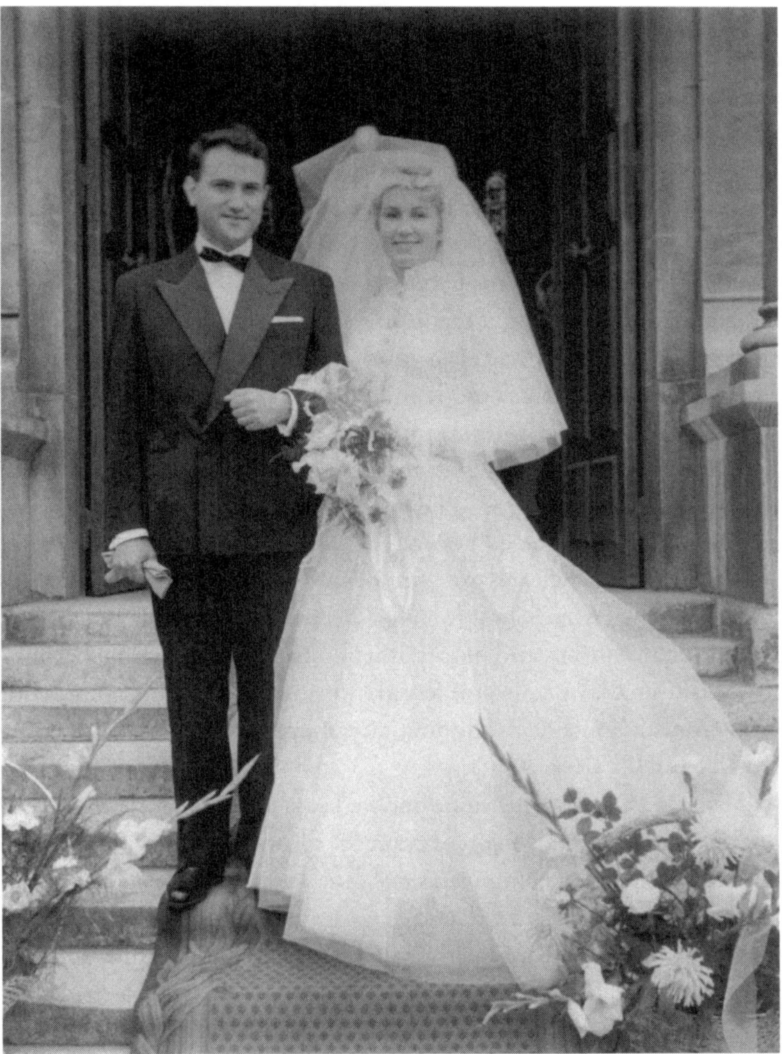

Wedding photograph of Isidore and Jacqueline, 27 July 1957.

middle-class enclave in the heart of what would later become proletarian Seine-Saint-Denis, just outside northern Paris.

The honeymoon night was booked in at the Ritz, where Isou had already briefed all the staff to call him 'Doctor' or 'Professor'. The only problem was that he did not have enough cash to pay the bill and Jacqueline convinced him to cancel the reservation just in time.

Having escaped from the embarrassment of the Ritz, Jacqueline had paid for train tickets to Juan-les-Pins, their honeymoon destination. She also discovered that Isou thought it was a wife's job to carry all the luggage

– this, she learned, was apparently how Goldstein Père had treated Isou's mother throughout their life. As Jacqueline tried to clamber aboard the train at the Gare de Lyon (second-class of course), weighed down by suitcases as the lordly Isou took his seat, a kind gentleman tried to help her. Isou flew into a rage, accused her of flirting with the man and sulked all the way down to the French Riviera. Jacqueline, meanwhile, thought carefully about her new husband, how little she really knew of him, and wondered where all this was taking her.

She had always thought that Isou was more worldly wise and mature than she, but now she had seen another side of him. He had revealed himself as no more than a spoilt child. For all of this, he was still handsome, intriguing and entertaining. She decided there and then that she did not really love him, but for some reason she *liked* him. When they got back from Juan-les-Pins they settled into a tiny apartment at number 22 on the rue de l'Hirondelle, a tight medieval corridor next to Place Saint-Michel, and even settled into a kind of domesticity, or at least as much as *lettrisme* allowed for. According to Jacqueline, the flat contained no library and hardly any books. This was mainly because it was too small. Isou also preferred, however, to keep his mental life away from and outside the domesticity of married life, reading instead in cafés and libraries.

Back in Paris from her honeymoon, Jacqueline first of all also found out that she was now an object of desire for Maurice Lemaître, who always fancied himself as a champion *dragueur* (seducer) and pleaded with her to sleep with him to show that she was an independent woman and as part of his friendly rivalry with Isou. She always refused him and was more interested in planning a family.

———

Catherine Goldstein was born on 5 July 1958. Everyone was delighted, including the parents on both sides. The Goldsteins and Fanny travelled over from Israel to meet their new granddaughter. Isou decided that his first-born, like him, would obviously be a genius, the first of a new generation, even a new species of human being who, being born a *lettriste*, would change human history. Jacqueline, declared Isou, was the *lettriste* version of Elsa Triolet – the writer and wife of Louis Aragon, whom he hated but also thought of as the most eminent poet of the period – and their new daughter a magical child destined for great works.

He was very pleased to have a daughter but he was now looking towards wider horizons. There was a side to Isou, said Jacqueline, that was very conventional and craved respectability, and even in their tiny apartment it was important to be clean, tidy and correct; there was none of the slapdash bohemianism that was the hallmark of the rest of the Left Bank. But family life, he said, did not really interest him. More to the point, he didn't have the time. It was Jacqueline's duty to understand this, to bring up Catherine in the correct way, but never to involve Isou too deeply in the concrete running of their everyday lives. For the time being, Jacqueline accepted the role, and they went on being married, unhappily or not.

She now also started to notice patterns in his behaviour. More to the point, everything with Isou was all or nothing. He never spoke about the war, for example, and certainly never about Romania or his experiences. When they went on holiday again, this time to Cannes, Isou did everything in Cannes exactly as he did in Paris – the only concession to being in the South of France was to sit for half an hour each day – no more and no less – to take in the sunshine. For all of his faults Jacqueline's parents were tolerant and accepting of Isou, still believing that in marrying this smartly dressed, well-connected and erudite young man, she had found a good match.

Jacqueline and Isou stayed together in a ragged but workable relationship for the next four years, until 1962. Even then they did not divorce. This was partly because Isou did not want to be properly separated from her, even if they (Jacqueline, in fact) had already decided that they would live separate lives. 'You are my wife,' he said to her in a moment of hurt and angry tenderness. 'You will always be my wife.' Through the next few decades Isou took other lovers, but they never divorced or lost sight of each other, or stopped feeling somehow affectionate towards each other.

Anyway, Jacqueline had then her own life and business to run. With a little money borrowed from her father she was able to buy, near her parents' place, a lingerie shop which specialized in young and modern styles (the shop was at first called Sexy, a name she hated and changed as soon as possible). Jacqueline soon extended the range of her shop, first by selling blouses similar to those of the television presenter Catherine Langeais, a fashionable figure on the Parisian scene (and a former lover of François Mitterrand), and soon after a variety of stylish clothes. She moved with their daughter near to the shop.

Isou, although he could not bring himself to say it, also truly loved her. He had been attracted to her because she looked like a film star or a model, but he also discovered something deeper in her femininity. She was alone among his acolytes in mocking him, although in a gentle manner. She teased him that *lettriste* poetry was just gibberish and that Isou wrote that way because he could not write 'proper poetry'. In response he wrote her a love poem, which was, as far as is known, the only poem that he ever wrote in classical French. He called it 'À ma femme, pour lui prouver que je sais faire un poème à mots' (To My Wife, to Prove to Her That I Can Write a Poem in Words).

It reads:

Frémissant d'au-delà de ma
naissance
Caresse née de ma chair antérieure
Attendu par mes fibres inférieures
Ces cordes attachés à la voyance

Incarnée dans une étoile nécessaire
Harmonieuse quintessence des détails
enfantins
Voilà ton parfum même est précis
comme tes mains
Comme ton front, tes yeux ou ta
bouche tortionnaire

Mais au tournant du plaisir
C'est ton visage
Tes regards éclatent en astres intérieurs
Tu redeviens pur désir, navigateur

Ton corps près de moi s'éloigne
comme une plage
Néantisée en sable
Tu redeviens absence,
Mon acharnement personnel.[4]

Quivering from beyond birth
Caress borne of my earlier flesh
Anticipated by my inferior fibres
The cords attached to visions of the unseen

Incarnate in a necessary star
Harmonious quintessence of childish details
There is even your perfume even which is precise
Like your hands,
Like your forehead, your eyes or your torturer's mouth

But at the turn of pleasures
It is your face
Your expressions break open into interior stars
You become again pure desire, navigator

Your body next to mine fades into the distance
Like a beach
Turned to nothing in the sand,
You become again absence,
My personal fury.

Jacqueline knew nothing about it. The poem appears in one of his secret journals of the period. At one level it seems to be a fairly conventional love sonnet, with traces of the nineteenth century and in particular Charles Baudelaire. There is also an echo of French Symbolist poetry in the Occultism and quick movement between microcosm and macrocosm (*astres intérieurs*/interior stars and so on).

For all his 'Frenchness', Isou noted in his journals that he would never entirely lose his origins and the traces of his homeland in his language and thought. The best he could do was to acknowledge his status as an exile. In this, Isou echoed the work of Ilarie Voronca, a Moldavian Jew from a slightly earlier generation than Isou, whose world was self-described as 'Post-Symbolist'. Like Isou, Voronca believed in manifestos, dreams, insults and a geometrical, or 'constructivist' approach to building a poem. He was close to the Dadaists and Surrealists and for a while one of the best-known Romanian figures in France, having moved there in 1933 and working variously for Radio France and several literary magazines, as well as having links to the Resistance. He killed himself after returning to Paris in 1946 after a brief trip to Bucharest, where he had been a witness to the wreckage of the old Jewish life he had known there before the war. He was 42 years old.

Isou knew of Voronca's work and admired it. He also wrote his poem to Jacqueline as he was passing through a period of nostalgia for Bucharest, and remembering Voronca. In a note in his journal, written alongside the poem, Isou also compared himself to Joyce, who carried Dublin with him wherever he went. Joyce always refused to forget, wrote Isou. 'I love my wife like I love Catherine, my daughter, who is French,' Isou wrote. 'But my work cannot be contained within the contingencies of a homeland.'[5]

fifteen

The Erotics of God

Isou's work was not confined to one single form of activity either. In the late 1950s and early 1960s, he was busier than ever. Having married and started a family, Isou also needed money and so set himself for the first time to salaried work as a ghost writer. This was mainly for the publisher Éric Losfeld, a provocative young Belgian on the make in Paris who had several simultaneous careers in publishing. He was known first for his allegiance to the Surrealists, in particular André Breton, and had set up a publishing house called Arcanes (after a Surrealist text), which was also a bookshop on the rue du Cherche-Midi in the 6th arrondissement. Losfeld concentrated on the likes of Benjamin Péret, Eugène Ionesco or Marcel Duchamp.[1] The atmosphere in the bookshop was fiercely intellectual. The publishing house was renamed Le Terrain Vague (The Waste Land) on the suggestion of André Breton in 1955. In 1959 Losfeld published, first anonymously, then under this imprint, the first of the *Emmanuelle* series of erotic novels by Marayat Bibidh, which went on to be filmed and make him both famous and rich.

Losfeld also had another less respectable career, however, as a purveyor of pornography which was published without an imprint and distributed illegally. In this he was the great rival of Jean-Jacques Pauvert, publisher of Sade and Bataille, among others, who was constantly testing the limits of the law. On the grounds of his reputation as a great lover of sex, and indeed as a self-styled expert in all of its ways and methods, Losfeld recruited Isou as one of his chief writers (Losfeld himself entitled his own autobiography *Endetté comme une mule* – 'Hung Like a Mule').

Isou was pleased to be paid but also saw this as an opportunity to increase his notoriety as a perverted and subversive enemy of bourgeois morality. Through the late 1950s and early '60s he wrote more than thirty 'sexy novels' (this is what he called them), with titles such as *Mémoire d'une maquerelle* (Memoir of a Madame), *Les Orgies d'un séducteur* (The Orgies of a Seducer) and *Les Plaisirs d'une dépravée* (Pleasures of a Depraved Woman). The literary quality was variable as Isou often sub-contracted the writing tasks to save time and energy (this was often to Maurice Lemaître). He insisted, however, as far as possible, on having his name on the cover, although he did also sometimes use the name Catherine Noël when trying to write about sex from a woman's point of view (these books would some-times be prefaced by a certain 'Isidore Isou'; Isou also received a fine of 13,000 francs for these, forcing him to turn again to his prestigious liter-ary sponsors – Cocteau, Breton and others – for financial help).[2]

The content of these books was often extraordinary, going well beyond the norms of pornography into orgies of bad taste. In *Mémoire d'une maquerelle*, for example, Isou described such 'terrible vices' of man-kind as cannibalism, a taste for eating shit, a steel condom used to murder a woman, and the death of a distinguished French politician crushed to death by a female elephant having just ejaculated into the trunk of her 'pederastic elephant partner'. In every sense, this writing was hysterical. Unsurprisingly, much of this output was immediately banned on publication.

Isou's erotic writings also contained barely occluded autobiographi-cal details. In the 1955 book *Belles d'Europe*, for example, he constructed a fictional travelogue out of his dangerous and illegal journey from Bucharest to Paris, describing the sexual delights to be found in cities along the way such as Vienna and Budapest. The *adorable Roumaine* Catinca puts in a cameo appearance during the Bucharest section of the book, then quickly disappears and is overshadowed by a longer section called 'The Hungarian Girl with Smelly Feet' – a description of a young Hungarian resistance fighter turned prostitute who aroused herself before sex by inhaling the stink from her unwashed boots.[3] Repulsed at first, the narrator – a loosely disguised Isou – learns to do the same; it is a return to the animality of sex. Later, smell is also an erotic perversion: a young German, a former Nazi, says that he was aroused by the smell of the poisoned gas used to kill Jews in the death camps.[4]

Isou now also wrote regularly for the magazine *V*. This magazine, founded in the 1940s, went through a variety of names – *Voir* or *Voilà*, for example – but its content was always pretty much the same: photo stories, some good journalism (the distinguished novelist Joseph Kessel was one of the contributors, for example) and prurient photo features on long-legged lovelies, *les top-models*, or young starlets. It was the precursor to the likes of the soft-focus soft-porn of *Lui* magazine. In *V*, Isou published extracts from his novellas or otherwise wrote pieces about a variety of sexual practices, testing them out as an expert.

Jacqueline's mother Raymonde, in particular, was fond of Isou. Jacqueline, a skilled typist, usually typed up the pornographic stories that he was writing for *V*. Sometimes Raymonde would dictate sections to Jacqueline but they spent most of the time laughing at his ludicrous stories. They actually thought that the stories were hilarious. The important thing at the time, however, was that Isou was thus making a living – of sorts.[5]

In the meantime Isou's old enemies on the Left Bank had not yet gone away. Chief among these was Guy Debord, who for some reason – no doubt jealousy – had not forgotten Isou and could not bear the fact that Isou still existed, despite the disparaging remarks he made about how Isou was now abandoned and isolated.

In 1957 Debord had made himself effectively the leader of a new avant-garde group called L'Internationale Situationniste (The Situationist International). This group, or movement, had been founded in July 1957 at a meeting in a bar in Cosio d'Arroscia, high in the Ligurian Alps. The meeting brought together eight representatives of three deliberately mysterious groups. The largest was the International Movement for an Imaginist Bauhaus, led by the Danish painter Asger Jorn, which had its base in the Italian towns of Albisola and Alba. The second group was the Internationale Lettriste, led by Guy Debord. The third 'group' at Cosio was the London Psychogeographical Committee, a rather notional affair represented by its only known member, the Newcastle-born artist Ralph Rumney. Rumney took photographs of the meeting at Cosio, which portray the delegates in various symbolic or ludic sites around the village; the most famous shows the group, with Debord and his wife (and chief collaborator) Michèle Bernstein at the centre, staring down into the camera from the edge of a sheer drop, in front of a dilapidated house.[6]

Under Debord's influence the Situationists developed a common line on Isou, despising him as a mystic and therefore the enemy of real material revolution which, they thought, had to happen and in fact was about to happen. It was Asger Jorn who launched the Situationists' main assault on Isou in the July 1960 issue of their own journal, *Internationale Situationniste*. Jorn's argument was simple: if Isou worshipped 'Youth' as the sole revolutionary value, how could he square this with the simple and plain fact that he was himself ageing every day?

Worse still, with his still stunning good looks and charm, Isou had once presented himself as the incarnation of 'Holy Youth!', as a godlike figure. But this did not make him a revolutionary leader. He was in fact more like an ageing God; a God in fact only in his own head. Everything about Isou's method was wrong or false, and therefore of no use to the coming revolution and the avant-garde revolutionaries who would make it. Jorn wrote:

> Isou's *religious* problem is complicated by a paradox on the following theme: 'I am god, seeing as how god is youth; seeing as how I am Isou, the point of origin'. He has to choose between personal originality and that of the system which he has created, and which automatically excludes him from the sphere of originality at the end of youth. The reservations which Isou has as regards his own system are easily explained. Put simply, he is getting older, my friends!

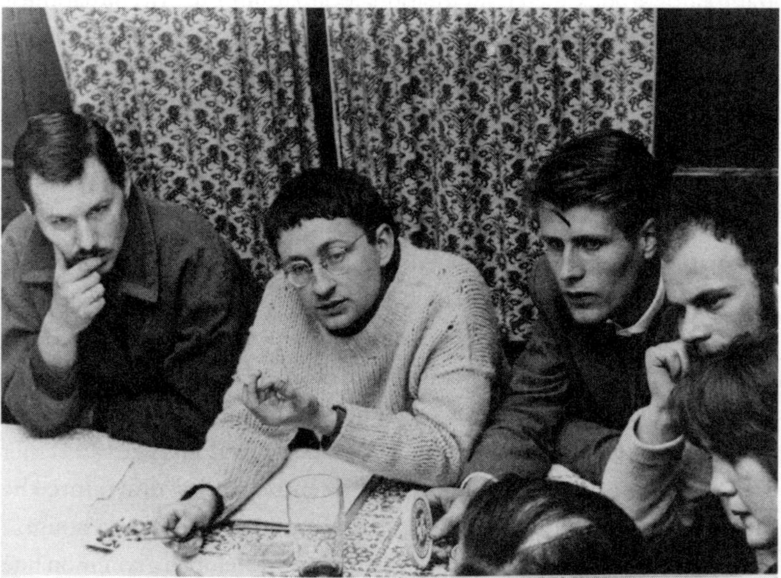

Guy Debord, Lothar Fischer and H. Houdejans at the third conference of the Situationist International held in Munich, 1959.

Thus, the elderly Isou sees the new youth start to overthrow him by virtue of his own system, and he flees to a more assured place, protected by the books of Breton.

This is how the drama goes: it's simply that Lettrism has superseded surrealism. In this way it will retire to claim its part in literary immortality. What joy! Holy youth! It returns all the time, and it is always the same.[7]

The Situationists' insults were not entirely wide of the mark. Even some of Isou's most faithful followers were beginning to think that his ideas were increasingly opaque and impenetrable. The closest intimates were being told by Isou that if they studied hard enough then the secret language of the Universe would be revealed to them. Isou began to refer to himself as *Dieu-Isou* (God-Isou) and peppered his talks and writing with references to the Hermetic tradition and Jewish mysticism. *Lettrisme*, he insisted, was now neither art nor science; it was no less than the reinvention of all human knowledge.

This included, of course, human sexuality. Isou's next big project, accordingly, was the book *Initiation à la haute volupté* (Initiation to High Voluptuousness), which was published by Éditions aux Escaliers de Lausanne in late 1960. In some ways, this was his most ambitious work so far. It was indeed intended as the follow-up to *Les Journaux des dieux*, which was now ten years old. Unlike the mere 150 plates that made up *Les Journaux des dieux*, which told the story of Genesis, *Initiation à la haute volupté* was a narrative novel of 500 pages, accompanied by 208 'plates of super-writing', which, like the pages of *Les Journaux des dieux* were complex, multi-layered illustrations whose meaning was never immediately self-evident.

Isou's intention was that this book would be his retelling of the Song of Songs, sometimes known as the Song of Solomon. This is the only part of the Hebrew Bible which makes no mention of the Law or the teaching of God but is given over entirely to a celebration of sex and eroticism. In the Jewish tradition the purity of the love which is celebrated in the text is often seen as an allegory of God's love for Israel. In the more esoteric tradition of the Kabbalah, the uninhibited sexuality described in the text is also seen as the flow of Divine Emotion, which is also Divine Knowledge, and Knowledge of the Divine.

Isou had already written about this aspect of sexuality before in *Isou ou La Mécanique des femmes* and a later text, *Je vous apprendrai l'amour*

(I Will Teach You Love). These were entirely separate from the 'sexy novels' he wrote for Éric Losfeld. They were, rather, attempts by Isou to develop what he calls an 'erotology' – a scientific system for understanding sex and erotic love. The ultimate aim was to refind the state of Humanity once known as 'Paradise'. In *Initiation*, accompanying a drawing of a naked woman surrounded by signs and hieroglyphs, Isou wrote: 'You could say that if Adam had never sinned, there would no such thing as an orgasm. Sexual techniques are an attempt to destroy the states of being fallen, to take Humans back to the original Paradise.'

The drawings in *Initiation* all contain an erotic motif which ranges from an imitation of a photograph of the 'Miss France' competition as featured in *V* magazine, to illustrations of pan-sexual orgies, featuring an Isou figure and a variety of men and women whose features all belonged to real friends of Isou. The figures are featured in scenes of masturbation (Isou was by his own confession excited by the sight of women leading themselves to solo orgasm). There are scenes of group sex, mild flagellation and bestiality. Isou accompanied one series of these scenes with the statement: 'Humans are not limited to themselves but appeal also to animals, vegetables, inanimate objects, and to invented gods.' In one of the scenes a young man, kneeling, is investigating the vagina of a brunette wearing plaits with a long-range telescope.

For all of this, *Initiation* also contains a reasonably straightforward narrative. Such as it is, the plot tells the story of Didier, who is hired by a gangster called Moshé to kill a beautiful teenage girl. In pursuit of his quarry, Didier passes through a succession of orgies, before finally falling in love with her – he realizes this after he has already killed her. He is then shot dead by Moshé's hitmen. There are two other significant characters: the lawyer, L'Agneau, who represents justice and human kindness, and Jean the Hypergrapher, who is no less than Isou himself, following and recording the action.

There are obvious echoes here of Isou's long-standing obsession with murdering a woman, especially one he loved. This impulse first appeared in his youth when, with Solly, he had dreamed of, and planned, the murder of Irina Galia in Bucharest. That story also, however, may well have been fiction.

There were, however, also other influences at work. One of these was again Georges Bataille, who in 1957 had published a book called *L'Erotisme* (Eroticism) with Éditions de Minuit. This was a sprawling work which, as was usually the case with Bataille, ranged over a wide range of topics without any great unifying theme or theory. Its main subject was, however, the mystery of human sexuality and how perversity – a form of artistry in some ways – was one of the defining aspects of what made sexuality 'human', as opposed to the purely 'animal' fulfilment of a biological need. Bataille linked this notion to religion, seeing in the work of great Christian mystics, for example, a passion for transcendence that not only mirrored sexual experience but actually was a form of sexual passion.

Isou understood this idea straightaway. His own account of sexuality, 'erotology', described sexuality in similar terms. In particular Isou identified with Bataille's description of erotic experience as a form of excess – an unnecessary but irresistible overflowing of the limits of ordinary, non-erotic experience. Isou wrote: 'Eroticism is an excess, a cable pulled towards an irresistible sun, and pulled by an increase in tension . . . a heightened delirium which ends in a fall.'[8]

Isou was also fascinated by the demarcation line between the 'human' and the 'animal', which he saw as ambiguous.

Sensuality is more than just physical. Eroticism is also beyond animality, if we understand animality to be mere biological features of a species. We don't know enough about the brain to understand the difference between the vision of a beast (which also sensual) and the vision of human beings; we cannot ever know if there is such a thing as a perverse animal, that is to animal behaviour which corresponds the 'erotology' of human beings.[9]

There was also a religious allegory at work in the novel's narrative, revealed at the end when Didier is compared to God, the original Creator, and Moshé to Moses, a teacher and prophet. Didier is revealed indeed as one of the 'masks' of God, indicating the Kabbalistic symbolism also at work in the book. God can never be named, in the Kabbalistic mode of thinking, but his Divine presence can be indicated in certain signs. These include the use of the Tarot, through which God also works his hidden meanings.

The use of the term 'Initiation' in the title of the book is a further indication of the book's esoteric content, with its echoes of Éliphas Lévi's famous work *Initiation à la magie*. Lévi, whose real name was Alphonse-Louis Constant, was a nineteenth-century occultist and Kabbalist whose work was known and admired by many, including Victor Hugo.

Lévi was also a kind of utopian socialist, who was at one point close to the feminist and socialist Flora Tristan, and his ideas on the perfect society, 'heaven on earth', were also close to those of Charles Fourier. Lévi, like Fourier, believed that 'Socialism' – the path to heavenly order – would be brought about by an elite of initiates who would eventually lead the people to freedom. This is how Isou describes himself in this book, and how he thought of himself in real life.

The most challenging and ambitious aspect of *Initiation à la haute volupté* is neither its convoluted detective-story narrative nor its esoteric meaning, but the series of new alphabets created by Isou, which sit alongside the erotic drawings. These are beautiful but mainly incomprehensible and grow increasingly predominant in the drawings to the extent where they finally cover most of the page. They seem like the obsessive creation of a madman.

This applies also to the mathematical formulae that are introduced as translations of the text and the new alphabets. It is as if Isou is reducing every sexual possibility and permutation to a mathematical code, which, like the Kabbalah, will then reveal new meaning of its own. To this extent, the book, like the first *lettriste* works of Gabriel Pomerand, is a *grimoire*, an enchanted text that can never properly be decoded but which has a transformative, magical effect upon the reader.

This was why Isou dedicated the book to André Breton, whose first Surrealist writings aimed at the same effect; they were meant not merely as entertainment but as transformative life experiences for the reader. 'So, he will know how to discover what is important in this book,' wrote Isou about Breton.[10] The book was praised by Jean Cocteau as the most important literature since Proust or Joyce.[11]

Someone else who grasped many of the book's hidden meanings, many years after its publication in 1960, was Isou's daughter, Catherine Goldstein, who is now a number theorist and historian of mathematics, with an international reputation. As a child, Isou doted on her. He was particularly delighted that she excelled in every subject in school. 'The children of the *lettristes*', he would say often, 'will always be more brilliant than all other children.' Her mother, Jacqueline, did not quite believe this but she too was proud of her gifted daughter – she told me, beaming with maternal pride, that Catherine could do anything, and as a child she had been a brilliant dancer as much as she was a scholar.

After the separation between Isou and Jacqueline in 1962, the young Catherine was forced to spend two Sunday afternoons per month with her father. For most of her childhood, she found the routine a bit boring. From the earliest age, besides going to museums or the cinema or in summer to the Jardin d'Acclimation (an amusement park), Isou insisted on schooling her in poetry, literature or art.

Much later, when she was an adult, they would develop another routine of eating – always in one of two restaurants – and then going back to Isou's place to have a discussion. Most often Isou would lecture on his genius and her duty to follow him. He would also read letters from the family. According to Catherine, as far as she could remember, Isou's behaviour was always at a far remove from the ordinary family life she enjoyed with her mother and grandparents.

Mathematics first appeared as a central part of Isou's art in the series of paintings called 'Les Nombres' (The Numbers), which were exhibited in the Galerie Palmes in Paris in the autumn of 1953. It was of great significance to Isou that written numbers and words had appeared in human civilization at the same time, alongside figurative drawings. The aim of this *lettriste* painting was to put these separate categories of thought and knowledge back together, to reassemble that which had been fragmented back into a totality.

Dealing with maths alongside literature was a massive ambition, noted Catherine, but it was not necessarily mad. One of the keys to deciphering *Initiation à la haute volupté*, following this logic, is to remember that mathematics in many ways accompanies written language and has always been an integral part of making art, from 'the perspectives of Piero della Francesca to the lines and angles of Kandinsky, from the regular pavings of the Alhambra to the fractals of [the contemporary German artist] Jürgen Partenheimer'. Around the late 1950s Isou also began to talk about works that he termed 'infinitesimal art'. These were pieces that borrowed from the mathematical concept of the 'infinitesimal'. The concept of the 'infinitesimal' belongs originally to the world of mathematics, explaining how to use infinitely small quantities to build and compute finite ones. In the same way, Isou's 'infinitesimal art' could only be imagined, never seen.

Despite these recurrent links between his art and mathematics, and even some attempts from him to write directly on mathematics (for instance on the point), Isou was, said Catherine, often deeply bored by the topic in itself. In the 1990s, he would ask her to teach him some basic mathematics (for example, second-degree algebraic equations), but quickly stopped listening, only to say that everything in this field, as in others, should be created afresh.

Among Isou's most shocking ideas during this period was to exhibit a human corpse covered in *lettriste* signs and symbols. He called this the new 'necrophile art'; the idea was to go beyond the representation of death in art towards the presentation of its reality. The model was Rembrandt's famous painting, *The Anatomy Lesson of Dr Nicolaes Tulp*, which depicts the preparation of a corpse for dissecting in front of a paying audience. Isou called for artists to remember the Nazi torturers who made beautiful objects out of human (Jewish) skin. Finally, this art would be painting which really stinks of truth![12]

sixteen

Madness in May

Throughout the late 1950s and early 1960s, Isou also concentrated on recruiting a 'second generation' of *lettristes*. This was composed of a faithful hard core of talented younger artists called Jacques Spacagna, Roberto Altmann, Roland Sabatier and Sabatier's brother Alain Satié (who had changed his name so as not to be confused with his brother Roland). This new wave would soon be joined by the so-called *femmes lettristes*, women *lettristes*, led by the likes of the painter Micheline Hachette. It was still fairly unusual for an avant-garde group in Paris in the 1960s to admit women into its central core, but it was part of Isou's belief, later pursued in his further writings on sex, that sexuality was always fluid and never fixed, and that each sex had its own powers.

As the 'second generation' of *lettristes* was being recruited, the world that Isou had grown up in was fast moving into history. This was marked most notably by the death in 1963 of Tristan Tzara. The *lettristes* made it a point of avant-garde honour never to attend funerals, even those of their best friends. But Isou also thought it was equally a point of honour to attend the funerals of 'true Creators' like Tzara, if only 'to make an intervention' to 'demystify' any myths around them, and to expose the 'professional jackals of the cemeteries' who only venerated artists when they were dead. Tzara, once the greatest man alive for Isou, had obviously been more than worthy of such an intervention.

Isou turned up with Maurice Lemaître at Tzara's funeral at the cemetery of Montparnasse on a grey December morning. The two *lettristes* had not been invited and were there for a fight. Isou wrote later: 'I was ready to receive a few punches, and then to give some back.'[1] Their enemies were those members of the Communist Party who were attending the funeral. During the later part of his life, Tzara had spent a lot of time and energy courting the Communist Party and trying to reconcile their aims with his own avant-gardist principles. Isou and Lemaître regarded any form of collaboration with communists – or rather 'Stalinists' – as a betrayal and had come to the funeral to express their anger and disappointment with Tzara.

The 'Stalinists' were, however, just as uncompromising and aggressive as the *lettristes* and threatened them openly, saying: 'We're watching you. We're killers and if you say anything against Tzara we'll do you in, here or when you're at home.' When one elderly woman, evidently a communist friend of Tzara, heard that the two strangers at the graveside were the notorious *lettristes*, she walked up to Isou and, practically spitting with venom, told him that he was 'a ridiculous cunt' who should just 'fuck off'. Isou replied automatically in kind: 'Fuck off yourself, you old bitch.' There were black looks and muttering from the 'Stalinists', but no violence.

Isou then started to make a speech but was interrupted by cries that the family had wanted the funeral to pass in silence. Isou shouted out: 'It's shameful that poets should be once again buried by policemen!' The threats from the communists were not enough to silence Lemaître, however, who made a speech ignoring the whispered threats, and then went on to read his 'Epistle to Tristan Tzara', a poem he had written in 1959 and which began 'étli, tzara, jofué lochigran télebile sarkénidan'. When André Breton died in September 1966 it was similarly the end of an era, declared Isou, but not necessarily the avant-garde revolution.

Isou's own life was changing fast during the mid-1960s. On 26 November 1965, after years spent either in cheap hotels or lodging with the Enger family, having finally left the flat at rue de l'Hirondelle in 1963, Isou moved into the apartment at 42 rue St André des Arts where he would live until the end of his life. The apartment had no kitchen and measured no more than 24 square metres (258 sq. ft). The initial credit for the apartment was spread over 33 months at the extortionate rate of 18 per cent a month. This was, however, the first place that Isou could call a settled home since he had left Romania. The apartment, according to legend and later corroborated by Isou, was paid for by the sculptor Alberto Giacometti, who admired Isou and *lettrisme*. Isou wrote a poem – still unpublished – to thank Giacometti, which began: 'Fakeet xhleugoi xorvioooorviooo'.[2]

Most importantly, unlike the apartment at 22 rue de l'Hirondelle, which was literally around the corner, this was a place where Isou could build a library, stacking the walls with books that he began to refer to as his 'infinitesimal library'. Ultimately, he planned to have a collection which covered all forms of human knowledge, discovered and undiscovered. When he realized that space would not allow this, he settled for making the apartment as uncomfortable as he could. This was not a place for Isou or his visitors to chat and relax, but a working environment where to read standing up meant that you properly studied a work. His reading was wide and eclectic, and pages were often covered in his own scattered, scribbled notes. A quick glance at his withdrawals from the Bibliothèque Nationale de France, as well as his own collection, encompasses medieval literature, a great deal of psychoanalytical material, the Beats, works on magic and mathematics, Romanian works on occultism, Victor Hugo, Nietzsche, Casanova, Marx and Dadaism, as well as a fair amount of soft porn (*La Revue Naturiste Internationale* – The International Naturist Review – was a favourite). It was in this place that Isou's ferocious mind finally began to unravel, not all at once but soon, and with an apparently unstoppable momentum.

Isou had always suffered from insomnia but by now it was no longer occasionally acute but chronic. Isou justified his insomnia on the grounds that although it occasionally left him exhausted, he was using his time far more effectively than weaker minds who dulled their senses with alcohol and food. He boasted that he masturbated several times a day, much more than the norm, he insisted, and this was proof of his higher sensibility and capacity for pleasure. Eventually (but not yet) he decided that masturbation was a far more effective way of discharging the sexual urge than relations with real people, who could be boring and a waste of his time.[3]

When Isou couldn't sleep – which was increasingly the norm – he took to wandering the streets of Paris until dawn. He was aware that Samuel Beckett, whom he knew and admired, did this (he also claimed that Beckett reciprocated the admiration). To his fellow *lettristes* he talked incessantly of the brilliant ideas he had during these dark, illuminated hours.

Isou's artistic output was prodigious during this new period in his life. The year 1965 began with 'La Semaine de l'Art Moderne', held at the end of January at La Maison Spectateur on the prestigious Avenue Hoche. This was a series of lectures and performances covering the full range of *lettriste* activity from poetry through to cinema, theatre and ballet, culminating in an explanation of the 'infinitesimal art' by no less than Isou himself.

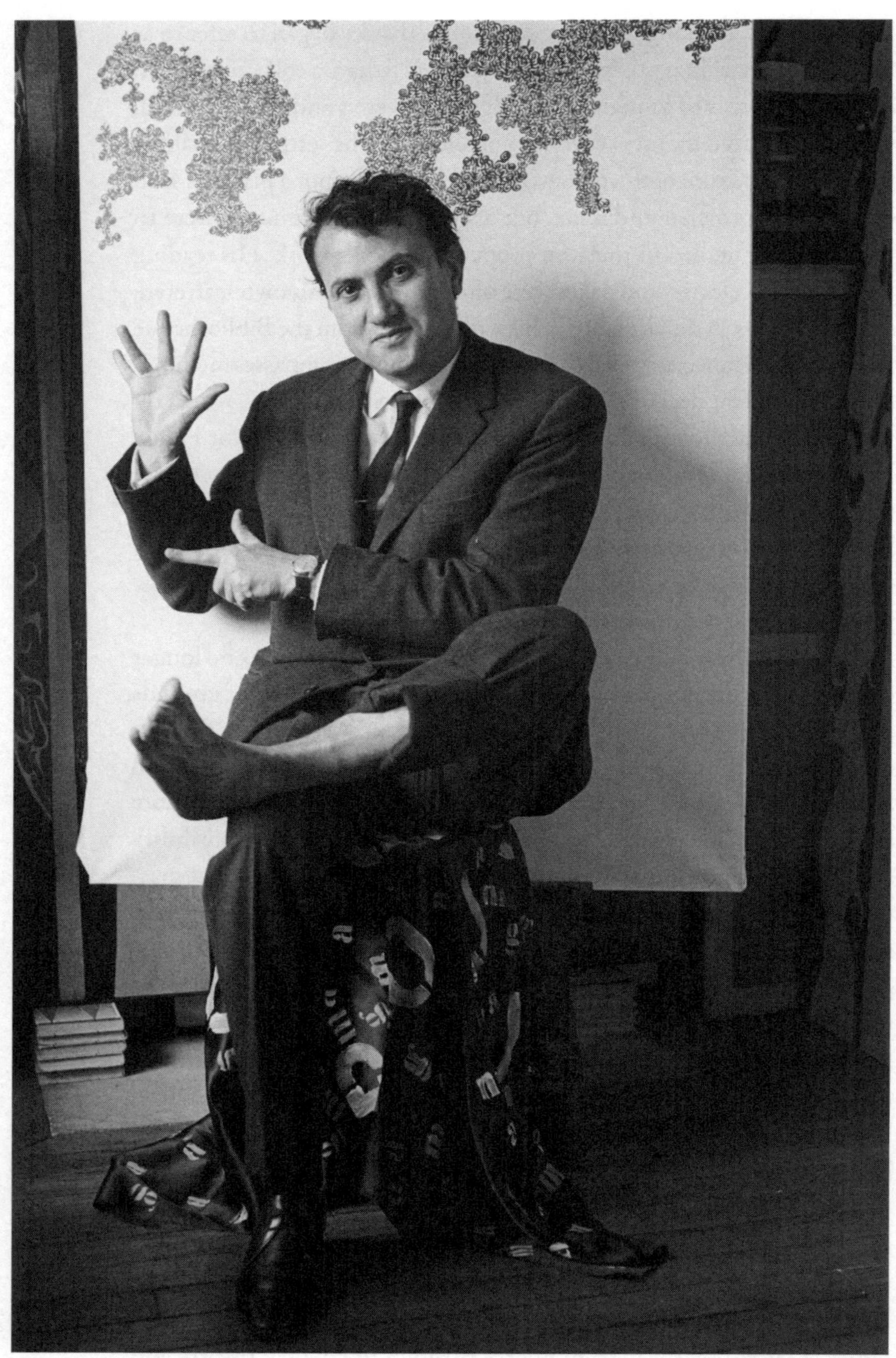

Isou posing barefoot with one of his artworks, 19 April 1965.

Not long after this flurry of activity Isou found himself once again featured in *Le Monde*, this time for his contribution to an exhibition called the 'Salon Comparaisons', organized by the distinguished artist Andrée Bordeaux-Le Pecq, who had championed work by Max Ernst, Leonor Fini and Yves Klein. Isou's contribution took the form of painted 'hypergraphic' plaques and 'moving sculptures', one of which was a frog, which visitors were persuaded to handle, and the other a tortoise with *lettriste* poems painted on its shell. The event was scuppered when, during a moment of inattention on Isou's part, the tortoise, spying its moment, made a successful bid for freedom. This, reported *Le Monde*, was the highlight of the exhibition: the Great Isou outwitted by a tortoise. The newspaper also featured a photograph of the crafty and disloyal animal at the Salon in the arms of a girl *lettriste*, but now presumably on the run somewhere on the Left Bank.

Isou did not care that outsiders occasionally found his efforts comic. The important thing was that the *lettristes* were still being talked about in the press and elsewhere. It did not matter anymore that they had lost – or 'discarded' as Isou put it – the first generation of activists. The *lettristes* were now composed of younger, fresher minds who, most importantly, were in touch with the fast-moving conflict of generations which would erupt in the 'events' of May '68. The younger *lettristes* wore long hair, leather or corduroy jackets, Chelsea boots and jeans. They liked rock music, sex and drugs. The most important thing of all was that they did not look or sound like any of the 'relics' of the Saint-Germain-des-Prés scene of the 1940s, the 'Zazous' or the Existentialists. The chic *femmes lettristes* looked as if they could have come straight out of a fashion magazine, while the boys could have been a rock band. The numbers were fairly fluid, but there were never less than forty or so at one time, a fairly high number held steady by the amount of free sex available within the group.

Isou himself was now forty years old and no longer the beautiful young man he had been. He was, however, still handsome, with the looks of a forgotten movie star from another era. He dressed the part with elegant suits and hat cocked to one side. He did not seem to belong to the mid-1960s but that didn't matter. *Lettrisme* was, however, still fashionable. Their work was, for example, still being praised by the likes of Michel Tapié, the prominent art critic who had first introduced Jackson Pollock and other Abstract Expressionists to Paris, and who would exhibit their work through the 1960s in his gallery on the rue de Seine. The only sceptical note came from a fellow Romanian, Paul Celan, who when asked by the critic Petre Solomon on a trip to Paris in 1966 whether Isou was to be taken seriously, described Isou as a 'charlatan', although still a treasured friend.[4]

Most significantly, the work of the *lettristes* was often compared to Fluxus – a fashionable 'neo-Dadaist' collective founded by the Lithuanian-born artist George Maciunas in New York. Fluxus collaborators or fellow travellers included the likes of John Cage, Yoko Ono, La Monte Young and members of the East Coast avant-garde royalty.

Fluxus believed in spontaneity, anti-art and chance. They termed their work 'intermedia', as it spans several disciplines. This was not *lettrisme* – far from it in fact (although one Fluxus artist, Wolf Vostell, did claim Isou as a mentor and had even painted a work in homage to Isou in 1959).[5] For another thing, the Fluxus artists saw their work as mainly a game, albeit one with revolutionary aspirations; for Isou *lettrisme* was life or death and the *lettriste* revolution – meaning the 'youth uprising' – certain, inevitable and terrible in its ferocity. But the two movements did have a shared belief in youth and change, and in youth as the sole agent of change in a revolutionary society.

From Isou's point of view, watching the rise of Fluxus in New York and then in Paris, it seemed as if the world might be finally catching up with him. Similarly, although Isou was indifferent to pop or rock music, he was nonetheless convinced that popular culture was moving in his direction. He attributed, for example, The Beatles' shift into avant-gardism in the mid-1960s to the direct influence of *lettrisme*. The proof was, Isou argued to anyone who would listen, that he had personally seen John Lennon, then an art student, at a *lettriste* exhibition in Paris in 1961 (this is not quite as far-fetched as it sounds; John Lennon had taken a long holiday with Paul McCartney in Paris just as they were on the cusp of fame and it was not impossible that Lennon, who was deeply impressed by the art scene in Paris, had dropped into a *lettriste* event).[6]

Anyway, Isou reasoned, the *lettristes* had been at work in popular culture for a long time, diffusing their work wherever they could – on film, on television, on radio, and even, in 1958, with a long-playing record by Maurice Lemaître. Called *Maurice Lemaître présente le Lettrisme*, this was released on Columbia Records (future home of Bob Dylan) complete with a colour reproduction of a painting and a black-and-white photograph of Lemaître in full *lettriste* flow.

The contents of the disc were hardly the rock 'n' roll of Elvis Presley or Johnny Hallyday, but it did contain readings by Isou, as well as a *lettriste* choir of male and female voices and, in reference to the new rock 'n' roll culture of youth, a sound poem, 'Lettre Rock', which imitated the noise and rhythms of the new music. The *lettristes*, Isou claimed, were always ahead of their time in whatever art form they practised; the proof of this was that everything they predicted always came true; this made sense as Isou was not only a messiah but a prophet.

———

Even Isou could not have anticipated, however, how quickly French culture was changing during the mid-1960s. Many of these changes were nothing to do with art but to do with the material quality of life: improvements in housing and sanitation for example. There were also huge shifts in the populations of the great cities, and Paris in particular, as overcrowded city centres were emptied of their inhabitants, who often moved to newly built, ready-made apartments in the suburbs. These new homes offered bathrooms, fitted kitchens, fridges, washing machines, televisions and all of the other amenities of modern life and in every sense were far removed from antiquated, often squalid, conditions that even many middle-class urban dwellers had grown up in.

The greatest cultural shifts that were happening were the direct results of the increased affluence that accompanied demographic changes. France, poor and broken after the Second World War, had become like America, a society of consumers who could afford not merely to survive, as had been the case only a few short years ago, but who now spent money on clothes, cars, records, home decor and other items, once deemed luxuries but now both desirable and within reach of ordinary people. Even the Communist Party declared that this period of expansion and development in French society was progress. Certainly, the working classes and lower middle classes embraced this new way of living.

The only dissenting voices, who were sceptical of this 'new France', and who were the greatest influence on the mood of May '68, came not from the mutually exclusive political Right or the Left but mainly from writers and artists, whose instinctive bohemianism scorned such bourgeois necessities as comfortable furniture and good plumbing. If not calling for revolution they at least anticipated the inevitable boredom that often went along with increased material comfort, and which would prove to have as much revolutionary potential as traditional proletarian class war.

In 1965 the novelist Georges Perec wrote a short novel called *Les Choses* (Things) about a young Parisian couple – a pair of market researchers, one of the fashionable careers of that moment in the French 1960s – who are dazzled by the new consumer society in which they live and seek to build their personalities from 'things' that they could acquire and own. Much to his own surprise, Perec, who was politically quite moderate, found his work praised in the Soviet bloc for his withering exposé of the contradictions of capitalism. Similarly, Jacques Tati's comic masterpiece *Playtime*, meant as satire, lampooned modern society and the newly mechanized city of Paris to the point of destruction. The film-maker Jean-Luc Godard, who genuinely thought of himself as a political radical, painted a nightmarish picture of murderous suburban anomie in his 1967 film *Weekend*.

These were only the best-known works of the period which, unlike the psychedelic flowering that was taking place in Anglo-American culture, was angry with the consumer society and ultimately unafraid to resist it with violence. If there was a great singular difference between the counter-culture in France and the Anglo-American world, it was that young people in the latter had found their own 'pop revolution' – which meant not only rock music, but fashion, drugs and free sexuality. These of course existed in France too but were often considered as illusory diversions from making the real revolution; these were the products of the 'Spectacular society' – a world of image and illusion, of 'things', which were not the same as the real expression of revolutionary energy, which would be the real youth uprising.

This was also the philosophy of Guy Debord's L'Internationale Situationniste, which now claimed leadership of the spontaneous 'youth front' who were the loudest enemies of the new commodity culture. The Situationists started to make themselves famous in 1966 by spreading revolutionary propaganda and agitation in French universities. Their greatest coup so far was the so-called 'Strasbourg Scandal' when, in November 1966, the Situationist-controlled Students Union deliberately bankrupted itself by spending all of its funding for a year on a beautifully produced pamphlet called *De la misère en milieu étudiant* (On the Misery of Student Life). The pamphlets had then been handed out at an inaugural ceremony of the university, with the Rector and the Bishop of Strasbourg present.

Students at Strasbourg were also encouraged by their Situationist representatives – all properly elected – to occupy the university and to steal books and food, while the campus psychiatric clinic was declared a centre of mind control. Mayhem and chaos were unleashed in 'a revolutionary festival' which in six short weeks of disobedience brought the university to its knees. The 'scandal' was reported widely not only in France but eventually across the world, where it was excoriated by the mainstream press as student petulance, and hailed as a revolutionary model on campuses in Berlin, London and San Francisco.

In 1967 Guy Debord published a book called *La Société du spectacle* (The Society of the Spectacle), a densely written work of pseudo-Marxist theory. Although the book was complicated and hard to read, severe and unforgiving in its style, its message was made clear in its title and Debord's insistence that his book was meant as a 'revolutionary weapon'. You didn't have to be a Marxist, or even to have read the book, to grasp that Debord was calling for an attack on the 'spectacular society' – the world of commodities and images which held youth in check and imprisoned them. This of course was the idea that Isou thought that he had first encountered with the *huliganii* of pre-war Bucharest, and which he had refined in post-war Paris in his description of the 'youth uprising'; this was a revolution that belonged to Isou.

As riots, led by young people, erupted all over Paris, and indeed across France, in May '68, briefly threatening to bring down the government of Charles de Gaulle and make a revolution, Situationist graffiti and ideas were everywhere. There were of course other groups too making trouble – Maoists, Anarchists and Trotskyists – but it was Debord's notion of the 'spectacle' which caught the mood of the hour and best explained the otherwise inexplicable anger of a young generation that had never known poverty or war, but which was nonetheless prepared to tear society apart because – apart from a life of enslavement to capitalism, to 'things' – they felt it had nothing to offer them.

The rebellion of May '68 began in March that year, when students at the University of Nanterre, a grim set of buildings in a dismal outer suburb of Paris, launched a series of strikes and occupations, protesting against conditions at the university and the draconian house rules of the campus. The university became a magnet for discontented students elsewhere in Paris and pamphlets and graffiti from the far Left, including the Situationists, were present everywhere in the buildings. The protests reached a boiling point when a group of pro-Situationist students who called themselves Les Enragés tried to take over the main building on the campus. They were soon kicked out but at the same time Situationist slogans – 'Never work!' or 'Boredom is counter-Revolutionary' – began to appear mysteriously all over the campus.[7]

The conflict went to a new level, however, attracting international attention, on 3 May, when the Nanterre rebels had disciplinary charges brought against them at the Sorbonne. A hearing was set for 6 May but by noon on 3 May there was already the possibility of serious violence in the air. The atmosphere was heightened by the presence around the Sorbonne of 'Occident', an extreme Right-wing student movement who were spoiling for a fight with the 'Bolsheviks'. The 'Enragés' and their fellow travellers began smashing up tables to use as clubs in 'self-defence' against the members of 'Occident'. At four o'clock that afternoon, the riot police moved in. By early evening a full-scale battle between stone-throwing students and the CRS (Compagnie Républicaine de Sécurité) was being fought on the Boulevard Saint-Michel. The fighting went on over 4 and 5 May, and then more sporadically over the next few weeks.

On 14 May a wave of strikes was declared in the name of solidarity with the students. Suddenly there was talk of a real Revolution. On 24 May, the most dramatic night of violence, barricades went up in Bordeaux, Lyons and Nantes, as well as Paris. The Élysée Palace, the Hôtel de Ville and other main buildings of State were placed under special guard. Although it was all over by the first week of June, the French government had only just avoided being destroyed by a revolt triggered by a group of straggly students.

———

During the first days of the revolt, as the student crowds grew larger and the violence against the authorities grew ever harder and bolder, Isidore Isou was exultant. Forgetting Guy Debord and the Situationists – as well as the other agitators on the Left – Isou claimed to his comrades, the disciples who had remained faithful through the past few years, that he had predicted it all, that this was all his work, that the *lettriste* revolution was finally happening, that the 'youth front' he had first described and theorized was about to change history and the world; that this was *the* moment when finally Isou the Messiah would be truly in command of history.

Isou never changed his mind about this; this indeed is what Isou told me when I met him over thirty years after the 'events' of May. He had by then, he said, already invented everything else of cultural importance in the post-war world: poetry without words, cinema without images, novels made up of 'hypergraphics' (complicated variations of the rebus), even the sexual revolution in his works of 'erotology'. Isou was aware that Daniel Cohn-Bendit, the student leader who acted as a spokesman for the rioters, had never read any of the *lettriste* texts on the 'youth uprising' but that he was familiar with Debord. According to Isou, Cohn-Bendit was making a historic mistake by reading Debord rather than Isou. Debord was really no more than a Marxist, as well as a plagiarizer, and therefore could not understand what was happening during May '68 or what would come next. Isou needed to talk to Cohn-Bendit and his followers to put them right. It was time for Isou to lead the Revolution.

The reality of what happened to Isou during May '68 is indeed complex. There are variations on the story, the time and the place and how it happened, but effectively Isou had a psychotic breakdown. The most repeated version of events is that at seven o'clock on the morning of 21 May, Isou was with his *lettriste* comrades in a café on the rue St André des Arts.[8] No one had slept for days, either attending demonstrations or riots, dodging the snatch squads of police operating in the area, or listening as the drama unfolded on the radio. Isou had by then already tried to commandeer a meeting at the Théâtre de l'Odéon, announcing himself as the leader of the uprising, explaining with mathematical formulae that he had invented all of this. Isou also thought he was being tracked with a hidden camera. He tried to gate-crash a radio programme at the ORTF, the French version of the BBC, to announce himself as leader of the French nation. On the Champs-Élysées, he tried to make sculptures out of broken biros and ice cream ordered from a nearby shop, then handed out 500-franc notes to the most beautiful girls who were passing.

In the café, Isou could not stop talking. Previously he had been out in the streets, walking calmly through the most intense violence, ignoring the police and walking through the hail of stones raining down from the student lines. He had started clambering onto the roofs of parked cars, some of which were still moving, walking and dancing, shouting slogans, pointing at the police and then the students, and declaring that a war had begun.

Back in the café, gathered with *lettriste* comrades, he started talking and talking, sometimes in languages that his comrades did not understand – fragments of Yiddish, German, Russian and Romanian, and languages which he claimed that he had just invented on the spot. He told his comrades that he was immortal. The riots in the streets were exactly the same as those he had seen during the war in Bucharest, and he had lived through the worst of them, including the pogroms. This was his, and their, destiny: the 'youth front in action'. He then started ordering ice creams, one after another, not even starting to eat the first. He wanted a mirror to smash up in front of his comrades, to cut himself up and smear himself in blood to prove that he was immortal.

He wanted to go out again into the streets, bloodied and naked. It was at this point that his *lettriste* comrades decided to save him from himself. François Poyet, one of the youngest and toughest of the latest wave of recruits to the *lettriste* corps, took it upon himself to telephone the renowned psychiatrist Gaston Ferdière to ask him to come immediately and to order an ambulance. Poyet had to manhandle Isou to calm him. Isou fought back, but Poyet was easily able to overcome him. Poyet worked by day as an apprentice undertaker and had developed a powerful physique from lifting coffins several times a day. (He told me that he very much enjoyed his job as an undertaker; he got to drive to different parts of Paris and usually got drunk at the funerals.[9])

Still raving, Isou began to pillage a nearby bookshop, as well as screaming at the schoolchildren at the nearby Lycée Fénelon, just arriving for the day, in an attempt to incite them to start a riot. Ferdière approached Isou calmly, greeted him in a courteous manner and shook his hand. Isou responded with equal politeness. The two men had in fact already met several times, and even lunched together as the psychiatrist was a great follower of the literary avant-gardes and had shown an interest in *lettrisme*. Isou mentioned the name of Lise Deharme, a novelist, intimate of the Surrealists, and a mutual friend, and they began a convivial chat. An ambulance arrived for Isou only minutes before a police car, which had been summoned by the local café owner, terrified of the wild Isou – who was now as elegantly civilized as ever.

Isou was driven, on Ferdière's orders, to the psychiatric clinic at Épinay-sur-Seine, a suburb to the north of Paris. Isou was first of all sedated as the doctors tried to piece together his story. A preliminary diagnosis was that Isou was suffering from a manic episode and was either hysterical or manically depressive (the term bipolar disorder was not in use at this point; manic depression was understood mainly as a pathological illness to be treated with drugs rather than a 'talking therapy'). Ferdière came to see him and the two men talked about art and literature. Then Isou was given a huge dose of benzodiazepine and put into a deep sleep.

This form of therapy has long since been discredited, but it was commonly used in France in the 1960s as a way of controlling the uncontrollable mood disorders that eventually led to the manic state. To this extent it was considered to be one of the most humane ways of protecting patients from themselves. The deep sleep therapy also enabled doctors to carry out treatments which patients might find distressing or intrusive during a waking state, especially if they were undergoing a psychotic episode. The most common treatment was ECT, or Electroconvulsive Therapy. What happens during this treatment is that an electric current is sent through the scalp to cause a brief seizure in the brain, which was meant to effectively reset how the brain works. The process takes place under a general anaesthetic and electrodes are applied to the head. The last thing the patient sees before slipping into unconsciousness is a blinding white light. The patient does not remember the treatment and is usually confused, red-eyed, spitting or frothing at the mouth, the central nervous system now reconfigured. There is no pain – at least according to the doctors who regularly adopted this practice. One famous survivor of this treatment was the singer and writer Lou Reed, who had been subjected to ECT by his parents to 'cure' his homosexuality. Throughout his life Reed's nightmares were dominated by the 'sad, off-white colour' of hospitals and fear of sleep. He wrote in a poem, 'How does one fall asleep / When movies of the night await / And me eternally done in.'[10] Reed was a lifelong insomniac.

When Isou awoke from his deep sleep 21 days after being admitted to the hospital, he had no idea what had happened to him, how he had got there or that he had been subjected to ECT (he found out about this later). There were problems too about who would pay his medical bill. But it did not take Isou long to remember the violent events of May '68 and to start to work out that the Revolution, *his* Revolution, had been stolen from him. To the end of his life he was still furious that he had been betrayed, that history had been made in his absence.

PART III

The Divinity of Isou (1968–2007)

I am going to die having understood nothing. The most
extraordinary joys of my life fade away into nothingness
in the face of the terror of the present moment.
ISIDORE ISOU, *Initiation a la Haute Volupté* (1960)

seventeen

'Demons are tearing me apart!'

On Isou's release from the psychiatric clinic at Epinay, France settled back into some kind of order, with the signing of agreements between the government and the main trade unions, which had stepped in to broker a way forward between the students and the government. Most French people were also by now sick of the disorder and ready for some kind of stability to be established.

Isou did not want to believe that the Revolution, *his* Revolution, was over. During one of his long walks in the Bois de Boulogne, he went to the nearby home of an old comrade called Robert Mitterrand, brother of François Mitterrand and a successful industrialist who, unlikely as it may have seemed, had funded early *lettriste* projects. On opening the door, Madame Mitterrand was confronted by a wild-eyed Isou, in full psychotic mode, haranguing for money and 'political support'. Terrified, she called the police, and Isou was immediately sectioned and interned in the psychiatric hospital of Sainte-Anne in central Paris. This was only a few weeks after he had last been interned.[1]

A few weeks later, when finally released again, Isou began to think seriously of suicide. He asked Gabriel Pomerand, with whom he had now renewed his friendship, to find him a gun. He had expected the 'youth uprising' of May to make him its leader; he was now wrecked, thin 'like a corpse', almost ruined by debt. He thought of going to live with his parents in Israel. Instead, he was looked after by friends and submitted to psychiatric treatment as an outpatient under Gaston Ferdière. The main place that he stayed in was the hospital of Sainte-Anne.

Sainte-Anne has been part of the Paris landscape since it first opened its doors to patients in 1867. It was then a crude and brutal place, applying primitive therapeutic methods. The main part of the hospital is behind a high, grey wall in a leafy part of the city's 14th arrondissement. It is almost directly opposite the prison of La Santé, which is guarded by the same high walls. The proximity of the two establishments is testimony to the late nineteenth-century French idea that hospitals and prisons are extensions of each other, as places where social and mental hygiene come together.

Right up until the 1950s, the inhabitants of the nearby *quartier* of Alésia grew used to the cries of the inmates of Sainte-Anne; the noise was part of the folklore of the area. The hospital only grew silent when, in the 1970s, the use of psychotropic drugs became the favoured form of treatment and the use of ECT was slowly abandoned. Inside the walls these days Sainte-Anne is the very opposite of a prison, and quite unlike La Santé. It is made up of gardens, arcades, galleries.

It is also an integral part of Parisian literary history – those who have trained and practised here include Michel Foucault (who was also a patient here) and Jacques Lacan, while its most distinguished literary patients include Antonin Artaud and Louis Althusser. Isou was proud that other Romanian inmates included the poet Paul Celan, a fellow Romanian Jew, and the Romanian philosopher Emil Cioran. He would later boast that the doctors made him sleep in Cioran's private room for its 'atmosphere'.

When he first got there, Isou recognized Sainte-Anne straightaway. He had read about it before in Louis-Ferdinand Céline's 1932 novel *Voyage au bout de la nuit* (Journey to the End of the Night), where the main character Bardamu takes a job in a private mental asylum. The place described in Céline's novel is fictional and set in the imaginary Paris suburb of Vigny-sur-Seine. But everything Céline describes was visible and real to Isou during his first days in Sainte-Anne. This includes Céline's sadistic chief doctor, the dank and desperate climate, the smell of old beds, the gardens which were meant to make the patients peaceful but could look like a nightmarish labyrinth to those whose minds were broken, and above all Céline's description of ECT: 'magnetic storms over the heads of the melancholics, assembled for this purpose in a hermetically sealed and pitch-black room'.[2]

Isou came to know Sainte-Anne very well. Over the next three decades he was in and out of the hospital, occasionally committed for his own safety but mainly as an outpatient, attending weekly 'talk therapy' sessions. Isou was often frightened in Sainte-Anne, sometimes scared of himself and the terrifying velocity of his thoughts and his inability to control them; at other times he was frightened of the other inmates, some of whom seemed capable of the worst kinds of violence. He found, however, that many of his fellow patients were highly intelligent and cultured, far more evolved in fact than many ordinary citizens; they were evidently incarcerated here as a punishment for having revolted against some aspect of 'ordinary society'. Really the problem was that they were drugged or made docile by electric shocks until they no longer knew what they were revolting against.

In 1968, despite advances in psychiatric medicine, the 'atmosphere' for patients in Sainte-Anne had in fact changed very little since the nineteenth century. The nurses were also guards, ready to meet any transgression with violence. There were a few isolation cells but very few barred windows. Patients who were not in the midst of full-blown psychosis could move around with relative freedom, but this did not make them any happier – it only exposed them to the varieties of mental disintegration among their peers.

This vision of hell inspired a book published in 1969 by Isou called *Les Démons me déchirent!* (Demons Are Tearing Me Apart!).[3] This was one of Isou's final attempts at a so-called 'erotic novel' – or at least it was published under this rubric. It is essentially a detective novel about a patient who escapes from Sainte-Anne. Its questionable 'erotic content' lies in the descriptions of the sadistic practices which take place there. Apparently, the idea was to appeal to those readers of Sade who were aroused by extremes of violence and punishment. But if the book has any real relation to Sade, it is because of its overwhelming atmosphere of claustrophobia and paranoia.

The book is also prefaced with a quotation from the gospel of Luke, who describes Jesus meeting a man possessed by demons and who, when asked what his name is, replies: 'My name is Legion: for we are many.' The clear implication is that psychiatric treatment is equivalent to the exorcism which takes place in the Bible story. But Isou did not want all of his demons to be exorcised; they were an essential part of who he was, his creativity, his status as a Creator. He called psychiatry and psychoanalysis 'medicine of the soul' and thought that he had to keep his soul, tormented as it was, intact, or he would not really exist at all. In other words, even if his 'soul' was sick, it belonged to him, Isou, and he did not want its uniqueness, the source of his creativity, to be 'cured'.

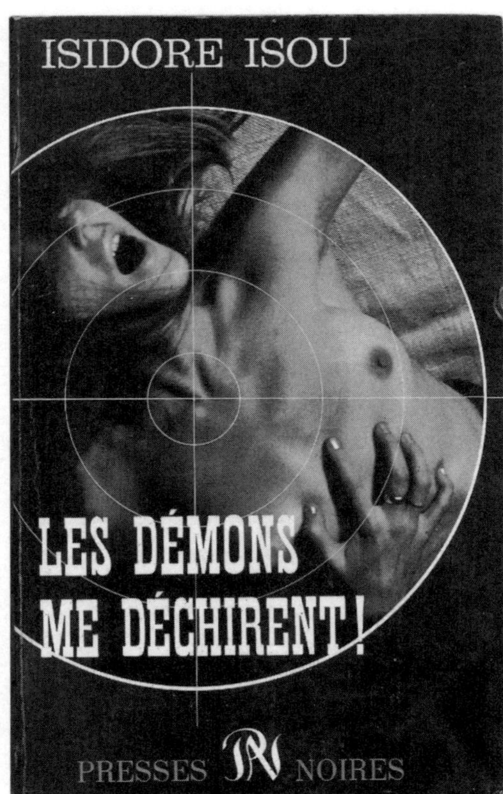

Cover of Isidore Isou's novel, *Les Démons me déchirent!* (1969).

This was worse than simply being murdered or killed by a random accident. It had been the project of the Nazis to wipe the Jews – every single one of them – out of history; and now this was happening to him in this hospital again. This was why his torturers were also Nazis. He described in the novel punching his doctor in the face, but it was useless: there was nowhere to go if you did escape, only deeper into the mind, and the mind was a labyrinth where you could too easily be lost. The psychiatric hospital, like Kafka's Castle, was a place that you could never understand but which controlled your life. For these reasons, Isou oscillated between hallucination and nightmare. This too is the substance of *Les Démons me dechirent!*, which fails as a detective thriller but is a true account of what Isou had lived through and seen in the hospital.

———

When Dr Ferdière began to treat Isou, he himself had already long been notorious in psychiatric circles for his relationship with the poet Antonin

Artaud, whom he had treated in the 1940s. Ferdière went on to write books about their dialogues. Many of his colleagues were suspicious about these, fearing that Ferdière was too vain to be a good doctor and instead prized literature over medicine.[4]

The doctor's relationship with Artaud was, however, far more complex than that. Ferdière had been introduced to Artaud by the poet Robert Desnos in 1943, as Artaud seemed to be in a state of complete collapse, about to starve to death in one of the many abandoned psychiatric hospitals wrecked by the war. Desnos had begged Ferdière to do what he could for Artaud, who admitted him to hospital at Rodez, deep inside Vichy France some 150 kilometres (90 mi.) from Toulouse. Desnos trusted Ferdière because throughout the 1930s he had been a friend and close supporter of the Surrealists, treating their work as seriously as his own scientific researches (he had along the way also known the young Céline, then working as a doctor). Ferdière had even started his career as a kind of Surrealist poet, sending André Breton his early poems published as a medical student in Lyon. He had also known René Crével, the Surrealist poet who killed himself in 1935, having spent the last night before his death with Ferdière at the psychiatric hospital of Sainte-Anne.

Ferdière was known to be wary of medical orthodoxies and believed in the value of listening to patients tell their own story, a practice which was a rarity at the time. Ferdière considered Artaud, as an artist, to be every inch his equal as a man of science and decided that they both had much to learn from each other. Although Ferdière considered Artaud's habits of writing magical spells and designing astrological charts as symptoms of mental illness, he was not always sure where to place them. Artaud suffered from delusions and psychotic breakdowns, but the spells and charts were also part of his method as a visionary artist.

Ferdière was a good psychiatrist and a good doctor. The difficulty for Ferdière was how to separate his admiration for art and his belief in medicine. Finally Ferdière decided that this was impossible, and in 1946 released Artaud back to a clinic near to his Paris milieu, where Artaud's critical reputation as a genius had never been higher. By 1948 Artaud was dead, killed most probably by an overdose of Chloral Hydrate, which he had been prescribed for his cancer. Once a stunningly handsome youth, he was now a shrivelled old man who looked far older than his 52 years of age.

Ferdière began his treatment of Isou by confirming the initial diagnosis that Isou, unlike Artaud who was a 'paranoid', was suffering from what was then called 'manic depression' but is now more commonly described as 'bi-polar disorder'. This had been first properly diagnosed as such in the 1850s by the psychiatrists Jean-Pierre Falret and Jules Baillarger, who identified the disorder first of all as a *folie circulaire* – a psychotic state with two extremes of manic euphoria and melancholia.

Isou's lifestyle seemed to corroborate this diagnosis. During the manic episodes the sufferer is euphoric, full of plans and projects and grandiose ideas, often totally uninhibited about behaving in an anti-social or irresponsible way; sleepless apparently without fatigue. The 'melancholic' state is characterized by chronic fatigue, sadness, dark thoughts, difficulty in accomplishing the smallest tasks, lack of pleasure in food or sex and suicidal thoughts. In their first studies of *folie circulaire* Falret and Baillarger drew bleak conclusions: that the condition was 'desperate, terrible and incurable' and most likely to end in suicide. The list of artists associated with this disorder is long and distinguished, but, as Isou came to know well, there is nothing romantic or glorious for those who suffer its agonies.[5]

Isou began to study the history of psychiatry. He also began to compare himself to Antonin Artaud, describing himself as his successor or even his 'second coming'. Isou was of course not only aware of who Ferdière was and of his relationship with Artaud, but had long been an admirer of Artaud, whom he recognized as a prophet of *lettrisme*. Most importantly, Isou believed Artaud's delusions, which psychiatrists took to be symptoms of his illness, to be political and religious realities. Isou also identified with Artaud's artistic works, particularly the drawings which Artaud began to produce in 1944, which he called 'hieroglyphs'; these were heavily inscribed works which were made up of symbolic objects, invented languages and alchemical symbols.

Most importantly, Isou thought that Artaud – like Isou himself – was not mad but a true mystic. At one point during the latter stages of the Second World War, Artaud began to believe that France had been taken over by the Anti-Christ. He thought that Jesus Christ alone could save the world from Hitler. He also believed that humanity needed a sacrificial victim, a redeemer, and offered himself up to fight for the immediate Empire of God.

This made perfect sense of course to Isou, but less so to Artaud's doctors. Dr Latrémolière – the doctor who delivered electric shocks to Artaud – took a more sober view, dismissing Artaud's apocalyptic beliefs with the remark that 'His terrible self-interested reasoning, in the end, made him build up his trivial personal needs into vertiginous intellectual edifices.' Isou was outraged by this dismissive attitude, mainly because it seemed to apply to his own thinking as well as Artaud's.

Ferdière had taken Artaud seriously, but only as a patient and a poet, and not as a prophet. This was a crime that Isou could not forgive, especially since, if Ferdière applied the same approach to Isou – which he did – it threatened everything that Isou had ever believed in; his whole life in fact. Ferdière was therefore immediately pronounced an enemy by Isou and Maurice Lemaître.

Lemaître also had to be punished by Isou. During a *lettriste* meeting in a bar on the Avenue Carnot, Isou denounced Lemaître for having signed the papers which had led to his internment, something which Isou's wife Jacqueline had refused to do (Lemaître had also recorded a telephone conversation with Isou in full manic flow; this recording is now in the Beinecke Library at Yale University).[6] As a punishment Lemaître was forced to follow Isou on his knees in the Luxembourg Gardens and duck his head in the basin of the fountain. A small number of *lettristes* resigned on the spot as Isou issued his orders. Worse still, Lemaître was forced to make the claim to Ferdière that he suffered from the same symptoms as Isou and persuaded the doctor to make him undergo the same sleeping therapy.[7] When he recovered, Lemaître went immediately onto the attack. He accused Ferdière in print of a fraudulent and retrograde way of thinking.

Both Isou and Lemaître soon intensified the assault; under the auspices of the *lettriste* group, they accused Ferdière of working for reactionary forces, possibly the French government, and deliberately sabotaging the near-Revolution of May 1968 by taking away its leader, the *conducator* (the Romanian term for 'chief'), which was Isou. By 'depriving the masses of their leader', Lemaître wrote in one of his tracts, Ferdière 'had provoked despair among young people and adults' and 'despair in France' generally. In 1969, under the auspices of 'social psychologists' at the Universities of Vincennes and Nanterre, the *lettristes* further accused Ferdière of cruelty, demanding that he be arrested in order 'to serve as an example, the Nazi doctor Gaston Ferdière, persecutor of the poets Antonin Artaud and Isidore Isou'. The *lettristes* distributed the texts as widely as they could

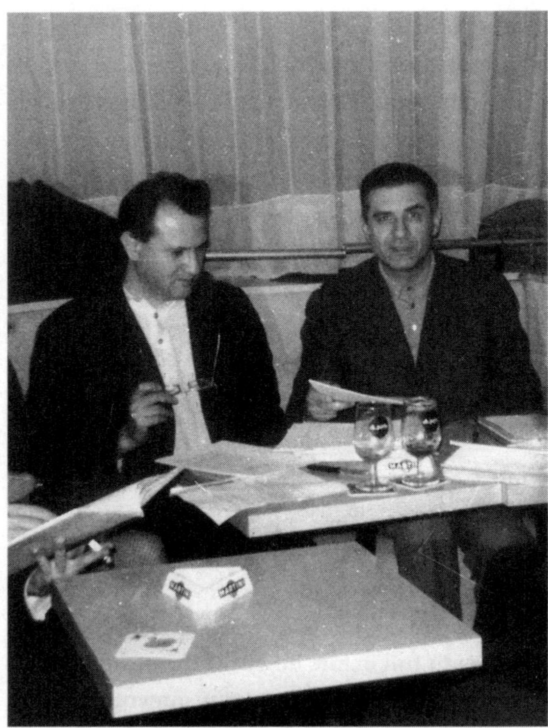

Isou and Lemaître, 1968.

but they were mainly lost in the post-1968 explosion of tracts on everything from sex to magic and Maoism.

The use of the term 'Nazi' was never innocent or gratuitous when used by Isou. He was always referring back to his experiences during the Second World War, his hatred and fear of the Nazis, the tortured bodies he had seen piled up in Bucharest, and the anguish that followed when he saw that they – the Nazis – wanted not just to kill him but, like Ferdière, wipe his name out of history.

Lettriste tracts were pasted up on the walls of the hospital of Sainte-Anne and the largest hospital in Paris, La Salpetrière. They read: 'Punish and reconvert the psychiatrists!' and 'All psychiatrists are demented. Dangers to themselves and others.' In September 1970 Isou published a text called 'Antonin Artaud, torturé par les psychiatres' (Antonin Artaud, Tortured by Psychiatrists). Although initially only read by a small group of disciples, the attacks on Ferdière soon started on a wider readership through the Paris press.

Finally, Ferdière had had enough of these public insults. He sued Isou and Lemaître for libel and defamation. The trial was heard on 21 April 1970. Isou was fined 500 francs while the editor of the weekly *Pariscope*, which published one of Isou's first attacks on Ferdière, was fined 2,000 francs. Another article had appeared in the Paris daily *Paris Jour* but received no sanction. Overall, however, Ferdière received a total of 20,000 francs as a final settlement (he was paid by one of Isou's supporters).

The libel suit partly revolved around the contents of a meeting held between Isou, his *lettriste* comrades and Ferdière in June 1968. The tone had been aggressive and Ferdière, who had agreed to the meeting, felt he was on trial rather than simply talking to a patient. Isou had asked Ferdière if it was true that Artaud had called Ferdière 'a swine who takes heroin'. Isou then speculated publicly that Ferdière – the aspiring literary artist – had taken heroin to improve his mediocre poetry. Lemaître had made all of this public in print, as well as accusing Ferdière of 'killing' Artaud and being responsible for the suicide of Gabrielle Russier – a schoolteacher in her thirties who had fallen in love with one of her sixteen-year-old pupils at the height of the revolutionary fervour of May '68.

Hounded by the press, Russier had become a heroine and martyr to the cause when she killed herself in 1969, tortured by the media spectacle. This sad story became a *cause célèbre* in France and later a successful film and then a hit song (sung by Charles Aznavour). Ferdière had never in fact met Russier. It was all of these aspects of the battle between Ferdière and Isou that turned a minor squabble between obscure avant-garde fanatics into a wider spectacle covered by the French media.

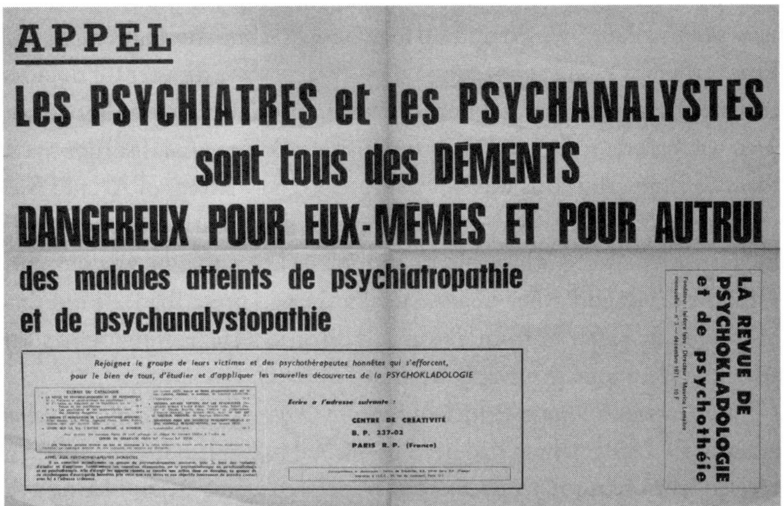

Isidore Isou, 'Les psychiatres et les psychanalystes sont tous des déments dangereux pour eux-mêmes et pour autrui', *La revue de psychokladologie et de psychothéie*, no. 3, (December 1971), poster.

This made the situation a pyrrhic victory for Ferdière. Despite winning his argument against the *lettristes*, Ferdière emerged from the battle as a melancholy and bitter figure. His lifelong ambition had been to marry literature and psychiatry, to create a new field of study called 'the science of the soul'. He never abandoned this ambition and worked on it until his death in 1990. But he never wrote poetry again, devoting himself instead to collating his papers on Artaud, trying to rescue a reputation that Isou and the *lettristes* had called so severely into question.

———

The *lettriste* 'war against psychiatry' (this had been the headline in *Paris Jour*) had not been taking place in isolation. In the aftermath of May '68, it became part of radical thinking that Freudianism was out of date and that the concept of 'psychiatry' as a form of healing only masked the truer more sinister aim of psychiatrists, which was mind control of the wildest and most uncontrollable people in society.

In the counter-cultural imagination, madness was not only hip but to be actively desired as an altered state which, like taking drugs, provided a shortcut to the universe and the universal. The *lettristes* were not drug-takers, but Isou's writings on psychiatry did seem, briefly, to chime with the mood of the times. More precisely Isou argued in his texts – most notably the long and rambling *Manifeste pour une psychopathologie et une nouvelle psychothérapie* (Manifesto for a New Psychopathology and a New Psychotherapy) – that conventional psychiatry was a disaster for doctors and patients because it was trying to do the impossible: to 'cure' the patient. This was based on the erroneous supposition that mental disorder was a form of 'illness', but this was not the case; as the writings of Artaud had shown, such disorder was in fact a form of illumination. Isou himself held a dual view of his 'psychiatric illness': he knew that he was sick and took the drugs and other treatments that he was prescribed; he did this as though he suffered from a stomach disorder. The real metaphysical struggles were something else, separate.

Isou owned a copy in French of *Self and Others*, by the Scottish psychiatrist R. D. Laing, which had been published in English in 1961 and in a revised edition in 1969. *Self and Others* created a cult around Laing as a kind of 'anti-psychiatrist' (a position that Laing always refuted), and he became a heroic figure in the counter-culture of the 1960s, albeit at the expense of the academic respect of his scientific peers.

In this book, Laing argues that what is termed madness, often diagnosed as schizophrenia, is in fact an entirely logical response to a world in which the 'mad person' feels inauthentic and unreal. Laing termed this state 'ontological security' in his later work *The Divided Self*. Laing went on to point out that as a defence mechanism the 'integrated self' of the 'mad person' is broken into component parts that do not always make sense. This is how the personality can disintegrate. This was not illness as such, posited Laing, but a perfectly reasonable response to a world that did not make sense; in other words civilization, and not the 'mad subject', caused the distress. The way out was not to 'cure' the sufferer but to listen, understand and even enter into their belief systems. Laing quoted Dostoevsky in *Self and Others* to explain all of these theories.

Isou admired Laing for his theories but had in fact come to the same conclusions during his own experiences in 1968 and '69. Isou was not mad – reasoned Isou – it was the world without Isou that made no sense. Isou was not alone either in his ideas and theories. Parallel to his attacks on psychiatry was the evolution of a group called SITIM, or La Société Internationale des Techniques d'Imagerie Mentale (The International Society of Techniques of Mental Imaging). This group was made up of a collection of students at the University of Paris who were already challenging the orthodoxies of French psychiatry by introducing the ideas of Carl Jung – still a discredited 'occultist' figure in French psychiatric circles – and Alfred Adler into their work, both of whom emphasized the importance of psychiatric symptoms as signifiers of a hidden purpose. They also embraced Depth Psychology, which meant trying to decipher the occluded language of the unconscious mind.

This new approach to psychiatry was entirely at odds with the mechanized, medicalized treatment that Artaud and Isou had undergone. Almost accidentally, therefore, Isou found himself involved in a highly politicized movement that would fundamentally shift the history of French psychiatry. Briefly Isou offered himself as a psychiatric consultant using the 'new methods' he claimed to have pioneered. He charged the same hourly rates as accredited psychiatric consultants. He had no clients.

———

It was in Sainte-Anne that Isou's wartime traumas, which he had so often repressed, started to return to haunt him. This is reflected in his writings of the time, many of which are not much more than fragments in his notebooks, or in plans for a future book. In one drawing, the psychiatrists at Sainte-Anne are depicted as Nazi camp guards, wearing swastika armbands. The patients are huddled together as they are harangued: 'Freud: come and lick my feet … Otherwise the concentration camps where they transform you into corpses will seem like a paradise, because believe me, I will torture you until you moult into dogs or pigs.' In another drawing Jews are crucified by a psychiatrist.[8]

As Isou saw it there was no difference between his conflict with the psychiatrists who were trying to treat him and his struggle against the Nazis, who had been trying to kill him. Isou knew that he was not sick, although he also knew that he was suffering, but thought instead that what was making him suffer was a religious problem. Put simply, psychoanalysis on its own was merely a science, a limited form of empirical knowledge in the hands of ignorant men, and it had no connection with the real, deep inner lives of human beings, which were dominated by love, hatred, anger, joy, despair and which could not be reduced to abstractions. Isou's whole belief system, the system that he thought had saved him from the Nazis, was based on the opposition between religion and science; in much more immediate terms, creativity versus psychiatry. This was why, in his war against psychiatry, the stakes were so high for Isou.

Isou decided finally that psychiatrists did not have a monopoly on understanding human catastrophe or human suffering. These were also religious issues. This was why they did not understand the Holocaust, or at least only understood it to a limited extent. It was not about trauma but religious experience.

During his periods of recuperation from psychiatric treatment Isou steeped himself in the literature of catastrophe – the writings of Wiesel and others who had questioned the meaning of the Holocaust. This was when Isou began his slow journey back to Judaism, suspecting that somehow it was part of the way out from his impossible situation, caught between madness and Messianism.

Until now Isou had firmly believed that the method and techniques of *lettrisme*, like the 'experimental science' of the Renaissance alchemists, would lead him towards the secret of immortality. But now he was starting to lose his faith. He found it difficult to accept at first but started slowly to understand that, like everyone else, he was going to die. This was of course the tragic knowledge that Isou had spent all of his life trying to avoid.

eighteen

Inside the Castle

The next decade was not easy for Isou. In 1972 he made a journey to Israel to see his parents, and tried unsuccessfully to launch a museum of his works in Be'er-Sheva. He tried to write a novel during his stay, a follow-up to *L'Agrégation* which was called *Voyage à Beer-Sheva ou Echecs sur le chantier de la société paradisiaque* (Journey to Be'er-Sheva; or, Failures on the Construction Site of the Paradisiacal Society). The result was an incoherent mess, a pastiche of Joyce which included an account of a flight to Israel, old arguments with Raymond Queneau, his views on Israel, relationships with his family. The volume was never published, not even in the underground format which the *lettristes* employed when they could not get published anywhere else. In Israel he harangued his family, argued with them and persecuted his teenage nephew, Fanny's son, on the grounds that he was wasting time if he did not become a genius like his uncle.[1]

On his return to Paris in late summer, Isou learned that Gabriel Pomerand had killed himself in June 1972 at the age of 46, having become a confirmed opiate addict. Isou was devastated by Pomerand's death, which to him clearly heralded the end of an era. That same year Isou was abandoned by long-term *lettriste* disciples like Jacques Spacagna, who felt that they could take no more of his excesses and delirium. No gallery would touch him. He was now also beginning to show the symptoms of hyperthyroidism and other as yet undiagnosed maladies, one of which made his eyeballs bulge out of his head. This was most probably exophthalmos, also known as proptosis, a condition related to hyperthyroidism. Having once stalked the streets of the Left Bank as a beautiful young god as handsome as James Dean or Elvis

Presley, he now sometimes looked as mad as the reputation which preceded him.

The *lettristes*, still with Maurice Lemaître as the staunch second-in-command, continued their campaign of pamphlets, propaganda and insults against all forms of official culture. But nobody took them seriously any more, or even paid much attention. They were a relic from an earlier era – the Saint-Germain-des-Prés of twenty years earlier. Claiming to be the leaders of the 'Youth Front', they were now starting to look distinctly like middle-aged men. Isou talked often of suicide and was interned in Sainte-Anne seven more times in the next few years. He thought of moving to Israel but when his parents died – his mother in 1975 and his father in 1976 – he did not attend the funerals. He published a tract attacking Islam, the prophet Mohammed and the current leaders of Israel and wrote an unpublished poem to his mother and her burial spot, comparing his work to Victor Hugo's great poem cycle *Les Contemplations* – a meditation on love, youth and death. His world was falling apart.

Isou fought on. On 17 January 1976 Isou was awarded a doctorate from the Université de Vincennes (Paris VIII). He did not actually produce a thesis but was given the award because of a change in the law in 1974 which meant that a doctorate could be awarded on the grounds of published work and an acknowledged contribution to thought. Isou's most important work, it was decided, was the 1,400 pages of *La Créatique ou la Novatique*, still in manuscript form.

The examination jury (which included the distinguished philosopher Jean-François Lyotard) gave him the highest grade possible – '*mention très honorable*' – but still Isou protested: 'Tell me please, has all my life been a failure? . . . Is this all I deserve?' A few months later, Maurice Lemaître proposed Isou for the Nobel Prize and a chair at the Collège de France. In a rare radio interview, Isou revealed to the world who he really was: 'When my work is looked at properly,' he said, 'you'll see that I am not just the inventor of *lettrisme* but in fact the creator of a new philosophical system.'[2] He went on to say that his only real rival in history was Leonardo da Vinci, but that Leonardo lacked Isou's focus and creativity.

Isou also still had a few supporters outside the *lettriste* faithful. In July 1976 the critic Bernard Teyssèdre (who had also been on the jury for Isou's doctorate) wrote an approving review of a modest exhibition of Isou's work at the Galerie Weiller in the rue Gît-le-Cœur. Teyssèdre placed the forgotten Isou alongside the much more famous American painter Cy Twombly, who was then exhibiting at the Muséé d'Art Moderne. For Teyssèdre Isou was the superior painter, with a wider diversity in style and able to use calligraphy in an imagined language, as evocative in its own way as any relics from the Mayas or ancient Egyptians. Teyssèdre was also sympathetic to the *lettriste* view that Isou was a Messiah; certainly, his capacity for endless creativity did indeed have something godlike about it, even if he was not quite a god. Isou was, Teyssèdre concluded, a genuine visionary who possessed 'distress in his humility'.[3]

Around this time, Isou also started psychiatric treatment with a new young doctor called Guy Maruani, who went on to become his friend and to treat Isou until his death in 2007. Maruani had originally trained as a surgeon but had turned to psychiatry because of his own literary interests and because it seemed to be a discipline halfway between art and science. Maruani also had another career behind him. In the late 1960s he had been a successful rock musician. With his brother André – both of them long-haired and good-looking – he had been part of a band called Classical M, which played bluesy pop and sounded not unlike the Small Faces, although Maruani's first and greatest love was The Beatles. Classical M were always on the cusp of making it big and breaking out of the Parisian rock music ghetto but eventually failed, blaming their lack of success on an inability to write convincing songs in English.

Most importantly for Isou, Maruani took him seriously as an artist and an intellect. Maruani was also a Jew and a Zionist. On hearing Isou praise Judaism so many times during their therapy sessions, Maruani asked Isou in Hebrew whether he spoke the language. Isou was incensed – of course he didn't speak Hebrew and how dare Maruani humiliate him by speaking to him in a language he didn't understand. Shortly afterwards Maruani seduced Isou's then lover, a beautiful dancer called Jacqueline Tarkieltaub. Isou never knew this but had decided to discard Tarkieltaub anyway, declaring once again that he did not have the time any more for human relationships and it was more efficient to masturbate in a porno cinema whenever the sexual urge overtook him.[4]

Maruani is also one of the characters in Isou's major novel of this period, which was called *L'Héritier du château* (The Inheritor of the Castle), published in the autumn of 1976 and intended as a sequel to Franz Kafka's final work *The Castle*. Isou was proud of this book and was fully convinced that it would win him at last the Prix Goncourt that he so richly deserved. In truth the book is a discordant mess, with no real plot but a series of anecdotes and incidents that veer from Israel to the island of Mykonos, but mainly focus on Isou's home territory, which was still the Left Bank of Paris. It is barely a novel but rather a thinly disguised autoportrait. Some of the characters have their names changed as in a *roman à clef* (Maurice Lemaître is renamed 'Pavel' and Catherine Goldstein called 'Caroline', and so on) but, as in *L'Agrégation*, the book mostly uses real names and real situations. For all this, *L'Héritier du château* is a powerful and deeply unsettling work – a visceral and disturbing account of a mind in free-fall. For this reason, it was published by the reputable publishing house Éditions Balland, and on its publication was praised by Armand Lanoux, a respected novelist and winner of the Prix Goncourt in 1963. Lanoux said that in this book 'Isou goes beyond Kafka and Dali.'

The book is narrated by a character called Claude Damiens, who is really Isou and who recounts through the course of the book his vast plan to transform society and the world through art, poetry, mathematics, political science and medicine. The novel is loosely related to Kafka's novel *The Castle*, in which a land surveyor is sent to a village and endeavours in vain to gain access to the mysterious authorities who run the territory from an impenetrable castle. The story is often interpreted as an allegory of totalitarian political control but is also sometimes read with a religious meaning: the castle represents a heavenly paradise that human beings can never enter. In Isou's novel, Claude Damiens purports to take us into the castle, revealing its secrets and thereby the pathway to what Isou/Damiens calls the 'Paradisiacal Society'. There are three essential secrets in the castle: how to overcome death, how to stop massacres, and how to create the Paradisiacal Society, which means to look God in the face without drugs.

It is not long before we realize that the castle has no real earthly existence but exists only in Damiens'/Isou's head. As such Isou's imagined 'castle' is the counterpoint to the all too real and earthly hells which his narrator encounters through the course of the book; these are mainly the lunatic asylums to which he is confined on a regular basis on the grounds of his 'excesses'. The mad could be dangerous and frightening (during one stay in a psychiatric hospital an inmate took exception to Isou's Oriental looks and threatened to 'cut his cock off'), and the guards were totally in control.[5] The world, evidently, had not moved on from Hitler or the Holocaust. Israel was no longer a safe haven for Jews, now that it had become an 'Americanized ghetto', drunk on aggression after the Yom Kippur War. The Situationists, who hijacked the near-revolution and conspired to steal it from the *lettristes*, were similarly denounced as 'neo-Nazis', no more than unreformed Hitlerites.

One of the most touching aspects of the story is that Damiens knows that he is ill and acknowledges that he may be mad. He wanders the streets and cafés of the Left Bank, wanting to 'clean the streets' to return the area to the paradise he had known in the 1940s, when its denizens believed in 'honour, courage' and had 'a taste for risk'. Now, all he sees are porno cinemas, fast-food joints, hippies and other drug-addled youths. This is not a safe place to let his daughter 'Caroline' walk alone. He takes books from shops without paying and is known to the waiters in the area as a bug-eyed madman, who talks to himself at a café table or explodes into rants against strangers. This is not necessarily an accurate self-portrait of how Isou really lived at this point in his life, but is inspired by some of his earlier experiences and the experiences of people he met, and there is a terrible pathos in the way that he describes it so lucidly and clearly.

He describes his various illnesses, and hospital visits, with the same accuracy. Particularly harrowing is an account of an arthritic attack which leaves the narrator paralysed in his apartment, unable even to get to the toilet to urinate; the paralysis is particularly agonizing because he has taken a powerful diuretic for his hyperthyroidism and is overwhelmed by the need to piss. Medicine is a 'pseudo-science', like psychiatry, but he still visits the doctor and takes his drugs. He is humiliated by being forced to attend at certain given times and writes to the hospital to complain that he is a genius and cannot be forced to wait in line as he has 'difficult books' to read. The self-portrait is that of a broken, brilliant mind, who knows that his body is betraying him but who holds on to his sense of self as a genius as the only identity he has.

There are other moving moments in the book. At one point, Damiens writes a long letter to his daughter 'Caroline'.[6] He says that she is the being that he has loved most in his life. He knows that her mother Jacqueline says that he is unwell and often delirious, like 'Hölderlin and Nietzsche'. But he is also full of paternal love (he compares their relationship to that between André Breton and his daughter Aube; Breton wrote to Aube often, always offering loving advice). Damiens advises Caroline to take up the study of medicine rather than engineering and mathematics, which was her first choice. This was because engineering as a career would take her to 'unpleasant provincial places', but above all it would take her away from the 'family tenderness', which was one of the most important things in life.

L'Héritier du château also contains an account of Isou's/Damiens' friendship with Emil Cioran, who was in fact a literary admirer of Isou (he reminded Cioran of another friend, Samuel Beckett). Isou knew that Cioran had been an antisemite and a fascist sympathizer in the 1930s and had been close to the ideas of Nae Ionescu. After 1945, when he was established in Paris and had begun writing only in French, Cioran never quite recanted his earlier fascism, but had moved away into a more apocalyptic form of nihilism. His reputation was built on two books, one in Romanian and one in French. The first was *Pe culmile disperării* (On the Heights of Despair), published in Bucharest in 1934, and *Précis de décomposition* (A Short History of Decay), published in Paris in 1949. Both works were driven by a philosophical pessimism and Cioran himself had often been overwhelmed by his feelings of despair and aching for suicide – which was why he had also been interned in Sainte-Anne so many times. Cioran lived a modest and isolated life on the Left Bank, but he was friendly with most of the Romanian literary diaspora, including Mircea Eliade and Eugen (Eugène) Ionesco. Isou was introduced to Cioran first of all as a Romanian and then as a writer.[7]

Cioran was in fact one of the first writers sought out by Isou when he came to Paris in 1945, on the recommendation of his Bucharest friends. At first Cioran thought that Isou was 'a madman, a mystic' but he was intrigued by him and came to acknowledge that Isou had achieved a great deal, if not quite everything that he had set out to do. The two men suffered from extreme insomnia and walked for hours together in the Luxembourg Gardens and through night-time Paris, talking in Romanian, until they could walk no more. Cioran described his insomnia as like falling out of life, falling out of time. This appealed to Isou, who was still – more than ever – in love with the idea of eternity, even if he now knew that his body would be destroyed before he got there. His friendship with Cioran was at its most intense throughout the 1980s.

Cioran kept a secret from Isou. He had been present in Bucharest during the pogrom of 21 January 1941, when Isou had almost been killed by the Romanian fascists called the Iron Guard. Cioran had been there that night and took part in the pogrom, willing on the Iron Guard to do their deadly work. When he had found out about this, Paul Celan had broken his friendship with Cioran. Even when Cioran's fascist past became public knowledge, and the source of controversy in Paris, the two men, Isou and Cioran, never talked about it.

They did talk about death, however. Isou/Damiens harangues Cioran for his pessimism and his nihilism, accusing him of inciting young people to suicide. Cioran responds that he does not think that this is the case, but he does concede that he was investigated by the police in Romania before the war when one of his students had killed himself. He had been found innocent.

There is one wartime enemy who is, however, explicitly attacked in *L'Héritier du château*. There is a reference to the fascist poet Horia Stamatu, who had been a legionary for the Iron Guard, briefly interned at Buchenwald and finally on arrival in Paris had been responsible for setting up the literary section of the course in Romanian Studies at the Sorbonne, along with Ionesco, Eliade, Cioran and other distinguished escapees from the war. He was not only a notorious antisemite, but with his prestige and honours, everything that Isou had wanted to be. In *L'Héritier du château* he is renamed Horia Poulamasu, a play on the Romanian profanity *pula mă-sii!*, meaning 'cocksucker'.

Above all, *L'Héritier du château* is meant to be a guide and introduction to the system of knowledge which Isou called 'Kladology'. This was Isou's grand unifying theory, which he had begun to develop as far back as 1966. The term is derived from a Greek root: *klados*, which means 'branch'. The term 'Kladology' was meant to describe the way in which all branches of human knowledge could be brought together in one universal theory, as defined by Isou.[8] These included arts and sciences, economics, medicine, psychology and religion, as well as poetry and art. The aim was to overthrow all established systems of knowledge and replace them with thought that came from the new culture, the new civilization that Isou called the Paradisiacal Society – literally heaven on earth – which was being forged by the *lettristes*. This was what Isou's follower Roland Sabatier, now describing himself as a disciple or an adept, meant when he said that *lettrisme* was like the Renaissance; it was literally the rebirth of human culture out of the wreckage of a failed civilization.

'Kladology' was not a theory but also a practice; its ideas could be activated to transform the world around you if you knew how to use them and used them correctly (that is to say according to the principles which were endlessly being defined by Isou). This was what made 'Kladology' so revolutionary in political and spiritual terms. Isou thought of it as similar to alchemy – the transformation of reality in the pursuit of invisible metaphysical realities. But 'Kladology' was also a refinement and advancement of the ambitions of the old alchemists of the Renaissance. Isou wrote that it was a kind of 'super-alchemy' – a divine method which did not so much reveal God as make its adepts into gods. These adepts – the *lettriste* disciples – were transparent. They passed for ordinary human beings but their project or mission was to follow Isou into the absolute, far from 'human animality'. All of Isou's work so far had been signs. He had yet to write 'the Bible of tomorrow'. But it was already in his head, which was the true castle that he also called 'a cathedral of the arts'. He compared himself to the twentieth-century alchemists Fulcanelli and Canseliet; but their work was far behind Isou, whose mind itself was an 'athanor' (the furnace used by alchemists to maintain a steady heat by burning its own fuel). He sometimes compared his apartment – packed with papers, books, drafts of manuscripts and paintings – to an 'athanor'.

All of this, at one level, was clearly a symptom of Isou's mental disintegration – or rather it was an elaborate defence mechanism against that disintegration. As Isou's external reality was being transformed by physical and mental illness, forces beyond his control, his own version of reality, 'Kladology', was a way of controlling his internal reality. The terrible pathos of *L'Héritier du château* is the way in which the main character Claude Damiens is able to hold his face up to these two opposing realities at once. His body and mind are crumbling, and he is aware of this, but he is conscious too of a 'super-reality' which transcends these facts. The book is not hard to read at a surface level but is packed with so many digressions and coded meanings as to be indecipherable to anybody without a detailed knowledge of Isou's thinking at this point. The book sold badly – less than a thousand copies.

'Kladology' is sometimes referred to as a form of occultism, a hermetic system of thought based on secrets and mysteries, but it is in fact closer to mainstream religion. More specifically, it is a sort of return to Judaism, although not necessarily to the form of Hasidism that he had known as a child in Botoşani. In his first writings on Judaism, mainly in *L'Agrégation*, Isou regards the Torah as containing the essence of Judaism – a sacred text which is sufficiently 'mystical' to withstand the domination of Christian dominance in Europe. The Torah also contains the Kabbalah – the signs and spiritual laws which guide the believer to the Creator. In Hasidism, the best-known Kabbalistic methods are known as Lurianic Kabbalah, named after its sixteenth-century founder Isaac Luria, a rabbi from Galilee.

These were the core of Isou's Jewish beliefs until the 1960s and '70s, when he found himself disappointed by the gulf between religion, especially the Jewish religion, and the changes in society and culture that he could see were happening all around him. His so-called 'Catholicism' was now long since abandoned, an expediency to help him get into bed with his future wife Jacqueline.

For Isou there had to be a connection between social change and the universe – this was the truth that he brought to the world as a Messiah. Isou's return to Judaism was not to make himself subservient to its messages and its laws but quite the opposite: to make Judaism, especially its esoteric, most divine methods, subservient to the laws of Creation as defined by Isou. This was what he meant when he spoke of rewriting the Bible.

This was of course a million miles away from the classical Marxism that was coursing through the body politic of France in the 1960s and '70s. In particular Isou's nearest rivals (and plagiarists) the Situationists seized on Isou's 'mystical' theories to prove that he was mad, as they had always said he was. In truth this was not madness but a philosophical system that was totally foreign to Western forms of Enlightenment and post-Enlightenment thinking, which posited Reason and Logic as the cornerstones for analysing and then implementing political change.

Isou had seen where Enlightenment thinking had led during the war and the persecution of the Jews, that the Rational could only be opposed by the Irrational, that Western thinking could only be undermined by Eastern mysticism.[9] His experiences in the psychiatric hospitals of France was only further proof of this.

This was one of the central ideas in *La Créatique ou la Novatique*, which was deposited in the Bibliothèque Nationale de France in 1977 with the sense that it was both a monument and a testament. Handling the original text takes great care – it is a large, unruly and disordered tome. To Isou it was as sacred as the Torah, a revelation from the Messiah or Holy Spirit, which of course was Isou.

In 1977 a change in French law also meant that the ban was lifted on Isou's erotic works, which were still officially banned (and entirely out of print in any case). It was also the year when he began work on a new novel called *Jonas ou le corps à la recherche de son âme* (Jonah; or, The Body in Search of Its Soul). It was finally finished seven years later. At this stage in embryonic form, it was to be the story of Isou, who like the biblical Jonah is trapped in the body of the whale, a metaphor for Isou in the psychiatric hospital. He had a sense that he was in a kind of prison, surrounded by invisible psychic walls.

In July 1979 he travelled once again to Israel. His paintings were actually selling at quite high prices as this time, which paid for his holidays. He wrote postcards back to Paris, including to Gérard Broutin, a publisher who had become a friend and *lettriste* disciple and would go on to finally publish *Jonas*: 'In this country inhabited by so many backward individuals, I have often thought of you as one of the superior personalities capable of helping us clean up the Holy Land and transform it into an Edenic place lived in by friends, living according to our nuclear economic conceptions.' In other words, Israel truly could be Paradise on Earth, if only it was cleared of its 'backward Jews'.[10]

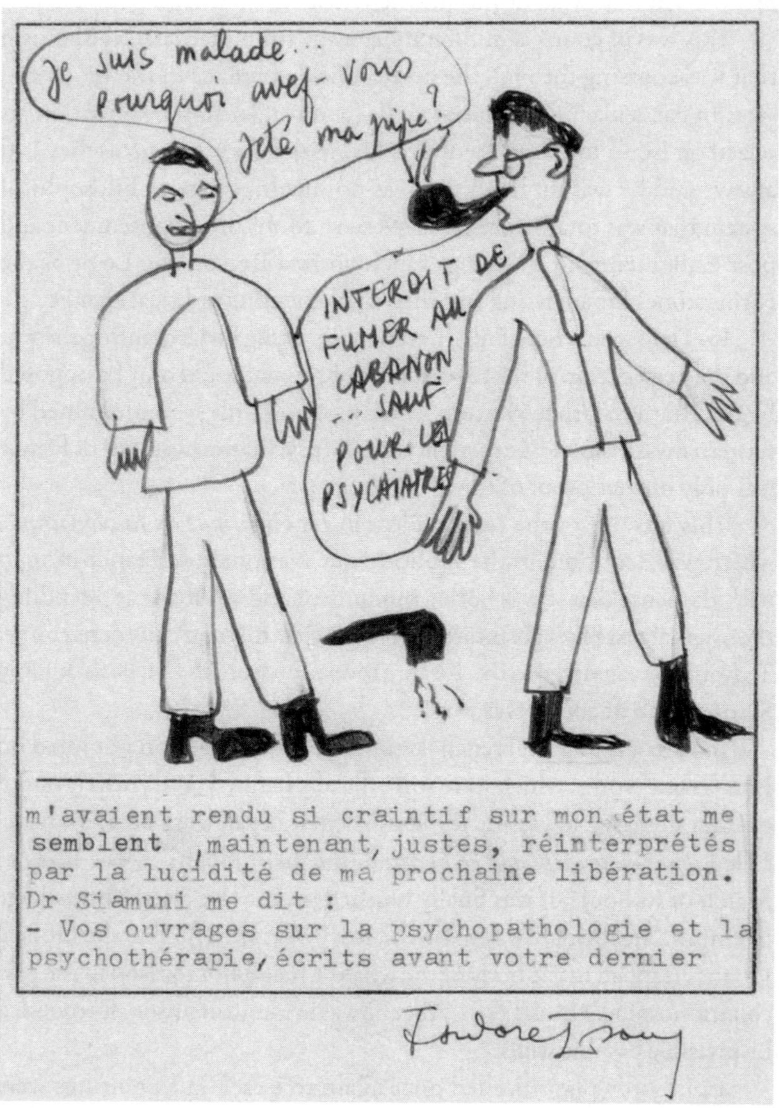

m'avaient rendu si craintif sur mon état me semblent maintenant, justes, réinterprétés par la lucidité de ma prochaine libération. Dr Siamuni me dit :
— Vos ouvrages sur la psychopathologie et la psychothérapie, écrits avant votre dernier

Isidore Isou, *Je suis malade . . .* (I am sick . . .), 1982, ink and collage on paper, published in *Jonas, ou le corps à la recherche de son âme* (1984).

nineteen

The Boy Who Thought He Could Live Forever

In one of the later sections of *L'Héritier du château* the narrator/Isou describes his life so far as consisting of three main episodes. It began 'in the Balkans a life of creation and no published work'. This was followed by his first years in Paris, which was 'a life of publishing and [as the] leader of a movement determined to take over the world'. The third part of his life was the most challenging part: after the collapse of May '68 he led 'a difficult life, trying to go forward in all ways, despite the hardships of illness'. He was trying 'to assume a fourth form of being, which would be paradisiacal – health in concrete immortality, happiness': he was still hoping, despite the scientific evidence to the contrary, that he would find the secret of eternal life.[1]

The alchemists had come near, or possibly even discovered it and kept it secret. Isou studied the Kabbalah again, trying to unlock its secret codes and inventing his own secret languages. Isou now described himself not as an artist, or at least not just as an artist, but also as a scientist. The model was, not for the first time, Leonardo da Vinci. In 1980, the same year that Isou was naturalized as a French citizen, he 'founded' the Université da Vinci. This was a university dedicated to *lettriste* methods of research into all forms of knowledge. It awarded no diplomas – this would have been reductive and stupid – but, under the statutes delivered to the Parisian Préfecture de Police, offered its students 'a total vision'.

A month after the arrival of François Mitterrand in power, in June 1981, Isou drew up a tract for the new president explaining the mission of the 'University'. The documents included a long list of distinguished individuals who had never finished school. It included Moses, Socrates, Thomas Edison, Jesus, Jack London and Ronald Reagan – all of whom,

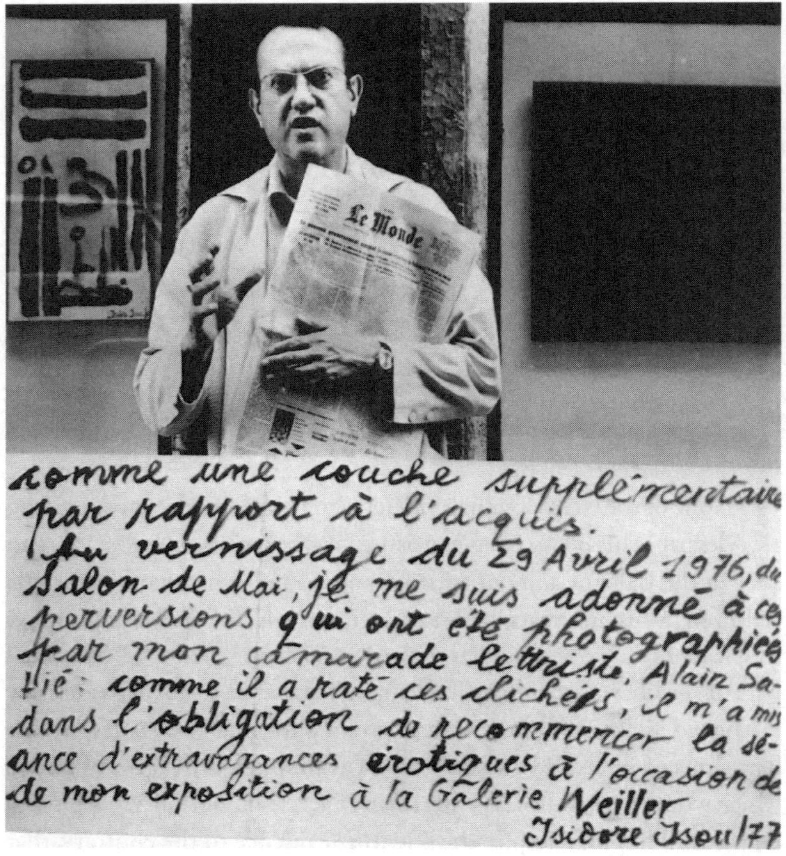

Isidore Isou, *Untitled*, 1977, pencil on photography.

in the absence of an official education, had somehow marked human history. This was what he, Isou, would teach: how to change the world. He set up court in the Librairie de la Pensée Sauvage, a bookshop on the Left Bank, where the students could register and pay fees with the aim of freeing themselves from 'backward education', which was like a 'prison or a pestilential trap'. In the meantime, preoccupied with politics, education and science, he informed his *lettriste* comrades that he was taking a 'pause' from painting.[2]

The 'pause', like the Université da Vinci, did not last long. Most significantly, Isou started painting again as a commentary on other painters, making *lettriste* pastiches of the work of the likes of Jules Pascin and Chaïm Soutine, both Jews from the East. He was also particularly fascinated by Van Gogh, not least because it seemed impossible to separate his genius from his mental condition. This had been part of an argument composed by Antonin Artaud in fragments that were published as a book called *Van Gogh. Le Suicidé de la société* (Van Gogh: The Suicide of Society). The notes which became the book were written in 1947, only a few months before Artaud's own death. Artaud was above all obsessed by the idea that there was no such thing as madness, only suffering, which came from the artist's consciousness of his alienation from society. Society at large refused to recognize this, condemned the alienated as being 'mad' and enlisted psychiatrists as the gatekeepers and jailers of the 'mad', who were in fact truly authentic human beings.

This was not so far in fact from the theories produced later by R. D. Laing, which Isou also admired, but they had a special resonance for Isou as an artist. Isou's reputation in Paris in the early 1980s was that he was not really a painter but someone who was mentally ill who used art as therapy – the term used today to describe such works would be *art brut* in French, or 'outsider art' in English. Isou was indignant at this categorization of his work and when he produced paintings during his therapy sessions, he refused to let them stay at the hospital. They were not 'symptoms' of a psychiatric disorder but real authentic creations. Isou was right. The work produced during this period is some of his best, a dynamic fusion of light, colour, signs and symbols. His reputation as a painter was ambiguous but his works did sell.

In Isou's mind they were entirely equal to any of Van Gogh's works. 'Nobody has ever written or painted, sculpted, modelled, constructed, invented, other than really to get out of hell,' Artaud wrote in *Van Gogh*. Artaud added: 'It [the madman] is a man who has preferred to become mad, in the socially understood sense of the word, rather than betray a certain superior idea of human honour ... a madman is also a man whom society does not want to hear, and whom it wants to prevent from speaking intolerable truths.'[3] Isou recognized himself in this statement.

In 1984 Isou published *Jonas ou le corps à la recherche de son âme*, which was now as near to being finished as it would ever be. This was not really intended to be Isou's last great work, but he would never again be able to construct a work of such complexity, invention and ambition. Isou was delighted with the sober cover art, which imitated the form and style of the Gallimard imprint and which seemed to present the work as a ready-made classic. The work consists of 484 pages, made up of 476 'hypergraphic' plates and other original drawings. Most of this content takes the form of photos in collage (including photos of his daughter Catherine), erotic sketches, framed by regular lines of signs and symbols drawn from mathematics, the Kabbalah, Hebrew, Greek and Sanskrit alphabets, musical scores and an invented alphabet. These are all deployed in the service of a novelistic plot and are deliberately rearranged into different ways of telling this story.

The book opens in Sainte-Anne, in the clinic of Dr Pierre Deniker – a distinguished pioneer of the use of chlorpromazine as an anti-psychotic drug. Deniker really did treat Isou but, according to Isou, did not recognize his genius. Isou is trapped in the hospital – like the biblical fable of Jonah in the whale's stomach – where his intelligence is stronger and more powerful than his failing body.

Although his body is weak and breaking down, Isou's mind is set free to roam, and he discusses with himself Georges Bataille, Plato, the Marquis de Sade, Fourier and the sixteenth-century Italian writer Pietro Aretino – a self-styled 'gossip, sodomite and pornographer' and the author of a sex manual called *The School of Whoredom* (often described as the founding text of modern pornography). Isou also discusses his own sex fantasies, including rape fantasies, or perhaps giving up sex altogether. He ruminates on his own failed marriage and the distance he feels from his daughter Catherine. Once again, psychiatrists are described as Nazi torturers and their techniques the purest form of cruelty. All of this thinking takes place over a single day in Sainte-Anne.

Isou thought that this book was easily the equivalent of works by James Joyce or Marcel Proust and said that it can be considered one of the most original publications of the post-war period. The result was text and drawing of sometimes shocking violence. This is not why *Jonas* is such a disturbing work, however; it is a work produced by someone who knows that he is unwell, possibly quite mad, and yet struggling to express his inner chaos in the form of an ordered external reality.

Isou therefore consistently resists diagnosis. When it is suggested in *Jonas* that his adoration of his mother is a straightforwardly Oedipal relationship, he responds that his love is of an entirely mystical quality: 'the splendour of my mother, for whom my feelings were mistakenly labelled as an "Oedipus" complex . . . [can be compared] to another splendour, which is my integration into a vision of the world, reinterpreted, recreated by myself.'[4] He adds, humiliated: 'Dr Latrémoine scolds me for not brushing my teeth.' There are other small humiliations: 'I am sick. Why did you throw my pipe away?' he asks in one section. The psychiatrist responds: 'It is forbidden to smoke . . . except for psychiatrists.'[5]

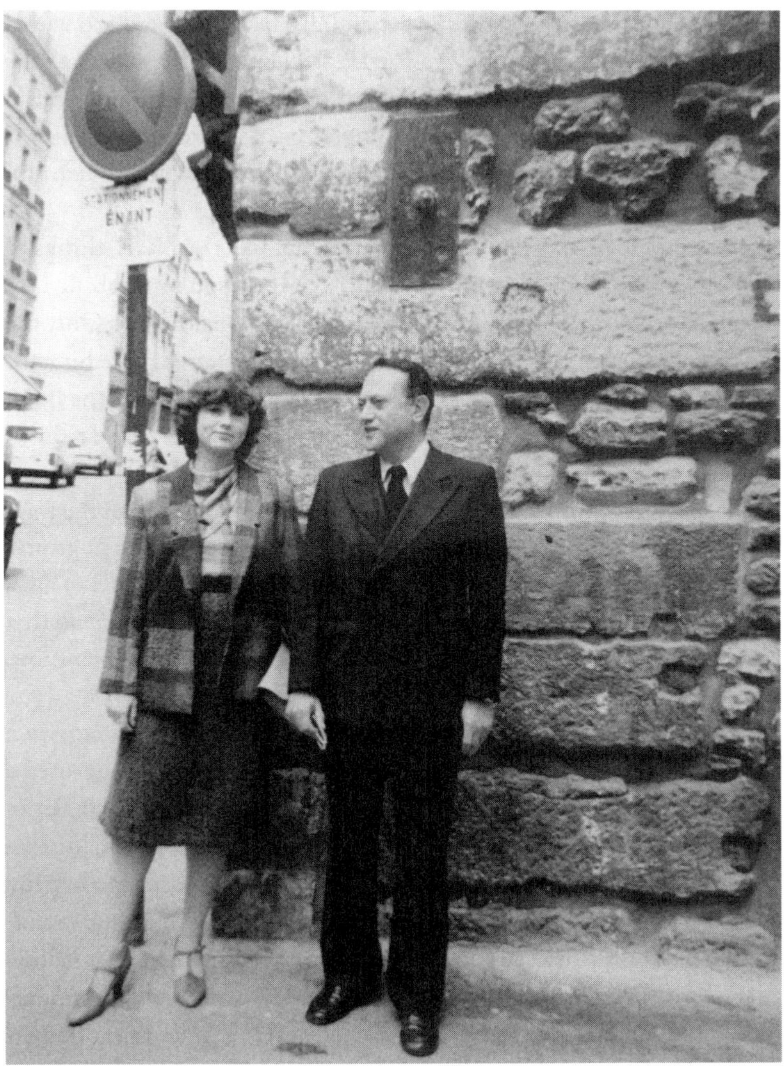

Isou and his daughter Catherine, 1980.

Isou describes his terror at being 'imprisoned': 'What bothers us most', he writes, 'is confinement, the reality that you can't get out of the asylum. So we are cruelly turned into prisoners of ignorant and exploited nurses who can throw us around without any rhyme or reason.'[6]

Isou is in constant dialogue with a Dr Siamuni (a thinly disguised Guy Maruani), whom he insults by saying that all of his work on psychoanalysis so far consists not of ideas but of mere definitions.[7] In one drawing the psychiatrist wears a cross identifying him as a 'Christian' and therefore a persecutor of the Jews (although Maruani was in fact a fervent Zionist).

The Isou figure wears a swastika armband; his face is covered too with a swastika and he implores the psychiatrist: 'Kill me! For the sake of all the madmen who didn't die for Berlin! Heil Hitler!' Dr Siamuni promises Isou that he 'will put the Oedipus complex back where he [Isou] lost it … You cannot deny that you were in love with your mother when you were a child,' says Dr Siamuni.[8]

The psychiatrist is not only a torturer but, like the Nazis, thinks of himself as a god, breaking Jewish law, crucifying Isou or stabbing him through the stomach, breaking every Jewish law along the way. Only the artist can become God, says Isou. This is why psychiatrists hate him, for his genius and because he is a Creator. As much as anything the book feels like a cry of anguish. Isou felt that he was under a curse and that his madness was the inward expression of this.

Isou always insisted to Guy Maruani that he had dealt with the traumas that he had lived through during the war, especially the pogroms, knowledge of the massacres of Jews happening in the northeast of Romania, and the constant threat of death in Bucharest. But it is clear in *Jonas* that these traumas kept on resurfacing for Isou, especially his fear of being lost, like so many Jews, in the great anonymous sweep of history.

Isou published another book in 1984 called *Histoire du Socialisme*, a far more sober and less tortured work than *Jonas*, in which he devoted a whole chapter to Hitler and 'Hitlerism'. Isou's argument was that Hitler was a kind of genius who represented a whole civilization – the Christian or Aryan civilization – but that he was doomed from the start to lose the Second World War. This was not because of geopolitics or military strategy but because Hitler had conceived of the Second World War as mainly a racial war, between Aryans and degenerate Jews. He could not understand therefore why the British, the French and the Americans opposed him, and he had to ally himself with the Japanese, who as non-Europeans were an inferior race. Part of Hitler's genius was that he understood the powerful energy of youth as a revolutionary force – as did Isou of course – and he had marshalled this in the service of his nationalism. Hitler's flaw, however, was that the Jews were a dangerous enemy: their culture was stronger and deeper than German nationalism, which had its roots only in the thin soil of German politics in the nineteenth century. Thus Hitler was doomed to lose the war and – despite the 6 million Jews who were killed – the Jews had prevailed again in history.

For all his sophistry it is clear that Isou did not, however, really believe this. As the texts of *Jonas* demonstrate, his real belief was that the Jews were the eternal victims in human history. He knew this himself as a Jew who had suffered during the war, and as a Jew who was suffering now. The Aryans or Christians were always there, always full of hatred for Jews; it was the defining fact of who they were. Isou still believed that another Holocaust might be on the way, this time from the Soviet East or the Arab world, or that it was already happening in the form of Leftist anti-Zionism in the West. Either way, the Jews were trapped once again by historical forces. This much was confirmed a few years later, in 1987, when Palestinians in the occupied territories of Israel began the uprising known as the first 'Intifada' and the world seemed to turn against Israel.

Despite his illnesses, Isou kept working. Over the next few years, there was a constant round of exhibitions, performances and publications. His work sold well enough but did not command anything like its previous prestige and rumours of Isou's madness grew ever more intense. In May 1985 Isou was invited to give a recital at a seminar in Milan. He decided to stun his audience by stripping down to his underwear, pronouncing a speech against sound poetry, and getting dressed again while burping into a microphone. The reaction in the room was sceptical hilarity. No one was shocked or stunned. He was humiliated – his sixty-year-old body was paunchy and tired, and invited pathos more than anything else. He did impress, however, an influential dealer called Francesco Conz, who decided to exhibit more of Isou's work in Italy, eventually republishing an expensive and luxurious edition of *Initiation à la haute volupté*.

Isou was now conscious more than ever of his frailty and mortality. Still he refused to believe that he would die, that he *had* to die, like everybody else. He had decided that he would be his own work of art, that his body would be his canvas and would therefore live as long as any other work of art. He wrote that one of his aims was 'to live for at least 10,000 years' and 'look exactly as I did when I was 21 years old or 35 years old'. These were the years when he had been at the height of his powers – artistically, intellectually, socially and sexually. He convinced himself that if he could only find the right method, beyond art and writing, and humanity itself, he could become God or godlike. In reality, he was trapped in an ageing body, with a fragile, restless mind that he could not control; his desire for eternal life was really just the desire to be frozen in time at the moment when he felt fully in command of the world, before his mind and body let him down.

Although Isou was naturalized as a French citizen in 1980, he had ambiguous feelings about this process, which was partly why it had taken him so long to apply after more than forty years in France. He did not necessarily feel 'Romanian' – Romanian Christians, the so-called 'true Romanians', had after all been those who had tried to kill him during the war. But he did feel that he was a Romanian Jew – a very different identity. Romania, and especially the Romanian language, never really left him.

His French nationality also allowed Isou to enter politics and in March 1993 he put himself forward as an independent candidate for the French legislative elections. He was funded and supported by Gérard Broutin, who also funded other *lettriste* candidates (Roland Sabatier, Frédérique Devaux and François Poyet). Isou began his campaign on 15 March with a public meeting at the primary school at 12 rue Saint-Benoit, in the heart of Saint-Germain-des-Prés. His programme was the same one he had delivered in the 1940s: he called for 'a youth uprising' which would change France, change the world and lead people towards the Paradisiacal Society – which was not a utopian fantasy but, like eternal life, a real and concrete concept which was near and attainable if only people understood this. There is a photograph of Isou, looking very much now a man in late middle age, casting a vote for himself, sporting a carrier bag from the supermarket chain Félix Potin under his arm and looking for all the world as if he is just about to collect his pension rather than lead an avant-garde revolution. In the end he received 184 votes, for a total of 0.58 per cent of the vote in his constituency.[9]

Later that year, partly as a result of the publicity surrounding Isou's doomed political campaign, the *lettristes* were invited to be part of the official French delegation to the Venice Biennale. Euphoria soon gave way to disappointment, however. The show was disorganized, despite the best intentions of Roland Sabatier, who had taken it on himself to co-ordinate the exhibition. Worse still, in the catalogue only one of the paintings by Isou was reproduced, out of the seventeen on display, while other works by lesser *lettristes* were mislabelled or simply printed the wrong way around. Far from looking like a tight and disciplined group who would change history forever, the *lettristes* seemed like a disunited rabble whose pretentious claims were matched neither by their talents – which were in any case hardly on show here – nor their tactics.

Isou's health grew worse. Shortly after the Venice Biennale Isou was diagnosed with a cerebellar disorder, otherwise known as ataxia. This may have been the result of a stroke, but its symptoms were unvarying: Isou now had difficulties with balance, walking, speaking, swallowing, reading and writing. He had a serious fall down the stairs in his apartment and did not leave his home any more than he needed to. When he did make a public appearance, he was now in a wheelchair and visibly diminished.

At the same time, he was becoming a mythical figure in Paris. The suicide of Guy Debord in 1994 had rekindled an interest in the Situationists and the post-war avant-gardes in general. This new interest was also fuelled by academic interest in the Situationists and the *lettristes* in the United States, where there were exhibitions and new publications investigating the *lettristes* and Situationists and their place in history. In Paris, the likes of Jean-François Bizot, doyen of the French underground, identified Isou as a key historical figure and celebrated him in his magazine *Actuel*. Isou was pleased with the attention, but also keen that his real place in history should not be obscured: he still described himself as one of the 'greatest men alive' and a 'great artist of the century, in fact any century'.

<hr>

On 4 April 1994 Isou received a visitor from a far distant past. This was 'Solly', or Serge Moscovici, whom Isou had left behind on the platform of the Gara de Nord in Bucharest in 1945 as he set off for Paris. Since then Moscovici had made his own way to Paris, where he was now famous, rich and distinguished. After his abandonment by Isou, Moscovici had thrown in his lot with the Romanian Communist Party. It was not long before he felt deceived and disillusioned and started working again with a Zionist underground movement to get Jews out of Romania. He was imprisoned for this in 1947 and determined to make his own way out of Romania. It took him a year to get to Paris, following much the same route that Isou had followed, through Hungary and Austria.

In Paris, supported by a grant for refugees, Moscovici studied psychology and became close to other literary members of the Jewish Romanian diaspora such as Paul Celan. He too was awarded his doctorate in 1961 and his career as a social psychologist gained an unstoppable momentum. He researched and taught at Princeton, Stanford, Yale and Cambridge as well as at the École Pratique des Hautes Études in Paris. He was awarded numerous prizes and became a prominent figure in politics. His son Pierre was by now also a rising star in French and European politics; Moscovici's world was a long way from wartime Bucharest. 'I was born twice,' he said often, 'once in Romania by chance, and then in Paris by choice.' But for all his worldly success, Solly had never forgotten his old friend Isidore Isou.

Solly had changed his name to 'Serge' in Bucharest in 1948, urged on by a friend called Krauze to take on a 'less Jewish name', one that 'made girls fall into bed with him', thinking that he was a pure-bred Russian and not a Jew. This was the name that Solly had brought with him to Paris. In the company of Isou, however, he was always Solly and always the faithful disciple, never the master thinker he had become elsewhere in the world.

During the five decades that the two men had lived in Paris, their paths had rarely crossed, and even then, only by accident. For the early part of his career, Moscovici had been close to Celan and another Romanian Jew called Isac Chiva, a survivor of the massacre at Iaşi (and a future anthropologist and collaborator with Claude Lévi-Strauss). They all lived in a small section of the Latin Quarter and it was inevitable that the *lettriste* Isou would sometimes run into the now serious and hard-working Moscovici; but as Moscovici climbed the social ladder, they grew further apart.

The circumstances are unclear, but in April 1994 Moscovici received a message from a third party that Isou wanted to see him. Apparently Isou had news to bring to Moscovici's attention: he had discovered the secret of eternal life and was going to live forever. Moscovici knew that his friend was unwell and lived in quite terrible poverty, but according to his diaries Moscovici also felt a need to see Isou. Moscovici was nearly seventy years old and starting to reassess his life, and in particular his early years in Bucharest where, like Isou, he had known hunger and persecution as well as a fear of death and of being trapped in a world that hated him. For a large part of his life, like many survivors of the Holocaust, Moscovici had managed to block out that part of his story. He noted that his close friend Paul Celan was unable to do this and spent every day tortured by the fact that he had survived an apocalypse, finally killing himself in 1970.

By 1994, Moscovici had not seen Isou for many years and so had no idea what to expect as he climbed the stairs towards the apartment. The staircase was old and rickety and smelt strongly of the various herbs that were stored at the back of the health shop which occupied the ground floor. This was a tiny corner of the Latin Quarter that had not yet been gentrified but was also not the old Romantic bohemian utopia of the 1940s or '50s. The street was littered with cheap kebab joints and fake art galleries for tourists, and an Irish pub. The only remnant of the avant-garde heritage of the area was the tiny, cluttered bookshop called Un Regard Moderne on the rue Gît-le-Coeur, piled high with counter-cultural literature including works on *lettrisme* and Situationism, and standing directly opposite the so-called 'Beat Hotel' where William Burroughs had finally finished *Naked Lunch*. The only other connection with the past was of course Isou himself.

As he opened the door, Moscovici squinted in the half-light. The place looked and smelled poor. The only place to sit was an uncomfortable wooden chair. Isou, who was no longer able to walk, sat on the floor, surrounded by books and dust. Moscovici understood why the place was in half-darkness when he saw Isou's swollen, bulging eyes, the symptom of hyperthyroidism, which meant that he could only tolerate the thin, yellow half-light coming in from the courtyard.

Straightaway, Moscovici could feel Isou watching him, judging him, daring him to judge the wretched conditions in which he had found himself. 'Solly' had once sincerely believed that his friend Isou, whom he had loved with a fierce devotion, would become one of the greatest men in the world. Within minutes of entering the room, Moscovici had become Solly once again and felt the same love and admiration for Isou he had known in the 1940s. He was impossibly moved to see Isou and was not depressed or disappointed by how he lived. Isou was faithful to himself; the world had changed, but he had remained the same. The dusty, bare room was a workplace. Isou was a Creator. There was a religious atmosphere in the air. Isou reminded Moscovici of a monk and the apartment felt as austere as a monk's cell. Perhaps this was where Isou's life had always been taking him, he thought.

Isou urged Solly to read the latest texts he had been writing, on medicine and spirituality and immortality, and obviously did not want the conversation to become too personal or emotional. But they soon fell into their old complicity and spoke of their old friends, Harry and Eddy and Maké, and how they had all finally escaped Bucharest. The two men spoke together in Romanian – the language which Isou had so harshly abandoned in front of Solly the last time that they had seen each other in Bucharest. Isou had never forgotten his mother tongue and still spoke Romanian in an accent that had a slight lilt that came from Yiddish. For all of his contempt for the *'petit pays de province'* of his youth, and the terrors he had known there, Romania had never really left him.

It was as if the two men had never been apart, with Solly in the familiar role of disciple and Isou as the master. Then they stopped talking. This was not new. They had often spent hours together in Bucharest without speaking. The silence allowed Moscovici to think and remember people, places and moments that he had forgotten, or thought that he had forgotten, a long time ago. He remembered meeting Isou for the first time and the strong bond, almost like love, which drew them together at once. Isou had a powerful life-force and unstinting belief in his genius and destiny that Solly also adopted. Solly remembered wandering the streets and avenues of Bucharest looking for girls and how successful and careless Isou could be with women. He remembered too how much Isou adored his mother and how Isou's mother had doted on him in return, treating him like a young lordling and believing that he could do no wrong. Isou venerated his family above all, but this did not stop him waging constant warfare against his father.

Solly's darkest and most deeply buried memory was of how Isou had escaped the terrible pogrom of the night of 23 January 1941, when the Legionaries of the Iron Guard slaughtered the Jews of Bucharest. Like Isou's family, Solly thought that Isou had been killed that night. He described how his heart leapt with joy when he saw that Isou had survived the massacres and he listened hard as Isou told him of how he had been arrested, imprisoned, beaten up with rubber truncheons, tortured and lectured on how the Jews carried syphilis and brought prostitution and pederasty with them. Then, in a darkened room, with thirty other young Jews, Isou winced with terror every time the door opened and another cohort were marched out to certain death. Isou somehow sneaked out into the street, where there was no lighting and he was bewildered and half-dressed, totally disorientated. He had lost his vision and walking was difficult. He smelled of piss and sweat.

Somehow he was either found by friends, or his father, or made his own way home. This is not quite the same description of that night given in *L'Agrégation* but it was close enough. According to Solly Isou never stopped talking about his experiences for days afterwards, telling and retelling the same horrors each time with a fresh terror. Solly thought the event had marked him for life. Isou always denied this, to his psychiatrists and to his disciples, but in 1994, Solly knew his friend well enough to sense his real feelings. He noted that these memories, still alive, had given Isou 'an elixir of fear' which never left him and the 'fear' had sustained Isou's whole career in Paris.

When Solly left Isou, it was late in the afternoon. Now returned to his identity as Moscovici, he could not get the tiny room, his friend and his memories out of his mind. He walked for hours along the Seine but might as well have been in Bucharest in the 1940s. He recalled too that

Isou had decided then that he had to live forever, that his mission in life was to find the secret of immortality. This was his revenge on the Nazis who had tried to kill him, and his revolt against the civilization which hated him and his fellow Jews.

Now, fifty years on, Isou was driven by the same obsession, except that illness and human frailty were driving him towards extinction. He communicated this much to Moscovici, saying to him that time was against him and that was why he had to work so hard. He calculated that he needed only 28 hours of sleep a week. He could no longer masturbate, which again saved him energy and time. Moscovici saw clearly, even if Isou did not or would not, that all of this was the consequence of his encounter with mass murder in 1941. For this and lots of other reasons – love, the dangerous and unsettling glance backwards at their former selves – Moscovici continued to think about Isou and write about him in his diaries long after this meeting. Had they been deluded? Had they failed? Had they misunderstood their own lives? At any rate, this was to be their last encounter, their last moment of intimacy.

As Solly left the stifling and stuffy apartment to find fresh air and walk along the Seine, Isou turned away from his friend and returned to his work. This was as it had been in 1945, on the hot August afternoon in the Gara de Nord in Bucharest, when Isou had turned his back on his friend, setting off for Paris and his destiny.[10]

Isou never spoke again to Solly. He told me that he never spoke to anyone about this, their final meeting, which was also their final separation.

Epilogue: Speaking East

So spake *Israel's* true King...
JOHN MILTON, *Paradise Regain'd* (1671)

The early evening of 6 March 2019 was bright and cold as I made my way up to the Galerie du Musée on the fourth floor of the Centre Pompidou in the heart of Paris. This building has always been ugly and is now starting to look grubby and run-down, an out-of-date relic from the late twentieth-century obsession with arrogant, high-tech flashiness in architecture. The views from the external escalator which takes you to the top are, however, always magnificent: a panoramic view of the rooftops of Paris, which that evening formed the perfect backdrop to the exhibition on the life and work of Isidore Isou which was due to open at the Galerie that evening.

The entrance to the exhibition was busy and quite festive with journalists and invited guests. The first person I bumped into was Catherine Goldstein, greeting all visitors with a warm smile. The exhibition had been made possible when she had originally donated Isou's immense archive to the Bibliothèque Kandinsky in the Centre Pompidou. The Pompidou had initially been slow to respond but now influential figures there talked about Isou in the same breath as Lautréamont or Rimbaud. Catherine introduced me to her son Thomas, who was tall but had all the same features as the young and handsome Isou of the 1940s. Catherine had told me that when Thomas was born Isou – with his usual grandiose manner – had wanted to send a hundred roses to Catherine to celebrate the birth of his grandson. Isou withdrew the offer when Catherine insisted that the roses, if any, be sent to her apartment, not offered publicly at the hospital.

I chatted too to Catherine's partner, a distinguished mathematician who had worked at King's College London but was now settled into a university job in Paris. Jim had met Isou only a few times, but while he found him at first an infuriating figure and was particularly angry at the way that he had treated Catherine over the years, he discovered that it was difficult to remain seriously angry with Isou face-to-face, because there was no meanness or cruelty in him. One of Jim's specialities is the history of physics. Isou had been intrigued enough by this to ask for Jim's help with his own theories in this field. Inevitably, they had disagreed. I asked Jim if Isou's physics was real and valid. Jim said no. 'It looked pretty as art,' he said, 'but there was no physics there.'

Did this make Isou a fraud? I did not think so, and Jim agreed. Isou may not have been a scientist in any real sense but he was quite definitely an artist and a poet; above all, he had been a theoretician of utopia, whose life's work was devoted to turning that theory into practice. Isou knew that he had failed to do this but, in his art, poetry, films and music, had seen glimpses of what success might have looked like. So had his followers, which explained why so many of his 'soldiers', disciples and friends had turned out on that chilly March night to celebrate his life and work. The atmosphere was like that of a good-natured wake and those who knew him and remembered him swapped stories as they admired the collection on display.

Isou had now been dead for twelve years – he had died on 28 July 2007. There had been other exhibitions before his death, a final public appearance in 2000, and since his death the beginning of academic enquiry into his life and legacy. But this was the first exhibition which put together the totality of his life, from his early years in Romania, the flight across Europe, the legend of the Left Bank, the pulp eroticism, the failed revolution of May '68, the settling of scores with old enemies, the mysticism, and finally the descent into illness and the realization that the utopia he had tried to create – the 'Paradisiacal Society' – could never be realized in his lifetime.

Isou's 'failure' has not, however, diminished the importance of his role in French history; if anything, Isou is indeed now being recast in history as the prophet of the 'events' of May '68. This process is being led most notably by the philosopher Michel Onfray, who argues that Isou, who was calling for a 'youth revolution' as far back as the 1940s, understood perfectly how the Second World War had eroded all previous historical class oppositions and generated a clash between the old and the young.[1] Isou had seen this at first hand in the streets of pre-war Bucharest during his days as a *huligan*. He had also seen how the energy of youth could be perverted into Fascism, whether into the Hitler Youth or the young Legionaries of the Iron Guard.

But he had also seen, in the courage of the young Zionists who were his friends and comrades, how a new world could be built out of the ruins of the old world, as long as you recognized that it was ruined and did not cling to false nostalgia or myths like the *Résistantialistes*, the 'old cunts' – Sartre, Aragon and all the rest whom he had met and hated in post-war Paris. Isou also learned all his shock tactics from the *huliganii* of Bucharest: to always be daring, to always be on the attack and to never compromise. This was his 'maximalist' philosophy in action.

These were all lessons that Isou had brought to Paris from his experiences at the eastern edges of Europe, and this is partly why the title of this book is 'Speaking East': its argument is that much of what we think of as component parts of Western modernity – Dada, Surrealism and especially Letterism/*lettrisme* – have their origins in Eastern Europe. This is not an 'Orientalist' reading of Western history but, as I have shown in this book, a straightforward historical fact. The reality is that, even though it has often been elided from European history, the supposed centre has often been shaped by the periphery. As I have already suggested in this book, Isou was not alone in bringing the East to the West.

But he did bring with him to the West, however, a religious sensibility which was more like a spiritual secret than any tangible political or historical reality. *Lettrisme* had begun as a response to the lies and propaganda that Isou had met head-on as a young Jew in the Holocaust of Nazi-occupied Romania. It was a form of psychic self-defence, opposing the 'controlling powers' of so-called objective reality with a reassertion of subjective 'poetic' reality. It soon became something else, something more: a complete system within a system that married avant-gardism and Jewish belief. Isou was not the first Jew from the East to do this: much of the radical creativity of Romanian inter-war culture had its origins in Eastern Yiddish – a fact which has often been lost or forgotten – as poets such as Tristan Tzara, Ghérasim Luca and others had made their way to the West. Isou was, however, the most stridently and avowedly Jewish among his avant-garde peers and predecessors; he never disguised it but made it the central point of his work: 'Judaism on the Attack!'

This was of course partly Isou's response to the Holocaust, to fight back and never again surrender to the 'Christians'. The more esoteric spiritual significance of his work also had its origins in the Jewish Orient. At one level, these themes inform the shape and content of the so-called 'hypergraphical' novels, which are not so very different from the calligraphic writing that appears in many Jewish prayer books. The deeper significance of this method of composition is that spontaneity and impulses of speech – the truth of communication – are often lost in writing; Isou's *lettrisme*, like the Jewish prayer books he studied in his youth, offer a way out of this snare. Most importantly, in this tradition, language is not only ultimately the word of God, but the pathway towards God. So *lettrisme* is not simply a new technique in art, poetry or painting but literally the voice of the Absolute. If you don't believe this, then it sounds simply insane, but no stranger perhaps than long centuries of 'illuminated' mystics who in all religions have sought to speak with God. Isou's life and work, seen in this way, is simply the twentieth-century version of an old tradition: a rejection of failed Western rationalism in favour of the irrational as the way towards divinity – literally 'speaking East'.

During our interview in 1999, I put it to Isou that reading his work was proof that the era of the avant-gardes was not yet dead, but still a living component of our present reality, and that their iconoclasm was perhaps needed now more than ever. Isou, now old but still a creator, smiled and said to me, 'Vous faites partie d'une élite, Monsieur, qui a compris que la tâche de l'avant-garde n'est pas encore achevée' (You are part of an élite, Monsieur, which has understood that the work of the avant-garde is not yet over).

By then, as he moved into the final part of his life, Isou had finally come to terms with death, accepting that, like everyone else, he too would eventually dissolve into the infinitesimal. But he never lost his faith in *lettrisme* – the theory of endless creativity which could literally bring the heavens to the earth. 'After my death, when my work will be better understood,' he wrote, 'Lettrisme or Isouisme will take over the world.'[2]

At his graveside in Père Lachaise, there is another quotation: 'Everything bad about me has already been said. It would be rarer and more original to discover the good in my actions.' This statement was chosen by Isou's cherished daughter Catherine Goldstein. It is not meant as an epitaph, as a full-stop. This makes sense: among the many challenges of writing about Isou is the fact that he does not often stand still or always make sense; he is grandiose, exasperating, self-regarding, brilliant, piercing and poetic, often all in the space of the same page.

Instead, ever faithful to a life lived as a continuous series of provocations, in turn poetic, philosophical and political, Isou is here again throwing down another final challenge: this time to his future readers.

REFERENCES

All translations from French or Romanian
are by the author unless otherwise stated.

Introduction: 'All Poets Are Yids!'

1 This interview took place in Paris, 26 April 1999. Photographs of Isou's apartment, its layout and Isou himself around this time can found in Bernard Plossu, *Trois heures avec Isou* (Paris, 2015). A diagram of Isou's apartment and an inventory of its contents can be found in Fabrice Flahutez and Camille Morand, *Isidore Isou's Library: A Certain Look on Lettrism* (Paris, 2014).
2 See the brief reference to Romania in the interview with the *lettriste* Roland Sabatier in Isidore Isou, *Précisions sur ma poésie et moi. Dix poèmes magnifiques. Suivi d'un entretien avec Roland Sabatier* (Paris, 2003), pp. 136–7. There are also semi-autobiographical references in Isou's novels *Adorable Roumaine* (Paris, 1978) and *Belles d'Europe* (Paris, 1955). See also Frédérique Devaux, *Entretiens avec Isidore Isou* (Charlieu, 1992), pp. 41–4.
3 Isidore Isou, *L'Agrégation d'un nom et d'un messie* (Paris, 1947), p. 135. Hereafter referred to as *L'Agrégation*.
4 Interview with author, 26 April 1999, Paris. See also *L'Agrégation*, p. 148.
5 See review of Mihail Sebastian, *Journal (1935–1944)*, www.franceculture.fr, 2007.
6 An account of this period in Romanian history is given in Tony Judt's essay 'Romania between History and Europe', in *Reappraisals, Reflections on the Forgotten Twentieth Century* (New York, 2008), p. 254. The Romanian Holocaust – by which I mean the systematic killing of Jews during the Second World War – is still a cause of argument and controversy. The key texts and documents are to be found in the three volumes of *Cartea neagra. Fapte și documente suferintele evreilor din Romania* (The Black Book: Acts and Documents of the Suffering of the Jews) by Matatias Carp, published in Bucharest between 1946 and 1948. Carp was a Jewish lawyer who was an eyewitness to many of the events which took place. The book was discredited during the communist period. It finally appeared in 2009 in French as *Le Livre noir de la destruction des Juifs de Roumanie 1940–1944*, translated and edited by Alexandra Laignel-Lavastine (Paris, 2009). The author introduces the Romanian Holocaust as 'Une Shoah oubliée' (A forgotten Shoah), p. 8. The French version was also partly the work of Isac Chiva, who knew Isou in Paris through their mutual friend Serge Moscovici.

7 *L'Agrégation*, p. 353.

8 This moment is clearly described in Frédéric Acquaviva, *Isidore Isou* (Neuchâtel, 2018), p. 14. See also Isidore Isou, *Précisions sur mon evolution dans l'art plastique, 1994–1988* (Paris, 1987), p. 12. References to this moment can also be found in Isou's journals from Bucharest held in the Fonds Isou, Bibliothèque Kandinsky, Centre Pompidou, Paris.

9 Isidore Isou, *Introduction à une nouvelle poésie et à une nouvelle musique* (Paris, 1947), p. 8. Hereafter referrred to as *Introduction*.

10 Tristan Tzara, *Dada Manifesto* (New York, 1978), pp. 78–9.

11 A full and excellent account of this history can be found in Tom Sandqvist, *Dada East: The Romanians of the Cabaret Voltaire* (Cambridge, MA, and London, 2006).

12 Author interview with Ralph Rumney, Manosque, August 2000. See also Ralph Rumney, *Le Consul* (Paris, 2018), p. 30, and Alan Woods and Ralph Rumney, *The Map Is Not the Territory* (Manchester, 2001), p. 177.

13 Ralph Thompson, 'In and Out of Books', *New York Times*, 6 February 1949, p. 8.

14 This took place March–May 2019: www.centrepompidou.fr/en/program/calendar/event/cpnBpG8.

15 See Ted Anton, 'The Killing of Professor Culianu', *Lingua Franca*, September/October 1992.

16 See 'Protest Sent to Romania over President's Holocaust Comment', *Haaretz*, 27 July 2003.

17 See 'Romanian Historian Publicly Denies Holocaust', *Times of Israel*, 7 March 2013.

18 See 'Paula Iacob colaborator al securatitii', *Ziare*, 6 October 2013.

19 Author interview (with Gavin Bowd) with Paula Iacob, Bucharest, 28 September 1996. See also 'Sympathy for the Devil: The Lonely Death of Nicu Ceausescu', *Times Change: A Quarterly and Political Magazine* (1997).

20 Interview with author, 26 April 1999, Paris.

21 This is in fact Celan's deliberate mistranslation of a poem by Marina Tsvetaeva which reads in the original Russian 'In this most Christian of worlds/Poet-Jews'. See the chapter 'Speaking East' in John Felstiner, *Paul Celan: Poet, Survivor, Jew* (New Haven, CT, and London, 1995), pp. 189 and 197.

PART I: A Romanian Youth (1925–45)

1 Yiddishland

1 Conversation with Mitchell Cohen, Paris, 2015. The book that Cohen was writing was *The Wager of Lucien Goldmann: Tragedy, Dialectics, and a Hidden God* (Princeton, NJ, 1994), a study of the Marxist philosopher Lucien Goldmann (1913–1970), a native of Botoşani.

2 A full account of Segal's early life can be found in Tom Sandqvist, *Dada East: The Romanians of the Cabaret Voltaire* (Cambridge, MA, and London, 2006), pp. 171–95. The same volume also contains several references and descriptions of Botoşani. See ibid., pp. 20–21, 172–4. 'Yiddishland' is also described ibid., pp. 271–89.

3 See Cohen, *The Wager*, p. 19.

4 Ibid., p. 20.

5 Ibid.

6 Leon Trotsky, 'The Jewish Question', in *The Balkan Wars, 1912–1913* (New York, 1980), pp. 413–14.

7 Ibid., pp. 20–23.

8 This quotation comes from Mihail Sebastian's novel of 1934, *De două mii de ani*, translated as *For Two Thousand Years* by Philip O'Ceallaigh (London, 2016), and is referenced as an example of Jewish self-doubt in Julia Elsky, 'How Do We Proceed? On the Translation of Mihail Sebastian's *For Two Thousand Years*', *Los Angeles Review of Books*, www.lareviewofbooks.org, 18 October 2017.

9 Much of this information is to be found in Isidore Isou, 'Le Père dans la création de son fils', in *L'Agrégation d'un nom et d'un messie* (Paris, 1947), pp. 28–39.

10 Isou, 'Fanny, ma chère Antigone', in *L'Agrégation*, pp. 24–7.

11 Isou, 'Entretien d'Isidore Isou et Roland Sabatier', in *Précisions sur ma poésie et moi. Dix poèmes magnifiques. Suivi d'un entretien avec Roland Sabatier* (Paris, 2003), p. 137. See also Frédérique Devaux, *Entretiens avec Isidore Isou* (Paris, 1992), p. 39.

12 Cohen, *The Wager*, pp. 16–17.

13 Ibid., p. 24.

14 Useful overviews of this period can be found in Traian Sandu, *Un fascisme roumain. Histoire de la Garde de Fer* (Paris, 2014), pp. 163–75. Also Traian Sandu, *Histoire de la Roumanie* (Paris, 2008). See also Dennis Deletant, *Hitler's Forgotten Ally: Ion Antonescu and His Regime, Romania, 1940–1944* (London, 2006), pp. 10–11.

15 Quoted in Robert R. King, *History of the Romanian Communist Party* (Stanford, CA, 1980), pp. 22–4.

16 This 'voice' is vividly defined in Patrick Leigh Fermor, *The Broken Road: From the Iron Gates to Mount Athos* (London, 2014), pp. 169–70.

2 Young Savage

1 See Igor Mocanu, '"Am plecat fără nici un act . . .": Isidore Isou și România', unpublished paper, Centre Pompidou, Paris, May 2019.

2 Isidore Isou, *L'Agrégation d'un nom et d'un messie* (Paris, 1947), p. 125.

3 Ibid., pp. 32–3.

4 Quoted in Andrew Hussey, *The Game of War: The Life and Death of Guy Debord* (London, 2001), p. 38. See Isou, *L'Agrégation*, p. 117.

5 Patrick Leigh Fermor, *The Broken Road: From the Iron Gates to Mount Athos* (London, 2014), p. 164.

6 For an overview of this process see Traian Sandu, *Histoire de la Roumanie* (Paris, 2008).

7 A full account of the Irina Galia story, partly ficticious or not, is given in 'Irina, ou la technique de l'influence', in *L'Agrégation*, pp. 43–56.

8 See Serge Moscovici, *Chronique des années égarées* (Paris, 1997), pp. 184–7.

9 *L'Agrégation*, p. 57.

10 Ibid., p. 46.
11 For an overview of Călinescu's literary attitudes see Mircea Zaciu, Marian Papahagi and Aurel Sasu, *Dicționarul scriitorilor români*, A–C, Editura Fundației Culturale Române, 1995.
12 This famous speech is quoted in Carla Baricz, 'Exile, Hooliganism, and Norman Manea's "The Hooligan's Return"', *Los Angeles Review of Books*, www.lareviewofbooks.org, 2 February 2014.
13 Isou, *Adorable Roumaine* (Paris, 1978), pp. 156–67.
14 *L'Agrégation*, p. 71.
15 The story of 'Bif' and Isou is told in 'Bif ou l'apprentissage de l'aventure', ibid., pp. 70–120.
16 Ibid., p. 77.
17 Ibid., p. 97.
18 For a definition of *umor* see Hussey, *The Game of War*, pp. 27–8.
19 Ibid., pp. 128–9.
20 Ibid., pp. 130–35.
21 This philosophy is explained at length in Gh. Al. Cazan, *Istoria filosofiei românești* (Bucharest, 1984).
22 A full explanation of the Iron Guard ideology is given in Sandu, *Histoire de la Roumanie*, pp. 197–235.

3 'God loves everything anti-Yid!'

1 For an explanation of the political background, see Traian Sandu, *Histoire de la Roumanie* (Paris, 2008), p. 355. See also Dennis Deletant, *Hitler's Forgotten Ally: Ion Antonescu and His Regime, Romania, 1940–1944* (London, 2006), pp. 65–7. See also Traian Sandu, *Un fascisme roumain. Histoire de la Garde de Fer* (Paris, 2014), pp. 353–55. For a full description of the atrocities committed against Jews during the 'uprising' see also Matatias Carp, *Le Livre noir de la destruction des juifs de Roumanie, 1940–1944* (Paris, 2009), pp. 142–68.
2 The following events and dialogue are recalled in Isidore Isou, *L'Agrégation d'un nom et d'un messie* (Paris, 1947), in the chapter called 'Livre de desagrégation', pp. 238–49, 250–52.
3 Sigmund Collin is listed alongside 'Izidor Goldstein' in Carp, *Le Livre noir*, p. 165, as one of the Jews taken to an Iron Guard headquarters at 37 Calea Calarasi.
4 F. Brunea-Fox, *Orașul măcelului* [1944] (Bucharest, 1997), p. 10.
5 This text is reproduced in Ion C. Butnaru and Renée Spodheim, *The Silent Holocaust: Romania and Its Jews* (New York and London, 1992), Foreword by Elie Wiesel, p. 85.
6 Quoted in C. Simpson, *Blowback: America's Recruitment of the Nazis and Its Effects on the Cold War* (New York, 1988), p. 255.
7 This is a reference to one group of Jews who were fed laxatives by the Iron Guard then left abandoned in a cell overnight. See Carp, *Le Livre noir*, p. 144.
8 Isou, *L'Agrégation*, p. 250.
9 Mihail Sebastian, *Jurnal* (Bucharest, 1991), p. 289.
10 *L'Agrégation*, p. 250.

11 For a full account of the massacres at Iași see Carp, *Le Livre noir*,
pp. 197–266. See also Jil Silberstein, *Les voix de Iași. Une epopée* (Paris, 2015).
12 Sebastian, *Jurnal*, p. 454.
13 *L'Agrégation*, p. 423.
14 Ibid., pp. 251–2.
15 Elie Wiesel, *Night* (London, 2015), p. 33.

4 Youth without Youth

1 Isidore Isou, *L'Agrégation d'un nom et d'un messie* (Paris, 1947), p. 161.
2 Ibid., p. 135.
3 Fonds Isou, Bibliothèque Kandinsky, Centre Pompidou, Paris.
4 Isou, *L'Agrégation*, p. 137.
5 Ibid., p. 140.
6 Isidore Isou, *Isou ou La Mécanique des femmes* (Paris, 1949), pp. 190–94.
7 Ibid., pp. 193–4.
8 Ibid., p. 194.
9 *L'Agrégation*, p. 148.
10 Ibid., p. 174.
11 The Morand story is recounted ibid., pp. 178–85. See also Isidore Isou,
Adorable Roumaine (Paris, 1978), pp. 194–204, for the fictionalized account.
12 Mihail Sebastian, *Jurnal* (Bucharest, 1991), p. 558.

5 Israelism

1 For a full account of the immediate post-war period in Bucharest and Isou's
response, see Isidore Isou, *L'Agrégation d'un nom et d'un messie* (Paris, 1947),
pp. 210–18.
2 Ibid., p. 215.
3 Ibid., p. 211.
4 Ibid., p. 213.
5 Mihail Sebastian, *Jurnal* (Bucharest, 1991), p. 570.
6 Ibid., p. 213.
7 Ibid., p. 556.
8 Ibid., pp. 560–63.
9 Isou, *L'Agrégation*, p. 216.
10 For an account of these friendships see Serge Moscovici, *Chronique de années
égarées* (Paris, 1997), pp. 259–60, 372–3, 375.
11 Ibid., p. 372.
12 Fonds Isou, Bibliothèque Kandinsky, Centre Pompidou, Paris.
13 Mica Gherghescu, 'L'Accumulateur d'immortalité. Du *Journal Roumain*
aux *Journaux des Dieux*', in *Isidore Isou*, exh. cat., Centre Pompidou
(Paris, 2019).
14 *L'Agrégation*, p. 223.
15 See Igor Moganu, unpublished paper, Centre Pompidou, 2019.
16 Ibid.
17 *L'Agrégation*, p. 225.
18 Ibid., p. 214.
19 Ibid., p. 229.

20 Isou discusses his jealousy ibid., p. 231.
21 See William D. Rubinstein, *The Palgrave Dictionary of Anglo-Jewish History* (London, 2011), p. 1059.
22 *L'Agrégation*, p. 302.
23 Ibid., p. 300.
24 Ibid., p. 341.
25 Ibid., p. 343.
26 This story is recounted ibid., pp. 341–40.

6 A Messianic Exercise

1 Isidore Isou, *L'Agrégation d'un nom et d'un messie* (Paris, 1947), p. 345.
2 The contents of this chapter, unless otherwise stated, are to be found ibid., pp. 345–60, 374–403.
3 Ibid., pp. 353–4.
4 Ibid., pp. 401–3.

7 Facing West

1 Isidore Isou, *L'Agrégation d'un nom et d'un messie* (Paris, 1947), p. 404.
2 Ibid., p. 409.
3 Ibid., p. 410.
4 Ibid., p. 412.
5 This part of Isou's journey to the West is recounted in *Isou ou La Mécanique des femmes* (Paris, 1949), pp. 20–28.
6 See ibid., pp. 30–55, 176, 250.
7 Isou, *L'Agrégation*, p. 24.
8 Ibid., p. 32.

PART II: Paris Seen by a Stranger (1945–68)

8 Making a Name

1 A brief account of this encounter is given in Jean-Paul Curtay, *La Poésie lettriste* (Paris, 1974), p. 12.
2 Isidore Isou, *L'Agrégation d'un nom et d'un messie* (Paris, 1947), p. 71.
3 Fonds Isou, Bibliothèque Kandinsky, Centre Pompidou, Paris.
4 Ibid.
5 Ibid.
6 Ibid.
7 Isou, *L'Agrégation*, p. 414.
8 'Notes pour Judaïser la France', ibid., pp. 413–14. A parallel description of early French reactions to the Holocaust can also be found in David Bellos, *Georges Perec, A Life in Words* (London, 1993), pp. 86–7. See also Alain Navarro, 'Le Grand Palais des Crimes Hitlériens', in *1945. Le Retour des Absents* (Paris, 2015), pp. 204–27.
9 Ibid., p. 495.
10 Ibid., p. 415.
11 Ibid., pp. 415–16.

12 Curtay, *La Poésie lettriste*, p. 13.

13 Introduction to Gabriel Pomerand, *Saint ghetto des prêts. Grimoire*, 1950, Bibliothèque Kandinsky, Centre Pompidou, Paris, unpaginated.

14 Curtay, *La Poésie lettriste*, p. 13.

15 Ibid., p. 12.

16 'La vieille chienne André Gide devant les lettristes', in *Appendices à une dictature lettriste*, Bibliothèque Kandinsky, p. 57.

17 Curtay, *La Poésie lettriste*, p. 1.

18 See p. 23 of Isidore Isou, *Initiation à la haute volupté* (Paris, 1960), where Isou states that there may well never be simply two sexes, 'just evolving states of one sexuality that evolves over the ages'.

19 Isidore Isou, *Isou ou La Mécanique des femmes* (Paris, 1949), pp. 140–41.

20 Ibid., pp. 143, 249.

21 Isidore Isou, 'Paris vu par un étranger', in *Introduction à une nouvelle poésie et à une nouvelle musique* (Paris, 1947), p. 344.

22 *L'Agrégation*, pp. 82–3.

23 Isidore Isou, *Lettre ouverte*, 1946, unpaginated, Fonds Isou, Carton 3, Bibliothèque Kandinsky. See also Curtay, *La Poésie lettriste*, p. 36.

24 The *lettriste* graffiti attacks on Éditions Gallimard became something of a tradition. See the cover of Roland Sabatier, *Le Lettrisme, Les Création et Les Créateurs* (Nice, 1979), for an example.

9 Poets for the Atomic Age

1 For an account of this fiasco see Guy Marester, 'Naissance du lettrisme', *Combat*, 5 July 1946. See also Christophe Bourseiller, *Vie et mort de Guy Debord* (Paris, 1999), p. 30.

2 See Maurice Nadeau, 'Les Lettristes chahutent une lecture de Tzara au Vieux Colombier', *Combat*, 22 January 1946. Also Jean-Paul Curtay, *La Poésie lettriste* (Paris, 1974), pp. 13–15. See also Serge Fauchereau, ed., *Tristan Tzara. L'Homme approximatif* (Strasbourg, 2015), pp. 40, 332.

3 For Isou's opinions on Paulhan see also *Appendices à une dictature lettriste*, Fonds Isou, Bibliothèque Kandinsky, Centre Pompidou, Paris, p. 63. Also 'Fleurs artificielles de Tarbes et leur Candide Jean Paulhan', in *La Dictature Lettriste*, Fonds Isou, Bibliothèque Kandinsky, Centre Pompidou, Paris, 1946, unpaginated.

4 Curtay, *La Poésie lettriste*, p. 15.

5 Ibid., pp. 15–16.

6 Ibid., pp. 32–3.

7 Isidore Isou, *L'Agrégation d'un nom et d'un messie* (Paris, 1947), p. 434.

8 For an analysis of Isou's view on Aragon and others see Fabrice Flatuhez, *Le Lettrisme historique etait une avant-garde* (Dijon, 2011), pp. 40–44. See also Isidore Isou, *La Créatique ou la Novatique, 1941–1976* (Paris, 2003), p. 1329, hereafter *La Créatique*. See also Curtay, *La Poésie lettriste*, p. 37.

9 Quoted in Eric Brun, *Les Situationnistes. Une avant-garde totale* (Paris, 2014), pp. 50–51.

10 *Appendices à une dictature lettriste*, p. 63.

11 All of these articles have been collected for reference in Frédéric Alix, *Penser l'art et le monde après 1945. Isidore Isou, essai d'archéologie d'une pensée* (Dijon, 2017), pp. xli–li.

12 Gabriel Pomerand, 'Sur la nécessité historique du lettrisme', also cited in Pomerand, *Le Cri et l'archange* (Paris, 1948).

10 Hatred of Poetry

1 Quoted in Fabrice Flahutez, *Le Lettrisme historique était une avant-garde* (Dijon, 2011), p. 24.

2 Isidore Isou, *Introduction à une nouvelle poésie et à une nouvelle musique* (Paris, 1947), p. 328.

3 Ibid., pp. 83–107. See also *Isidore Isou*, exh. cat., Centre Pompidou (Paris, 2019), p. 18.

4 Fonds Isou, Bibliothèque Kandinsky, Centre Pompidou, Paris.

5 Jean-Paul Curtay, *La Poésie lettriste* (Paris, 1974), p. 61.

6 Greil Marcus, *Lipstick Traces* (Paris, 2018), pp. 287–8.

7 Gabriel Pomerand, *Saint ghetto des prêts. Grimoire*, 1950, Bibliothèque Kandinsky, unpaginated.

8 The full original text of this poem is reproduced at François Letaillieur, www.lettriste-situationniste.com.

9 Isidore Isou, *Réflexions sur André Breton* (Paris, 1948, reprinted 1970), p. 10.

10 See Letaillieur, www.lettriste-situationniste.com.

11 Georges Bataille, 'La Divinité d'Isou', in *Oeuvres complètes*, Tome XI (Paris, 1988), pp. 379–82.

12 *Réflexions sur André Breton* (Paris, 1948), pp. 16–19.

13 Both of these conferences are described in Letaillieur, www.lettriste-situationniste.com.

11 Sex, Prison and Revolution

1 Jean-Paul Curtay, *La Poésie lettriste* (Paris, 1974), p. 6. Also François Letaillieur, at www.lettriste-situationniste.com.

2 Ibid., Letaillieur.

3 See Zoran Rosko, at https://zorosko.blogspot.com. Also Jacques D'Arribaude, *Cher Picaro. Journal des années cinquante* (Paris, 2003), p. 511.

4 Isidore Isou, *Isou ou La Mécanique des femmes* (Paris, 1949), p. 290.

5 See Marquis de Sade, *Les 120 Journées de Sodome* (Paris, 1975).

6 Isou, *La Mécanique des femmes*, pp. 138–40.

7 Apollinaire, *Alcools* (Paris, 1913), pp. 186–8. 'Que lentement passent les heures. Comme passe un enterrement'.

8 Frédéric Acquaviva, *Isidore Isou* (Neuchâtel, 2019), pp. 34–5.

9 Isidore Isou, *Front de la Jeunesse* (Paris, 1950).

10 Greil Marcus, *Lipstick Traces* (Paris, 2018), pp. 287–8.

12 The Heroic Period

1 A detailed account of Maurice Lemaître's early life is given in Frédéric Acquaviva, *Lemaître. Une vie lettriste* (Paris, 2014), pp. 8–12.

2 Ibid., pp. 7–8.

3 Ibid., p. 8.

4 Ibid.

5 Isidore Isou, *La Créatique ou la Novatique, 1941–1976* (Paris, 2003), p. 32.

6 L. F. Céline, *Bagatelles pour un massacre* (Paris, 1938), p. 54.

7 For the full correspondence from Céline see L. F. Céline, *Lettres à Pierre Monnier, 1948–1952* (Paris, 2015), pp. 257, 259–60, 268–9, 274, 293. See also Patrick Lepetit, 'Maurice Lemaître et l'Association israélite pour la réconciliation des Français', *Le Bulletin Célinien*, XXXVII/410 (2018).

8 Céline, *Lettres à Pierre Monnier, 1948–1952*, p. 268. See also Annick Duraffour and Pierre-André Taguieff, *Céline, la race, le Juif. Légende littéraire et vérité* (Paris, 2017), p. 771, and Henri Godard, *Poétique de Céline* (Paris, 1985), p. 21.

9 L. F. Céline, *À l'agité du Bocal* (Paris, 2018), pp. 8–11, 14.

10 Isidore Isou, *L'Agrégation d'un nom et d'un messie* (Paris, 1947), p. 423.

11 See Greil Marcus, *Lipstick Traces* (Paris, 2018), pp. 287–8, 310.

12 Ibid., p. 342.

13 Ibid., p. 315.

14 Isidore Isou, *Précisions sur ma poésie et moi. Dix poèmes magnifiques* (Paris, 2003), p. 97.

15 A full account of the presentation of the film at Cannes and its critical reception is given in Acquaviva, *Lemaître*, pp. 44–8. The photograph of Guy Debord and the graffito 'Isou' is reproduced in Acquaviva, p. 45. See also Andrew Hussey, *The Game of War: The Life and Death of Guy Debord* (London, 2001), pp. 35–6. For Rohmer's comments see 'Isou ou les choses telles qu'elles sont', *Cahiers du Cinéma*, 10 (1952).

13 Traitors

1 'Préface de Jean-Isidore Isou' to Maurice Lemaître, *Le Film est déjà commencé?* (Paris, 1952), pp. 2–5. Isou often used the prefix 'Jean' to his name at this point.

2 For an account of the sociological importance of *ciné-clubs* in France see Kaira M. Cabañas, *Off-screen Cinema: Isidore Isou and the Lettrist Avant-garde* (Chicago, IL, and London, 2014), p. 68.

3 'Préface de Jean-Isidore Isou', p. 36.

4 Ibid., p. 25.

5 See Jean-Marie Apostolidès, *Debord. Le Naufrageur* (Paris, 2015), pp. 68–71, 85–6.

6 Ibid., p. 88.

7 Asger Jorn, 'Originalité et grandeur (sur le système d'Isou)', *Internationale Situationniste*, 4 (1960).

8 Apostolidès, *Debord*, pp. 98–100.

9 Ibid., pp. 100–101. See also Andrew Hussey, *The Game of War: The Life and Death of Guy Debord* (London, 2001), pp. 65–7.

10 Guy Debord, *Correspondance, 1951–1957* (Paris, 2010), pp. 49, 78.

14 A Letter from Gaza and a Marriage in Paris

1 See 'Lettre de Gaza', reprinted in Frédéric Alix, 'Penser l'art et le monde après 1945. Isidore Isou, essai d'archéologie d'une pensée', doctoral thesis, Université Paris Nanterre, 2015, pp. 649–65.
2 Email from Guy Maruani, friend of Salomon and Isou's psychiatrist, Paris, 7 November 2018.
3 The following account is drawn from a lengthy interview with Catherine Goldstein and Jacqueline Enger, Paris, 21 September 2018.
4 Fonds Isou, Bibliothèque Kandinsky, Centre Pompidou, Paris.
5 Ibid.

15 The Erotics of God

1 Eric Brun, *Les Situationnistes. Une avant-garde totale* (Paris, 2014), pp. 31, 66–7, 137.
2 Frédéric Acquaviva, *Isidore Isou* (Neuchâtel, 2019), p. 88.
3 Isidore Isou, 'La Hongroise qui sent les pieds', in *Les Belles d'Europe* (Paris, 1955), pp. 39–45.
4 Ibid., p. 119.
5 Conversation with Jacqueline Enger, Paris, 21 September 2018.
6 Andrew Hussey, *The Game of War: The Life and Death of Guy Debord* (London, 2001), pp. 110–11.
7 Asger Jorn, 'Originalité et grandeur (sur le système d'Isou)', *Internationale Situationniste*, 4 (1960), reprinted in *Internationale Situationniste* (1997), pp. 134–8.
8 Isidore Isou, *Initiation à la haute volupté* (Paris, 1960), p. 66.
9 Ibid., p. 30.
10 Quoted in Frédéric Acquaviva, *Isidore Isou: Hypergraphic Novels, 1950–1984* (Romanian Cultural Institute in Stockholm, 2012), p. 63. This catalogue, created to accompany an exhibition held at the Romanian Cultural Institute in Stockholm in February–April 2011, is an indispensable guide to Isou's 'Hypergraphical' works.
11 Jean Cocteau, 'Le Cas Isou', in *Mes monstres sacrés* (Paris, 1970), p. 31, quoted in Acquaviva, *Isidore Isou*, p. 83.
12 Quoted in Acquaviva, *Isidore Isou*, p. 124.

16 Madness in May

1 For a description of Tzara's funeral see Isidore Isou, *Considérations sur la mort et l'enterrement de Tristan Tzara* (Paris, 1965).
2 Fonds Isou, Bibliothèque Kandinsky, Centre Pompidou, Paris.
3 Conversation with Guy Maruani, Paris, May 2019.
4 Petre Solomon, *Paul Celan: The Romanian Dimension* (Syracuse, NY, 2019), p. 57.
5 Quoted in Frédéric Acquaviva, *Isidore Isou* (Neuchâtel, 2019), p. 133.
6 A link between Lennon and Isou was made by Guy Maruani, 'The Semantic Bomb', paper given at the conference 'Invisible Republic', University of Lisbon, 25 October 2017.

7 An overview of Situationist involvement in the events of May '68 in Paris is given in Andrew Hussey, *The Game of War: The Life and Death of Guy Debord* (London, 2001), pp. 221–40.

8 Acquaviva, *Isidore Isou*, p. 163. Acquaviva's account of Isou's activities in May 1968 in most likely the most definitive and authoritative account, corroborated in conversation with other *lettriste* comrades.

9 Conversation with François Poyet, Paris, 2016.

10 Quoted in Victor Bockris, *Lou Reed: The Biography* (London, 1995), p. 15.

PART III: The Divinity of Isou (1968–2007)

17 'Demons are tearing me apart!'

1 Frédéric Acquaviva, *Isidore Isou* (Neuchâtel, 2019), p. 163. This incident is also recalled in Isidore Isou, *L'Héritier du château* (Paris, 1976), p. 271.

2 L. F. Céline, *Journey to the End of the Night*, trans. Ralph Manheim (Surrey, 2010), p. 335.

3 Isidore Isou, *Les Démons me dechirent!* (Paris, 1969).

4 For an overview of these events see Gaston Ferdière, *Les Mauvaises frequentations. Mémoires d'un psychiatre* (Paris, 1978); Antonin Artaud, *Nouveaux écrits de Rodez. Lettres au docteur Ferdière, 1943–1946, et autres textes inédits, suivis de six lettres à Marie Dubuc, 1935–1937* (Paris, 1977); Laurent Danchin, Jean-Claude Fosse and André Roumieux, eds, *Artaud et l'asile. 1. Au-delà des murs, la mémoire* (Paris, 1996); Laurent Danchin, Jean-Claude Fosse and André Roumieux, eds, *Artaud et l'asile. 2. Le Cabinet du docteur Ferdière* (Paris, 1996); also Emmanuel Venet, *Ferdière, psychiatre d'Antonin Artaud* (Paris, 2006).

5 A useful and accessible overview of this illness and art is given in Kay Redfield Jamison, *Touched with Fire: Manic Depressive Illness and the Artistic Temperament* (New York, 1993). See references to Falret and Baillaiger, pp. 35–6. An overview of the history of mental hospitals in Paris can be found in Benoît Majerus, *La Folie à Paris* (Paris, 2018).

6 Acquaviva, *Isidore Isou*, p. 165.

7 Ibid., p. 167.

8 See Isidore Isou, *Jonas ou le corps à la recherche de son âme* (Paris, 1984), p. 265.

18 Inside the Castle

1 Conversation with Catherine Goldstein, Paris, 2018.

2 Frédéric Acquaviva, *Isidore Isou* (Neuchâtel, 2019), p. 185.

3 Ibid., p. 186.

4 These aspects of Isou's life were discussed in many conversations with Guy Maruani, Paris and Lisbon, 2017–20. See also private correspondence between Maruani and Isou (1979) held in the Maruani collection.

5 Isidore Isou, *L'Héritier du château* (Paris, 1976), p. 237.

6 Ibid., pp. 119–25.

7 Ibid., pp. 221–8.

8 For an introduction to 'Kladology' see Roland Sabatier, *Le Lettrisme. Les Créations et les créateurs* (Nice, 1979).

9 See Sami Sjöberg, *The Vanguard Messiah: Lettrism between Jewish Mysticism and the Avant-garde* (Berlin, 2015).
10 Acquaviva, *Isidore Isou*, p. 197.

19 The Boy Who Thought He Could Live Forever

1 Isidore Isou, *L'Héritier du château* (Paris, 1976), p. 251.
2 Frédéric Acquaviva, *Isidore Isou* (Neuchâtel, 2019), p. 196.
3 See 'From Van Gogh: The Man Suicided by Society – Antonin Artaud', a version reproduced at http://theoria.art-zoo.com.
4 Isidore Isou, *Jonas ou le corps à la recherche de son âme* (Paris, 1984), p. 189.
5 Ibid., p. 238.
6 Ibid. pp. 58–9.
7 Guy Maruani is named and described in *L'Héritier du château*, p. 281. He is described as 'a controller' of Isou's 'normality' and in the same space as 'an evil genius . . . kind, brave and friendly'.
8 Ibid., p. 241.
9 Acquaviva, *Isidore Isou*, p. 252.
10 This final meeting between Isou and 'Solly' is recounted in Serge Moscovici, *Chronique des années égarées* (Paris, 1997), pp. 259–60.

Epilogue: Speaking East

1 Michel Onfray, *L'Autre pensée de 68* (Paris, 2018), pp. 10–11.
2 Isidore Isou, *Contre l'Internationale Situationniste* (Paris, 2000), p. 87.

BIBLIOGRAPHY

Selective Bibliography of Works by Isidore Isou

Isou wrote at least two hundred books, manifestos and tracts. Many of these were published by small and short-lived publishing houses and are not always easy to find. When I have reproduced images from these small presses all efforts have been made to find the copyright source. Copyright holders are encouraged to contact the author to ensure acknowledgement in future editions.

The most complete bibliographies have been established in print by Frédéric Alix in *Penser l'art et le monde après 1945. Isidore Isou, essai d'archéologie d'une pensée* (Les Presses du Réel, Dijon, 2017). Unpublished letters, tracts and journals can be found in the Fonds Isou, Bibliothèque Kandinsky, Centre Pompidou, Paris. This is a massive archive and its organization is ongoing work – certain references in the text may have shifted slightly therefore since this book was written. An important source is also the Fonds Lettristes in the Bibliothèque Nationale de France. There are also important *lettriste* holdings at the Beinecke Rare Book and Manuscript Library, Yale University. I began my own *lettriste* collection by buying a copy of *L'Agrégation d'un nom et d'un messie* almost by chance for a few francs at a *bouquin-iste* in Paris in 1994. God knows what that battered edition is worth now.

The following selection is intended as a guide to the most important aspects of Isou's thought, divided into different genres.

Economics
Manifestes du soulèvement de la jeunesse, 1st edn, preface by Roland Sabatier (Paris, 2002)
Manifestes du soulèvement de la jeunesse, 1950–1966, postface by Roland Sabatier (Paris, 2004)
Traité d'économie nucléaire. Le Soulèvement de la jeunesse (Paris, 1949)

Erotology
Adorable Roumaine (Paris, 1978)
Belles d'Europe (Paris, 1959)
Les Démons me déchirent! (Paris, 1969)
Initiation à la haute volupté (Paris, 1960)
Isou ou La Mécanique des femmes (Paris, 1949)

Je vous apprendrai l'amour, suivi de L'Érotologie mathématique et infinitésimale
    (Paris, 1957)
Notre métier d'amant (Paris, 1954)

Hypergraphic Novels

Amos ou Introduction à la Métagraphologie (Paris, 1953)
Jonas ou le corps à la recherche de son âme (Paris, 1984)
Les Journaux des dieux, précédé d'un essai sur la définition, l'évolution et le
    bouleversement total de la prose et du roman (Paris, 1950)

Manifestos

Manifeste de l'excoordisme ou du tëisynisme mathématique et artistique (Paris, 1992)
Mémoires sur forces futures des arts plastiques et leur mort (Paris, 2000)

Philosophy

L'Agrégation d'un nom et d'un messie (Paris, 1947)
Contre l'Internationale Situationniste (Paris, 2000)
La Créatique ou la Novatique, 1941–1976 (Paris, 2004)
L'Héritier du château (Paris, 1976)
Les Lettristes sont irrécupérables (Paris, 2005)
Mes définitions sur l'œuvre de Jean Cocteau (Paris, 2000)
Réflexions sur M. André Breton (Paris, 1948), reprinted with a preface
    by Philippe Blanchon (Paris, 2000)

Poetry and Literary Criticism

Introduction à une nouvelle poésie et à une nouvelle musique (Paris, 1947)
Précisions sur ma poésie et moi. Dix poèmes magnifiques (Paris, 1950),
    reprinted with an interview with Roland Sabatier (Paris, 2003)

Psychopathology

'Antonin Artaud, torturé par les psychiatres' (Paris, 1970)
Manifeste pour une nouvelle psychopathologie et une nouvelle psychothérapie
    (Paris, 1971)

Theatre and Cinema

Esthétique du cinema (Paris, 1952)
Fondements pour la transformation intégrale du théâtre (Paris, 1952)
Œuvres de spectacle [1951–4] (Paris, 1964)
Traité de bave et d'éternité (2000), DVD, Éditions Re:Voir (Paris, 2008)

Notable Individual Exhibitions by Isidore Isou

'Les Nombres', Librairie Galerie Palmes, Paris, 31 October–7 November 1953
'Isidore Isou. Exposition d'art infinitisémal', L'Atome, Paris, 27 May–11 June 1960
'Isidore Isou. OEuvres', Galerie Namher Paris, 18 May–11 June 1962
'Isidore Isou', International Centre of Aesthetic Research, Turin,
    25 March–30 April 1964
'Isidore Isou. Dessins et peintures de 1944–1975', Galerie Weiller, Paris,
    2 June–3 July 1976

'Les Tableaux les plus intelligents de l'histoire de la peinture et aussi les sculptures
    les plus intelligentes', Galerie de Paris, 26 May–10 July 1989
'Réponse à de Chirico', Galerie de Paris, 15 September–20 October 1990
'Dialogue avec Rembrandt', Galerie Rambert, 15 September–20 October 1990
'Initiation à la haute volupté', Fondazione Europea Cravanzola, Milan,
    18 March–30 May 1999
'Pour en finir avec la conspiration du silence', Institut Culturel Roumain,
    13 September–11 October 2007
'Isidore Isou: From Lettrism to Eternity', La Plaque Tournante, Berlin,
    29 August–29 September 2017

Selected Works on Isidore Isou

Again there is now a substantial library of writings on Isou. This collection focuses
on those that helped shape this book.

Special mention must be made of the excellent monograph *Isidore Isou* by
Frédéric Acquaviva (Éditions du Griffon, Neuchâtel, 2019), which is recommended
to any reader who wants to take their study of Isou further and deeper.

Place of publication unless otherwise stated is Paris. All other works consulted,
historical, political and cultural, have already been referenced in the text and
references above.

Acquaviva, Frédéric, 'Interview avec Isidore Isou', *Revue et Corrigée*, 49 (2001)
—, 'Isou, l'édité', *Revue d'Histoire du Lettrisme*, 2 (2007)
—, 'Isou 2.', catalogue *Isidore Isou, pour en finir avec la conspiration du silence*,
    Institut Culturel Français (2007)
—, *Isidore Isou: Hypergraphic Novels, 1950–1984*, Institut Culturel Roumain
    (Stockholm, 2012)
—, *Isidore Isou* (Neuchâtel, 2019)
—, *Lemaître. Une vie lettriste* (2014)
Alix, Frédéric, *Penser l'art et le monde après 1945. Isidore Isou, essai d'archéologie
    d'une pensée* (2017)
Bandini, Mirella, *Pour une histoire du lettrisme* (2003)
Bowd, Gavin, *Isidore Isou. Lettrisme et roumanité* (Chisinau, 2007)
Cabañas, Kaira M., *Off-screen Cinema: Isidore Isou and the Lettrist Avant-garde*
    (Chicago, IL, 2014)
Caron, Anne-Catherine, *Il lettrismo al di là della femminilitudine*, précédé
    de *L'Apport du Lettrisme et du Juventisme au mouvement de libération des
    femmes*, Isidore Isou, bilingual Italian/French edition (Sordevolo, 2008)
—, 'Isidore Isou sau zorii unei societati paradisiace' ('Isidore Isou ou L'Aube de la
    Société Paradisiaque'), *Revue Cultura*, IV/31 (2008)
Curtay, Jean-Paul, *La Poésie Lettriste* (1974)
Devaux, Frédérique, *Entretiens avec Isidore Isou* (1991)
—, *Traité de bave et d'éternité* (Leuven, 1992)
Eram, Cosana, 'L'Insurrection de L'Erotologie', *Mélusine*, 36 (2016)
Flahutez, Fabrice, *Le Lettrisme historique était une avant-garde* (Dijon, 2011)
—, and Camille Morando, *Isidore Isou's Library: A Certain Look on Lettrism*
    (2014)
—, Drost Julia and Frédéric Alix, eds, *Le Lettrisme et son temps* (Dijon, 2018)

Ghergescu, Mica, 'Les Journaux des dieux', *Histoire de l'art*, 71 (2012)
Girard, Bernard, *Lettrisme. L'Ultime avant-garde* (Dijon, 2010)
Home, Stewart, *The Assault on Culture* (London, 1991)
Hussey, Andrew, 'La Divinité d'Isou', *Forum for Modern Language Studies*, 36 (2000)
—, 'The Making of a Messiah', *New Statesman* (29 April 2019)
—, 'A-L Crea pe Mesia', *Steaua*, 7 (2019)
—, 'From Bucharest to the Beat Hotel', *L'Esprit Créateur*, LVIII/ 4 (2019)
Lemaître, Maurice, *Isou. Introduction à une biographie créatrice* (1954)
Liucci-Goutnikov, N., *Isidore Isou*, exh. cat., Centre Pompidou, Paris (2019)
Plossu, Bernard, *Trois heures avec Isidore Isou* (2015)
Robin, Guillaume, *Lettrisme. Le Bouleversement des arts* (2010)
Sabatier, Roland, 'Isidore Isou. La problématique du dépassement', in *Du Surréalisme en heritage. Les Avant-gardes après 1945* (actes du colloque éponyme, à Cerisy du 2 au 12 août 2006) (2008)
—, *La Bibliothèque d'Isidore Isou – et ses proximités* (2014)
—, *Propriétés d'une approche. André Breton et Isidore Isou, de la méprise à l'impasse (1946–1966)* (2014)
Satié, Alain, *Le Lettrisme. La Création ininterrompue* (2003)
Seaman, David, *French Lettrisme: Discontinuity and the Nature of the Avant-garde* (Amsterdam, 1994)
Sjöberg, Sami, *The Jewish Shtetl Tradition in the Franco-Romanian Avant-garde: The Case of Isidore Isou* (Uppsala, 2010)
Thomas, Jean-Jacques, 'Isidore Isou's Spirited Letters', in *Paris-Bucharest, Bucharest-Paris* (Amsterdam, 2010)

ACKNOWLEDGEMENTS

This book is dedicated with eternal love to my wife, Carmel, who has always been there for me, especially when I was recovering from serious illness in 2016 and about to to start writing this book. My parents, John and Doreen Hussey, my sister Dawn and her tribe in Canada all supported me with their love at that difficult time, too, and it is returned here.

In the making of this book I would like to thank Dr Louise Lyle, whose wit, intellect and sharp literary sensibility helped shape the tone and style of the book. Dr Guy Maruani led me through the labyrinth of Isou's mind, as well as educating me on Judaism and the politics of psychiatry in France. Catherine Goldstein and Jacqueline Enger generously told me about Isou as both a father and a husband. Roland Sabatier explained to me the art and philosophy of Isou. Luke Ingram, Sarah Chalfant, George Morgan and Stephanie Derbyshire of the Wylie Agency immediately grasped the significance of Isou's tale and kept the faith.

At Reaktion Books, Michael Leaman, Alex Ciobanu and Phoebe Colley turned the story of Isou into a book. Others who played a part were Frédéric Acquaviva, Frédéric Alix, Geoff Bird, Cristina Birsan, who taught me Romanian and about Romanians, my old comrade Gavin Bowd, who went with me on my first trip to post-Revolutionary Bucharest, Dennis Deletant has always been an invisible inspiration, Christine Donovan, Anabela Duarte, Cosana Eram, who explained Isou and 'erotology' to me, Fabrice Flatuhez, Valentine Gay, Catherine Gilbert, Oliver Harris, Arthur Hubschmid, Andrew Lees, Rob and Ange Merino for friendship and love, Igor Mocanu, François Poyet, Guy Stevenson, Sarah Wilson.

This book is also in memory of Brian Russell Ashcroft (1962–2010), musician, artist and founding member of The Last Chant. Among other things, Brian was a reader of Antonin Artaud, who would have understood this story perfectly. I am only sorry that he is not here to read it.

PHOTO ACKNOWLEDGEMENTS

The author and publishers wish to express their thanks to the below sources of illustrative material and/or permission to reproduce it. Every effort has been made to contact copyright holders; should there be any we have been unable to reach or to whom inaccurate acknowledgements have been made please contact the publishers, and full adjustments will be made to any subsequent printings. Some locations of artworks are also given below, in the interest of brevity:

All artworks by Isidore Isou – © Isidore Isou Estate/Catherine Goldstein

AcquAvivArchives, London: p. 205; akg-images/Mondadori Portfolio/Electa: p. 238; Beinecke Rare Book & Manuscript Library, Yale University, New Haven, CT: pp. 162–3, 217; courtesy Pierre Bismuth: p. 268; photos © Centre Pompidou, MNAM-CCI, Bibliothèque Kandinsky, Paris, 2021/RMN-Grand Palais/Dist. photos SCALA, Florence: pp. 85, 183; photos © Centre Pompidou, MNAM-CCI, Paris, 2021/RMN-Grand Palais/Dist. photos SCALA, Florence: pp. 164 (Georges Meguer-ditchian), 165 (Audrey Laurans), 167 (Philippe Migeat), 174 (Philippe Migeat), 181 (Audrey Laurans), 204 (Hervé Véronèse); photo Jean-Claude Deutsch/Paris Match via Getty Images: p. 248; courtesy Elke and Arno Morenz Collection (EAMC), Post War Avantgardes, Berlin: pp. 161, 168; courtesy Galerie Patrice Trigano: p. 284; courtesy Catherine Goldstein: pp. 30, 32, 124, 229, 287; collection of Guy Maruani (photo courtesy Guy Maruani): p. 166; private collection: pp. 20, 282; © René Saint-Paul/Bridgeman Images: p. 150; © Tallandier/Bridgeman Images: p. 114; photo Roger Viollet/LAPI via Getty Images: p. 127; courtesy Yad Vashem Photo Archive, Jerusalem: pp. 48 (3367/30), 53 (3367/2).

INDEX

Page numbers in *italics* indicate illustrations